Legendary Trains

The Great Locomotives of the World Past and Present

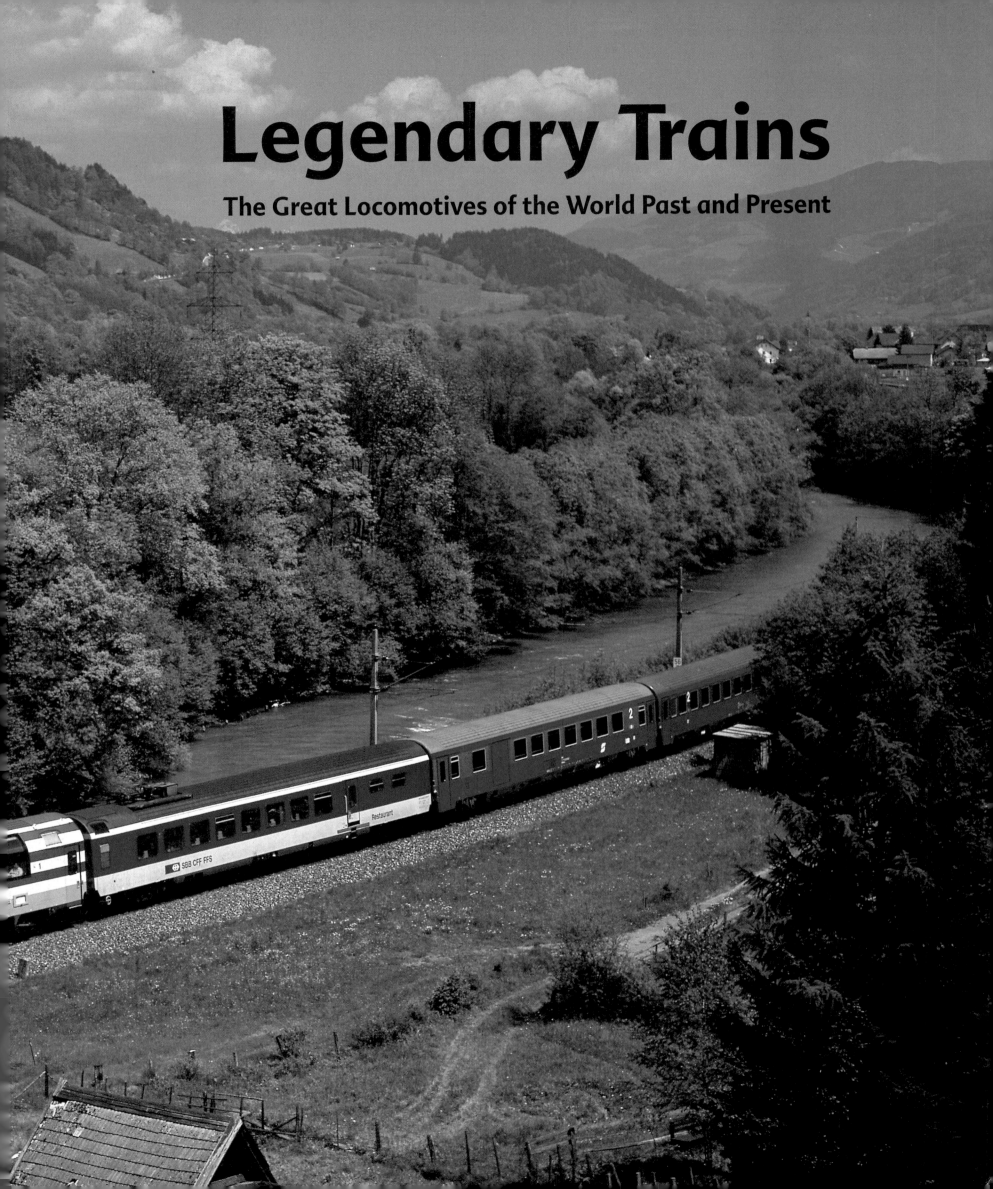

Legendary Trains

The Great Locomotives of the World Past and Present

© 2001 DuMont Buchverlag, Köln
DuMont monte UK, London

Cover illustrations: Michael Hubrich, Klaus Eckert
Text: Torsten Berndt, Ilona Eckert, Thomas Hornung, Thomas Küstner,
Dr. Franz Rittig, Bernd Vollmer

Translation and typesetting: Rosetta International, London
Parts: Übersetzungsbüro Braun, Köln

Concept and design: Klaus Eckert
Reproduction: Fotolito Varesco, South Tyrol

Printing and binding: Brepols, Belgium

Original edition

Printed in Belgium

ISBN 3-7701-7081-4

CONTENTS

Today it is quite amazing to think that there was ever a time when people fled in panic at the sight of a steam locomotive. Contemporary illustrations and descriptions depicted the terrible dangers to body and soul of the smoke and soot spewed forth by these roaming monsters, not to mention the breakneck speed of the trains. These fears marked the pioneering times of the railway in the early 19th century, when this new means of transport began to spread throughout the world.

Today in the 21st century speed is part of life and the rare sight of a steam locomotive arouses feelings of nostalgia within us. Even the familiar system of the flanged wheel and steel rail is slowly but surely reaching the boundaries of technological progress. So the Transrapid, which is in fact no longer a rail-bound means of transport, is the final chapter of a long and interesting history of the development of the railways, illustrated in this book with a large number of rare, spectacular photographs of locomotives, trains and railways.

The steam locomotive conquers the world of rails

In the beginning was the steam locomotive. The history of railways is therefore first and foremost that of steam traction. It was steam that determined the development of the world of railways throughout the world with lasting effects. Yet today, apart from a few preserved lines, steam locomotives have become now museum pieces.

Above: The Adler, or rather a reproduction of it dating from 1935, can be seen year after year pulling special trains on local railways in southern Germany.

Right: Preserved steam locomotives are still very popular with tradition-loving tourists on narrow-gauge railways such as this one in the Harz mountains. This is how it is still possible to take wonderfully nostalgic photographs of steam locomotives today.

Following double spread: One of the last real "working" steam locomotives in the world can be found on the Jingpeng Pass in China where it is still in regular service.

Above: A locomotive of series 139 is pulling a regional train through the Upper Bavarian countryside. For years a daily sight, this picture has a very special meaning in 2001 because it is showing one of the last 139 painted in green.

Right: Taken out of service by the ÖBB, locomotive 1020 004 travelled from Innsbruck to Germany in June 1994, passing through Mittenwald and Garmisch-Partenkirchen. It is seen here with the Karwendel mountains in the background.

But the fascination of steam locomotives has survived unabated, an enthusiasm reflected in the large number of special trains that are running today. The enormous popularity of the "iron horse" and the nostalgia of railway enthusiasts for the age of steam has provided us with some wonderfully atmospheric pictures of trains pulled by steam locomotives. This book will transport you through the ages and all over the world, presenting you with a wonderful panorama of many of the most interesting locomotives, landscapes and trains.

The choice of these locomotives was based on several criteria. A selection had to be made because even in a book of 440 pages it is not possible to illustrate every single interesting locomotive. As well as the locomotives and motor-coach trains that played an important part in the technical history of rail transport, the choice also includes railway lines passing through spectacularly beautiful landscapes, which are therefore of great tourist value. In all, this book will give the reader a lively and fascinating picture of the railways of the world, past and present.

Naturally, we illustrate the most important locomotives that were produced in the largest numbers. But we have also included many examples of more exotic locomotives, of which in some cases only a single example may have been produced. In the end, all selection is subjective and should be considered in that light.

Lively technology

One of the striking features of this book are the large number of photographs that are not completely dominated by the locomotives themselves. The dramatic, expressive photographs also show the surroundings in which these locomotives and trains operate. The locomotives and trains are set off against a variety of backgrounds such as high mountain ranges, roaring mountain

Above: This sparkling locomotive caused a sensation among the inhabitants (Sir Lowry's Pass).

Previous double spread: Travelling on the "Rocky Mountaineer" is a delightful way to discover and enjoy Canada's magnificent landscape.

Right: Luxury trains pulled by steam locomotives were a South African tradition. Nowadays they will only be found in museums.

Following double spread: Trains and bridges have one thing in common: they overcome distances. The EuroCity express from Cologne is travelling to Vienna and consists entirely of Austrian coaches. The locomotive is a DB-101.

torrents, rolling hills and peaceful villages. These powerful engines hauling their coaches or wagons are shown in their natural environment where they reveal their power, elegance and character.

The colour photo graphs of the last three decades are complemented by historical photographic material that brings back to life a past that has long vanished. The book has been arranged in such a way as to provide a general survey of the history and development of railways. In the chapters dealing with the development and description of the various types of steam, diesel and electric locomotives, we start out in Europe and travel round the rest of the world. Another chapter is devoted to high-speed trains, dealing with Germany's ICE trains and France's TGVs among others. Later chapters concentrate on the most spectacular railway lines in Europe, the United States and other continents. Thus the reader will discover in words and pictures the famous Swiss mountain railway lines, the impressive long-distance tracks of North and South America, the pleasant countryside of New Zealand and the dramatic landscapes of Africa and China. All are pictured in breathtakingly beautiful photographs.

This book contains such a variety of information and illustrations that it will appeal not only to railway enthusiasts but also to those who enjoy travelling by train and enjoying the sight of spectacular landscapes. There is also a glossary of technical terms and an index that will help the reader locate particular locomotives or trains. The information is up to date as of 2 May 2001.

Finally, we would like to thank all those who contributed to this vast project and made this book possible. We wish you, dear reader, the same joy in reading and looking at this book as we have had in producing it.

Above: George Stephenson with a model of the *Rocket*.

"The rail and the wheel go together like husband and wife."

A dmittedly it is not proved beyond doubt that George Stephenson made this remark. But it expresses succinctly and accurately the challenge that faced the inventors of the railway. More than one inventor? Yes, because even the great pioneers who advanced the railways in significant ways only solved problems in comparatively small, defined areas. It is simple and correct to attribute the invention of movable metal type solely to Johannes Gutenberg, for example. But the responsibility for the development of the steam locomotive, appropriate rails and the many other facilities of the track that today are obvious is shared among a large number of not always amiably public-spirited people.

After the invention of the wheel, thousands of years passed until the "gloomy chant of wheels upon the track" (Reinhard Mey) could everywhere be heard. In early antiquity people already recognized that heavy objects could be transported more easily if they were rolled on logs made of tree trunks lying on the ground. It is hardly surprising that the person who first had this breakthrough of an idea cannot be identified today. The same applies to the idea of slicing a tree trunk into round pieces. When this was done, the wheel was born. Later the wheels were enhanced by putting a box on top of them, thus creating the first cart. But the rail for the wheel, the "husband for the wife", was still missing.

At first nobody thought of rails. Traffic was first tied to a track by furrows, which were initially created entirely by chance. After heavy rain, the wooden wheels of carts sank deeply into the softened earth of the track. Once the sun had dried the mud, carts travelling along the track subsequently would be guided by it. The whole resembled the grooved rails for trams recessed in a tarmac street, but with the difference that tramways are manufactured from steel and are less vulnerable to the weather. But what would happen to other wagons with the wheels set a different distance apart? It was after all unlikely that all wheels would be the same distance apart. The result was that the wheels threatened to lurch sideways into one of the furrows of the track. This might damage the goods being carried, and at the worst the cart could topple over. Since transport liability insurance had not yet come into existence, the ancient carriers would have been very unhappy with the furrowed tracks.

Although the Romans clearly made many technical innovations, it is not certain that the idea of guiding traffic along organized, standardized tracks occurred to them. The paved streets of that time admittedly show miscellaneous track grooves. Whether they originated by chance or consciously it is impossible for anyone to say with certainty. The problem in the early days was that "husband and wife" did not match. Whether Chinese, Greeks or Romans — all these peoples failed to create a viable combination of wheel and track groove. Even in ancient Israel, whose calendar has now reached the year 5760, track-guided carts should not have been unknown.

In the early Middle Ages, there were carts in mines that were equipped with a device called a "track nail". This stuck into a gap between the wooden planks laid on the ground and consequently steered the cart. But even then nobody came up with the idea of standardizing the gauge of the carts and other vehicles.

The first rails in England

The first rails originated in the transitional period from the Middle Ages to modern times. Mine operators laid parallel tree trunks on the ground and rolled the mine wagons along them. The wheels had flanges on both sides, but the system was not satisfactory. The heavily-laden cars were derailed again and again because the naturally-grown trees were not straight or accurate enough. Also many trunks were too weak to support the heavy loads and broke. The system did not make the transport of heavy loads much easier either, since the wooden wheels ran very heavily on the wooden trunks.

The next thought was to use iron, bringing the pairing of "husband and wife" closer together. In the second half of the 18th century the first cast iron rails were made. At about the same time, the idea of fitting iron tyres to the wooden wheels occurred. According to tradition, a mine owner took this crucial step in Coalbrookdale in England; traditionally the date was 13 November 1767. But serious historians question the historical validity of this date; to them it sounds like a well-executed public relations story. It is certainly true

Above: Model of the "Rocket", which was the winner in the Rainhill Trials held in 1829.

Left: The first locomotive running on iron rails dates from 1804. Built by Richard Trevithick, it was in operation for a short time in South Wales.

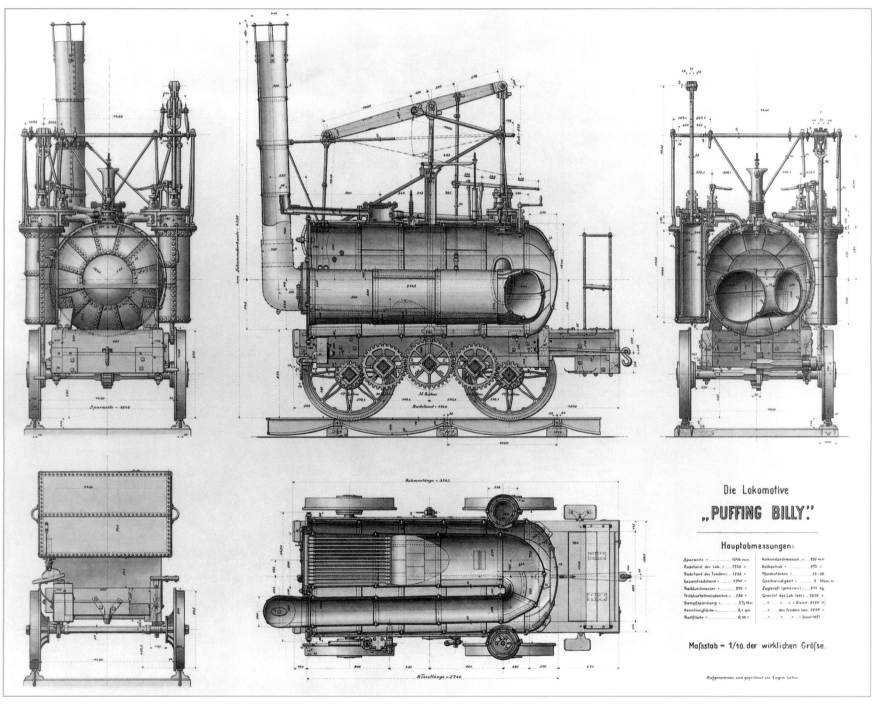

Die Lokomotive

„PUFFING BILLY."

Hauptabmessungen:

Maßstab = 1/10. der wirklichen Größe.

Above: Technical drawings of the "Puffing Billy" locomotive.

Right: The "Locomotion".

Opposite page, top: A steam-powered vehicle from France. It was actually more a car than a locomotive.

Opposite page, bottom: James Watt, the inventor of the steam engine.

that the iron tracks proved themselves, but still not well enough to challenge the comfort provided by a horse-drawn carriage. However, comfortable journeys in carriages were not available to most people, and at that time the length of trip the majority of the population could make was limited to a mile or two. Whether on foot or using that four-legged oat-powered means of transport, the horse, only high-ranking well-off people who did not have to spend their lifetime with hard work could afford to travel any significant distance. In order to bring mobility to the masses, thus taking the first steps to a global economy, faster, less expensive transport was needed. It was no use moaning and complaining: a replacement for the horse had to be found.

At that time, the only possible replacement for the horse was the steam engine that the British industrialist James Watt had developed. But how could its immense strength be harnessed to the rails? Watt's original steam engine was stationary and could drive weaving looms and similar machinery.

Another obstacle was that when a small, harmless steam engine had been fitted with wheels, it had scared and terrified the passers-by who saw it. The French Joseph Cugnot had even succeeded in building a half-way working steam car. Contrary to common opinion, this rather clumsy machine was not so much the first locomotive as the world's first automobile, since it drove on ordinary surfaces, not on rails. Its performance was enough to drive itself slowly along.

It was evident that James Watt's design of low-pressure steam engine could not be made small enough to power a locomotive. Another English engineer Richard Trevithick, took an important step. He did not simply put the steam engine on wheels. Trevithick had earlier worked out a way of increasing the power of the hissing monster by using high-pressure steam. His patent for a high-pressure steam engine, granted in 1800, was a vital contribution to railway history. Until then, boilers produced steam at a comparatively low pressure, which was enough for the performance required of them in driving stationary engines. In Trevithick's steam engine, the steam was raised to such a high pressure that its desire to escape enabled it to carry out heavy work.

"Catch me who can"

Four years later, in 1804, Trevithick introduced his first steam locomotive. This ran in a mine in Penydarren and is thought to have been called "Invicta." A little later Trevithick presented another locomotive, called "Catch me who can". This name was indeed apt in that nobody could catch it when it reached a maximum speed of up to 30 km/h (19 mph) on the straight. But Trevithick's innovative experiments ended sadly. His locomotives were simply too heavy for the cast iron rails used at that time and Trevithick had to give up. He then emigrated to South America to try his luck, but in vain. He died in 1833, completely impoverished.

William Hedley was somewhat more successful with his designs, which were based on those of Trevithick. He presented his "Puffing Billy" in the summer of 1813, and this locomotive ran until 1862.

Rails and wheels complemented each other like "husband and wife". If the wheel is too heavy for the rail, it will collapse. So what can be done? Steam locomotives are intrinsically heavier rather than lighter — the constantly increasing efficiency had its price. George Stephenson, who had built his first locomotive, the "Mylord" and followed it with other locomotives for the coal

mines, found a solution. In 1814 he had an idea that was to play a decisive part in the development of the railway. As chief engineer on the Stockton and Darlington Railway he decided to use malleable iron rails on half the line instead of cast iron rails. The experiment was successful. As he had expected, the rolled rails were better able to handle the load and also more stable than cast iron ones. Later on, the volume and the mass of the rails also changed. The principle of using rolled steel is still applied everywhere in the world.

George Stephenson also produced the right locomotive for the Stockton and Darlington line. On 27 September 1825 the "Locomotion" pulled the first passenger train in the world. But this was not the only reason that Stephenson's name became famous. The "Rocket" developed by Stephenson's son Robert was a real breakthrough. It showed its worth in October 1829 at the Rainhill Trials.

Naturally locomotive competitions are different from other kinds of racing. In these trials all the entrants in the competition had to travel the distance of

3.2 km (2 miles) 20 times without any problems. Only the the "Rocket" survived this demanding test, which it did so triumphantly. Robert Stephenson and the inventor of the tubular boiler, Henry Booth, were awarded the prize together. This helped to overcome the scepticism that was then prevalent towards the steam locomotive, demonstrated by the fact that on most railway lines for steam locomotives there were originally also many trains pulled by horses. In fact, according to one anecdote, whinnying was heard from the entrails of one of the competing locomotives, namely the "Cyclopede".

German railway plans

On the continent too there were plans to build railway lines. In Munich Joseph Baader had suggested building a railway line between Munich and the Danube as early as 1807. In 1812 he presented a memorandum that he entitled "For the introduction of artificial iron roads into the kingdom of Bavaria" in which he encouraged industry and trade to support the infrastructure with investment, which is a quite modern concept even today. But Baader did not only use political and economic arguments; he also covered the subject of technological developments. His paper contained a description of an as-yet undeveloped project for a road-rail vehicle and a trolley for transporting heavy coaches. But Baader still clung to the concept of "four legged" power provided by horses.

In 1825 Friedrich Harkort proposed a railway link between the North Sea and the Rhine in which he was more progressive in his thinking. Such a distance would have been too demanding for horses. However, his first task was to solve the local transport problems by building a suspended railway, pulled by horses, in Wuppertal in 1826. This suspended railway was followed in 1828 and 1829 by a double track for horse-drawn carriages near Hattingen and between the Hardenstein region and Elberfeld. In 1832, freight was transported on the 7.5-km (4½-mile) track from the Schlebusch region to Hagen. However, the plan to build a track almost 45 km (28 miles) long to transport coal in the Ruhr region was not carried out. Meanwhile steam power had been developed.

Among those who did not consider only the technical aspects was the political economist Friedrich List. He advocated political and economic

reforms that made him a dangerous enemy of the state in a country still governed by bureaucratic absolutism. Even the liberal middle-classes who shared his passions were suspicious of List's rigorous thinking and his matter-of-fact approach, because they believed that one should not oppose the State too forcefully. As a result, the champion of democratic reforms and a customs union for the states of Germany had no followers but many enemies, and he was imprisoned.

When List had served his term he left for the United States where he was entrusted with the task of building railways. He subsequently returned to his native country in his new capacity as consul and began immediately to campaign for this new means of transport. To do this he did not develop individual railway lines or try to solve regional transport problems. List had a grander vision, to create an all-German railway network that disregarded all the boundaries of the numerous German states. But the small States did not like his ideas. Almost all turned away from the troublesome thinker in spite of seeing their aims within reach. The railway committee that built the first German long distance line between Dresden and Leipzig effectively sacked him, giving him complimentary gifts that barely covered his costs. Nevertheless, there is no doubt that List introduced the concept of a national Germany railway system powered by steam locomotives . It would be left to others to put it into practice.

The Budweiser horse tram

The first line opened for passengers was the stretch between Linz and Budweis, 127 km (79 miles) long. The section between Linz and Kerschbaum was inaugurated at the end of September 1828 and four years later, it was extended to Budweis. Franz Anton Ritter von Gerstner conceived the entire line but then distanced himself from the project when his comrades in arms began to deviate from his large-scale, pioneering plans. Parts of the line were built to standards that at best met the requirements of a mining railway. But in the end, it was impossible to use standard locomotives because of the unsuitable layout of the most recently built part of the line. This led to an expensive process of conversion work on the line.

Above: The Budweiser railway line for horse-drawn carriages operated from 1825 to 1832. This water-colour by Christian Martin was painted in Vienna in 1924.
Opposite page: The legendary race between the "Rocket", the "Sanspareil" and the "Novelty" locomotives at Rainhill, which was won by the "Rocket".
Below: Passenger train with four coaches on the Linz-Budweiser railway line for horse-drawn coaches, the first on the European mainland.

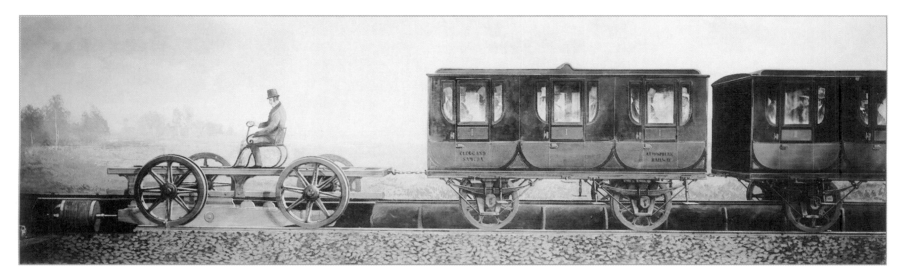

Above: The picturesque railway line between Exeter and Totnes in England was only in service for one year, from 1847 to 1848.

Right: The Adler, the first locomotive put into service in Germany. This is a photograph of an accurate reproduction of the original, built in 1935.

Opposite page: The Augsburg-Munich railway line caused much horror and alarm among the local population.

Meanwhile, Gerstner had started working on new projects. He tried unsuccessfully to persuade Tsar Nicholas I of Russia to build a railway from St Petersburg to Moscow. Nevertheless, in 1837 he was commissioned to build the first railway from St Petersburg to the imperial residence at Tsarskoe Selo.

This stretch of line was 27 km (17 miles) long and had a broad gauge of 1,829 mm (6 ft 0 in), rather than the standard European gauge of 1,435 mm (4 ft 8½ in), was inaugurated on 30 May 1837. In the end, however, yet another gauge became standard throughout the former Soviet Union and former Russian Finland, and is still in use today. This is 1,534 mm (5 ft 0 in) and it was first introduced on the Moscow-St Petersburg line. The choice of gauge was taken on the advice of an American expert, and not, as is often reported, out of animosity towards the rest of Europe.

Random railways

The standard gauge of 1435 mm (4 ft 8½ in) came about virtually by chance. In the early days of railways Stephenson's locomotive factory held a kind of monopoly. It produced locomotives with a standard gauge and the railway companies of other countries had to build their railway lines accordingly. But

no formal agreement was ever made, and other gauges were used in various parts of the world. Thus, even today at the border between France and Spain, for instance, it becomes evident that "each husband matches a particular wife". For instance, French wheels, which are standard gauge, cannot run on Spanish rails and vice-versa because the gauge in Spain is 1,676 mm (5 ft 6 in). Portugal originally built standard gauge railway lines but ultimately settled on broad gauge so that it could connect directly with the Spanish railway network. As it happens the Portuguese gauge is 4 mm (⅛ in) narrower than the Spanish but this difference is not enough to matter. Railway traffic moves freely between the two countries on the Iberian peninsula, which only acquired national railways in 1941 and 1947.

The first horse-drawn coaches travelled on the railway line for horse-drawn coaches from St Etienne to Andrézieux on 1 October 1828, only a few days after the opening of the Linz-Kerschbaum stretch. The first steam locomotive in continental Europe travelled for the first time from Brussels to Mechelen in Belgium on 5 May 1835. Belgium was also the first country in the world with a national railway system.

In America the age of the railways started on 28 December 1829 when the

first steam locomotive travelled the 24 km (15 miles) from Baltimore to Ellicots Mills. The American settlers immediately recognized the great advantages of this new means of transport to help them establish themselves across this vast continent. Only a decade later, the railway network in America was larger than that in Europe. In 1869, the first railway line from San Francisco to New York, linking the east and the west coast was completed. Like the other railways of America it was the product of private initiative.

The government's involvement was restricted to supporting the railway companies by providing the land as its financial contribution in kind. The large expanses and the enormous amounts of goods to be transported stimulated many pioneering projects. Many technical developments such as the bogie came from America. European locomotives and coaches still had their wheels rigidly connected to the frame. As locomotives became longer, the wheelbase increased, making it harder to negotiate curves. In America the problem was solved by mounting two or more wheels in a bogie that pivoted beneath the locomotive. The effect was that each bogie acted as an independent vehicle that could travel on the rails without derailing. Bogies were soon used everywhere in Europe. But there was another American innovation took much longer to arrive, namely the corridor coach.

The first European coaches resembled mail coaches. At first they were similarly short with a superstructure consisting of one compartment. Later coaches came to consist of several compartments, each compartment having its own door for access. A footboard on the outside of the coaches made it possible for the guard walk along the train. In Prussia where the railway companies bought many such compartment coaches, the antiquated coaches survived until the first half of the 20th century The first railway company to use corridor coaches were the Württemberg National Railways — a name indicat

ing that in the early days of railways, the foundation of the German Reich was still a long way away.

At first each little state or "Land", each little kingdom muddled merrily through on its own. This had tragic results in south-west Germany. Being rather short-sighted, the Grand Duke of Baden rejected the standard 1,435 mm (4 ft 8½ in) gauge, opting instead for a gauge of 1,600 mm (5 ft 3 in). The Grand Duke's government declared that Prussian, Bavarian or Württemberg coaches would never be able to travel on Baden railways. However, the grand duchy paid dearly for its narrow-mindedness because already by the 1850s it was forced to convert certain stretches to the narrower standard gauge. From the beginning Baden had built its railway lines at public expense while elsewhere governments had wondered whether it was their duty to provide a working infrastructure. Baader's realization that the quality of the communication network contributes to the economic development of a country had not yet been understood by everyone. In Prussia the government promoted economic development in a different way — economically underdeveloped regions were encouraged by billeting a regiment of the army on them. History showed that both Baader and Prussia were right. Obviously private investment in the railways required fewer taxes unless the State took over private railways. But in fact that most governments thought they could stand in the sidelines without making a decision. There was also ideological confusion.

Beginning in Nuremberg

The first German railway was the result of private initiative. At the beginning of 1833 two applications were made shortly after each other to build a railway from Nuremberg to Fürth. The first one was drawn up by Erhard Friedrich Leuchs, publisher of the "Allgemeine Handlungszeitung" newspaper, which

had first promoted for this new means of transport in 1817. The second appeal had been drawn up by a committee of prominent citizens of the town. From the very beginning they made it clear that they supported a steam railway: "Railways for steam locomotives are without any doubt among the important and influential inventions of our time; they are the fastest, least expensive means of transport for people and goods". Investments, running costs and revenue were calculated in minute detail: the line, two locomotives, five people and two freight coaches would cost 132,000 guilders. With an annual revenue of 29,200 guilders and expenses of 12,800, the railway was calculated to give a return on capital of 12. 5%.

The 132,000 guilders of equity capital was soon raised. On 18 November 1833 the shareholders formed the "Ludwigs-Eisenbahn-Gesellschaft in Nuremberg". After their attempt to appoint a British engineer to build the railway failed because of the high salary demanded, they employed a district engineer who had studied railway building in the United States and in Great Britain: Paul Cammille von Denis. He was to prove a fortunate choice for the Ludwigsbahn. Within three months Denis was able to propose plans and estimates for the

whole line and defended them against any wishes for changes to his proposals. The line's smooth operation later confirmed Denis's genius.

On the other hand, there were problems with the materials. Chairs for the rails and track fastenings were available on the spot. However, rolled rails had to be imported from the Prussian Palatinate because only Remy & Co in Raselstein near Neuwied could roll steel. Contrary to what was stipulated in the original plans, the Ludwigsbahn made do with one locomotive, which naturally was built by Stephenson. Having been dismantled it arrived in separate pieces in Rotterdam on 23 September 1835. From there the parts were transported by boat and cart, a journey that took over one month. Assembling the hundred or more separate pieces took three weeks. Finally, on 16 November 1835 the locomotive, which had been christened "Adler", steamed from Nuremberg to Fürth. Because of the lively interest of the population in this new means of transport, the railway organized public rides between the two towns as well as the test run. The Ludwigsbahn officially started services on 7 December 1835. Contrary to what was announced but in accordance with the shareholders' decision, horse-drawn coaches as well as steam locomotives used the line.

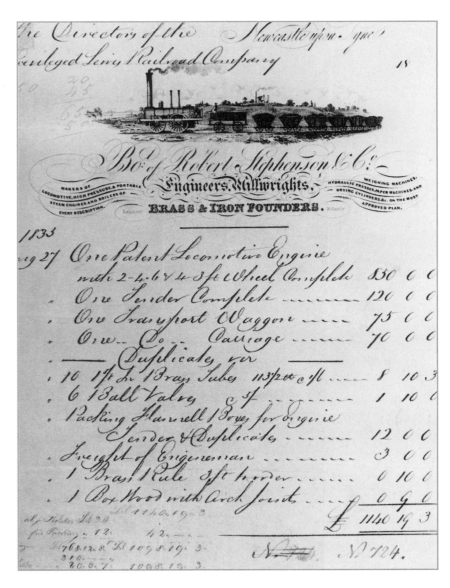

Above: This bill detailing the cost of the "Adler".
Left: The maiden journey of the "Adler" shown in a contemporary picture.
Below: A test run in November 1837 in the Austrian station of Floridsdorf.

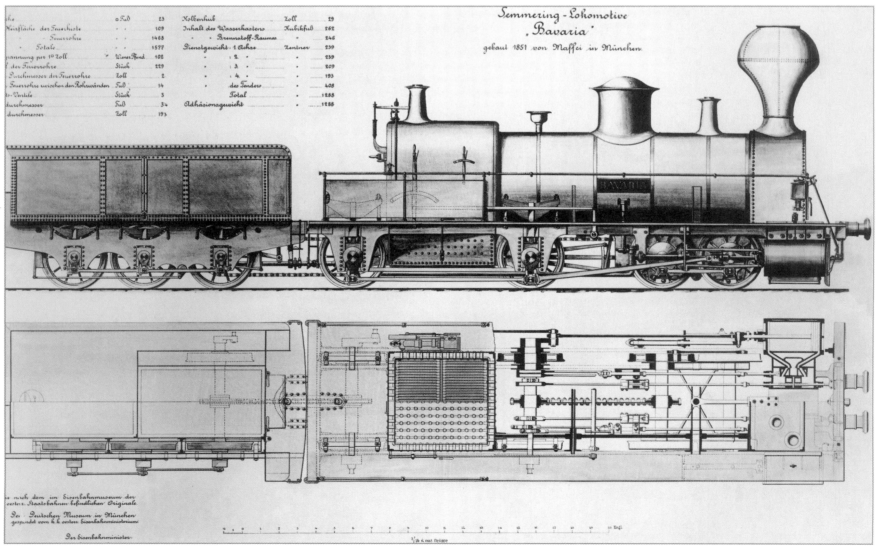

Opposite page, top: Henschel built its first locomotive, the "Drachen" ("Dragon"), in 1848.
Opposite page, bottom: The "Bavaria" built by the Munich firm of Maffei in 1851 took part in the Semmering trials.
Above: The "Beuth" built by Borsig in Berlin.
Below: August Borsig, whose factories built thousands of locomotives.

During the day there was already a timetable. Even in the first year an average of 615 passengers travelled the 6-km (4-mile) stretch every day in both directions. But the railway did not just improve transport conditions. Its example also improved organization, because all trains travelled absolutely on time. Many passengers missed their train because they relied on the clock of the Catholic church in Fürth. After complaints the magistrate ordered that the church clock should be adjusted to show the same as the station clock.

The first main railway lines

Strictly speaking the Ludwigsbahn belonged to the category of steam tramways, because it did not link up with any other railway lines. In the end it had to give way to electric tramways and the steam locomotives were removed from service on 31 October 1922. However, Prussia's first railway inaugurated on 29 October 1838 was of particular importance. Admittedly, like the Ludwigsbahn it only linked two neighbouring towns — Berlin and Potsdam. But from the start there were plans to extend to Magdeburg and if possible to Hamburg. It was July 1845 before the government eventually approved the plans, and at the same time the exact route of the Berlin-Hamburg railway was set down. It crossed three States — Prussia, Mecklenburg and Denmark — as well as the free Hanseatic cities of Lübeck and Hamburg. On 7 August 1846, the first train travelled from Potsdam to Magdeburg.

There it linked up with a line to going through Hanover to Cologne and Antwerp.

The first main line

By then a whole series of main lines had been built. The Leipzig-Dresden railway was first opened over its entire length on 7 April 1839. It was the first time in Germany that a railway line went through a tunnel and the first time that a large bridge was built for a railway line. In addition, the railway had the "Saxonia", a locomotive that had been specially designed for it. This locomotive built at the Übigau locomotive factory under the supervision of Johann Andreas Schubert with two driving axles and one carrying axle placed under the driver's cab is considered the first German locomotive. But this is not absolutely true. In 1816 Heinrich Friedrich Krigar built a locomotive for the Königliche Eisengiesserei (Royal Iron Foundry) in Berlin. Whether it ever ran has never been proved. However, there is no doubt that the "Saxonia" was the first German steam locomotive to have been used operationally.

But Schubert and the Übigau locomotive factory played no further part in the development of German railways. The railway pioneers of the 1840s were August Borsig, Joseph Anton Maffei, Emil Kessler, Carl Anton Henschel, Richard Hartmann, Ferdinand Schichau, Louis Schwartzkopf, Georg Egestorff and Georg Krauss. They followed British and American examples but also contributed with their own developments.

At the beginning of the 1840s the concept of new standard locomotives was introduced from England. The main handicap of the so-called patented type of construction with the 1A1 (2-2-2) wheel arrangement was its low performance because of its very small boiler. Without any more ado, the boiler was extended by the addition of an extra section to the individual segments of the boiler jacket. This did not improve the appearance of the locomotive particularly, but it brought about a considerable improvement in performance. At that time no attempt was made to lengthen the wheelbase because it was feared that it would affect the way it performed round curves. The first long-boiler locomotives appeared in Germany in 1842 with the patented 1A1 (2-2-2) axle arrangement. Later locomotives were fitted with two driving axles, like Schubert's "Saxonia". In 1843 the first long-boiler loco appeared with three pairs of wheels driven by connecting rods.

The large overhang of the long boiler encouraged the pitching and hunting movement of the locomotives. Edmond Heusinger von Waldeck, who invented the steam driving gear control named after him, warned of the dangers of large overhangs as early as 1844. His warnings were proved right by a series of accidents from the mid-1840s. After an accident in Gütersloh in 1851 the Prussian government set up a commission to investigate the running of the long-boiler engine, and in 1852 long-boilers were finally prohibited from pulling fast trains.

The problem of jolting and rolling of long-boiler locomotives was also known in Britain, the country where railways were born. But what was the solution? The driving axle had to placed under the boiler, which had to be as low as possible, while the other wheels could not be too far away from the driving axles so that the locomotives could negotiate curves. The problem was only solved with the arrival of the bogies from America, where they had been invented. Later engineers also realised they were wrong in believing that the

Above: The "Saxonia" at an exhibition in Radebeul/Ost in August 1939.
Below: The "Limat" was the first railway line in Switzerland.

boiler should be placed as low as possible. A lower centre of gravity had very little effect on the running of the locomotive because of its great weight. The pioneer German locomotive builders were influenced not only by English locomotives but also by American concepts of locomotive building; the latter was the predominant influence on Borsig's first locomotive built in 1841, modestly named after its architect. However, it was unable to prove the superiority of its construction on the Prussian lowlands. More important was the decision of the Royal Württemberg National Railways to buy locomotives with the 2'B (4-4-0) wheel arrangement for the Cannstatt-Untertürkheim section. A little later the Württemberger put a heavy, triple-coupled locomotive on the Geislinger Steige, a steep mountain section. The so-called "Albklasse" (Alpine class) became the progenitor of all German freight locomotives.

Power station in the rocks

The triumphant progress of railways quickly became unstoppable. In France the first steam locomotive was launched on 26 August 1837 on the line between Paris and St Germain. By 1839, the Netherlands and Italy had also instituted national railways. The first Danish railway line, which went from Altona to Kiel, was opened in 1844. The line between the capital Copenhagen and the cathedral town of Roskilde in Schleswig-Holstein, which later became Prussian and thus German, was first opened on 26 June 1847. In the same year

Left: This locomotive of the B IX series displaying factory number 1000 was built by Krauss in 1874.

Left: In about 1880 the American engineer Heigs from Boston developed a new overhead railway system. It was never built, however.

Above: The exceptionally large driving wheel of an English "single" steam locomotive.

the first railway was inaugurated in Switzerland. The "Spanisch-Brötli-Bahn" ran from Baden to Zurich. Its name was inspired by a typical Baden confectionery that is now eaten hot from the oven for breakfast in Zurich.

Railways in Sweden

In Sweden, Norway and Finland, the age of the railways began during the 1850s and 1860s . In these thinly populated countries, the railways played a particularly important part in transporting raw materials. Passenger services were never as important in Scandinavia as they were in the rest of Europe, although the 200 km/h (124 mph) X 2000 motor-coach train of Swedish National Railways recently caused quite a sensation. The most important stretches were the Lulea-Kiruna-Narvik line, which was electrified between 1915 and 1923. A hydro-electric power station was built in the rock near the Porjus Falls. The double locomotives used today for the transport of heavy mineral ore trains are among the most powerful and impressive-looking locomotives in Europe.

The first Finnish railways date from the time when Finland was under Russian rule, which is why they have broad gauge tracks.

Railways in outer Europe

Parts of Poland, whose national railways came into being when the country recovered its independence in 1918, had also been under Russian rule. At the same time, a large part of the 16,000-km (10,000-miles) network was in the former Prussian part. Other sections had been built by Austrian railways. When the Austro-Hungarian monarchy collapsed, Slovakia, Slovenia and Hungary also regained their independence. Hungary had in fact developed its railway network independently from the Austrian railways. Legal separation took place on 30 June 1867 and Hungarian railways as they exist today were founded on 30 June 1868. The Greeks on the other hand had to wait until 18 February 1869 before the first train travelled from Athens to the harbour of the Piraeus.

... and Asia

Steam locomotives arrived in Asia in 1852. In India, there was a line linking Bombay and Thana. The British colonial government encouraged the development of a sizeable rail network. India boasted over 15,000 km (9,300 miles) of railway lines as early as 1880. Even today India still has the largest railway network on the Asian continent. Japan had to wait until 1872 before the first train travelled from Tokyo to Yokohama. The line had been built at public expense with British help. Subsequently the government was obliged to sell concessions to private railway companies because of lack of money. In 1900 Japan had built up a network of over 6,000 km (3,700 miles). The lines were mostly on the main island and largely separated from each other, so the railway companies had to build a network of linking tracks amounting to roughly the same length again.

Above: The "Maxburg" locomotive shows the developments made in locomotive building. The driver's cab already had a roof.

Left: Typical steam locomotive as they could be seen everywhere in America before the turn of the century.

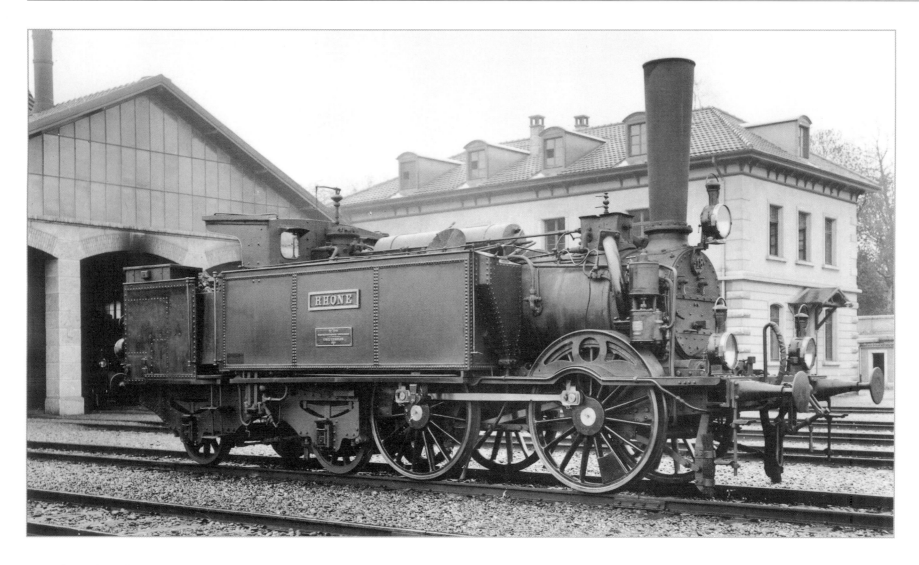

In China, the railways were built mainly by foreign countries such as Russia, Japan and Great Britain. The Chinese did not build many kilometres of line on their own. The superstition of the population and also the negative attitude of the Tsing dynasty resulted in a successful self-blockade. The first railway went into service in 1876, although trains only used the 17-km (10½-mile) track between Shanghai and Wusung for one year. This was followed by a period of peace, when a British company was given permission to build a coal mine railway line. In 1889 this was to develop into the first major railway in the country. However, by 1900 China still only had 650 km (400 miles) of track. Ten years later however this had risen to about 8,600 km (5,350 miles). Germany also took part in the development of China's railway network. In 1908 the engineer Julius Dorpmüller was appointed chief engi-

neer of the Chinese National Railways. It was under his management that the Tientsin-Pukou track was built. He subsequently managed it after it was completed and remained in charge until 1917.

In that year China joined the war on the side of the Allies, and Dorpmüller was therefore forced to leave the country. Back in Germany, he joined the Deutsche Reichsbahn whose chairman he became. In 1937 he combined this function with that of transport minister in the National Socialist government.

At the beginning of the 20th century Turkey became one of the great powers, controlling large parts of Asia Minor. Even so the first railways were built by the British. The rivalry between the great European powers resulted in France and Germany also becoming involved in the Middle East. The most important project was the Baghdad railway line whose first section was built

Above: An original construction, the "Rhone".

Right: A Garratt built by Krupp for South Africa.

Opposite page, top: Magnificent set of coaches of the Bavarian King Ludwig II.

Opposite page, bottom: Type U.1. Garratt built in England.

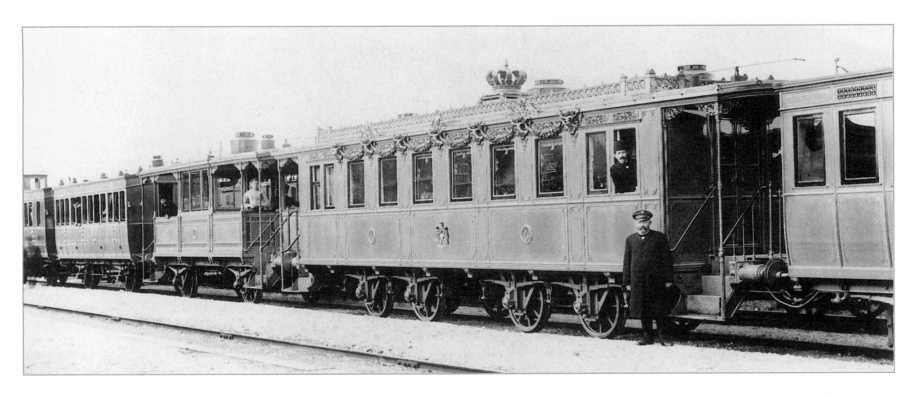

with German support. It was completed by the British and the French, who had carved up the Middle East between themselves after 1918.

It was only in 1940 that the first passenger train was able to travel from Baghdad to Istanbul. Today the line has suffered from the whimsical behaviour of the Middle Eastern depots, which are forever closing certain sections. The Haj line between Damascus and Medina suffered the same fate, remaining in service for only seven years between 1908 and 1915. During the World War I the line was fought over by the Turks, who had joined the German side, and the Allies. The British were also supporting the independence movements of the Arabs in order to weaken Turkey. Many attacks were carried out against the line, and subsequently only the Damascus-Amman section was rebuilt. Attempts to completely rebuild the line have failed in spite of an agreement between Syria, Jordan and Saudi Arabia.

The first railways in Africa

Egypt was the first African country in which railways were built. In 1856, the line linking Cairo to Alexandria was built on the initiative of the British. Four years later the Egyptians had almost 450 km (280 miles) of track, while in the rest of the continent the only other line was the 12-km (7½-mile) line between Cape Town and Wellington in South Africa, where in the course of time the

largest railway network was developed. In the early days the development of the railways was slowed down by the rivalries between the independent Cape regions. The creation of the Union of South Africa also meant that the railways were put under the same management.

At the time the network covered some 15,000 km (9,320 miles). Many railway enthusiasts associate South Africa and Africa in general with the Garratt steam locomotives. These are articulated locomotives , effectively consisting of two engines linked together. The fuel tender usually rests on the rear engine while the water tank rests on the front engine. The boiler works like a bridge between the two. This gives the locomotive an extremely unusual appearance. Garratt locomotives can hardly be surpassed as far as performance is concerned.

1854: the start in Australia

In 1901 Australia consisted of seven independent colonies. The various lines were built by private companies and used various gauges, but they were almost completely nationalised already before the creation of the federal state. Everything started in Victoria in 1854. A railway resembling a tramway was built to link Melbourne and Sandridge harbour 4 km (2½ miles) away. It was opened on 13 September. The railway network developed particularly in

Rax 2009 m. *Semmering. Kalte Rinne*

the south-east of the country, reflecting the settlement structure. The coastal railway line Brisbane-Sydney-Melbourne-Adelaide-Port Augusta branched off into numerous branch lines. However, there was no line linking the north and the south. In the south the line went as far as Alice Springs, while in the north it ended in Larrimah. In the west, the dead-straight line covering 528 km (328 miles) crossed the desert of the Nullarbor plain. The building of the line started in 1912 and was completed five years later. Looking after the 3,000 building workers was quite a problem, with temperatures rising to 50° C (122° F) in summer and falling to -15°C (5° F) in winter.

A railway 900 metres (1,000 yards) long

Even the Vatican and Liechtenstein have joined the world-wide railway network. But the two countries do not have their own nationalised railways. The 900 m (1,000 yd) of track in the Vatican is managed by Italian National Railways. Mainly freight wagons arrive at the little station with a platform, sealed off by sliding gates. The few kilometres of track in Liechtenstein are managed by Austrian railways. They run from Feldkirch on the Arlberg line through Schaan-Vaduz to the Swiss border station of Buchs.

In Austria, where the first steam locomotive was launched in 1837, travelling from Vienna to Florisdorf, there were soon plans to build a line crossing the Alps. In 1848, building had already started on a track crossing the Semmering Pass. Even experienced railway engineers doubted the success of this venture. In fact, Robert Stephenson had calculated that a steam engine should be able to tackle a gradient of 1 in 61. Bold engineers like Karl Ghega

who built the Semmeringbahn, which was opened in 1854, did not bother with such calculations. They just tried it out and — it worked, although an ingenious stratagem was used. In order to reduce the gradient, the trains were diverted through a number of side valleys. Twenty years later, when building the Brenner railway line, the Italian engineer Achilles Thommsen had the idea of building spiral tunnels. Now the track could also be built higher up the mountain. The builders of the Gotthard line were particularly clever in their approach, incorporating several spiral mountain routes to overcome steep gradients.

Competition on the Semmering

In order to discover the best locomotive for mountain tracks, the Südbahn organised a competition in which four locomotives took part. The Munich-based firm Maffei sent the "Bavaria", Cockerill based in Seraing sent the "Seraing", the Vienna-based Günther sent the "Wiener Neustadt", and the Südbahn itself sent the "Vindobona" built by John Haswell. While Haswell first proposed a locomotive with four fixed driving axles attached to the loco frame, the other three attempted to transfer the driving power across several articulated drive units linked together, using curious solutions. Against all expectations, it was the "Bavaria", the least convincing from a technical point of view, which won the competition. However, it did not work out in the long run. The driving chains with which the locomotive transferred part of its power to the tender axles were constantly breaking. The "Vindobona", in spite of bringing up the rear of the competition, eventually became the ancestor of all heavy

Die Brennerbahn. Kehrtunnel bei St. Jodok

Opposite page: The Semmeringbahn, opened in 1854, was the first mountain railway in the world.

Left: The principle of the spiral mountain route and tunnel was applied for the first time in building the Brenner line. It enabled the gradient to remain a tolerable 1 in 40.

Below: The Series Ae 6/8 locomotive built in Italy for the Lötschberg railway.

freight locomotives. The Belgian "Seraing" later inspired the Fairlie type of construction. In principle, it resembled two steam locomotives, coupled back to back, sharing a common continuous frame.

The first transit line

The Semmeringbahn was the first real mountain line in Europe, but at first it was only of national importance. The Gotthard line, opened in 1882, was the first transit stretch that linked central and southern Europe. It became possible for the first time to persuade several countries in a fragmented Europe to take part in a large-scale joint project. Germany and Italy contributed millions to finance the project, which was realised with a lot of support from Bismarck. At first the Gotthard line was owned by a private company but in 1909 it came under the management of the Schweizerische Bundesbahnen (SBB), Swiss Railways.

The entire project would have been doomed to failure if the railways had not finally decided to bring their technical developments into line with each other — at least in part. A common gauge was not enough to enable coaches to move freely on the European railway network. The type and height of coupling, the type of brakes, the width, length and height of the coaches, the size of the tunnels, the approved weight per coach axle, the height of the wheel-flange, the width of the wheel tread surfaces, identification of the vehicles understandable to all, the height of bridge clearances — all these had to defined and agreed upon, years after each railway had already developed its own technical approach.

BERN LÖTSCHBERG SIMPLON

Above right: The first electric locomotive was built by Werner von Siemens. It was shown to the public at the 1879 Berlin Industrial Exhibition.

Below: This electric train was also displayed at the Berlin Industrial Exhibition, but this photograph of it was taken at the 1882 All-Russian exhibition in Moscow.

The "Verein Deutscher Eisenbahnen" (Association of German Railways) was created in the mid-1840s. The association developed a manual of rules and specifications that was adopted in 1856 by the railways of countries including as Austria-Hungary, Romania, the Netherlands and Switzerland. On a political level, the railways of Germany, Italy, France, Austria-Hungary and Switzerland signed an international agreement on "technical standardization". In the course of time the remaining countries in Europe whose rail-

way tracks had a standard gauge joined the international agreement. Nevertheless, it was only in 1913 that a standard gauge for vehicles was set down. On the other hand, other attempts at standardization failed. For instance, even today there is no standard signalling in Europe. Almost every country has its own train protection system. Any attempt at building a truly European locomotive will fail for the foreseeable future if only because of the different safety devices. Even the electric power supply of the various European railways does not go together.

It is true that Germany, Austria-Hungary, Switzerland and Sweden had agreed to use single-phase current of 15,000 volts and 16.67 cycles as early as 1912. But that did not prevent the other countries from experimenting with other electric systems. France did not even succeed in standardizing the electric train operation in their own country — even today there are still two networks of electric lines that do not match.

The German empire was founded in 1871, but this did not immediately imply the creation of national railway network. Only an "Imperial Management of Railways" was created, which was supposed to cover the Reich but was in fact mainly the Prussian Railway Administration. In 1873 another office, known as "Reichseisenbahnamt" ("Federal Railway Bureau"), was created in Berlin.

But its authority was so minimal that even very independent-minded Ger-

man states approved its creation without opposition. Otto von Bismarck remarked maliciously about the department that "it produced many documents and gesticulated a lot without anyone taking any notice". Articles 4 and 41 of the constitution of the Reich, which put the Reich in charge of the railways, were ignored from the very beginning. In the mid-1870s a tactical Prussian proposal to hand over all national railways to the Reich was rejected by the other states.

At least they succeeded partly consciously and partly accidentally in converting all the individual states to the concept of national railways. Baden, Braunschweig, Oldenburg and Württemberg had all set up national railways. The Bavarian government supported the building of a national railway network but was not always able to pay for it. In Prussia, the situation remained unclear and directionless for almost three decades. The government was aware that many railway connections favourable to the development of the country would not be profitable for private companies, such as the Ostbahn Berlin- Königsberg line. Nonetheless, the government waited optimistically for enlightened investors to bring about a turn for the better.

Among the first railway lines built with financial help from the state were the Thuringian Halle-Kassel and Cologne-Mindener lines. The Ostbahn was even entirely paid for by the state. Other projects failed because of lack of money or interest, especially after the Manteuffel government came to power in 1848, which at the same time made it difficult for private companies to build railways. In return, the state bought a series of railway companies that were in trouble. Others were put under the management of the state, sometimes justifiably but sometimes under rather transparent pretexts that often nonetheless benefited the railways so that they flourished. It proved that state involvement could in fact be beneficial. So for example, the government introduced the concept of night trains and also the so-called penny tariff for coal transport, which led to a reduction in heating costs in Berlin and other places. But the squabbling and bickering of officialdom resulted in unnecessary duplicated transport, grotesquely bad investments and a lack of coordi-

nation between individual lines. Thus in the Ruhr region rival railway companies would build lines several miles apart without there being any link between them.

It was only after the foundation of the Reich that Bismarck took drastic measures to put an end to this muddle, which had long been disapproved of by the military. It is not known whether the military played a decisive part in the nationalisation of the railway. But it did not need to. In a military state like the former Prussia, everything was so subordinate to the government that no direct intervention would have been necessary. Railway companies were also happy with Bismarck's railway policy because the state paid well for the lines and the directors received substantial compensation. It was "Bismarck's Socialism" as Friedrich Engels mockingly described it.

Nationalized or private railway?

But the situation was not much better in neighbouring countries, such as Austria-Hungary and Switzerland for instance. After the failed revolution attempt in 1848, the Dual Monarchy was almost constantly involved in small wars. On one hand, some of the regions of this vast empire were fighting for their own independence, while on the other the Habsburg monarchy was trying to achieve supremacy in the German field of influence. It was therefore not surprising that the state had no money to invest in new railways. But the Austrians pursued their goal in a resolute and single-minded manner. They not only stopped building new railways but they also sold all the existing ones. Later, the wheel was turned back. New important railway lines were built and economically weak ones were bought back by the state. Even so it took until 1923 before the last important private railway — the Südbahn — was bought back by the state. But this policy was also the state's undoing. After the collapse of the Habsburg monarchy, the railways lines were scattered in four countries which were not always friendly to each other, and obviously not interested in making a compromise because of the continued existence of a private railway.

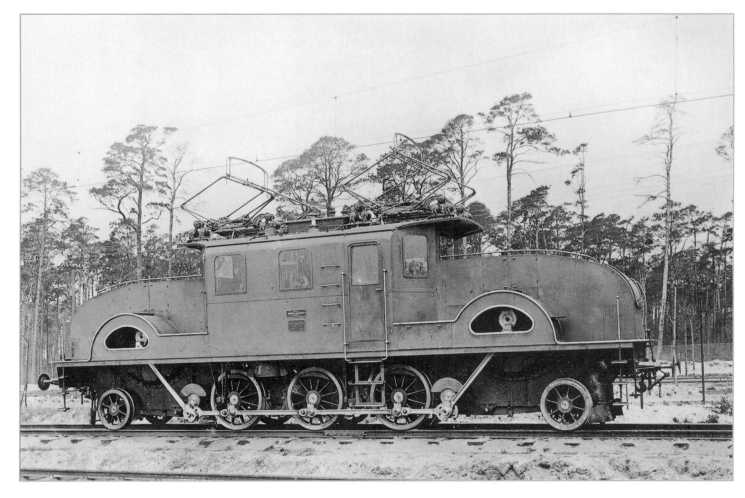

Right: Electric locomotive of the Wiesentalbahn with two engines alternating current, built in 1910.

Below: The first high-speed electric loco-motive entered service in 1911. This picture was taken on the Dessau-Bitterfeld line.

Opposite page: E 69 01 on the electrified section between Murnau and Oberammergau.

In Switzerland, the central state bought the railways for a 1,000 million francs. It then unceremoniously passed on the certificate of indebtedness to the Swiss Railways that were set up in 1903. Only two cantons, Bern and Graubünden, rejected this proposal and kept their railways. The Bern-Lötschberg-Simplon railway line, known as the BLS, is still independent today but has recently been working in close collaboration with the SBB, especially for freight transport. Nevertheless, there is still stiff competition in other areas because, among other things, BLS also works closely with the German freight train transport company, DB Cargo. The decision of the Graubünden railway company and the Rhaetian line not to become part of the federal network was based largely on operational reasons. They run on metre-gauge tracks, which means that interchange of rolling stock with other lines is hardly possible. In addition, there are a many small railway companies in Switzerland in which the canton or municipal corporations are majority shareholders. But legally they are considered as private railways.

Birth of the electric railway

In 1879, the steam locomotive was threatened by the appearance of a rival. One of the exhibits at the Berlin Industrial Exhibition was a little locomotive that hummed quietly and odourlessly along the track. The electric locomotive was born. At first this new type of traction proved itself as a tramway. In 1881 electric trains travelled to Lichterfelde near Berlin. It was only in the 1890s that this new type of vehicle became powerful enough to be used on the railways. The first electrified stretch in the world was the line between Meckenbeuren and Tettnang. In 1895 the first railcar was used in the small Swabian capital. Even the electric power supply was reminiscent of that of tramways, although the first electric railways used direct current of a fairly low voltage.

At the turn of the century, the voltage in the overhead contact wires was increased. At the same time, there were also experiments with three-phase and single-phase alternating current. But as in the early days of the railways it was not always simple to bring "husband and wife" together. In fact, it was not enough to suspend a cable over the track and establish a link between it and the train. It was only after lengthy experiments that engineers succeeded in transferring the current safely and reliably to the vehicle by means of two pantographs. The difficulty had been to prevent brief interruptions of current that would be damaging to the electric system of the locomotive. The so-called Wippe pantograph was invented later: it had two contact surfaces, one of which was always in contact with the overhead wire. However, at the turn of the century there were only fixed pantographs.

An overhead contact wire was hung above the tramway track while the return line was through the rails. The same principle was applied when the lines were electrified with single-phase current. In contrast, the use of three-phase current required multipolar overhead contact wires. But suspending them over points and crossings proved extremely difficult, which is why the use of three-phase current was normally restricted to test tracks. Elsewhere, for instance in Italy, main lines like the Brenner section were equipped with double-pole overhead contact wires. Later, the Italians switched to direct current.

200 km/h — or 124 mph

Already at the turn of the century electric railcars were able to break the 200 km/h (124 mph) mark. In 1903 a six-axle railcar with three-phase converter built by Siemens reached the incredible speed of 210 km/h (130 mph) between Marienfelde and Zossen near Berlin. However, in everyday life the railcar travelled at a more leisurely pace, not least because of the heavy current consumption. In 1904 experiments with single-phase current took place on the Swiss stretch between Seebach and Wettingen. The following year the Murnau-Oberammergau private local railway electrified the track in the Werdenfeld region of Bavaria.

Naturally, the countries in the Alpine region proceeded as fast as possible with the electrification of their railways since hydro-electric power provided an unlimited supply of energy. In addition — and this is particularly true of Switzerland and Austria — electric locomotives were better suited to mountain tracks with large number of tunnels than steam locomotives. Strong exhaust fumes would not only bother the locomotive crew but also damage the walls and rails in the tunnel. So electrification was a real blessing for Alpine countries. Already by the end of World War II almost all trains in Switzerland were electric. In Germany on the other hand there are still non-electrified main lines.

A difficult birth

The Reichsbahn was created after the end of World War I. The state and industry were going through a depression and the individual states could not pay for the rebuilding of their railways. The obvious solution was to transfer them to the state and receive compensation. It was agreed that the Reich should pay 39,000 million German marks for old, worn out locomotives and coaches, tracks in bad condition and crews that were demotivated by the war.

Above: The Mallet articulated locomotives were at home on the gradients of the low mountain region areas of Germany.
Below: The New York Central railroad also used Mallet locomotives. They had an additional bogie at the front with front and rear axles.

By the Treaty of Versailles, Germany lost well over 70,000 km² (27,000 sq miles) of its territory, an area almost corresponding to the size of the Austria today, and about 8,000 km (barely 5,000 miles) of track. The Reich now had 53,559 km (33,280 miles). Much of the Prussian network had been removed by the territorial losses brought about by the Treaty, but even so with a length of 34,443 km (21,401 miles) it was still about about 80% longer than the rail networks of all other German regions put together. The foundation of the German Federal Railway or Deutschen Reichsbahn changed the legal form of the railways, but it did not solve its problems. Those responsible were not empowered to carry out fundamental alterations themselves, and the state-owned enterprise had to suffer to achieve the economic goals of the state in other areas. So, the politicians still organized the regional railways themselves and reappointed all their own railway staff. Consequently the total number of employees increased by almost half while the traffic performance deteriorated by more than 50%. This could not be satisfactory, as even the politicians might have foreseen.

In addition the federal railway system also had to contend with another problem: all the railways of the individual states had developed their rolling stock to their own criteria. The south German lines were far ahead technically. In Baden, Bavaria and Württemberg, ultra-modern locomotives were built with bar frames, twin expansion compunding and other sophisticated touches. The performance of the locomotives was impressive, but they required intensive maintenance and were consequently expensive to run. Too expensive, in the opinion of Robert Garbe, the head of the Prussian locomotive department, who believed that a good locomotive could be repaired in a cow shed in the furthest corner of east Prussia if necessary. Garbe favoured super-heated steam, which would not condense in the cylinders. Consequently, they needed less fuel to achieve the same performance. Garbe's developments were impressive for their simplicity, which made his a more robust technology. Locos such as the P 8 quickly demonstrated this in a way that everyone could see. In World War I, the Prussian locomotives were aklways found at the front, while their south German colleagues spent much of the time in workshops well away from the front, immobilised by minor problems.

Later, the "Beautiful Württemberger", the 18.1, and the Bavarian S 3/6, often described as the most beautiful locomotive in the world, had long ago been fed to the blast furnaces while the Prussian engines were still performing

Above: The Württemberger C Class was a very successful design both visually and technically. It hauled express and passenger trains.

Below: The six-coupled K locomotive was originally built as a heavy freight locomotive for the Geislinger Steige. In the 1930s it also operated in Austria as the Series 59.

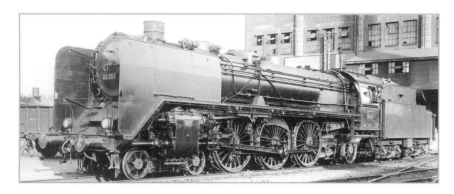

useful service. Only in the early 1970s did the flame go out for ever. To attribute their long, effective life only to the large numbers built by no means tells the whole story.

While the great variety of locomotives and rolling stock is very interesting to railway enthusiasts today, it caused substantial problems to the German national railway system. In its first fiscal year it had revenues of 18 billion marks against an expenditure of 33.6 billion marks. In economic circles therefore the alleged panacea of denationalization was recommended. But this would have been pointless, because the Versailles Treaty had virtually given away the Reichsbahn already. German and allied politicians had simply pawned the railway system in payment of reparations. After the defeat it was the most important asset of the individual states, but the question of whether it belonged to the countries or the empire was of little interest to the Allied powers. Their attitude was that the German government had to sign the Treaty no matter what. Ironically it was the collapse of the German monetary system that first brought relief to the German states.

In 1924, the Reichsbahn changed to become the politically, administratively and financially independent Deutsche Reichsbahngesellschaft, the federal

Top left: Express locomotive Number 03 051 of the Deutsche Reichsbahn.

Top left, below: Number 03 193 received a complete disguise when it was decorated in 1936 as an advertising locomotive for the Olympic Games.

Above: Maffei delivered the magnificent locomotive S 3/6 3644 to the Royal Bavarian National Railway in 1914.

Top right: The Series 43 freight locomotives were robust and economical.

Right: Locomotive 01 053, specially painted for photography.

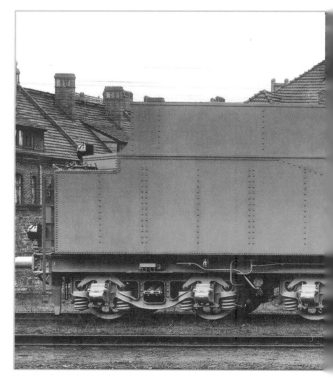

German railway company. On 30 August the German railway act was passed, burdening the railway company with a bond of 11,000 million gold marks in favour the victors. This decreed that between 1926 and 1964, the new Reischbahn had to find 660 million gold marks for reparations each year.

Second flowering

Despite this enormous burden, the railway was remarkably successful in the years that followed. Without any exaggeration, it is possible to speak of a second flowering of German railways. Now built to standard criteria, large numbers of locomotives left the factories, including the legendary Series 01. Modern express train coaches replaced a much of the old rolling stock inherited from the regional state railways. With the introduction of the ES 04 in 1927, an electric locomotive was produced in considerable numbers for the first time in Germany. On test runs, this proved that speeds of over 150 km/h (93 mph) were possible on existing lines. This provided the cornerstone of the programme for the high speed network.

Flying trains

This network does not refer to the development of the tram system, which incidentally, was substantially supported financially by the Reichsbahn from 1933. Rather, the Reichsbahn from the outset developed a new generation of diesel trains, the so-called "Fliegenden Züge" or "flying trains." With their light-weight construction and efficient engines, these achieved maximum speeds of up to 160 km/h (99 mph). Record average speeds were also set. The record holder was the FDt 16, that in 1936 averaged 132.3 km/h (82 mph) between Hanover and Hamm. For 50 years, only few trains exceeded this speed. Between 1933 and 1939, the express train network had 6,000 km (3,700 miles) of track.

Somewhat slower than the "flying trains" was the E 18 series of locomotives introduced in 1935. These six-axle electric locomotives had a maximum speed of only 140 km/h (87 mph), but this was a notable achievement given that they had to haul heavy passenger trains. In 1937 the ES 19 was developed from the E 18, and this could reach a speed of 180 km/h (112 mph). But its production was curtailed by the outbreak of war.

Steam locomotives too ventured into new levels of performance. The 01 had a maximum speed of 120 km/h (75 mph), and its smaller sister the 03 could reach a maximum of 130 km (81 mph), even though it had two cylinders instead of four, and simple steam expansion. The end of the 1930s saw the introduction of three-cylinder compound locomotives of the 01.10 and 03.10 series that were in no way inferior, with the ES 18 achieving a maximum speed of 140 km/h (87 mph). Experimentation and test runs demonstrated that there was much more potential in steam locomotives than many had believed. The Borsig 05 002 reached a speed of 200.4 km (125 mph) on a test run in 1936, while the Henschel-Wegmann train had of a maximum 175 km/h (109 mph) , hauled by a streamlined Series 61 engine. It is true that these locomotives were not typical, but steam locomotives proved in everyday life that they were certainly able to meet the demands of the time. The legendary "Flying Hamburger" reached an average speed of 124.7 km/h (77 mph), while an

Top: The "Flying Scotsman" ran non-stop between London and Edinburgh.
Above left: The E 04 once broke a record with a speed of 153 km/h (95 mph).
Above: The futuristic "Henschel-Wegmann" train with the streamlined 61.

Above: Majestic and unbelievably elegant. These were only some of the attributes of the beautifully streamlined locomotive 05 001.

Below: The German Reichsbahn operated some very fast trains. The diesel-electric, six-axle express railcars ran between Berlin and the most important cities of Germany. Many of the journey times they achieved were not reached again until today.

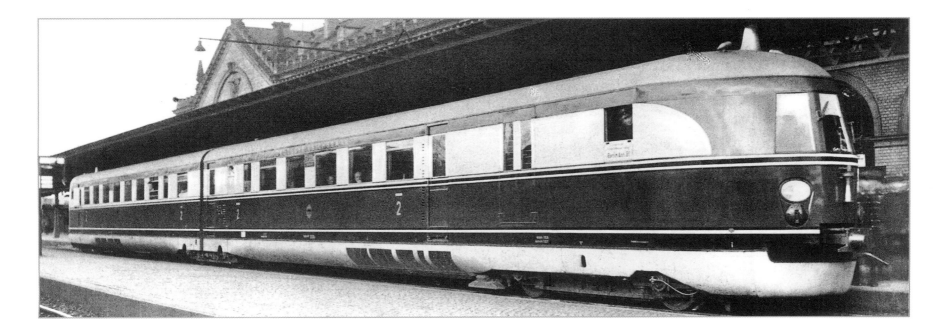

Above: A fast German Railways train under the overhead contact wire. The ET 11 entered service in 1936.

Below: There were many variations of "flying trains". This is the SVT 137 153, Leipzig type, on display.

Bottom: The Henschel 45 001 freight train locomotive had a tender with five pairs of wheels.

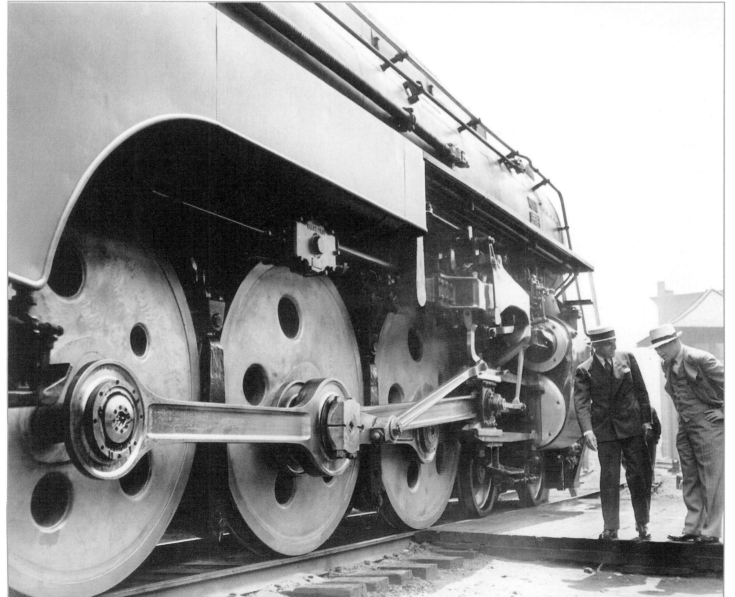

Above: In Britain too some steam locomotives were streamlined. Here the largest of them, a four-coupled (2-8-2) engine, leaves London heading for Doncaster.

Left: The "New York Central Flyer" was a non-stop train running between New York and Chicago. The first journey took place on 15 June 1938. The travel time was 16 hours.

Above: Locomotive 03 1080 in the Vienna West locomotive depot in 1941.

Right: After the war locomotives from the United States arrived in Europe. This is a CSD Series 456 freight locomotive, built in the US in 1945.

Below right: A large diesel locomotive of the V 188 series. It was given the computer-number designation 288 and was operated by the Deutsche Bundesbahn.

Opposite page, above: The first much simplified Series 52 war loco, 1942.

Opposite page, below: The Series 85 that ran on the Höllentalbahn/Schwarzwald.

express train hauled by a streamlined locomotive was only insignificantly slower with a speed of 119.5 km (74 mph). But the outbreak of World War II ended any further development. The military demanded simple, immediately available engines such as the Series 52. Some locomotives that had been developed before the war, including the 44 series of freight locomotives, continued to be built in a somewhat simplified form.

Trains to the death camps

But the wheels did not only turn for victory. The transport of the Jews to the extermination camps mostly took place by rail. It succeeded all too well in preserving the appearance of normality, because the ten or twenty daily trains travdelling to the death camps did not stand out among the total of 20,000 trains a day running on the network Ordinary officials at all levels put the trains together; they were run as special passenger trains composed of goods

Above: There is little more to be said about the legendary "Big Boy". It is enough simply to introduce it as the largest steam locomotive in the world.

Opposite page, top: A rare sight: the T 18 1002 trial locomotive with its forward drive system and condenser tender.

Opposite page, below: The E 93 dates from 1932. It went into operation on the Geislinger Steige, where among other things it hauled heavy freight trains.

wagons. The clients were the SS, the head office of government security and other state authorities, and initially payment was made at the third class tariff. Even before the start of the programme of systematic mass murder, the Reichsbahn had offered tickets at reduced rates for group travellers. Everything happened in broad daylight, and it was certainly officially arranged; but of course after the liberation nobody felt responsible. Even Albert Ganzenmüller, a participant in the Hitler "putsch" of 1923, bearer of the extermination orders and since May 1942 the secretary of state in the German transport ministry responsible for rail traffic, had claimed not to be aware of the murder of the Jews. "Really it was not easy to see these things in relation to that ... and as for me, I was a simple citizen", he explained when he finally stood in court in 1973. It is true that for the Nazi leadership the railways were only a means to an end. Its management did not put up any resistance to the crimes, but rather the opposite: they even collaborated with the perpetrators, as for instance with the special tariff. The Nazi regime did not have to give the Reichsbahn any special orders.

Wheels stood still

World War I ended with the defeat of Germany, while World War II ended with the country's complete military and moral breakdown. After the invasion the Allied Forces tried to prevent all railway operations by numerous air raids on intersections and marshalling yards. About 10,000 bombs were dropped in 25 raids on the marshalling yard of Hamm alone. Also, German units had destroyed many railway bridges and other installations as they retreated. All wheels were still on 8 May 1945.

But within a few weeks, the railway workers had succeeded in reconnecting the surviving tracks into a modest network, on which mainly freight trains ran. At first the Allied Forces allowed passenger transport only in empty freight trains. The coaches were used for onward transport of refugees from the lost eastern part of the country. The Allied Forces forbade the Germans from repairing their own locomotives, but brought their own materials into their zones. Naturally the Reichsbahn was divided between east and west. The only exception was in the four zones of Berlin, where the Reichsbahn managed the traffic for all areas of the surrounding Soviet zone. In the years to follow, the railways system underwent a series of politically motivated changes.

USA: no longer the country of the railroad

So far as the United States was concerned, serious developments took place, partly political and partly economic. In the United States the car had started its triumphal march much faster than in Europe. The endless expanse of the country and its existing sources of raw materials had promoted great changes in the transport sector. Also the structure of the railroads played a decisive role, in that private rather than state-owned railroad companies had always been favoured in the USA.

This had not necessarily been an advantage for rail transport. Ordinary public companies can only conditionally repel the takeover bids of rivals. Deliberately dishonest decisions are indeed punishable even in the country of limitless opportunity. But if the majority of the owners of a public company sees great profit potential in other areas, there is no way to prevent the company from neglecting its original main business. Also, it is not even possible to prevent railroad investment and profits being directed into other businesses, thus eroding the original business. But not all the economic difficulties of the railroads were caused by structural changes arising from the growing competition of road and aircraft travel. Some problems were brought about consciously, and even local railroad operators have not been spared from such behaviour. Until today the railroads of North America tracks have been quietly wasting away. Wonderful rolling stock, such as the "Big Boy" or the advanced F7 locomotive that is the begetter of a whole family of engines, and the use of freight trains 1 km (⅝ mile) long, often laden with two stories of containers, cannot conceal the fact that for a long time the United States has not been a railroad country. The renaissance of the railroad, which is at least indicated, will take some time to arrive, particularly since there is complete silence on the subject of the financial resources that the reconstruction of the system would require.

Double new beginning

The railways in West Germany had to pay for the consequences of World War II largely from its own revenue. The state withheld both direct and indirect financial support, concentrating all its investment on road transport. Since

Above: An FS (Italian Railways) Series 428 direct current electric locomotive.
Below: The V 80 was the first postwar diesel loco of the DB (German Railways).
Bottom: DB's "Rheingold" luxury express, hauled by locomotive E 10 1244

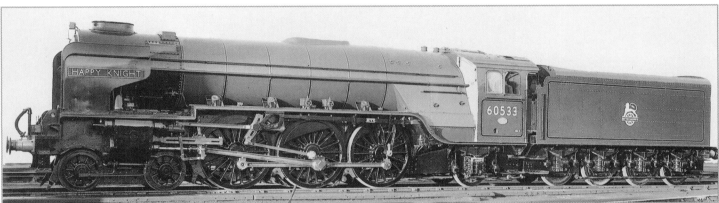

Above: Locomotive number 241 023, a French Mikado class steam engine.

Left: A British Railways express steam locomotive. It weighed 101 t (121 tons) without its tender.

Links: British Railways Pacific (4-6-2) locomotive, built in 1954.

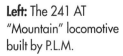

Left: The 241 AT "Mountain" locomotive built by P.L.M.

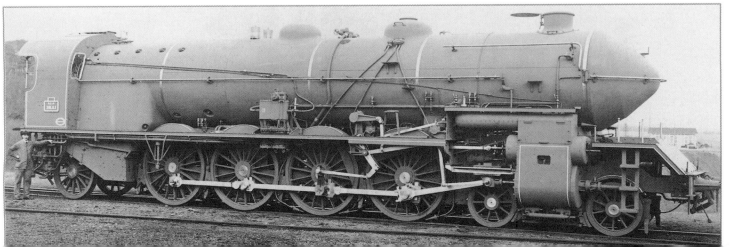

Only two examples of the Series 10 entered service. This is locomotive 10 002.

1960, 150,000 km (93,000 miles) of new highways have been built at a cost of 450,000 million marks. This compares with 700 km of new railway lines, to which the state contributed 56,000 million marks. Advantageous credit terms were only given to private companies, and did not apply to the state railway company. In order to repair the network and rolling stock, the Bundes-bahn founded in 1949 had to obtain funding from the capital market. The interest payments ruined the railwa . Experts such as Wolfgang Schneider also spoke of the "historic deficit" of the state-owned enterprise.

Meanwhile the railways' share of the transport market continuously declined. Before World War II, the direction of traffic was mainly east-west. The industrial centres were in the Ruhr, central Germany and the Neckar region. The rest of the country was devoted to various kinds of agriculture. The division of the country led to an increase in transport in the north-south direction. The necessary roads were built quickly, while the construction of railway lines proceeded more slowly; for instance, the electrification of south German lines continued according to plan, while the Feucht-Altdorf line near Nuremberg was completed in the 1950s.

Export goods shipped from Hamburg still trundled round the harbour under steam power until 1965. The construction of an efficient north-south route between Hanover and Würzburg began only in the 1970s. By that time, railways had essentially lost the race with the road transport system. As the first real newly-built route in West Germany became operational, already there were no longer two Germanies.

In East Germany too, politics absolutely impeded the existing positive foundations. The xreation of goods and passenger services with similar speeds had been quite easy to achieve, and this single fact made the system easier to run. Until the end of the GDR, passenger trains reached at most a speed of 120 km/h75 mph), while freight trains ran with a maximum speed of 100 km/h (62 mph). Passenger and freight trains did not get in the way of each other as they did to the west of the demarcation line, where the fastest passenger trains reached up to 200 km/h (124 mph) and rarely gave way to the freight trains. But it cannot be claimed that the speed limits in the GDR were an expression of strategic considerations. Rather, the reason was that the GDR did not have the economic resources to strengthen its network to handle the higher speeds. Technically, there would have been no problem in building locomotives and coaches with a top speed of 160 km/h (99 mph). Among the first to prove this was the 212 001, with which LEW, as the con-demned Hennigsdorfer AEG factory was called, tried to point the way. As a prestige project this was a success at the expensively funded party conference of the SED (Socialist Unity Party) . But in a country where an artificial short-age of locomotives prevailed, there were other problems to solve.

The artificial shortage of locomotives meant that there were admittedly enough locomotives available for the service planned. But the circulation timetables had become hopelessly confused because of excessive delays in the whole network. The operating controllers had perforce to use reserve engines for the trains, sometimes even setting off with inappropriate locomo-tives in order to be able to get the trains running on the line at all. But the development of the track was not only hindered by the system-induced short-age of locomotives. With the conversion to a different form of traction, the state leadership twice changed the direction of its policy. First, it promoted

Above: The "Golden Arrow" luxury train of British Railways.

Below: Four units of the TEE II, RA 1051-1054, put into service by the SBB. The trains could operate on four different electric systems.

electrification, using the Series E 11 and E 42 engines that were at its disposal. But in 1966 the politburo decided henceforth to use diesel-powered locomotives. These locomotives would come largely from the Soviet Union, which would also supply cheap oil. But as the oil price escalated in the 1970s, the state leadership encountered the disadvantage of this course of action. Now electric power was the one to have. However endless squabbling meant that until the 1980s only steam and diesel engines reached Berlin, the centre of the GDR, and the sea port of Rostock had to wait even longer even longer for modernization tokelp it in its competition with Hamburg.

Technically, the GDR followed the Garbe route of using robust, efficient engines. The motto would have been "No experimentation", had it not

already been too busy with other matters. The Bundesbahn had indeed taken one risk: as early as the 1970s it had tested trains using tilting technology. The interests of the management however primarily turned towards practical high technology. There was little recognition of the requirements of everyday life, or of the needs of the traveller.

Speed, speed

France has been the keenest advocate of high-speed traffic on selected main lines. In this centralist country, all the important lines radiate from the capital Paris. High-speed running began in 1981 on the rebuilt Paris-Lyons route. The TGV HPS reached up to 270 km/h (168 mph). In this age of European harmony,

Above: A very successful design: the DR's Series E 11.

Right: The prototype V 320 001. The locomotive remained the only one of its kind.

Opposite page, top: A large number of examples of the Series E 41 were built. It is still in operation today.

Opposite page, middle: The year 2001 is likely to be the last year in which the unique Series E 03 is used. E 03 001 was first shown to an astonished public in 1965.

it might have been expected that the railways of other countries would have adopted the French concept. But this degree of European unity has not been reached. Each country developed its own technology. Some train sets, the German ICS 1 and 2 for example, cannot use all the lines in its own country, because it exceeds the allowable loading gauge. In Sweden, the choice has been for moderately high speeds with tilting technology, while in France and Germany the high-speed trains run on specially designed or rebuilt lines. Recently the InterCity express with tilting technology has been put into service by German Railways. The Italians and Spanish have built new lines and acquired newly built trains, some of them equipped with tilting technology.

But Japan is the unambiguous front-runner so far as high-speed trains are concerned, with its Shinkansen dominating long distance traffic. Work began on the line in 1964. First, it connected Tokyo and Osaka at a speed of 210 km/h (130 mph), later raised to a maximum of 250 km/h (155 mph). The Shinkansen does not have to assert itself on the world market, although it runs on standard gauge tracks. Elsewhere , the narrow gauge of 1067 mm (3 ft 6 in) is dominant in Japan.

The largest exporter of high-speed trains is the French company Alstom, the builder of the TGV. Sometimes the French government has helped it with favourable loans, an action that the Federal Government tends not to follow. Nevertheless Siemens, which was in charge of the ICE consortium, has succeeded in exporting several trains. Thyssen-Henschel has done even better with the magnetic levitation (MAGLEV) train, the "Transrapid." For the reference route in Peking, the German government opened its coffers and granted generous support.

German policy is to have an export success of a particular type. Several German regions have copied this in a positive manner, acting together after the sensible railway reform of 1994. At that time the rail network was not only opened to the competition that was extremely welcome. The track, long-distance passenger services, short-distance passenger services and freight transport were separated into individual units. While competition from private or local railway companies grew only slowly, the individual divisions of the Deutschen Bahn managed to give themselves a difficult time. The clearest example appeared with the new railcars acquired by DB Regio for local traffic. These have automatic Scharfenberg couplings that are not compatible with the conventional screw-coupling system with a coupling hook. This old fitting admittedly has to be modernized, in order to haul increased weights of freight traffic, which is particularly necessary in the transit through the Alps . All locomotives of German Railways are prepared for adaptation to an automatic coupling system. But not all European railways can afford to make the changeover to a new coupling system, and there is a tendency to remain with older methods. So far it is only the railcars of the German regional traffic that can no longer haul freight wagons. The German Federal Railways had already made this mistake with the procurement of the first diesel locomotives of the 627 and 628 series. Later a large sum of money had to be spent converting the screw couplings to Scharfenberg ones.

However freight traffic will soon only takes place on few, heavily used sections of the network. The goods lines extending to many businesses have been abandoned, because they did not appear in the DB's commercial view of the situation. There is no doubt that it is unprofitable to pick up a single

loaded flat wagon using a large, busy diesel locomotive with driver and shunter. The shunter cannot be dispensed with because the driver has no view of the coupling. In any case, at many points of the rail network freight traffic is no longer admitted. The regional railway also runs on single-track sections at hourly intervals and occupies all the passing loops. There is no longer any free capacity for freight trains. Where possibilities still exist for mixed freight trains, the DB network generously sets the points to alternative routes. But however well this is done, it is not satisfactory because freight trains and passenger trains belong together like the wheel and the rail. For a view of where the thoughtless fragmentation of mature structures can lead, it is worth looking at the British Isles.

There, the Conservative party of the day (subsequently voted out) decided to privatize the railway. Obviously it could not sell British Rail as a whole, or there would have been a private monopoly. Therefore, the government established many small rail companies, each of only limited importance in the market. The customers did not get a look-in. Timetables of the individual companies did not coordinate with each other. Quality, punctuality and safety rapidly declined. On British lines nothing any longer fits together and the balance sheets of the lines will not correct this for a long time. Nonetheless, there are regional ideologists in Germany who consider that the British way is promising for Germany too.

Dead-ends and experiments

Over the years, a number of unconventional railway tracks have appeared. The serious intentions of the inventors cannot be denied, even if some of the experiments soon seemed absurd.

In the very earliest days of railways, strange-looking locomotives were developed with toothed wheels engaging with toothed rails. Their inventors included John Blenkinsop, who believed that there would not be sufficient friction between the smooth iron wheel and the rail to move the locomotive forward. Later the builders of mountain railways took up the idea again and created rack locomotives that could manage extremely steep gradients.

Thomas Russell Crampton introduced a first express train locomotive in 1846. He mounted a gigantic driving wheel under the cab and simply supported a long boiler on two or sometimes three carrying axles, like the locos from the USA. The steam reached the cylinder directly without being obstructed and the locomotive had excellent acceleration and high speed. But the Cramptons, as they were soon known, had a crucial disadvantage. The driving wheels carried only a little weight, so the traction of the locomotive was correspondingly limited. The Cramptons pointed to a dead end. It is true that locomotive factories went on to develop some Super Cramptons in the USA, which broke the locomotive speed record. But in the end these speedy locomotives were merely an episode. The last new Crampton rolled onto German tracks in 1864.

One of the most popular ideas among inventors was the abandonment of

the second rail. The best-known monorail system is the suspended railway in Wuppertal, the Wuppertaler Schwebebahn, where indeed the coaches hang from a rail. Since they execute a calculated pendulum movement swinging outwards with increasing speed, they cannot fall or crash from the rail. But the system is not proof against derailment if a foreign object is fixed to the rail. In 1999 there was a serious accident caused by a forgotten clamp that was not removed by construction workers after finishing their work. Because the Wuppertaler Schwebebahn is free of intersections it is the most reliable and punctual means of transport in the world.

On the whole, other monorails have not fulfilled their promise. What is the advantage, for instance, of having a single rail in contact with the driving wheel, if there have to be two guide rails on the left and right of the train to direct it? Yet this was normally the case, for example in the 16-km (10-mile) long monorail of the Listowel-Ballybunion Railway built in Ireland in 1887. The two-cylinder locomotives had two boilers, connected together in order to remain balanced. There were three driving wheels. The track ran until 1924 and transported both passengers and goods. Another monorail was built in India. In this case two wheels ran on the single rail, with two more running on a parallel concrete roadway.

The German engineer Franz Kruckenberg, who came from the aircraft industry, turned his attention to driving rail vehicles. He developed a diesel train with propeller drive. This "rail Zeppelin", as the aerodynamically streamlined vehicle was named, reached the fabulous speed of over 230 km/h (143 mph) on a record-breaking attempt in 1931. It was however not

very suitable for train services, since it could only run at a much lower speed in the other direction. Admittedly separate tender locomotives also had to be turned at the final destination, but in that case it was a simple matter of attaching a second engine to the other end of the train. The "rail Zeppelin" would have had to drive onto the turntable, and of course it was not allowed to do this with passengers. The air suction generated by the propeller also caused concern as to its effect when passing through a suburban station at speed, for instance. But the rumour that the "rail Zeppelin" would whisk up the gravel along the line was quickly dispelled when a railway worker put a newspaper on the track. It was not the railcar but the freight train driving past afterwards that generated more turbulence and blew it about all over the place.

Recognizing that in the widest sense all track-guided vehicles are railways, the track-bus qualifies. This was a street bus that ran in a special concrete roadway. The driver did not steer the vehicle but simply operated the accelerator and brake .The track-bus was installed in Essen and Adelaide, and on conventional streets it behaved like its rubber-tyred brothers.

The overcoming of steep gradients had caused railway surveyors and builders considerable headaches in the 19th century. This was hardly surprising, when one remembers how even Robert Stephenson had underestimated the capability of the steam locomotive. A large number of ideas were proposed to solve the problem, including among other things the use of chains or suction or compressed air.

The chain-operated railway would be powered by a stationary steam engine that pulls the train up the hill, sometimes with its locomotive to continue under its own power. The suction or compressed air railways used a vacuum or air pressure to transport the coaches in the same way as the pneumatic tube system used in some department stores to convey documents and the like. Another idea for overcoming steep gradients consisted of a train rolling downhill, pulling another train uphill. This principle has often been applied to smaller hill and mountain railways, using steel cables that are controlled by a drum at the upper station.

FORMER GERMAN STATES STEAM LOCOS

At the beginning of the last century, the lack of a powerful express locomotive also able to be deployed usefully in hilly terrain had been noted in Prussia. Whilst the Maffei S 3/5 and S 2/5 models with compound drive pulled the heaviest expresses between Spessart and Karwendel in Bavaria, Prussia had to make do with rather lame engines, some of which originated from the previous century. Robert Garbe, the locomotive expert of Prussian State Railways and orthodox advocate of the superheated steam principle with simple steam expansion, therefore formulated an idea for an express steam locomotive on these principles with three coupled driving axles in 1905. If reports of that time are to be believed, Garbe intended that the engine should be capable of being repaired by a village blacksmith in the most far-flung corner of eastern Prussia.

P 8: The first locomotive for Europe

Berliner Maschinen AG delivered the first engine designated P 8 with the characteristic final axle displaced to the rear as early as 1906. The streamlined driver's cab underlined Garbe's aim of getting the engines approved as express locomotives for speeds of 110 km/h (68 mph). But the miserable running characteristics of the P 8, an unerring fault in many of Garbe's designs, prevented the model from becoming a real express locomotive. With a top speed of only 100 km/h (62 mph) and without the strikingly arrowed front to the driver's cabin, the P 8 initially began its march to glory rather modestly. Although test runs in 1906 confirmed the capacity of the P 8, even at the head of heavy express trains, the teething problems of the model were also mercilessly exposed. Only numerous changes through the course of the years made the P 8 into what is regarded as today: one of the best locomotives of all time. A good 2,300 P 8s had already been built by numerous engine builders by the end of World War I, and the locomotives did not just remain the preserve of Prussian railways. The State Railways of the Grand Duchy of Baden, among others, acquired 40 of the universal locomotives.

The stock of P-8s in Germany was reduced by about a quarter, with the delivery of engines to Poland, Belgium and France as part of the reparation payments required by the Treaty of Versailles. In order to close the glaring gaps in its fleet, the newly established Reichsbahn ordered the P 8, later given its own new designation of 38.10, right through until 1923. Apart from its home stretches, the P 8 also ran in Bavaria and Württemberg, and even supplanted other tried and tested models there. About 3,800 examples of the P 8 were made, counting the machines built under licence in other European countries. In the chaos following World War II the indestructible model could be encountered throughout the continent. Denmark relied just as much on the P 8 as Romania, Poland and the two Germanys. Some 1,200 engines formed the backbone of the Bundesbahn's express and passenger train service, while about 700 more were indispensable to the Reichsbahn in East Germany. Whilst the Bundesbahn extended the range of numerous engines in the 1960s with the tub tenders of former war locomotives, Giesl

Right: Locomotives of the P 8 series were in passenger train service in southern Germany until the 1970s. Often the old Prussian steam locomotive hauled three silver coaches, or other rebuilt coaches.

ejectors with their characteristic flattened chimneys considerably improved the economy of several Reichsbahn engines. Number 38 1182, today a museum engine, signed off from service as the Reichsbahn's last locomotive at Bw Aschersleben. Three years later, at Bw Rottweil, she was followed by 038 772-0, likewise preserved in a museum, which was only removed from inventories two years before its successor, construction Series 23, some 40 years younger.

Series 74: not just on the Berlin Urban Railway

Robert Garbe, the locomotive expert of Prussian State Railways and the spiritual father of several Prussian steam engines, thought that Prussian locomotives ought to be powerful, economical and, above all, fulfil their purpose. These qualities apply without restriction to the Prussian T 12. At the turn of the century, a powerful tank locomotive also able to pull passenger trains at up to 65 km/h (40 mph) was precisely what Prussia lacked. True to the Prussian creed of austerity, the locomotive engineers continued to develop the proven T 9.3, a small tank locomotive, which was particularly at home on branch lines. Steam superheating, which had only recently been effectively applied to locomotives, presented an effective option for further increasing the locomotive's economy.

Thus in 1902 the T 12 with superheated steam transmission emerged from the T 9.3 as a larger, more powerful, although not necessarily better-looking engine. The new superheated steam technology was apparently viewed with little confidence and at first only four examples of the engine using it were produced. From 1903 the T 11, with saturated steam drive but much the same structural design, was preferred for mass production. But there was to be no stopping the glorious march of the superheated steam engine, as foreseen by Garbe in this case. Two years later Borsig, the Berlin engine builder, began to produce the T 12 in large numbers. In a short space

of time the T 12 became not just a classic model on the Berlin Urban Railway, but also one of the most successful tank locomotives of its time. By 1916, numerous engine builders had supplied a total of 929 machines of type T 12 to all the Prussian administrative districts.

Then in 1918 and 1919 the Prussian T 12 inventory was severely reduced by the new borders in Europe and reparations to the victorious powers. Nevertheless, together with the 40 engines subsequently supplied to the former administrative district of Berlin in 1921, Deutsche Reichsbahn was still able to categorise 899 machines as construction Series 74 in its new numbering schedule of 1925. Over the course of the years, these machines were joined by a further ten locomotives from Saarland Railway, whilst the nationalised Lübeck-Büchener Railway added 11 engines to the fleet, some of which even had streamlined cladding. The T 12 had long since been in use on other lines away from its home tracks in Prussia. Machines of construction Series 74 proved themselves both in suburban transport in Stuttgart and on Bavaria's local railways.

The former Berlin Urban Railway machines continued to be indispensable in both Germanys even after World War II. The Bundesbahn did not decommission the last 74 until 1968 at Bw Düren.

S 10: Prussia's Pacific answer

The P 8 was actually intended to become the standard express locomotive of Prussian State Railways. The project nevertheless failed because of the poor running characteristics of the machines, even below the magic 100 km/h (62 mph) speed barrier. The Prussians tried to prevent the unbalanced masses of the two-cylinder P 8 moving to and fro with an ingenious move. The high-performance P-8 boiler was simply installed on a underframe with four-cylinder driving gear and simple steam expansion, which ran on driven wheels with a diameter of 2 m (6 ft 6 in). The express locomotive designated

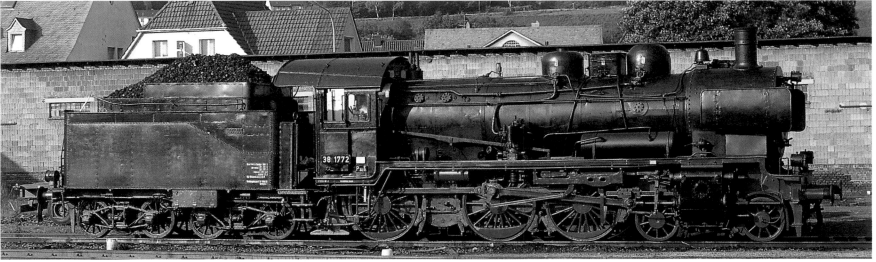

Opposite page: A P 8 hauls a passenger train towards Freudenstadt in 1971.

Top: The P 8 was also a native in Poland. There they were known as Type Ok 1. The picture was taken on the turntable at the Wollnstein locomotive depot.

Above: Number 38 1272 is a privately-owned museum locomotive.

Left: A special train hauled by a Series 74 loco near Langenorla in October 1989.

Series 17.0, 17.6, 18.1, 18.4 and 38.10				
Wheel arrangement	2'Ch4 (4-6-0)	2'Ch4 (4-6-0)	2'C1'h4v (4-6-2)	2'C1'h4v (4-6-2)	2'Ch2 (4-6-0)
First delivery	1910	1906	1909	1908	1906
Last delivery	1914	1906	1921	1931	1923
Withdrawn from service	1954	1956	1955	1967	1974
Quantity	202	6	41	159	3502
Length overall	20.75m (68'1")	20.545m (67'5")	21.935m (72'0")	22.862m (75'0")	18.59m (61'0")
Total wheelbase	9.1m (29'10")	8.5m (27'11")	11.04m (36'3")	11.19m (36'9")	8.35m (27'5")
Bogie wheelbase	1.98m (6'6")	1.905m (6'3")	1.8m (5'11")	1.87m (6'2")	1.75m (5'9")
Wheel diameter	1.0m (3'3")	1.065m (3'6")	1.25m (4'1")	0.95/1.206m (3'1"/3'11")	1.0m (3'3")
Working weight	77.2t (85 tons)	73.3t (81 tons)	87.8t (97 tons)	94.7t (104 tons)	78.2t (86 tons)
Maximum speed	110km/h (68 mph)	100km/h (62 mph)	115km/h (71 mph)	120km/h (75 mph)	100km/h (62 mph)
1-hour rating	854kW (1,145hp)	n/a	1,372kW (1,839hp)	1,336kW (1,791hp)	861kW (1,154 hp)

Above: The Prussia S 10 was a convincing locomotive. This photograph shows the Deutschen Reichsbahn locomotive number 17 107 in a classic pose.
Opposite page: The Series 78 could be seen in southern Germany until in the 1970s, at the Rottweil depot. The type was particularly used for light passenger train services.

S 8 was born. Prussia rejected a steam engine built using the compound principle because of alleged start-up problems. The fact that the S 10.1 with compound drive was triumphant only a short time later is another story.

After the generally good results with the two S 8 engines, particularly in comparison to the P 8, mass-production began in 1911 with minor changes and the engines were thereafter designated S 10. The high steam consumption nevertheless remained the problem with the four-cylinder S 10. In the same year the S 10.1 impressively demonstrated the advantages of a four-cylinder compound drive in direct comparison with the normal four-cylinder S-10. There was certainly no lack of experiments in subsequent years as the search to find the ideal steam engine for the standard Prussian express locomotives were finally followed in 1914 by the S 10.2 with a normal three cylinders. Although it did not achieve the economy of the compound engines, it required considerably less steam to produce the same performance as its four-cylinder sister.

Even though the original S 10 may have appeared more elegant than the other two models, its high steam consumption, and therefore fuel use, always put it at a disadvantage. Despite this, all three S-10 construction types shared the main load of the heavy express service in equal measure at Prussian State Railways. Some engines even had the honour of transporting the German Kaiser and the King of Prussia, Wilhelm II, in the royal train.

The popularity of the S 10 among other rail operators was demonstrated after World War I. Of the former 207 machines, the Reichsbahn could only categorise 135 locomotives as construction Series 17.0 in its new numbering schedule. A total of 64 of the four-cylinder express locomotives ended up on foreign railways as reparation payments or as a result of territorial changes.

Accidents, too, reduced the stock of S 10s. After its spectacular crash from the Trogenbach bridge in Ludwigsstadt in Upper Franconia, the S 10 Trier 1013 had to be decommissioned even before it was redesignated. The star of all S 10 construction models began to wane after World War II. By 1948 the last machines with three- and four-cylinder drive had come under the cutting torch. DB's last S 10.1 with compound drive followed in 1952. Only the S 10.1 with the Reichsbahn in East Germany was able to keep on going until April 1964: a late triumph for the compound technology originally scorned by Prussia.

T 18: Prussia could also build elegant locomotives

Prussian engines were never going to win any beauty contests, particularly not in Robert Garbe's era. But in 1912 Prussia's locomotive engineers proved that they could be different. With elegant, harmonious forms almost reminiscent of locomotives bearing Maffei's hallmark, the first T 18 rolled out from the Vulcan locomotive works in Stettin after just over a year under construction. The beauty and elegance of the T 18 was no mere chance. After years of building engines with austerity under the aegis of locomotive expert Robert Garbe, the T 18 now put into service by Prussia fulfilled all the expectations placed on it. When a railway ferry ran for the first time from Sassnitz on Rügen to Trelleborg in Sweden in the early years of the 20th century, those responsible at Prussian State Railways quickly noticed that the small Series T 12 tank locomotives used in heavy express train service were hopelessly inadequate on the steep ramps to the ferry loading terminals. Similar complaints were heard about the T 10, another machine designed by Garbe under minimalist principles, which ran at the limits of its capacity in

heavy express service between Frankfurt and Wiesbaden. The T 18, drafted under Garbe's successor, Hinrich Lübken, offered a solution to the problems in the Rhine-Main area and at the Rügen ferry terminals.

The engines were massive by Prussian standards and easily exceeded the demands placed upon them. Once the tank locomotive with its three driven wheels and two twin-axle bogies had got over its early teething troubles, it was superior even to the much praised P 8 in almost every way. There was reason enough to keep ordering the T 18 until 1927. The last engines rolled out of the production shops ready painted in uniform black and with the new Reichsbahn number 78. The Reichsbahn took delivery of 460 machines from Prussia and 20 locomotives that had been ordered by Württemberg. The Reichsbahn's fleet was supplemented over the course of the years with further engines belonging to Saarland Railways and the Eutin-Lübecker Railway (ELE).

The 78 continued to be indispensable even after World War II. The Deutsche Bundesbahn (DB) operated 424 of the former T 18 in its fleet, and the Deutsche Reichsbahn (DR) deployed 53 machines of Series 78 in the GDR. DB operated the T 18 for longer than some newly-built steam engines. As the last of its class, number 78 246 only ended her career on 30 December 1974 at Bw Rottweil. 78 425 closed the active service life of the T 18 in the GDR at Bw Pasewalk. The last machine to be removed from stock was 78 110 on 31 January 1972, although this had been sitting in the sidings since 1969. 78 009 was spared decommissioning and entered Dresden Transport Museum as a non-functioning exhibit on 15 September 1971. Another was restored to working order in 2000.

The T 18 lasted as long in France as in the two Germanys. Of the total of 27 engines delivered to the Alsace-Lorraine State Railway, only number 8419 remained with the Reichsbahn after World War I as 78 093. The remaining 26 machines spent the rest of their service lives in France. The last engine was 1-232 TC 423, which was decommissioned by the French national railway SNCF at Depot IIᵉ Napoléon in Mulhouse on 27 December 1966.

Series 58: a tough goods locomotive

The loads pulled by goods trains had increased considerably since the start of World War I. The engines of Classes G 8.1 and G 10 were acquired in large numbers before then were no longer powerful enough. Prussian State Railways therefore asked Henschel to develop a 1'Eh3 (2-10-0) locomotive. In order to prevent the loads on bearings and tappets becoming too high and to ensure even power at start-up, it was decided to use the three-cylinder drive successfully deployed in the S 10.2. The six-axle underframe was required because of the long boiler. The first locomotives of the G 12.1 class were ready in August 1915. Despite favourable coal consumption they were not really convincing. On the one hand they consumed a great deal of water. On the other hand the maximum axle load of 17.1 t (19 tons) meant that they could not be run freely on all main lines and branch lines. It was 1916 before Henschel finally received the order for the revision work.

The Armed Forces likewise had major grumbles. The state railways provided many different locomotives for wartime use. This complicated the supply of spare parts immensely and the workforce was occasionally confused by the operating features of the different machines. The military consequently demanded that a uniform model be developed with a maximum axle weight of 16 t (17.6 tons).

Above: Locomotive number 58 503 hauling an extremely long freight train near Altoberndorf. The picture was taken in the year 1937.

Opposite page: At the head of a special freight train, this operational 58 311 in East Germany was being filmed for a video recording in February 1993.

Although Henschel broke with several principles of Prussian locomotive building, the goal was never really achieved. The axle load was a little higher, but a number of railways in the south of the country continued to pursue their own designs at will. Nevertheless, a first step had been taken. By 1924 the Reichsbahn and the state railways in Baden, Prussia, Saxony and Württemberg had purchased 1,499 examples of the Class G 12, the forerunner of the uniform locomotives.

A Prussian locomotive was given a through-going sectional underframe for the first time. The boiler rose to unimagined heights, with its centre point 3 m (10 ft) above the track. Instead of a narrow firebox, as propagated by the earlier locomotive expert Robert Garbe, the engine received a broad rear boiler. Henschel moreover developed a new type of suspension. The G 12 pulled 1,330 t (1,466 tons) on even stretches at 65 km/h (40 mph), its top speed, and still managed 1,000 t (1,100 tons) at 25 km/h (15½ mph) on a 1 in 100 gradient.

The Reichsbahn deployed the machines in all areas with uphill stretches. With the exception of the few locomotives in Hanover, northern Germany was the only place where it was not possible to find the G 12, designated as Series 58 from 1925. The Bundesbahn rapidly decommissioned the G 12s remaining in the West after World War II.

A longer service life was foreseen for the Prussian engine in the GDR. Engines in the original design were indispensable up to 1976. There were two types of engine conversions besides this, those fired by pulverized coal and those retrofitted with a newly-built boiler.

Pulverized coal firing had already been experimented with before the war. The principle did not make much impression in practice, however, because the mechanical transport of the fuel to the firebox did not work as envisaged. Hans Wendler developed a compressed air feed system for the GDR Reichsbahn. The first pulverized coal engine was ready early in 1950 in the form of locomotive 58 1208. Initial trials were not promising. Neither sufficient pulverized brown coal nor enough combustion air reached the firebox. Wendler installed a narrow chimney with a tapered blast pipe. During the second series of trials it was established that the coal bunker, taken from a pre-war design, was unsuitable because large volumes of residues remained. The Reichsbahn finally divided the bunker into several segments, and thereafter pulverized coal firing worked relatively smoothly. A total of 55 Series 58 engines were converted in subsequent years. Apart from these, locomotives of the Series 44 and 52 were also fired in this way. The last of these locomotives were withdrawn from service at the end of the 1960s.

A longer service life was foreseen for the machines with newly-built boilers, the Reko 58 or 58.30. Welded boilers with combustion chambers, as had been developed for newly-built engines of Series 23.10 and 50.40, were fitted to 56 locomotives between 1958 and 1963. A Trofimoff-built pressure compensating piston valve improved the idle running properties significantly. The boiler pressure rose from 14 to 16 bar (203 to 232 psi).

Reko 58s managed to gain acceptance after some early teething troubles caused by inaccurate workmanship. Their coal consumption was up to 25% lower than that of mass-produced models. Traction force was increased by 12 to 15%t and extended into the range of the Series 44. The instruction manual stated that the boiler could be fed with up to 65 kg per m² (13¼ lb per

Series 58, 59, 78.0, 95 and 96					
Wheel arrangement	1'Eh3 (2-10-0)	1'Fh4v (2-12-0)	2'C2'h2t (4-6-4)	1'E1'h2t (2-10-2)	D'Dh4vt (0-8-8-0)
First delivery	1917	1918	1912	1922	1913
Last delivery	1921	1924	1927	1924	1923
Withdrawn from service	1982	1957	1975	1981	1954
Quantity	1499	44	534	45	25
Length overall	18.495m (60'8")	20.2m (66'3")	14.8m (48'6")	15.1m (49'6")	17.7m (58'1")
Total wheelbase	8.5m (27'10")	9.9m (32'6")	11.7m (38'4")	11.9m (39'0")	12.2m (40'0")
Bogie wheelbase	1.4m (4'7")	1.35m (4'5")	1.65m (5'5")	1.4m (4'7")	1.216m (4'0")
Wheel diameter	1.00m (3'3")	0.943m (3'1")	1.00m (3'3")	0.85m (2'9")	–
Working weight	95.7t (105 tons)	108t (119 tons)	105t (116 tons)	127.4t (140 tons)	131.1t (144 tons)
Maximum speed	65km/h (40mph)	60km/h (37mph)	100km/h (62mph)	65km/h (40mph)	50km/h (31mph)
1-hour rating	1,124kW (1,507hp)	1,401kW (1,878hp)	832kW (1,115hp)	1,182kW (1,584hp)	1,190kW (1,595hp)

sq ft) per hour. In practice, 8 to 20% more than this was possible without problem. The Reichsbahn used the 58.30 primarily in central Germany. Only Bw Aue was not able to accommodate the machines because its 19-m (62-ft) diameter turntable was too small. The Reko 58 steamed on until 1982. The museum engine 58 3047 was preserved for future generations.

S 3/6: The loveliest steam engine in the world?

Even though the S 3/6 is today regarded as the very essence of Bavarian locomotive building, its roots lie on the other side of the Atlantic. The most attractive locomotive ever built in Germany has American parents. This is not to say that good engines could not be built in Bavaria. The express locomotives of the C V class were proof of the high art of locomotive building between Spessart and Karwendel. But the designers at Maffei, the largest engine builder in Bavaria, realised that it was possible to go one better during a visit to America. Alongside several design features, such as a steel firebox or the four-cylinder compound transmission developed by Samuel Vauclain, in which the high-pressure and low-pressure cylinders were arranged above one another, the Bavarians were particularly taken by the sectional underframes of American engines.

After ordering two goods locomotives from Baldwin in Philadelphia, Royal Bavarian State Railway followed this up with two express locomotives designated S 2/5 with Vauclain drive and sectional underframes in 1901. The American S 2/5s engines of the Atlantic class with a 2'B1 (4-8-2) wheel arrangement were a roaring success. A short time later Bavarian

State Railways ordered two similar engine types from their main supplier, Maffei, based on the American precedent. In place of the American style, slightly reminiscent of the Wild West, Maffei's head designer, Anton Hammel, came up with his own design with unpretentious, elegant lines and a high-lying boiler, the beauty of which was never captured again. The uneven-running Vauclain drive made way for a traditional compound drive with four cylinders in a row and a von Borries drive unit. The only basic difference between the engine types was the wheel arrangement: Whilst the S 2/5 transmitted power to two wheels 2 m (6 ft 6 in) in diameter, the S 3/5 had three driven wheels of just 1.87 m (6 ft 1½ in) diameter. This meant that the small trailing axle below the driver's cabin had to go.

The start came with the S 3/5 3301 in 1903. This rolled out onto Bavarian rails as the first European locomotive with a sectional underframe and with the elegance typical of Maffei's creations. Anton Hammel's design prevailed. After no less successful Atlantics for Baden State Railways (II d) and Palatinate Railways (P 4), and also the legendary S 2/6 high-speed engine for Bavaria, Maffei then turned its hand to a locomotive with a 2'C1' (4-6-2) wheel arrangement, the first Pacific in Germany. This did not remain in Bavaria, but went on to enter railway history in the neighbouring state of Baden as the IV f. Its debut in the Rhine valley and on the slopes of the Black Forest was, however, only a moderate success because of the poorly adjusted transmission. Although basically a faulty design, the IV f still has the honour of being the direct predecessor of the most successful express locomotive by far in the era of the state railways, the Bavarian S 3/6.

Following the experiment in Baden, Maffei made fundamental improvements to several details and unveiled its first Bavarian Super Pacific, with the operating number 3601, on 16 June 1908. The S 3/6 did not just win friends for its technical qualities alone; its elegant exterior form soon made it a contender for the most attractive steam engine anywhere. The second S 3/6, number 3602, rolled out of the workshops only four days later and virtually made straight for the "Munich 1908" Exhibition. The royal coat of

Opposite page: For filming purposes, locomotive 58 311 was restored as 58 1620 in the period style of the GDR's Reichsbahn.

Below: An express train is hauled up the Frankenwald gradient by 18 546 in 1932.

arms on both sides of the smoke chambers, a golden chimney cap, bright boiler rings and the brass-covered cylinder and valve heads underline the elegance of the ochre-coloured S 3/6.

Five further S 3/6 prototypes followed up to November 1908. The S 3/6 passed its trial by fire in test runs and in hard everyday use, so nothing stood in the way of series production. All ten machines of Series a made between September and November 1909 rolled out unchanged to the prototypes and into the care of the central workshop in Munich. In 1910 Maffei inserted an S 3/6 designated as Series b into the running production of other machines at short notice for the World Exhibition in Brussels. With shining blue sheet cladding and all kinds of brass trimmings, it was as lavishly equipped as the exhibit from 1908. Another five Series c locomotives followed unchanged in May and June 1911; then Maffei's engineers had a rethink.

Although the S 3/6 excelled in hilly terrain with its 1.87-m (6 ft 1½ in) driving wheels, Bavaria needed a racehorse on the long rolling stretches along the Danube, Main and Lech. Maffei's designers in Munich began to think back to earlier fast runners with large wheels. The driven wheel diameter of the S 3/6 was therefore increased to 2 m (6 ft 6 in) for the Series d and e produced in 1912 and early 1913. The streamlined form of the driver's cab, superfluous in practice, made way for a straighter design, as with the other Bavarian engines. The expectations were fulfilled. Long-distance runs from Munich to Würzburg or between Nuremberg and Halle became the domain of "long thighs", as the personnel soon came to call the large-wheeled engine. The flip side of the coin was that the more agile, older machines had the clear advantage on the gradients of Frankenalb and Frankenhöhe and in the Fichtel mountains. Higher-quality bearings and improved lubrication oils, however, soon mad possible longer runs and constant high speeds for the series with smaller wheels. The 18 engines with 2 m (6 ft 6 in) driving wheels remained a well-intended intermezzo, but one that was technically unnecessary.

Above and below: On the initiative of the model train manufacturer Märklin, the only operational S 3/6 was given a fashionable blue livery. From time to time it hauls special trains from Munich to Füssen. There, passengers can see the musical about Ludwig II, the legendary Bavarian king.

Below left: The home of the loco is the Bavarian railway museum in Nördlingen.

Rights: Loco number 3673 in operation after being restored and painted in the original Bavarian green.

Opposite page: Number 95 027 is one of the most evocative locomotives of German railways. Here it is pulling a freight train at a steam display event through the heavenly winter landscape of the Erzgebirge mountains.

The original appearance of the S 3/6 with its streamlined driver's cab and small driving wheels again came to the fore in 1913–14. Major technical changes were not required until 1914 when Palatinate Railways ordered ten Series g locomotives. As the engines had to fit onto the small Palatinate turntables, which were 19 m (62 ft) in diameter, Maffei shortened the distance between the front bogie and first coupling axle by some 16 cm (6 in) in all subsequent series of the S 3/6. Maffei's designers only intervened again in the penultimate series with the abbreviation i of 1917. They increased the axle weight of the engine from 16 to 17 t (17.6 to 18.7 tons), whereby the transmission could now generate 1,715 hp (1,279 kW) of tractive force instead of 1,660 hp (1,238 kW).

After World War I, Bavaria was obliged by the Treaty of Versailles to hand over 19 of its 89 type S 3/6 express locomotives to the victorious powers as reparations. The French national railway ETAT took delivery of 12 brand-new machines delivered free of charge from Maffei's workshops in the Hirschau district of Munich. In addition, numbers 3602 and 3618 with their lavish brass fittings had to leave their old stamping grounds and travel westwards. Why the comparatively old 3605 and 3622 engines were part of the reparation package remains a mystery to this day. If sources of the time are to be believed, crafty Bavarian railwaymen knocked some years off a few old machines, including the three locomotives for Belgium, by swapping their rating and number plates with those of younger models, and so saved the newer machines from being handed over.

Shortly after its establishment in the year 1920, Deutsche Reichsbahn was only able to present vague draft designs for an express locomotive of the future. Although it was to take up the first place in the new numbering schedule as 01, it was simply too heavy for the majority of lines. Faced with a much reduced fleet of locomotives, the only alternative open to the new national operator was to continue purchasing proven state railway models; so the S 3/6 had an Indian Summer as the 18.4-5. A successor also appeared for the S 3/5, technically rather overshadowed by its big sister. In 1921 Maffei placed the S 3/5's more powerful superheated steam boiler onto the underframe of the former, somewhat lame P 3/5 N from 1905. With this, the new P 3/5 H was born, a small passenger train locomotive, but one that was also not out of place at the head of express trains. Although many believed that the Bavarian four-cylinder had passed its zenith with the establishment of the Reichsbahn, the most successful time for the S 3/6 now began.

Reworked in a number of technical details, Maffei started to build engines of type S 3/6 again from 1923. With its side walls drawn inwards towards the top, the driver's cabin was already oriented to the draft designs for the later uniform locomotives. The last S 3/6 supplied by Maffei in full Bavarian livery was the 3709 for its stand at the Technical Railway Exhibition in Seddin. Just as elegant as the machine for the World Exhibition in Brussels in 1910, number 3709 was also painted blue and equipped with numerous brass fittings. The new Reichsbahn numbers now adorned all subsequent locomotives, which were designated as 18.5 in its new number schedule, on the still green boiler. All 18.5s up to model Series n had rolled out of Maffei's workshops, but when the Bavarian company went bankrupt in 1930, the Reichsbahn had to order the last series with operating numbers 18 531 to 18 548 from Henschel in Kassel.

The S 3/6 then proceeded to find homes outside Bavaria. Osnabrück, Halle, Berlin, Bingerbrück and Heidebreck in Silesia were stations for the 18.4-5. The star S 3/6 train was undoubtedly the "Rheingold" express running between Mannheim and Emmerich. The decline started after World

War II. Of the large-wheeled engines, only 18 451 was given a stay of execution up to 1953 as a fast, long-distance locomotive in test runs for the Bundesbahn's Head Office (BZA) in Minden. Numerous other machines had ended their careers under the cutting torch of the locomotive scrap works in Desching near Ingolstadt by the end of the 1950s. The Bundesbahn only had big plans for a few 18.5s.

New, welded, high-performance boilers were fitted into a total of 30 engines of the youngest series from 1953 onwards, first at Krauss-Maffei and later in the Ingolstadt repair works, turning them into true power packs. Compared to the other locomotives, the powerful machines with the new numbers 18 601 to 18 630 developed up to 2,220 hp (1,641 kW) of traction power. Despite a few technical inadequacies, the S-3/6 conversion proved itself in heavy express service until 1966. The "Concerto bavarese" in 4/4 time only died out in 1969, when the fire of the unconverted 18 505 was extinguished for ever by the Bundesbahn's Head Office in Minden. By this time the overwhelming majority of S 3/6s had long been melted in the blast furnaces. What is left for enthusiasts of what was perhaps the most attractive locomotive of all time are the seven machines preserved in museums, of which the 3673 at Nördlingen Railway Museum is in working condition and will hopefully keep enthusiasts' pulses beating a little faster for a long time to come.

Series 95: The Mountain Queen

Seen from a southern German perspective, everything in Prussia was flat, the wide plains only broken by the occasional, hardly noticeable hill. Why then did Prussia need uphill locomotives such as the T 20?

Anyone looking a little closer will see that there were respectable mountains in Prussia. From a railway history viewpoint, another factor was that Prussian State Railways was also active in neighbouring states, which either could not or did not want to afford their own railway. These included Anhalt and Hessen, as well as other states with names which sound rather exotic today, such as Saxe-Coburg-Gotha and Saxe-Weimar.

Uphill stretches were mainly built as rack-and-pinion railways in the 19th century. Many experts doubted that adhesion locomotives could also cope with steeper inclines, but measurement and trial runs then proved that adhesion traction was clearly superior to the rack-and-pinion system at inclines of up to 1 in 16$^{1/2}$. It was also possible to bring the train to a halt reliably, even under difficult conditions. The so-called "Animal class" engines belonging to the Blankenburg-Halberstädter Railway were among the first adhesion locomotives for uphill stretches.

The positive results finally convinced the transport ministry, which ordered an initial ten 1'E1' (2-10-2) tank locomotives from Borsig. These were first categorised as T 20, following the Prussian numbering system, but were later given the designation 95. The ten machines in the first series were on the rails in 1923. By 1924 Borsig and Hanomag had supplied a further 35 locomotives. Although they counted as Prussian engines, the Reichsbahn also stationed them in Dresden-Friedrichstadt and Geislingen from the start. Locomotives had been taken in at Bw Rothenkirchen and Neuenmarkt-Wirsberg even before 1945. This had nothing to do with providing competition to the proven Bavarian classes, such as Series 96, at all

costs. Rather locomotives of the same series now stood ready on both sides of the Frankenwald and Saale railways, which made services easier to operate. The feared Frankenwald gradient nevertheless did not count among the uphill stretches.

There may be a certain contradiction here to the original purpose of Series 95, but it nevertheless still corresponds to the Prussian application principles. The size of the countryside and the huge differences in the population density required very economical running. Technical ingenuity and experiments were left to others. The Series 95 was able to show its full qualities on runs such as the Saale Railway and the Frankenwald gradient. It attained a speed of 65 km/h (40 mph), which was sufficient for goods trains; it had enough traction force for inclines, and it was economical to maintain thanks to its simple method of construction.

In 1945, 14 machines remained in West Germany and 31 in East Germany. The Bundesbahn classified Series 95 under the sub-classes. Bw Pressig-Rothenkirchen and Neuenmarkt-Wirsberg soon handed their machines over to Bw Aschaffenburg. The "Mountain Queen", as the 95 was named by railway enthusiasts, then ran exclusively on the Spessart incline. Once the Aschaffenburg-Würzburg line had been electrified in September 1957, the locomotives were put into the sidings.

The Reichsbahn stationed its machines primarily in rail shops in Thuringia and in the Harz region. East of the demarcation line they also worked much more frequently after 1945 in their planned areas of use than was at first the case. Thus they ran on the Rübeland line, which was taken over by the state in 1949, and on various lines in the Thuringian Forest. Although locomotive 95 028 stayed a few weeks in Sassnitz in 1967, there is no evidence to suggest that it put in any service worthy of note there.

The Reichsbahn modernized its locomotives in the 1950s and at the start of the 1960s. The most important project, the conversion to oil firing, began in 1964. A total of 24 locomotives were provided with the new firing system. It would have been possible to increase the performance, but this was rejected by the head administration in order to spare the boilers and underframes. In addition to this the Reichsbahn fitted ten locomotives with newly-built boilers between 1966 and 1975.

By this time the traction change had also progressed a long way in the GDR. The Soviet Union supplied a large number of diesel locomotives month after month. Romanian Railways had moreover ordered the Series 119. Series 95 was withdrawn from service. Number 95 10027 pulled the official farewell train between Steinach and Saalfeld on 28 February 1981. At the end of April and beginning of May it steamed out again, this time on a scheduled run between Sonneberg and Saalfeld, because there were not enough diesel locomotives available. It was then definitively decommissioned. Numbers 95 009 and 016 have been preserved, both locomotives with newly-built boilers, and also number 95 027, which was converted back to conventional grate firing.

Opposite page: The Series 95 was in operation for many years on the stretches around Sonnenberg. In order to be prepared for winter sessions with the steam rotary snow plough, practice runs took place in late autumn. Since the steam snow plough cannot drive itself, it is pushed and pulled by locomotive 95 016.

Above: After its refurbishment, locomotive 01 150 undertook its first test run round Nuremberg (1985).

Right: The classic front of an express steam locomotive. With its large Wagner smoke deflectors, Number 01 111 can be seen in the Neumarkt-Wirsberg museum.

The creation of the Deutsche Reichsbahn on 1 April 1920 marked the beginning of an organised, unified railway system. Its management was faced with a variety of types of locomotives and coaches dating back to the time the "Länder", the individual regions of Germany. There were also different types of permanent way, railway equipment and signalling systems. All this made it very difficult to assess the situation and to control it. Rational and economic management required that the approach should be standardized as much as possible. This is why the "Select Committee for Locomotives" ("Engere Ausschluss für Lokomotiven") was created with the objective of unifying the locomotive fleet.

The Committee was faced with an almost insoluble problem in that the united regional railway stock of Prussia, Bavaria, Saxony, Baden, Württemberg, Mecklenburg and Oldenberg consisted of locomotives from 210 different design series and sub-series. The task was to unify the stock of locomotives while ensuring that in future the Reichsbahn would be left with as few different types as possible. There were two possible ways of achieving this. Either the best and the most recent locomotives could be selected and declared as the standard for the entire Reichsbahn; or a logical programme could be planned for the construction of new locomotives based on the most modern developments. This second option was the most likely to create an effective standardization of locomotive parts with the aim of producing an economic unit construction system. Such a system would allow the planned long-term exploitation of a design series while also allowing the development and construction of new types and series.

The idea of standardization was not a new one. During World War I a series of locomotives had been created that was produced and used in all the "Länder" of Germany. Under the series designation G 12, Prussia developed a heavy three-cylinder freight train locomotive. This war-produced standard type was used both on the front lines and in the country away from the front. It was invaluable on military railways, reducing the enormous difficulties

caused by the considerable technical differences that existed between the numerous other locomotives of the "Länder". Encouraged by the military, locomotive factories in Baden, Saxony and Württemberg produced the Prussian-developed G 12, following the original Prussian plans. This is how the first standard locomotive was created. However, as a new and independent series, it would not have spare parts interchangeable with other series. Therefore it could not yet be described as the basis of a unit construction system common to all series.

Temporary postwar production

However, the Select Committee was able to fall back on a series of important experiences when it met for the first time between 18 to 20 May in Oldenburg. The successful deployment of the G 12 greatly helped to clarify the question of which locomotives from the various regional railways should be acquired until the standardization programme with its entirely new locomotives could be completed. This point was an absolute priority in view of the enormous reparation payments Germany had to make: by the terms of the Versailles Peace Treaty, Germany had to hand over more than 8,000 locomotives to the victorious powers . Naturally, the further production and deployment of regional series locomotives was only a temporary solution. In fact, these locomotives helped meet the gap that would otherwise have arisen between the disappearance of the last, reliable regional locomotives and the arrival of the first, new standard locomotives.

But temporary measures sometimes continue for a long time. For some years after the creation of the Reichsbahn central office, the Select Committee and a special Standardization Office for Locomotives, a wide range of locomotive types were still being acquired, sometimes in large numbers. These included for instance, the Prussian P8, G 8.1, G 10, G 12, T 14.1, T 16.1 and T 18, and also Saxon locomotives such as the XII H2 and XX HV as well as the famous Bavarian S 3/6 and last but not least the Baden VIc.

Above: Bellowing large clouds of smoke and steam, locos 001 211 and 088 leave the station in Bamberg in the direction of Hof.

Right: Number 01 118 has become a museum train. On 1 September 1985 it pulled this colourful special train.

Opposite page: Locomotive 01 1066 is still operational as a museum locomotive. Here it too is hauling a special train.

In spite of this impressive list of the most successful locomotives ordered in the largest numbers, and in spite of the omnipresent financial constraints, standard locomotives remained on the Reichsbahn's agenda. In the long term nothing could replace the development of new construction principles and concepts — not even a careful selection of successful regional locomotive types that could be modernized if necessary. It is true that the wide-ranging experience of the German locomotive industry provided a solid base for future developments. But the construction of new and modern locomotives based on standardized principles was only possible through the elaboration and discussion of new projects.

With this in mind the Berlin Borsigwerke presented to the Oldenburg meeting a first well-rounded series of projects for seven types of steam locomotives for the major deployment areas. Publicly encouraged by Hinrich Lübken of the Railway Central Office, Borsig proposed two locomotives with separate tenders for slow stopping passenger trains, two tender locomotives for freight trains, and three tank locomotives of equal power — at least to judge from their appearance. The inspiration for the tender locomotives was the new heavy locomotive for passenger trains, the Series P 10 with 1'D1'h3 (2-8-2) wheel arrangement. On the other hand, the three tank locomotives were based on the powerful T 20 series, a 1'E1'h2 (2-10-2) locomotive.

A rival project from Henschel

In appearance all the locomotives in this series already revealed a certain degree of standardization. It was evident that Borsig had increased the total weight of the train without losing any speed, resulting in locomotives that were extraordinarily compact and powerful. They also looked very modern with their raised boiler. Immediately after the Oldenburg presentation to the Select Committee Borsig revised the series once more, while Henschel & Sohn in Kassel worked on similar projects for freight trains and tender locomotives. This standard series was based on Henschel's most recent and successful design, the Prussian series G 8.2, which itself was inspired by the reliable G 12 developed during the war.

Both the Borsig proposals and Henschel locomotives had construction and design features that were unmistakably Prussian. These proposals were discussed on the occasion of the second meeting of the Select Committee in Überlingen between 14 and 16 September 1921, finally leading to fundamental agreements about several points regarding the concept of the standard locomotive. This included the structure gauge — the overall clearance — of the new locomotives, the construction of the frame, the boiler pressure, the axle load, set at a maximum of 17 t (18.7 tons) and the wheel diameter.

On the other hand, the Select Committee did not come to any decision regarding the category of express train locomotives. Indeed, they were not the primary concern. In the opinion of the Reichsbahn Central Office, so far as express train locomotives were concerned it would be possible to make do with regional railway passenger locomotives for a while longer. The extraordinarily rapid technical developments, in particular the increase in maximum speeds, and the creation of a pioneering high-speed network could not be foreseen at this point of time. As a result locomotives similar to the Prussian series S 10.1 and P 10, the Bavarian S 3/6, the Saxon XX HV and the Series IV from Baden seemed capable of meeting passenger requirements for the time being.

The third meeting of the Select Committee took place between 10 and 12 May at Hildesheim. This time the subject of the meeting was different. Germany's Ministry of Transport had come to a far-reaching decision that had a direct impact on the work of the Select Committee. This decision was to increase the approved axle load to a maximum of 20 t (22.0 tons), which widened the scope for the development of more powerful, more efficient locomotives, especially for freight trains. For the first time the idea of a standard express locomotive was mooted, for which, according to the Ministry of Transport, the four-cylinder compound system similar to that of the south German locomotives would be a possibility. While the Select Committee had decided at its first meeting to opt for the Prussian S 10.1 and Saxon XX HV as a kind of "standard type" for the time being, the time had now come to choose a new type of standard express locomotive.

Series 01, 01.10, 03, 03.10 and 24					
Wheel arrangement	2'C1'h2 (4-6-4)	2'C1'h3 (4-6-2)	2'C1'h2 (4-6-2)	2'C1'h3 (4-6-2)	1'Ch2 (2-6-0)
First delivery	1926	1939	1930	1939	1928
Last delivery	1938	1940	1938	1940	1940
Withdrawn from service	1982	1975	1982	1980	1968
Quantity	231	55	298	60	95
Length overall	23.94m (78'7")	24.13m (79'2")	23.905m (78'5")	23.905m (78'5")	16.995m (55'9")
Total wheelbase	12.4m (40'8")	12.4m (40'8")	12m (39'4")	12m (39'4")	6.3m (20'8")
Driving wheel diameter	2.0m (6'7")	2.0m (6'7")	2.0m (6'7")	2.0m (6'7")	1.5m (4'11")
Bogie wheel diameter	1/1.25m (3'3"/4'1")	1/1.25m (3'3"/4'1")	1/1.25m (3'3"/4'1")	1/1.25m (3'3"/4'1")	0.85m (2'9")
Working weight	108.9t (120 tons)	114.3t (126 tons)	100.3t (100.6 tons)	103t (113.5 tons)	58.5t (64.5 tons)
Maximum speed	120km/h (75mph)	140km/h (87 mph)	130km/h (81mph)	140km/h (87 mph)	90km/h (56mph)
1-hour rating	1635kW (2192hp)	1715kW (2299hp)	1445kW (1937hp)	1314kW (1761hp)	672kW (901hp)

The Pacific gains acceptance

Obviously these unexpected developments at the Select Committee's third meeting in Hildesheim did not go unnoticed by the locomotive industry, which reacted immediately to the decisions from Berlin by submitting new proposals to meet the new requirements. Besides a 1'D' (2-8-0) type, the proposals also included a project for an express locomotive with a 2'C1' (4-6-2) "Pacific" wheel arrangement. After lengthy discussions about the merits of these various proposals and debates between the representatives of the various schools of locomotive constructors and the Reichsbahn Central Office, the legendary Series 01 was born. In spite all kinds of difficulties and various teething problems, this modern express locomotive became the symbol of the German standard locomotive.

What had already become apparent after only three meetings was confirmed later. From the start the Select Committee had searched tirelessly and doggedly to find the best constructional solutions. All those involved aimed to submit proposals for the most economical deployment of locomotives and the achievement of the best practical railway services. Engineers with remarkable knowledge and skills distinguished themselves in the process. The concept of the standard locomotive was developed by men such as the chief designer Lübken who worked for the Reichsbahn Central Office and Georg Meyer, the chief designer who looked after Saxony's interests. The practical implementation of the standard locomotive programme was embodied in a man who had already become a legend in his lifetime, Richard Paul Wagner, chairman of the Committee for many years. He was recognized by his contemporaries as being amazingly knowledgeable and highly qualified, with incredible energy and a phenomenal ability to assert himself. These were

invaluable qualities because creativity, inventiveness and decisiveness were prerequisites for getting such a project off the ground. But it later became clear that Wagner's attitude to the project was too dogmatic . Wagner's biography explains a serious deficiency in the standard locomotive programme — the very fact that its creators believed it would last forever. Wagner's impatience towards critics and criticism continued when the progressive construction and design principles of the 1920s gradually reached a dead end in the 1930s. The sad fact is that Wagner and many of his collaborators were determined to ignore new engineering techniques.

It was clear from the start that the great standardization programme was being pulled between two opposing objectives. On one hand, the aim was to meet the requirements of the already highly specialized areas of locomotive deployment, which ranged from shunting duties in marshalling yards, local stopping trains, heavy freight transport and express train services, used in terrain ranging from level lines to hilly stretches and steep mountain tracks. On the other hand, components had to be interchangeable and standardization was to be as comprehensive as possible, which meant that the number of locomotive types should be as few as possible. There were also differences of opinion over the type of construction. The South German locomotive industry favoured a four-cylinder system while Wagner favoured two cylinders. Which was best?

Finally, it was decided that the best approach was to specify a wide-ranging programme of types for the various services. With its internal logic, its functionality and technical standardization, the series specifications were without parallel and set international standards of high technical expertise. At the time these series specifications established a coordinated system on which new and modern locomotives would be based, depending on requirements.

In other words, locomotives would be built in accordance with set guidelines, produced economically and — after extensive testing — put into service with the greatest effectiveness:

1. Express and passenger locomotives with separate tender:
Series 01 – 39

Series	Wheel arrangement	Axle weight
01	2'C1'h2 (4-6-2)	20 t (22.0 tons)
02	2'C1'h4v (4-6-2)	20 t (22.0 tons)
20	2'Ch2 (4-6-0)	20 t (22.0 tons)
22	2'D1'h3 (4-8-2)	20 t (22.0 tons)
24	1'Ch2 (2-6-0)	15 t (16.5 tons)

2. Freight locomotives with separate tender:
Series 40 – 59

Series	Wheel arrangement	Axle weight
40	1'Ch2 (2-6-0)	20 t (22.0 tons)
41	1'Dh2 (2-8-0)	20 t (22.0 tons)
42	1'Eh2 (2-10-0)	20 t (22.0 tons)
43	1'Eh3 (2-10-0)	20 t (22.0 tons)

3. Passenger tank locomotives:
Series 60 – 79

Series	Wheel arrangement	Axle weight
60	1'C1'h2t (2-6-2)	20 t (22.0 tons)
62	2'C2'h2t (2-6-4)	20 t (22.0 tons)
64	1'C1'h2t (2-6-2)	15 t (16.5 tons)

4. Goods tank locomotives:
Series 80 – 96

Series	Wheel arrangement	Axle weight
80	Ch2t (0-6-0)	17 t (18.7 tons)
81	Dh2t (0-8-0)	17 t (18.7 tons)
82	Eh2t (0-10-0)	17 t (18.7 tons)
83	1'D1'h2t (2-8-2)	20 t (22.0 tons)
84	1'E1'h2t (2-10-2)	20 t (22.0 tons)
85	1'E1'h3t (2-10-2)	20 t (22.0 tons)
86	1'D1'h2t (2-8-2)	15 t (16.5 tons)
87	Eh2t (0-10-0)	17 t (18.7 tons)

5. Narrow gauge locomotives for 750 mm (29½ in) gauge:
Series 99

Series	Wheel arrangement	Axle weight
99.73	1'E1'h2t (2-10-2)	9 t (9.9 tons)

For various reasons, Richard Paul Wagner's fundamental principles of construction as made clear in the specification table were not always formulated

On 8 October 1971, locomotive 001 2202 leaves the station of Neuenmarkt-Wirsberg with a train of rebuilt four-axle coaches.

or handed out to those involved in the form of costly instruction manuals. A few of the fixed points, especially those defined by Wagner himself, were not written down anywhere, but were often quietly agreed on after long debates, purely out of respect.

Standardization and interchangeability

Perhaps the most important principle consisted in being able to use as small a number as possible of standard components in as many series as possible. This made it possible to interchange the parts when the need arose, irrespective of the series. As a result the processes of construction, production and spare part maintenance, including holding stocks, were technically efficient and economical. The pool of spare parts was easy to manage. Whether in Hamburg or Munich, in Breslau or Cologne, the standard locomotive offered the railways and main repair shops everywhere in Germany the best conditions for trouble-free maintenance and minor repair work. It also saved time on conversion work as well as in the execution of the increasingly important renovation programmes. There were further advantages, such as the simplification of training and qualification of repair workshop personnel. The opportunity of using the same component in many different series was consistently applied to many spare parts, including entire units such as boilers

and controls, driver's cabs, cylinders, bogies, pumps, valve gear, connecting rods and so on. While Wagner's principles were clearly formulated, the situation was quite different in the case of the driving mechanism. There was often tacit agreement because Wagner enforced his view on standard locomotives that two-cylinder locomotives were the best in principle. It is indeed true that this was recognized as the second, characteristic feature of the standard locomotive, but it was never formulated as a published standard — largely because of the resistance of the south German school who favoured the four-cylinder compound design.

A third feature, which this time was put in writing, was the use of the bar frame instead of the plate frame. The fourth feature concerned the superheater and feed pump for main line locomotives. In addition, an almost square grate was also an unwritten law for all standard locomotives. Serious problems with the trapezoid-shaped outer firebox of the Prussian P 10 had apparently contributed to the decision that a long, narrow grate was no longer to be permitted. Wagner was convinced that this had a decisive effect on the tubular heating surfaces. All main line locomotives of the standard type were to have leading bogies. There was another external feature that applied to express standard locomotives whose name perpetuates that of the person who inspired it: the use of the famous, large Wagner

Above: Locomotive 001 126 photographed on the turntable of the Hof depot, the last stronghold of the very popular 01 series. It was taken out of scheduled service here in May 1973.

Left: Locos 03 001 and 01 137 pulling the D 2755 at a steam locomotive event on 30 August 1992. In the early 1990s railway enthusiasts "exchanged" the scheduled diesel locomotives for operational museum steam locomotives at these events, which attracted great crowds.

Opposite page: Locomotive 003 131 hauling a wonderful set of Reichsbahn express coaches on 4 November 1971 on the stretch between Ulm and Friedrichshafen.

smoke deflector became a characteristic feature of modern, high-speed German locomotives. Contrary to popular opinion, these were not fitted for aerodynamic reasons. In fact their purpose was to guide the dispersing smoke upwards so as to clear the train driver's view of the track. Further criteria of the standard locomotive were the design features of the driver's cab, the footplate with skirts over the front buffer beams that were all similar in principle, and finally a similar overall appearance even in locomotives destined for different uses, indicating that they belonged to one and the same family.

The start of the Series 02

Between the creation of the Deutsche Reichsbahn and the appearance of the first standard locomotives, just six years elapsed in the course of which many changes took place. At the beginning of the project there was not yet a programme for a standard express locomotive. But the Series 02 launched in 1925 marked the beginning of a series of new standard locomotives. The following year the first locomotives of Series 01 and 44 were produced. These were followed in 1927 by Series 24, 43, 64, 80 and 87. In 1928, Series 62, 81 and 86 as well as the narrow gauge locomotive series 99.73 came out.

The practical testing of these series was supposed to help answer those questions of daily management for which the Planning Committee had not yet found a satisfactory answer or on which there was no agreement. This would sometimes lead to irritation and friction that might perhaps have been better avoided. But the basic idea was achieved: as early as the period 1925 to 1928, standard boilers or at least standard boiler parts were used in several series. The principle of interchangeability was also applied to engine parts, including running gear and cylinders as a result of standardization.

The first standard locomotive to enter service was number 02 001 delivered by Henschel in October 1925. A few days later it was followed by locomotive 02 002. From January 1926 it was used as a test locomotive, and especially as a locomotive to compare with number 01 001 that was delivered a little later.

At first glance, both series seemed identical in appearance and technical design, not least because of the high level of standardization of the parts and units from which they were built. However, the construction of the power unit clearly differed considerably in the two locomotives, and as before this represented controversial opposing positions. While Series 01 with a 2'C1' (4-6-2) wheel arrangement was a two-cylinder locomotive, Series 02, which had the same wheel arrangement, was a four-cylinder compound locomotive — as had been discussed at the third meeting of the Select Committee. The two-cylinder locomotive was favoured by the chairman and locomotive engineer Wagner, while the four-cylinder one was a concession to the so-called "south German faction of the four-cylinder school".

Left: The new type of boiler used in some locomotives of Series 01, 01.10 and 41 was a controversial subject among experts. In the end it failed to fulfill the expectations of higher performance. Locomotive 001 180 was one of the 01 series fitted with the new type of boiler.

Above: Locomotive 009 of Series 24 has been preserved for posterity. It is often used to pull special trains.

Opposite page: A few locomotives of the 41 series were oil-burning and were fitted with a new type of boiler. One of these was locomotive 41 360, here seen performing for filming purposes, pulling a freight train near Brilon Wald in Sauerland.

Below: The Reichsbahn in the German Democratic Republic rebuilt many Series 01 locomotives. These powerful locomotives fulfilled all expectations.

Above: Locomotive 03 1010 is seen pulling the D 647 at a speed of 130 km/h (81 mph) in the evening light on 21 October 1991.

Opposite page: For many years the "Jumbos" of Series 44 represented the epitome of the freight train locomotive. Locomotive 044 654 was photographed on 23 February 1973 near Neukirchen on its way to the steelworks at Sulzbach-Rosenbach.

The compound steam locomotives were fitted with high- and low-pressure cylinders. After the energy of the live steam had been partially released in the high-pressure cylinder, the steam passed into the low-pressure cylinder where it carried out further mechanical work by means of a second expansion. This more efficient use of steam led to a reduced fuel consumption. In addition the four-cylinder engine contributed to remarkably smoothing running. But because Wagner — who from the start had favoured the two-cylinder engine — was in a position of power and did not actively prevent or want to prevent serious defects creeping into the Series 02, it was the Series 01 that eventually triumphed.

The powerful and economical Series 43

Even when buying heavy freight train locomotives, the Reichsbahn did not immediately decide logically on the type of construction. In addition to the ten locomotives of Series 44, a relatively expensive type of three-cylinder compound engine, it decided to acquire ten Series 43 two-cylinder freight locomotives that apparently had not been planned at all. As with the high-speed Series 02 and 01 locomotives, the aim was to compare whether the two-cylinder versions would be less expensive. Apart from the number of

cylinders and the drive concept, the two rival locomotives were broadly similar. Series 43 had a such economical fuel consumption that it was decided not to purchase the Series 44 for the time being. It was therefore not surprising that Series 43 had the highest overall efficiency of the first standard types of rationalized freight locomotives and their developments. This is why the Reichsbahn came to the decision to buy 25 locomotives of Series 43. This included locomotive 43 013, which during extreme testing was coupled to a train of 5,000 t (over 5,500 tons). Contrary to all expectations, it succeeded in pulling this extraordinary load over the designated stretch.

Series 24, 64 and 86: abortive developments?

It is true that these powerful locomotives for heavy express freight trains were based on modern, pioneering concepts, but they were often accompanied by indecisiveness as to which of the various possible solutions should be adopted. Several wrong choices were made and there were also some professional errors.

Thus, on the one hand, Series 24, 64 and 86 provided excellent model examples from the point of view of the extensive interchangeability of their

Above: Only 15 Series 62 locomotives were put into service. Locomotive 62 015 is still in working order and it is often used to pull special trains.

Opposite page: Replacing a diesel locomotive, locomotive 44 1616 is pulling a heavy salt train on the Hohenzollern Regional Railway to Gammertingen in November 1993.

components. On the other hand, all three series had design solutions that fell short of realizing the full constructional possibilities of local railway locomotives.

Because the network still needed drastic modernization, the type specification provided for these three light local railway locomotives to meet various different requirements. Series 24 was suited to long secondary lines because of its separate tender, which meant that it could undertake long journeys without stopping to replenish its supplies of coal and water. Originally conceived for passenger services with a maximum forward speed of 90 km/h (56 mph), and also suitable for use on following railways, it was intended to be used for passenger trains and light freight trains. Because of its separate tender it was only approved to a maximum speed of 50 km/h (32 mph) in reverse running, and it therefore had to be rotated on a turntable at its destination station.

Series 64 also met these requirements, but with one difference: as a tank engine, its area of deployment was limited to short branch terminal lines and junction railway lines. Compared to the Series 24, it had the advantage of being able to travel at the top speed of 90 km/h (56 mph) even in reverse running, so that the Reichsbahn did not have to build a turntable at every one of its destination stations.

The specifications for both locomotives were very similar as far as construction was concerned. In addition, apart from the framework and the way the framework was assembled, there was a similarity between the components that went further than what would have been considered for standard locomotives. But for obvious reasons the water tanks and coal bunkers of the Series 24 tender loco could not match those of the Series 64 tank engine.

The third locomotive in the group was the Series 86, which deviated a little more from the other two in that it had a smaller wheel diameter. Its nearest relations were Series 80, 81 and 87.

A puzzle for the Traffic Operating Department

The disadvantage of all the three series acquired in large numbers was that, instead of the modern Krauss-Helmholtz bogies for the carrying wheels, they were fitted with the comparatively more primitive, already obsolete pony truck bogies. The bogie actually consisted of an axle that was secured through a shaft to a bogie pin on the frame. At higher speeds the riding stability decreased considerably because of its fairly simple construction. The Krauss-Helmholtz bogie linked the carrying wheels with the first pair of coupled wheels. The link between the driving wheels and the carrying wheels, had a very positive effect on the handling of the locomotive. The use of the pony truck bogie instead of the Krauss-Helmholtz amounted to a technically retrograde step in several German locomotives at this time. The Series 86 for example had four pairs of rigid coupled wheels and had a tendency to derail; this was a puzzle that the Standardization Office handed over to the chief motive power engineer.

Series 62 — the "little 01"

On the other hand, the Series 62 was a complete success. In the systematic classification of standard locomotives, it was to a certain extent a bridge between the large tender locomotive and the more manoeuvrable tank locomotive. For this reason the locomotive crew and engineers described the Series 62 as the "little 01". The locomotive with its symmetrical axle arrangement 2'C2' (4-6-4) had a rather inelegant appearance because of its third pair of coupled wheels placed further towards the back. But this was beside the point because as far as efficiency and operation were concerned this unusual locomotive left most other standard locomotives far behind, and in Thuringia it was certainly used as a slower Series 01.

Nevertheless, in spite of its advantages there was a serious problem. There was no suitable deployment area for the large, heavy, fast locomotives because with their limited coal and water capacity they could not carry out the long, uninterrupted runs of express services. Also the highly reliable, far from ancient T 18 was still running on short sections because of its reduced axle loading and it could not be withdrawn from service completely. As a result, a total of only 15 tank locomotives with their large smoke-deflecting "Wagner ears" or "elephant ears" survived.

Series 80 and 81 with their 17.5 t (19.3 tons) axle weight fell in between the secondary line locomotives and the heavy main line locomotives. As modern, robust shunting locomotives the 80s in the large passenger train stations and the 81s in freight terminals proved that superheated steam had advantages over saturated steam even in shunting services, as well as being cheaper to run. In 1943 the Series 89 employed for shunting operations used saturated steam again, but it only confirmed what the 80 and 81 had already proved earlier on.

Series 41, 42, 44, 50 and 52					
Wheel arrangement	1'D1'h2 (2-8-2)	1'Eh2 (2-10-0)	1'Eh3 (2-10-0)	1'Eh2 (2-10-0)	1'Eh2 (2-10-0)
First delivery	1936	1943	1926	1939	1942
Last delivery	1941	1949	1949	1959	1951
Withdrawn from service	1987	1969	1981	1989	1989
Quantity	366	1063	1989	3446	6330
Length overall	23.905m (78'5")	23.0m (76'5")	22.62m (74'2")	22.94m (75'3")	22.975m (75'4")
Total wheelbase	12.05m (39'6")	9.2m (30'2")	9.65m (31'8")	9.2m (30'2")	9.2m (30'2")
Bogie wheelbase	1.6m (5'3")	1.4m (4'7")	1.4m (4'7")	1.4m (4'7")	1.4m (4'7")
Wheel diameter	1/1.25m (3'3"/4'1")	0.85m (2'9")	0.85m (2'9")	0.85m (2'9")	0.85m (2'9")
Working weight	101.9t (112.3 tons)	99.6t (109.8 tons)	110.2t (121.5 tons)	88t (97.0 tons)	89.1t (98.22 tons)
Maximum speed	90km/h (56mph)	80km/h (50mph)	80km/h (50mph)	80km/h (50mph)	80km/h (50mph)
1-hour rating	1387kW (1859hp)	1314kW (1761hp)	1533kW (2055hp)	1285kW (1723hp)	1182kW (1484hp)

Above left: In the German Democratic Republic the Reichsbahn used the Series 86 with great success on short secondary lines.

Above right: The driver of locomotive 86 1501 evidently enjoys his job.

Opposite page: In the 1970s the Series 64 tank locomotives with their characteristic converted three-coupled wheel arrangement were often seen on secondary lines in southern Germany.

Left: Locomotive 64 393 seen here in the Bayreuth depot is rather unkempt.

Series 64 and 86		
Wheel arrangement	1'C1'h2t (2-6-2)	1'D1'h2t (2-8-2)
First delivery	1928	1928
Last delivery	1940	1943
Withdrawn from service	1974	1976
Quantity	520	774
Length overall	12.5m (41'2")	13.92m (45'8")
Total wheelbase	9.0m (29'6")	10.3m (33'10")
Bogie wheelbase	1.5m (4'11")	1.4m (4'7")
Wheel diameter	0.85m (2'9")	0.85m (2'9")
Working weight	75.2t (82.9 tons)	88.5t (97.6 tons)
Maximum speed	90km/h (56mph)	80km/h (50mph)
1-hour rating	693kW (929bhp)	752kW (1008hp)

Right: On the secondary line from Nuremberg to Unternbibert-Rügland, long out of service, locomotive 086 457 is seen pulling away with a local train of 4-axle coaches on 5 July 1971.

The Series 87 showed that there were also problems to be solved in following the standard locomotive programme. The five-coupled (0-10-0) locomotive for use on the tight curves of the Hamburg harbour station had a special undercarriage with gear-coupled wheels attached to the boiler of a Series 86.

Enforced delay because of lack of funds

The world economic crisis of 1929 temporarily stopped the standard locomotive programme. There were not enough funds to pursue the programme in a consistent, logical manner. This affected the production of new locomotives as well as the expansion of the programme itself. Until the second half of the 1930s only ten series-produced locomotives of Series 44 had been built. Meanwhile the Reichsbahn saw no further need for the otherwise successful Series 62. Deviating from the original programme, the decision was now taken to make a variation of the Series 01 that was given the designation Series 03, and with an axle load of only 17 t (18.7 tons). The derivation of a new series from the 01 series and its production were evidently more advantageous financially than rebuilding all the main lines to take an axle load of 20 t (22 tons), a programme that was only happening very slowly because of the shortage of funds.

Experts immediately — and quite rightly — recognized locomotive 03 001, launched on 2 July 1930, as a copy of the 01. The 03 was only lighter because of its use of lighter components as had been planned. The very short development phase was the result of the principles of standardization and the fact that the mistakes and teething problems of the heavier, older sister locomotives had successfully been avoided.

In 1936 Series 41, a fast, elegant 1'D1'h2 (2-8-0) freight locomotive with the characteristics of a universal locomotive was developed. It was also vaguely reminiscent of the 03 — for instance it had the same type of boiler. Originally conceived as G-8.2 replacement, the engine ran unexpectedly smoothly even at a speed of 100 km/h (62 mph). The 03s and 41s clearly revealed the potential of the German standard locomotive programme. The fact that a light locomotive could be derived from a heavy one was evidently a positive direct result. That it was possible in addition to derive an almost universal locomotive for freight trains from an express train locomotive was a tribute to the systematic, pioneering approach of the creators of the programme.

From a historical and technical point of view, however, both locomotives

were somewhat lacking in innovation, in spite of their excellent test results. The only real innovation of the Series 41 was its adjustable compensating balance beam by which the axle loading could be set at 18 or 20 t (19.8 or 22 tons) according to need.

On the whole, it is apparent that in the 1930s the original concept was no longer applied as rigidly as it had been in the past. The choice of particular types and the design of a new series were no longer based on the projects included in the programme with its well thought-out, wide-ranging spectrum of locomotives conceived for particular purposes. Instead they were designed to meet the particular requirements of the various railway companies.

Series 85: a heavy tank locomotive

The Series 85 was created in 1932 for entirely pragmatic reasons. Because the Reichsbahn wanted to end the obsolete, cumbersome gear changing on the Höllentalbahn as quickly as possible, it commissioned a 1'E1'h3t (2-10-2) locomotive that was very successful, not least because of the numerous parallels with the Series 44, many of which were also externally visible. Experts considered the massive locomotive the culmination of technical perfection that surpassed even the pioneering success of the Prussian T 20, the DR Series 95. Series 85 successfully put an end to the expensive use of gearing in Baden.

The attempt to apply the concept of the standard locomotive for special uses had already borne fruit with the Series 87. In 1935 a second attempt was made, this time to develop a tank locomotive with five pairs of coupled driving wheels that could easily negotiate the small-radius curves of the new Dresen-Heidenau-Altenburg line. But there were clear constructional differences between the 12 locomotives of what became known as the Series 84. Numbers 84 001 and 84 002 had three cylinders. Their carrying wheels were mounted in a Schwartzkopff-Eckardt pony truck bogie that was linked to the adjacent coupled driving wheels, so that the undercarriage no longer had a fixed wheelbase. In addition the central wheel was turned into a flange-less driving wheel. The only fixed points and therefore also the limits of the fixed wheelbase were the aligned bogie pins of the two bogies.

Locomotives 84 003 and 84 004 had two cylinders and Luttermöller-type, gear-coupled end driving wheels, resulting in shortened coupling rods that only connected the central three driving wheels. In 1936 numbers 84 001 and 84 002 clearly showed their superiority in test running. The large locomotives could be used on all small-radius curves without any difficulty.

The Luttermöller-type two-cylinder locomotives were more economical in their use of steam but they ran very noisily and unevenly because of the heavy weight of the gear mechanism connecting the end driving wheels. The

Reichsbahn therefore ordered eight more locomotives with Schwartzkopff-Eckardt bogies. These locomotives remained outsiders that were expensive and sometimes frustrating to operate, because of their technical complexity. However they provided very useful experience and are recognized as interesting, creative episodes in the history of the standard locomotive.

Series 05: the high point of the programme

In the mid-1930s this period in the history of the standard locomotive reached its high point with the high-speed locomotives of Series 05 and to a certain extent Series 61. These locomotives were developed because the newly developed express railcars were proving serious competition to the steam-powered express trains as far as maximum speed was concerned. But since the relatively short diesel railcar was unable to replace the long, heavy high-speed train, the steam locomotive clearly remained the better bet at least as far as heavily-used express services was concerned.

The development of the Series 05 was marked by two important innovations. The first of these was the perfectly streamlined body. This was not only to emulate the attractive, sleek body of the diesel railcar but also to reduce wind resistance substantially when running at high speeds, thus increasing the haulage capacity while maintaining the same steam consumption.

The second innovation may not have been visible but had a very lasting effect. Unlike the previous design, the new express locomotives had a symmetrical 2'C2' (4-6-4) wheel arrangement that ensured outstanding performance because of its two carrying bogies. For the first time in Germany the diameter of the driving wheels rose to 2.3 m (7 ft 6½ in), not of course to impress with their size, but to reduce the number of revolutions over a given distance. The three-cylinder compound drive, which differed from the previous concept applied in the 01 and 03, also contributed to the locomotive's outstanding running qualities. Even the tender was new: as the body of the locomotive became more streamlined, it now also became five-axled with a two-axled bogie and three fixed axles in the frame. Its water tank could hold 38 m³ (1,342 cu ft) of water.

Already the first experiments with locomotives 05 001 and 05 002 in 1934 showed that the construction team, led by chief engineer Adolf Wolff von Borsig, had achieved a fantastic success. The locomotives were able to haul trains of 300 t (330.7 tons) at a speed of 175 km/h (109 mph) without difficulty and maintain a punctual service. The test run that took place on 11 May 1936 became famous when locomotive 05 002 pulling an express train of 200 t (220.5 tons) reached a record top speed of 200.3 km/h (125.5 mph) between Berlin and Hamburg. The maximum power developed was equivalent to 2,340 kW (3,137 hp). The driver's cab being placed very much at the back of the locomotive, there were fears about the train's safety when running at high speeds. For this reason locomotive 05 003, which came into service in 1937, was fitted with a forward driver's cab. To be precise, the boiler with the outbreak of World War II development ceased and they were unable to reach their potentially satisfactory level of construction and operational performance. The excellent undercarriage later became the basis for conversion to the DR-Edelrenner 18201.

World War II also prevented the final development of the high-speed concept using exceptional steam locomotives. The excellent results obtained with the streamlined shape and three-cylinder drive resulted in the latter being used in Series 01.10 and 03.10 in 1939. But there was a striking difference. In order to be able to maintain the engines more easily and to ensure the unrestricted intake of combustion air to the firebox grate, the locomotive did not have a streamlined skin.

Series 06 and 045: the largest locomotives

In 1936, two locomotives became famous for being the largest and most powerful of German steam locomotives. They joined the Series 05 and 61 that had the distinction of being among the fastest and most beautiful German steam locomotives. But that was all there was to them. However, in the judgement of experts both the 06 and the 45 were failed locomotives that had been created to achieve political prestige rather than to provide improved technical solutions.

The enormous boiler of the two locomotives with an absurdly large area of tubular heating surfaces clearly showed where Wagner's dogmatic sticking to certain principles could lead. What kind of superhuman fireman would work in these driver's cabs? Elsewhere the incorporation of mechanical stokers and large fireboxes had brought definite advantages. However the ageing yet still powerful Richard Paul Wagner closed his mind to such progressive solutions. Consequently, these locomotives were designed to be operated by two stokers without mechanical assistance. So although these impressive, gigantic locomotives with 2'D2'h3 (4-8-4) wheel arrangement in the case of the Series 06, and 1'E1'h3 (2-10-2) in the case of the Series 45, were the most powerful German steam locomotives ever made, they were also the most uneconomical of the standard locomotive series.

Series 50: a great success

If the Series 06 and 45 left a rather negative impression, the locomotive conceived to replace the reliable G 10 from the Prussian school in 1939 was a great success. Thousands of Series 50 locomotives, a technically successful and economically advantageous 1'Eh2 (2-10-0) design, were produced in the course of time. It also reflected a slight deviation from the dogma of Wagnerian by opting for a new ratio of panel heating and tubular heating surfaces. Consequently, the new, externally harmonious locomotive differed from previous types of construction in its relatively large grate area — fitted for the first time with an outer firebox made from steel — and a fairly low level of superheating.

It is true that the front carrying axles were still of the old, traditional type used in standard main line locomotives, but they worked very well in this case because the Series 50 was a light locomotive with an axle load of only 15 t (16.5 tons), and compared to the old G 10 it was also able to reach a higher permissible maximum speed. In many services, it occasionally even moved into the field of operation of the Series 41 universal locomotive.

Left: Left: Number 50 622 is also a museum locomotive. It still used to pull special trains as well for film and video purposes. Here it is seen on a lovely spring day, hauling a freight train manned by staff dressed in the style of the 1960s.

had been turned in this version of the 05, so that the locomotive was effectively running in reverse. The special fuelling system using pulverized coal did not prove satisfactory, so the third 05 was not followed by any others.

Henschel had produced a streamlined 2'C2'h2 (4-6-4) express locomotive, designated Series 61, as early as 1935. This pulled a streamlined Henschel-Wegmann train that had been specially designed for it at a top speed of 175 km/h (109 mph). Although it was able to reach a speed of 160 km/h (99 mph) within 6 minutes, it ran very unevenly at this speed because of its two-cylinder drive. In addition, the coal and water capacity was barely sufficient for uses comparable to that of a high-speed railcar. In 1939 a sister locomotive was produced with a 2'C3' (4-6-6) wheel arrangement and three cylinders, which resulted in much smoother running; it also carried more coal and water. But

A new passenger train locomotive was developed almost in parallel with Series 50, namely the Series 23. Just as the Series 50 had replaced the old G 10, the 1'C1'h2 (2-6-2) locomotive was developed to replace the P 8. Fitted with the successful boiler of the Series 50, the Series 23 with its top speed of 110 km/h (68 mph) was a successful new development. Nevertheless, only two test locomotives were produced because World War II intervened and prevented further production.

The belligerent Nazi regime required modern, reliable locomotives that were also as straightforward as possible. In addition, production had to be quick and economical. The ideal locomotive for the purpose was the Series 50, which could be rigorously simplified to meet these requirements. The fast, unpretentious freight train locomotive soon proved itself and became known as a transitional war locomotive. In the interests of economy it lost a number of non-essential parts over various intermediate stages, such as the feed water heaters, piston feed pumps, cylinder safety valves, sludge separator and axle-box wedges. Welding was used first for the drive shafts and connecting rods and later also for the boiler, while the older, less expensive steel plate frame construction came into use again instead of a bar frame. Because of the cold winters in the east, an all-enclosed driver's cab in the Norwegian style was used. The separate tender of the Series 50 was turned into a body tender.

War locomotives: the Series 52

In 1942 the famous Series 52 war locomotive was born. This was a sleek, somewhat stark locomotive with the required functional performance for what was intended to be a short period of use. This was followed in 1943/1944 by the Series 42. With an axle-load of 17 t (18.7 tons) it was slightly more powerful than the Series 52 and was also able to pull greater loads on certain stretches because of its larger, better-performing boiler. It thus closed the yawning gap that the transitional war version of the Series 44 had tried to fill. Interestingly it had a bar frame again instead of a steel plate one.

It might be disputed whether the overall concept of the war locomotives still reflected that of the standard locomotives, and indeed whether war loco-motives could be considered standard locomotives. Richard Paul Wagner had refused to participate in the conversion of the standard locomotive to the war version and resigned. A total of 6,100 Series 52 and 840 Series 42 war loco-motives were purchased. From 1943 onward the Reichsbahn took delivery of 500 Series 52 locomotives every month.

In spite of the pioneering unit construction system used to build these clas-sic standard locomotives, some parts were quite expensive to build and the designs were not really suited to being produced on such a large scale. But both types — the classic standard locomotive and the functional, economical-ly produced war locomotives — gave rise to countless constructional solu-tions, providing much valuable experience and proving a lasting source of inspiration. Both locomotives introduced innovations that influenced the

Right: This photograph of a freight train pulled by locomotives 052 769 and 052 440 was taken on 27 October 1973. Both locomotives have a cabin in the tender for the guard who was then always present on a freight train.

Right: The tank tender and the closed front windows of the driver's cab recall the locomotive's origin as a war locomotive.

Below: The steep stretch between Nuremberg and Sulzbach-Rosenberg demands all the reserve capacity of loco 050 737.

Opposite page: Converted to oil, the 01.10 series was able to demonstrate its excellent performance as an express locomotive on the plains of North Germany (Emden-Rheine).

postwar German locomotive industry. They therefore deserve their place in the technical history of locomotive production.

Installation of oil firing

Almost all the standard locomotive series survived until well into the 1970s in West Germany and into the 1980s in East Germany. Both railway administrations partially modernized the standard locomotives. Thus the Bundesbahn developed new boilers and new mixing feed water heater. Small smoke deflectors of the Witte type replaced the large Wagner ones. The Bundesbahn installed controls to regulate the superheated steam on Series 01 locomotives fitted with the new boilers. However, these controls were often difficult to operate because flying ashes collected inside them and jammed them. In other locomotives the Bundesbahn experimented with new feed water heaters but these proved unsatisfactory. On the other hand, the conversion of locomotives of Series 01.10 and 44 to oil burning was more successful. It greatly increased the performance of the locomotive and the job of the fireman became very much easier.

The Reichsbahn also installed new boilers on a large number of standard locomotives and converted other locomotives to oil. However, at the beginning of the 1980s, the reverse process took place and oil-fired locomotives were fitted again with a traditional fire grate. The reason was simply that oil was becoming increasingly expensive, while there were very large reserves of brown coal in the Lusatian Hills and central Germany. Brown coal has a relatively low calorific value and is not ideal as a fuel for steam locomotives, but it is possible to use it. In order to save the country's foreign exchange reserves, the government declared that there should be as few imports as possible. The damage to the environment caused by the intensive use of brown coal was not taken into consideration.

From a technical point of view, the modernization programme of both German states was to a great extent successful. However, the change in the type of traction from steam to diesel or electric could not halted. Many fine steam locomotives have survived for posterity, some still in working order and others as museum pieces.

Above: The Series 10 certainly qualifies as one of the most elegant steam locomotives of all. But its construction came too late and it was actually superfluous.
Opposite page: The Series 23 locomotives built for medium-heavy passenger service were very successful.

I n the first years after World War II, the development of new steam locomotives ceased in all four occupation zones. The consequences of the war itself prevented the realization of any forward-looking projects, but so too did the initial prohibitions of the occupying powers. Ideas for the construction of modern steam locomotives certainly existed. They resulted mostly from the experiences with the unit-locos. At first the repair of the damaged locomotives was more important than building new ones. The first, promising activities for the procurement of newly developed steam locomotives began at the end of 1947 in the western occupied zones. In the then dual zone, from 12 May 1948 there was also once more a special body called the "Technical Committee for Locomotives", itself in the tradition of the "Select Committee for Locomotives" of the German Reichsbahn.

Friedrich Witte took on the chairmanship. Born in Hanover in 1900, the engineer had already come in contact with the Standard Locomotive Programme as a young official. However, having sat on the Locomotive Committee since 1934, Witte had also learned the dogmatism and stubbornness of his patron Richard Paul Wagner.

Three years after the war Witte tried to combine the lessons of efficient wartime construction and production practice with the best traditions of the standard loco era. This resulted in a program of modern locomotives that were distinguished for the smooth, unfussy appearance following the model of the war locomotives, resulting from the application of welding technology instead of endless rows of rivets, details such as small, elegantly acting smoke deflectors, and many improved technical details such as for instance combustion chambers and feed water heaters. Soon people came to refer to the "Friedrich Witte building principles". An extensive procurement programme of originally 15 types was already revised again in 1949. In the same year, three series first took shape on the drawing board. Between September 1950 and February 1951, the construction patterns left the studios of Henschel and Krauss-Maffei.

Witte's handwriting

The Series 23 was to replace the Series 38.10. It is true that such a designation was already carried by two construction pattern locos from the standard loco program that remained in the East Zone. However only the operating program tied it to the Series 23 of the old Reichsbahn. Technically, the new 1'C1'h2 (2-6-2) locomotive of the DB clearly deviated from its older sisters. With its welded boiler and sheet metal frames, the completely enclosed Norwegian driver's cab inherited from the model of the war locos, and equipped with side-operated superheated steam regulator and central lubrication, the new Series 23 symbolized the Friedrich Witte construction principles in compact form.

The installation of a firebox with combustion chamber went back to an unrealized design by Schwartzkopff. The resulting boiler, much smaller than the old Series 23, together with the other features of Witte construction, gave the impression of a fairly compact locomotive. Even the separate tender showed the close connection between the war locos and the postwar philosophy: the tub-like water reservoir of the Series 42 and 52 was now inverted with the Series 23 and arched over the bogies, giving the whole an unusual, powerful appearance.

The Series 23 easily achieved a speed of 110 km/h (68 mph). It was therefore suitable for fast stopping trains and light express train service. For a long time it even hauled the "Rheingold Express" between Cologne and Venlo. Altogether, the Bundesbahn acquired 105 of thee locomotives. Within the series, however, there were various differences. Locomotives 23 001 to 023 and 026 to 052 still had the conventional surface pre-heaters of the Knorr type of construction. The feed water heater had meanwhile become technically mature, and was first installed from locomotive number 23 053, but different types were used contributing to an irregular overall picture.

Series 23 locomotives operated throughout almost the whole of West Germany. Still in 1970, individual engines were hauling fast stopping trains in Emsland as well as between Ulm and Aschaffenburg. Saarbrücken even put its locomotives into reversing operation, for which this construction with its high speed and its tender design was excellently suited. Isolated critics were irritated by the external appearance of the new-built loco and would have wanted a "reprint" of the Wagner design principles, including among other things the installation of large smoke deflectors.

Secondary new development: the Series 82

On the other hand, the Series 82 was marked by continuous, clear design. Following the wishes of the railway operating department, this locomotive was to be a universally usable successor to the Prussian T 16.1 heavy shunting engine, but capable of working sections with steep inclines that were beyond the capacity of the predecessor. It was even hoped that it would be able to replace the Series 87 with its five-coupled wheels and maintenance-intensive gear-driven end axles, used successfully on the Hamburg harbour line with its tight curves. Viewed from the engineering point of view, the careful design of the 82's running gear was impressive. The front and rear, laterally-adjusting coupled wheels were linked to the Beugniot bogies, so that with this type of bogie in front and behind, good performance of the very compact locomotive

on curves was guaranteed. In operation, the Series 82 at first received conflicting evaluations; but ultimately the predominant opinion was "excellent".

Only 37 locomotives were built and there were differences among them. Numbers 82 001 to 012 as well as 82 023 to 037 had no feed water heater. Numbers 82 013 to 022 were fitted with the Knorr pre-heater. Locomotives 82 038 to 82 041 were the first to be fitted with new feed water heaters in the factory. Fundamentally this locomotive, which incorporated all the experience learned from its predecessors, was ready for production in quantity. But this did not in fact take place, because the DB was still very cautious in taking decisions and reluctant to take any risks in relation to steam locomotives.

Series 65: too slow, too heavy and too weak

The third newly developed design was the Series 65. Designed as a 1'D2'h2t (2-8-4) passenger locomotive, it was to serve the same wide range of uses as the Series 78, 86 and 93. Whatever the advantages of its large coal and water capacity of this shapely machine might be, the loco was inadequate in operation, failing to match the performance of the 93 series that had also proved itself in heavy shunting duties and hauling heavy pick-up goods trains. Even on stretches where the nimble, weaker-performing Series 86 with its troublesome uncertain running was in operation, the 65 was not particularly welcome, because with its axle loading of 17 t (19 tons), it could not be run on lighter tracks. Nor was the new locomotive a satisfactory replacement for the fast Series 78, because of its small driving wheel diameter. Experts summed it up frankly: it was too slow for the fast passenger trains on main line, it was

too heavy for service on branch lines, and it was too weak to pull heavy freight trains.

Nevertheless, no faulty detail design was found in the 18 examples of the 65 that were built. There were some areas of use where it performed very reliably and was a very popular engine. With its maximum speed of 85 km/h (53 mph) in both directions and with its very powerful starting traction, it seemed as if it had been designed specially for the demanding suburban and rush-hour traffic in and around city centres; also light goods traffic offered a suitable load for the 65. A modern, impressively high boiler with its firebox contributed to the impressive capability of the engine. Some locomotive drivers and firemen who had handled the engines with heavy goods trains between Essen and Düsseldorf were well aware of this. Also in the Odenwald or between Aschaffenburg and Miltenberg, drivers and firemen were happy to replace the puny 64 at the head of their trains with the modern Series 65.

The superfluous Series 10

The Series 10 is unusual among new locomotives. Its development began with specific, ambitious requirements. But the undoubtedly impressive appearance of the 2'C1'h3 (4-6-2) high-speed locomotive could only outdo the smaller Series 66 in size and appearance. From a technical point of view, the concept of this locomotive was inconsistent in many respects. For instance, it had adopted the axle arrangement and three-cylinder engine of the 01.10, one of the last standard locomotives. The delays in production of the Series 10 reflected the dreadful lack of interest on the part of the manufacturer.

Ordered in 1953, the construction of the locomotives took almost four years.

From a historical-technical point of view, the cylinder block is particularly interesting because it is made from a single piece of cast steel welded onto the loco frame. However, the opportunity to create with this locomotive a modern variation of the much debated, highly-performing and technically efficient four-cylinder power unit was not taken. Although the 22-t (29-ton) axle loading and boiler pressure of 18 bar (261 psi) produced an enormous tractive effort, it was impossible to exploit this advantage, even in combination with its impressive top speed of 140 km/h (87 mph). The few stretches capable of taking such a high axle load were soon electrified because of their important position in the rail network. The Series 10 was therefore superfluous from the very beginning.

However, its appearance was very exciting, a very successful compromise between an elegant body and problem-free, safe access to the engine and its running gear. The members of the locomotive crew of number 10 002 were particularly happy with the oil firing installed in this engine, which removed the burden of strenuous coal-firing. But however impressive they looked, the life-cycle of steam locomotives was coming to an end. The Bundesbahn acquired the first modern electric locomotives such as the E 10 as early as the mid-1950s, and it put new diesel locomotives into service such as the V 200.0, pulling trains with impressive-sounding names and showing off with elegant high-speed railcars of the Trans-Europ Express. Even technical innovations such as those of the Series 66 could not stop this development.

Above: Locomotive number 18 201 occupies a very special position. It was developed from the 61 002 and 45 024 locomotives and is distinguished for its impressive speed. The locomotive is still in good working order and is used to pull special trains.

Right: In 1985 the Deutsche Bahn museum acquired number 23 105, the very last steam locomotive to be built in West Germany.

Opposite page: Series 65 played a subordinate role. It ran on the Aschaffenburg-Miltenberg section where it was used to pull light passenger trains.

New types of steam locos of the German Railways

In the Soviet-occupied zone that later became the GDR (German Democratic Republic), the development, production and introduction of new types of steam locomotives took place under different conditions. It was only in 1951/52 that serious work began on a design of locomotive that in its capacity of universal locomotive could be used for both freight and passenger service. The delay had been caused by a variety of political impediments, that remained rooted in the ubiquitous occupying forces until the end of the Communist regime. Moreover, the supply of hard coal dried up with the increasing tensions between the Eastern bloc and the west. This caused great difficulties because the standard locomotives and those of the regional railways were not prepared or suitable for the low-energy brown coal or lignite that was mined in East Germany. The lignite fell through the grate without having burned completely. Gradually the problem was tackled, albeit unsatisfactorily, with simple solutions, particularly the "dead man's fire-bed" formed of a layer of pebbles.

It was evidently clear that new steam locomotives would also have to be fed with lignite. Since the poor condition of the rail network still did not high axle loads or high speeds and there was no improvement in view, the locomotive specification could be rewritten roughly as follows: lignite-burning, maximum speed 80 km/k (50 mph), later 100 km/h (62 mph), maximum axle load 18 t (20 tons), and usable on all different services.

The successful Series 41 new-built design was quickly eliminated, and not only because of its hard coal fire grate; the locomotive was too expensive and its technical conception was too elaborate. Once this was eliminated, a locomotive similar to the Series 41 without trailing axles began to specify itself: simple in construction, undemanding in maintenance and operation, with a grate suitable for lignite and lignite briquettes, and capable of versatile service, it would fulfil the old dream of a universal locomotive.

Also in 1952, the concept of a Series 25 was on the table. This 1'Dh2 (2-8-0) type combined features from a range of modern steam locomotive designs in one. But however desirable the idea of a universal locomotive was always assumed to be, the railway management continued to ask for engines *designed* for particular uses.

So while the Railway Rolling Stock Committee in Berlin-Adlershof was seeking the philosopher's stone of locomotives, cynics composed a list with seven new-built locos for different purposes as a precaution. It seemed that the Series 25 was not a pointless exercise after all. While the separate tender may have prevented the promise of universal use, the engine itself was a practical test vehicle for new solutions in firebox technology, steam technology and frame construction.

The list did not come from the Adlershof but emerged from the central design office of the GDR's united locomotive and freight wagon construction company, known by the abbreviation LOWA. In this office, connoisseurs of the conceptual worked in advance - and disadvantages of the standard locomotives. As in West Germany under Friedrich Witte, in East Germany a break also occurred with the outdated Wagner building specifications. This is very clear from the example of the proposed express train locomotive, the 01.20, which was actually designed as 2'C1'h4v (4-6-2) engine! But should the former south German way now be abandoned in favour of an energetic, quietly running high-performance express locomotive?

To replace the P 8, LOWA also designed a 1'C1'h2 (2-6-2) locomotive developed from the model of the construction patterns of the Series 23. Turning to the needs of medium and heavy freight train services, a 1'Eh2 (2-10-0) locomotive was designed, the 42.10. Witnesses at the time recall a joker who defined this locomotive as a cross between the powerful 44 and the simple, robust 52. In fact this summed up the needs of the East German railways rather accurately.

For rush-hour commuter traffic a rapid, heavy tank locomotive was designed, later designated 65.10. Plans for this 1'D2'h2t (2-8-0) locomotive design had already existed for some time, but neither the standard locomotive programme nor the regional railway systems had a prototype from which it could be assessed.

Nevertheless, consideration was also given to a light universal locomotive similar to the Series 64 for the less important branch line network, which also included the narrow gauge railways that had been taken over in 1949. Finally, this important project required a replacement for the numerous existing, still indispensable Series 94 locomotives, the former Prussian T 16.1. The new locomotives were to be fuelled with lignite. The firing technology used included the enlargement of the firebox area, representing a definitive ending to the over-long tubes of the final Wagner designs.

After being sanctioned, the plan for the 01.20, the Ersatz-64 and the replacement of the T 16.1, was carried out by the Minister of Transport and the Reichsbahn's general manager, Erwin Kramer. At that time however there was no plan for the construction of a modern high-performance express train locomotive. Apart from the condition of the rail network and the maximum speeds possible on it, first thoughts were towards the electrification of the important main lines. The function of the Ersatz-64 could include carrying out the smaller tasks of the 1'C2'h2t (2-6-0) locomotives. It was expected that the Series 94 would probably be replaced by diesel locomotives.

Also at the German Railways there was a highly experienced engineer, who was strongly committed to the construction and operation of new steam locomotives: Hans Schulze, 1903–62. He knew how to explain difficult technical situations in layman's language. His first task on joining the reconstruction programme in 1952 was the series production of new narrow-gauge steam locomotives. The 750-mm (2 ft 5½ in) line in Saxony and the metre-gauge (3 ft 3⁵⁄₁₆ in) lines in the Harz mountains and the Thuringian forest badly needed new engines. Numbers 99.73-76 and 99.22 were modern steam locomotives designed by consistently overhauling and developing every aspect of the prewar series. Engines 99 771 to 794 for 750 mm and 99 231 to 247 for the metre gauge lines entered the technical history of the railways as the very first new locomotives of the reconstruction programme of the GDR-Reichsbahn.

The DR Series 65

When Hans Schulze joined the technical central office of the engineering technology department of the railways as an adviser in May 1953, , the series-production of the Series 25 was already no longer an issue. Nonetheless, two locomotives that were ready and equipped with the newly developed feed water heaters and superheated steam regulators. Both engines had sheet metal frames, which proved to be important in connection with the development of the four-coupled driving equipment for the Series 65.10 heavy main line tank engine. Prototype locomotives 25 001 and 65 1001 were both shown to great interest at the Leipzig autumn fair in 1954. The remarkable size of the Series 25, the huge tender with a capacity of 9 t (10 tons) of coal on a bogie with outside frames and the two side tanks that reached all the way to the cab, gave it an appearance that clearly distinguished from the less powerful operating Series 65 of the DB, locomotive 65 1001. Following modern principles, the sheet metal frame was welded, as was the boiler. The superheated steam regulator and the feed water heater caused many difficulties on the first test runs. As a locomotive for severe rush-hour traffic, the 65 1001 was at first disappointing, and with a power of only about 600 hp (448 kW), it appeared that the loco was not very suitable for anything.

However Schulze and his small team did not give up. Convinced of that the 65.10 would be a universally employable, agile, nimble and above all powerful tank engine, they spared nothing in trying out an ultimately successful series of trials and experiments. After the elimination of serious faults and extensive reworking, the measured performance was eventually raised to 970 kW (1,300 hp).

Essentially serious problems caused the little sister of the 65.10, the Series 83.10, whose production put in front the Federal-track a series-construction of the 65.10. Because the railway management claimed that it needed this light but very powerful machine urgently, series production began with numbers 1001 and 1002 before the test runs of the 83 had been completed.

But noone was happy with the series-produced locomotives that were eventually delivered in 1955. Within the modern, rationally designed concept of the 83.10, there was a fundamental constructional deficiency. Incorrectly rated cylinders were already known to be a problem with feed water heaters, and the heavy demands of the unreliable superheated steam regulators caused difficulty from the start. The boiler proved to be too small, which led to lack of steam again and again. In operation, this caused serious disruption to the trains.

At first glance, locomotives 65.10 and 83.10 were very similar externally.

Series 10, 23 (DB), 23.10 (DR), 65 (DB) and 65.10 (DR)					
First delivery	1956	1950	1957	1951	1954
Last delivery	1956	1959	1960	1956	1957
Withdrawn from service	1968	1977	1981	1972	1982
Quantity	2	115	113	18	86+5
Length overall	26.503m (86'11")	21.325m (70'0")	22.66m (74'4")	15.475m (16'9")	17.5m (57'5")
Total wheelbase	12.525m (41'1")	9.9m (32'6")	10.1m (33'2")	11.975m (39'3")	13.3m (43'8")
Bogie wheelbase	2.0m (6'7")	1.75m (5'9")	1.75m (5'9")	1.6m (5'3")	1.6m (5'3")
Wheel diameter	1.0m (3'3")	twin 1.0/1.25m (3'3"/4'1")		0.85m (2'9")	1.0m (3'3")
Working weight	118.9t (131 tons)	82.8t (91 tons)	87.2t (96 tons)	107.6t (118 tons)	121.7t (134 tons)
Maximum speed	140/90hm/h (87/56mph)	110/85hkm/h (68/53mph)	110km/h (68mph)	85km/h (53mph)	90km/h (56mph)
1-hour rating	1,825kW (2,246hp)	1,303kW (1,747hp)	1,240kW (1,662hp)	1,080kW (1,448hp)	1,095kW (1,468hp)

Possibly the most obvious difference appeared in the undercarriage, where the 83.10 had a driving wheel diameter of only 1.25 m (4 ft 1 in) compared with the graceful 1.6 m (5 ft 3 in) of the 65.10. The small driving wheel diameter made possible unusually quick acceleration for a steam locomotive. On good track experienced drivers could make the light locomotive leap away on starting.

The 83.10 combined many design requirements in order to become an ideal locomotive for the use on secondary lines in the flat and hilly country; it even came to replace the noisy Series 86. However the over-hasty move to series-production, the inconsistent weeding out of consequent problems and the time it spent in the maintenance sheds led to only 27 locomotives being manufactured. Not sure where to use them, the Deutsche Reichsbahn pushed these engines from department to department. When it appeared in the Thuringian forest, it was never allowed to be used for the purposes it had been designed for.

Fortunately, many of the mistakes were avoided with the production of the 65.10 that immediately followed it, which had a negative effect on the 83.10. So the 88 engines built proved successful after the resolution of some teething troubles. In this model the railway management possessed a good locomotive developing a power of over 1,082 kW (1,450 hp). So, the great four-coupled locomotives with their high cabs gave way almost easily before the heavy occupation trains, providing suburban services in centres such as Berlin and Dresden and assorted services on busy branch lines, finding many friends among the locomotive workers.

But as the full P-8 replacement, the first series was the 23.10. Its construction was a distillation of all the good and bad experiences of the Series 25, 65.10 and 83.10. The example of the excellent Series 23.0 locomotives could not be followed, since they had remained in East Germany at the end of war. One must nevertheless credit the designers and Johannes Töpelmann of the Committee of Rolling Stock for not succumbing to the enticements of a direct copy of the 23.0, but instead to pursue new directions in a logical manner.

23.10 and 50.40: visually successful

So, modern steam technology found a very wide application. The locomotives had a boiler with a combustion chamber that proved to be extremely successful in its performance, reliability and economy. In order to spare itself the trouble of the unreliable superheated steam regulators, the tried and tested steam regulator made by Schmidt & Wagner was used, and proved satisfac-

Above: The DR's Series 65.10 was a very successful design. The tender locomotive had been developed for heavy passenger train service on main lines. Locomotive 65 1049 is a surviving operational example.

tory. As the test programme had already shown, version 23.10 of the 23.0 series operated with higher speed and greater economy. Hans Schulze also established that the engine would also run remarkably smoothly above the allowable maximum speed of 110 km/h (68 mph).

Externally too, Schulze had a formative influence on the appearance of the 23.10. Unlike the 23 of the DB, the 23.10 had a continuous horizontal line from the separate tender to the smoke box. The cab and other features unmistakably interpreted the classic locomotive architecture. With the large driving wheels of 1.75 m (5 ft 9 in) and connecting rods sensitively arranged in context with the the rest of the locomotive, the result was a very aesthetically attractive locomotive. Good steam development, smooth running and low slippage on gradients made the 23.10 ideal for the express train services in the areas where the old S 10.1, the 03, and — roughly in the Elbtal between Dresden and the Czechoslovakian border — the 01 had operated. In Mecklenburg, they were even regarded as an excellent substitute for the 41 in express freight train services.

Parallel to the 23.10, the Series 50.40 was created. The 42.10 project had been dropped in favour of a development of the Series 50. The 50.40 possessed the same boiler, the same feed water heater, the same cab and the same separate tender as the 23.10. Both machines also had the same row of instruments. Once again, Töpelmann and Schulze had adopted use-

ful modern ideas and combined them in a locomotive that was also visually pleasing.

The Series 50.40 also contributed to the reduction of the precarious raw material situation in the GDR. Like the 23.10, despite the fire being fed with very poor quality lignite briquettes, it turned in considerable performance. Even the experienced Hans Schulze was quite amazed when the test runs showed that a fuel-savings of over 8% could be achieved with the 50.40 compared with the successful old-built 50.0 series. But in contrast with the 23.10, this economically successful locomotive with advanced combustion technology suffered in that its sheet metal frames were not strong enough. Experts attributed the frequent damage suffered by the frames to a policy of continuously overloading the engines with extremely heavy freight trains in the north of the GDR. Since the engine ran amazingly quietly at 80 km/h (50 mph), it was even used for passenger trains, in some cases pulling scheduled holiday expresses on secondary lines quite successfully.

With the completion of the last of the 88 examples of the 50.40 on 4 January 1961, the production of steam locomotives in Germany came to an end. Apart from unhappy Series 83.1, the new-built locomotives remained in operation for quite a long time, some of them well into the second half of the 1970s. Unfortunately, the opportunity of acquiring a 50.40 and a 83.10 for posterity has passed.

Above: Locomotive 118 621 with train N 5806 waiting to depart from Görlitz.

Below: A long train of wagons hauled by locomotive 118 569 at Haldensleben.

Opposite page, top: An everyday scene in the 1980s, with locomotive 120 048.

Right below: It was not uncommon for the side stripe to be missing on the 118 series. Locomotive 118 316 at Bad Lausick on 9 May 1987.

When steam began to give way to diesel traction, the East German State Railway, the Deutsche Reichsbahn, also decided to opt for hydrodynamic transmission. In the first locomotives hydraulic transmission units converted the horsepower of the diesel engine into driving torque. It was only when the DDR bought locomotives from the Soviet Union that the diesel-electric locomotives entered the picture. In these the diesel engine powered a generator that produced current for the traction motors. Although the Reichsbahn put almost 1,250 diesel-electric locomotives into service between 1966 and 1982, its acquisition programme opted for another diesel-hydraulic locomotive.

It all started with design series V 180. 0

This multi-purpose diesel locomotive was above all intended to replace all the Series 23.10 steam locomotives, pulling passenger and freight trains. Locomotive V 180 01 was ready for delivery at the end of 1959, performing its first drive on the track on 12 February 1960. Up to 1963 the Babelsberg-based locomotive builder "Karl Marx", formerly known as Orenstein & Koppel before it was expropriated, built three more pre-series locomotives. V 180 003 and 004 were later delivered to the Deutsche Reichsbahn, while the other two locomotives were taken out of service. Their engines and transmissions ended up in the VT 18 1601 and 02 express railcars.

This in fact illustrates one of the fundamental principles of the diesel locomotives in the early days of the German Democratic Republic (DDR). All the locomotives — the V 180, V 100, V 60 and VT 18.16 — used engines of the same family. This made the substitution of engines relatively easy. In addition, when the engines were further developed technically, the industry or the Reichsbahn itself was able to install the more powerful version in several locomotive series at the same time.

The V 60 had normally aspirated engines, while the rest of the locomotives had units with pressure charging. The Reichsbahn also paid attention to ease of substitution when acquiring transmissions that had been developed several times from DDR production. There was a starting torque converter and two similar running running torque converters for different ranges of speeds. The first V 80s still had gear systems produced by the West German manufacturer

After the DB withdrew the V 180 series from service, three locomotives went to the independent company ITL, which painted them green. Here on the Dortmund-Obereving line is locomotive 118 003, partnered with V 200 002 of the same company, hauling a freight train to Neuss.

Voith. In 1963 LEW started the series production of design series V 180. Up to the end of 1965 some 83 locomotives, soon known as sub-series V 180.0, were built. While the locomotives were being built the engine manufacturer managed to increase the performance of the units from 662 to 736 kW (887 to 987 hp). The Reichsbahn consequently classified the locomotives produced from then on as sub-series V 180.1, of which 82 were built. The two versions differed in appearance in the number of side windows: the V 180.0 had four while the 180.1 had two. LEW had replaced two of the windows by two ventilator grills.

The Reichsbahn subsequently also installed the more powerful drive units on the V 180.0, which by now had become the 118.0. Because the control and monitoring systems were also modernised, the locomotives were given series number 118.5. The Reichsbahn tested two engines with an output of 1,100 kW (1,475 hp) in the 118 124. This was the Reichsbahn's most powerful diesel-hydraulic locomotive with a drawbar performance of 1,570 kW (2,104 hp) thus exceeding that of Series 132, which had a power of 1,500 kW (2,010 hp).

Already during the development of V 180 series it became clear that the four-axle locomotives would have an axle load of 19 to 20 t (21 to 22 tons). Naturally, this was too much for local railway services. In order to be able to replace the Series 38, 55 and 57 steam locomotives, the Reichsbahn ordered a six-axle version of the V 180 with a maximum axle load of 15.5 t (17.1 tons). This was based on the V 180.1 and prepared for conversion to a maximum

speed of 140 km/h (87 mph). But the conversion of the gear system never happened. All the locomotives of Series V 180 had a maximum speed of 120 km/h (75 mph) during their lifetime.

Locomotive V 180 201 undertook its first test run on 28 January 1964. The following year a second pre-series locomotive was launched, numbered V 240 001 by the manufacturer. This revealed that the locomotive had two engines each with an output of 900 kW, about 1200 hp. The experiments finally resulted in a type of construction similar to that of the Series V 180.

The six-axle locomotives of Series V 180.2 were soon running. The Reichsbahn bought 206 locomotives of this series up to 1970. The following year the Reichsbahn acquired V 240 001, which it renamed 118 202. In the meantime this had been equipped with engines of 883 kW (1,184 mph). A year later the Reichsbahn began installing 900-kW (1,206 hp) engines on the 118.2. It also modernised the control system and monitoring system to match those already fitted to the newly-engined 118.0. The converted locomotives were given the designation 118.6. In 1980 the Reichsbahn tried out diesel engines with an output of 1,100 kW (1,475 hp) on locomotives 118 625 and 118 805.

The rise of fuel prices in the early 1980s led the Reichsbahn to rethink its approach. The government decided to reconsider electric traction. Slowly but surely the diesel locomotives lost their operational area. The Reichsbahn wanted to take the four-axle locomotives out of service by 1995, and the final collapse of the DDR only speeded up the process. In the unified German numbering system, under which 118 acquired the designation 228, only the sub-series 228.1, 228.2, 228.5 and 228.6 still survived. The aim was to scrap the series by the end of 1994, but in practice it was only in 1998 that the last 228s were sent to the blast furnaces.

Series V 100: efficient mid-range locomotives

Besides the main-line diesel locomotives of Series V 180, the Reichsbahn also needed a diesel locomotive of medium power. It wanted to buy this from the Soviet Union, but it was not available for delivery. As a result, the Institut für Schienenfahrzeuge (Institute for track vehicles) and LKW were commissioned to develop an internal combustion engine with an output of 736 to 875 kW (987 to 1,173 hp). The plan was to order further locomotives at a later date with an output of 985 kW (1,320 hp). The transmission was of course to be hydrodynamic. The locomotive had to be able to run at 65 km/h (40 mph) in shunting yards while reaching a maximum speed of 100 km/h (62 mph) on main lines. It was stipulated that the axle arrangement should be B'B', a locomotive two two-axle bogies and a driver's cab in the middle. The Reichsbahn ordered two locomotives that were to undergo an ambitious test programme.

Instead of two prototype locomotives, three were constructed. LKM built locomotives V 100 001 and 002 with an engine output of 662 and 736 kW (887 and 987 hp). The third locomotive, which also had a motor output of 736 kW (987 hp), was built at the AEG factory in Hennigsdorf, renamed LEW after nationalisation. LEW took over the series production of the V 100, of which there were six versions. Series V 100.1 went to the Reichsbahn, which from 1970 onwards designated it Series 110. Similar locomotives intended for export to China were classed as the V 100.2 by LEW, which became the

Series 110, 112, 118.0 and 118.2				
Wheel arrangement	B'B'	B'B'	B'B'	C'C'
First delivery	1964	1979	1959	1964
Last delivery	1978	1998	1965	1970
Withdrawn from service	1999	–	1991	1998
Quantity	867	512	83	206
Length overall	13.94m (45'9")	13.94m (45'9")	19.46m (63'10")	19.46m (63'10")
Total wheelbase	9.3m (30'6")	9.3m (30'6")	15.6m (51'2")	14.51m (47'7")
Bogie wheelbase	2.3m (7'7")	2.3m (7'7")	3.4m (11'2")	2 x 1.8m (5'11")
Wheel diameter	1.0m (3'3")	1.0m (3'3")	1.0m (3'3")	1.0m (3'3")
Working weight	63.7t (70.2 tons)	64t (70.5 tons)	78t (86.0 tons)	90t (99.2 tons)
Maximum speed	100km/h (62mph)	100km/h (62mph)	120km/h (75mph)	120km/h (75mph)
1-hour rating	736kW (987hp)	883kW (1184hp)	1324kW (1775hp)	1472kW (1973hp)

Above: Better together. In the 1980s DR steam locomotives were still in service. Here locomotive 110 541 supports a hardworking 50.35.

Left: On 26 September 1991 large numbers of people were still using the lines in East Germany. Here locomotive 112 515 hauls a passenger train through the romantically situated Neumühle station in the Elstertal.

Above: The V 200 series leaves Leipzig. On their last day in service, 28 May 1994, locomotives 220 269, 353, 268 and 295 are seen in front of the loco shed.

Opposite page: Locomotive 120 274 takes on a freight train of twin-axle wagons at Mohlsdorf in September 1991.

Below: A shot of locomotive 120 036 taken in July 1991.

V 100.3 when technically modified. For industrial operations LEW built the V 100.4 without a heating boiler. The Reichsbahn put these locomotives into service under the designation 111. LEW also constructed locomotives equipped for main lines under the designation V 100.5, which the Reichsbahn called Series 110.9. The V 100.6 was to be given a new gear system, with a hydrodynamic reversing mechanism instead of a mechanical one. But the V 100.6 series was never built. Locomotives with electrically operated reversing gear, called the Series 108, were created from converted 110s.

The Reichsbahn bought 867 of this standard series. The first 171 had a two-speed gear, fast and slow. It had emerged in the factory that the slow speed was only very rarely used, so the Reichsbahn decided to do without slow speed from number 172 onward. These locomotives, which bore the factory number 110 201, were therefore classed as the first locomotive of a new sub-series. On 15 March 1978 the Reichsbahn took delivery of the last locomotive, number 110 896.

As it had been with the V 180, the Reichsbahn was also interested in increasing the motor output of the V 100. In 1972 it equipped 110 457 with an engine with an output of 900 kW (1,206 hp). In 1977 and 1978 two more locomotives followed. As early as December 1972 LEW had built locomotives 110 511 and 512, which were already fitted with 900-kW (1,206-hp) engines. Admittedly, subsequent locomotives were again fitted with the 736-kW (987 hp) engines. But in 1979 the Stendal repair shop replaced these with more powerful ones during scheduled maintenance operations. Twenty locomotives of Series 110.0 retained the gear system with slow and fast speeds, and these were classed as Series 112.0. The 512 converted 110.2s were redesignated 112.2. The conversion of locomotives only ended in 1998. At that time the first 202s, as the locomotives had been called since 1992, had already been taken out of service. Locomotive 202 353 was in service for the incredibly short period of 29 days. The locomotive left the factory on 17 July 1998 and on 15 August the Deutsche Bahn took it out of service. At the end of the year 2000, the DB still had 82 Series 202 locomotives.

But 900 kW (1,206 hp) was not enough for the Reichsbahn. In 1981, it fitted the 112 203 with an engine of 1,100 kW. Because this corresponds approximately to 1,500 hp, the locomotive should been classed as Series 115. But this number had already been allocated to a V 100 with electric heating (albeit a variation that was then never built). This is why the 65 converted locomotives were given number 114. They were all based on the 110.2, so they too did not have the two-speed gearbox. They were not destined for a great future. First, DB acquired new diesel locomotives for local railway services. Secondly, DB Cargo wanted to close large numbers of branch lines, so that there was not enough work for the locomotives. In addition, the Bahn had reduced the top speed of the 202 and 204 to 80 km/h (50 mph). The reason for this was the wear on the track caused by the horizontal forces exerted by the locomotive. DB did not consider the possibility of modernising the bogies.

However, the many modernised locomotives owned by private railway companies clearly show that improvements were possible. Private railways had recognised the fact that these good, efficient locomotives could be modernised at very little cost. But some experts at Deutsche Bahn must have recognised the potential of this family of locomotives because the Series 111 shunting locomotives underwent a thorough modernisation programme. In the course of this modernisation programme, the locomotives were fitted with radio remote control and electric reversing gear.

Imports from Ukraine: Series V 200

In 1966 the Politbüro of the DDR made a decision that had serious consequences. Instead of continuing to electrify the main lines, it opted for diesel power. The Soviet Union would provide the necessary locomotives. The "Oktoberrevolution" locomotive constructors, based in Lugansk in the

Ukraine, had already built 3,000 diesel locomotives for the Soviet Union which ran very reliably in the country's harsh weather conditions. According to the DDR government: "Learning from the Soviet Union means learning how to triumph". As early as 1962 the Lugansk factory developed a large diesel locomotive adapted to meet European requirements. Hungarian Railways were the first to use the M 62. In December 1966 the Deutsche Bahn acquired two locomotives. These were designated V 200 001 and 002. In fact, buying the locomotives had been like buying a cat in a bag because the railway had no experience with diesel-electric traction. In addition, the bogies did not entirely meet European standards . The standard instructions in Cyrillic characters made the work of the mechanics in workshops even more difficult.

Slowly by surely the staff learned to get on with these primeval creatures. In particular, the regulation of output caused great problems. Even the Soviet co-workers could only help to a certain extent. Reichsbahn train drivers also found that they could distinguish between "strong" and "weak" locomotives. It was only 1970 that the problems were brought under control. At that point 287 locomotives had been produced. By 1974, the Reichsbahn had acquired 378 locomotives. which since 1970 were known as the Series 120.

However, after these initial teething problems these powerful locomotives proved reliable and very robust. Because there were no facilities for train heating these locomotives were mainly used for freight transport. The char-

acteristic noise of the two-stroke diesel engine infuriated people living along the tracks. Admittedly, the Reichsbahn tried to reduce the noise by installing sound insulation, but nonetheless the 120s remained among the noisiest locomotives. It was given the nickname "Taiga drums". But the disappearance of the DDR and the decline of rail freight transport made many 120s redundant. In any case, the railways were not very interested in these "Russian diesels". From June 1991 onward, it was decided that main overhauls would no longer be carried out. But it was only in 1995 that the DB was able to take the last "Taiga drums" locomotive out of service.

Universal locomotive: Series 132

Three of the four types that succeeded it did not fare much better. Series 130, 131 and 142 were all scrapped by 1995. Only the two 130s that had been converted for railway maintenance survived. But the almost all the locomotives of Series 132, which were built in large numbers, are still in service.

Because of the delays in the electrification of the tracks the Reichsbahn was in urgent need of diesel locomotives with a greater output than the 1,472 kW (1,973 hp) of the "Taiga drums". It is true that in theory it was possible to use the 120 in double traction, but in practice, this presented serious technical and operational problems. The Lugansk locomotive factory has already proposed a successor for the 120 in the shape of 2,200 kW (2,949 hp) TEG 109. At first the Ukrainians planned two versions: one for passenger service and one for freight transport. From the start, the passenger train

131

locomotives were to be fitted with an electric heating system for the coaches. But because its development had not yet been completed, the Reichsbahn acquired first a freight train locomotive without heating system in 1970.

Like the 120, the six-axle locomotives of the Series 130 had been constructed with a maximum speed of 140 km/h (87 mph). In the DDR they were allowed to run a top speed of 120 km/h (75 mph). Up to 1972 the Reichsbahn had acquired 82 Series 130 locomotives. Subsequently, the Lugansk factory supplied another 76 constructionally quite similar locomotive with maximum speed reduced to 100 km/h (62 mph). The starting effort of the Series 131 was 340 kN (76,432 lbf), clearly higher than the Series 130 with 250 kN (56,200 hp). Because there were no plans to use the locomotive for passenger trains, construction was slightly simplified. For instance, there was no anti-skid device.

The arrival of the "Ludmilla"

In 1972 the Reichsbahn was able to put the first two locomotives with electric heating into service. There were numbers 130 101 and 102 and they were already very similar to the following Series 132. The train heating did not appear to be ready for series production yet, which is why the purchase of series 132 was delayed until the middle of 1973. The 132 was efficient, it had a top speed of 120 km/h (75 mph) and it was suitable for both freight

transport and passenger service. However, the high axle load of 20. 5 t (22.6 tons) proved to be a problem. The so-called "Ludmilla" locomotives were simply too heavy for many sections of the network. The problem was aggravated by the axle-hung motors. The electric traction motors rested half on the locomotive frame and half unsprung on the axle. In order to put the locomotives into operation, the Reichsbahn had to strengthen the track on many stretches. This diesel-electric locomotive had problems that needed solving, and it was intrinsically better suited to the vast expanses of the Soviet Union than to a relatively small country like Germany. Particular attention was paid to the adjustment of the motors during the scheduled tests carried out on the locomotives.

In spite of the various problems, the 132s were soon among the most important locomotives on the Reichsbahn tracks. The East German State Railway acquired no fewer than 709 Series 132 locomotives. After German reunification, the railway authorities recognised the potential of these sturdy, reliable locomotives. Redesignated the Series 232, the locomotives were modernised and fitted with new diesel engines. The Reichsbahn converted 60 locomotives to a maximum speed of 140 km/h (87 mph) so that they could be used for InterCity services. Ten locomotives were equipped with even more powerful engines and renamed the Series 241. These were to be used for pulling heavy freight trains to Belgium and the Netherlands. The 232, 234 and 241 are unlikely to disappear in the near future.

Opposite page: The Series 232 will be used by DB Cargo for the foreseeable future. Here locomotive 232 434 awaits a new task, while 508 already has a freight train coupled to it.

Above: Hauling a fertilizer train, this 232 is still painted in the original DR colour scheme.

Left: Before the 232 came into service for express trains, this "Ludmilla" leaves Lübeck station on 27 July 1991, at the head of train D 1037.

Above: A Series 119 at the head of a regional train.
Right: This 119 014 is travelling between Sonneberg and Probstzella.

Import from Romania: series 119

Prospects for the Series 119 Romanian diesel locomotive are less favourable. It rapidly became known as the "Karpatenschreck" ("Carpathian Terror"). The Series 119 was to be used on secondary lines, on which the Ukrainian diesel locomotives were not permitted because of their high axle loading. In 1977 the Reichsbahn received two pre-series locomotives, and series production began in 1978. The DR acquired 200 locomotives of the Series 119 between 1978 to 1985. Its design was based on the V 180 and it was intended to be "Only the best for the Socialist sister nation".

However, shortly after putting the 119 into service, the Reichsbahn already began to modernise the locomotives, using many parts borrowed from the Series 118. After conversion the 119 had roughly the same output power as the Series 118. In 1990/1991 20 locomotives were sent to the Krupp workshops where they were fitted with much more powerful motors to enable them to pull InterCity trains and to provide the necessary power. The trains' air-conditioned carriages needed much more current than conventional electric heating. As a result, the 119, redesignated 219 in 1992, could only pull InterCity trains in double traction. The re-engined 229 had two units each with an output of 1,380 kW (1,850 hp).

Nevertheless time seems to be running out for the imported Romanian locomotive. The technology of the original 119 is now obsolete and the 140 km/h (87 mph) locomotives are no longer needed operationally. Instead of trains pulled by these locomotives, the Bahn prefers to see the Series 605 ICE-VT gliding silently through the low mountain ranges. Unlike the Ukrainian diesel locomotives, the Romanian 119 will not be saved by private railways.

Series 119, 120, 130, 132				
Wheel arrangement	C'C'	Co'Co'	Co'Co'	Co'Co'
First delivery	1977	1966	1970	1973
Last delivery	1985	1974	1972	1982
Withdrawn from service	–	1995	1992	–
Quantity	200	378	82	709
Length overall	19.5m (64'0")	17.55m (57'7")	20.62m (67'8")	20.82m (68'4")
Total wheelbase	14.51m (47'7")	12.8m (42'0")	15.85m (52'0")	16.05m (52'8")
Bogie wheelbase	2 x 1.8m (5'11")	2 x 2.1m (6'11")	2 x 1.85m (6'1")	2 x 1.85m (6'1")
Wheel diameter	1.0m (3'3")	1.05m (3'5")	1.05m (3'5")	1.05m (3'5")
Working weight	96t (105.8 tons)	116t (127.9 tons)	115t (126.8 tons)	122t (134.5 tons)
Maximum speed	120km/h (75mph)	100km/h (62mph)	120km/h (75mph)	120km/h (75mph)
1-hour rating	1980kW (2654hp)	1470kW (1971hp)	2200kW (2949hp)	2200kW (2949hp)

In talking to gatherings of railway enthusiasts, it quickly becomes apparent that a bulky, impressive second-generation diesel locomotive probably has the largest community of fans in Europe. They have accumulated a variety of descriptive pet nicknames in various countries — primarily "Nasenloks" ("nose locos") or "Nohabs", but also "round snouts", "potato beetles", and "round noses". These all describe the same type of locomotive: later-built examples of the United States Series FP 7, acquired by Sweden and Belgium in the 1950s and 1960s .

The FP 7 passenger locomotive belonged to a family of locomotives, no fewer than 6,333 examples of whose members were manufactured in North America alone. EMD, a subsidiary of the General Motors group of companies, had not made the decision entirely on the basis of its own free will, however.

Shortly before the USA entered World War II, the "US War Production board" declared that the Series FT, a Bo'Bo' locomotive designed 1939 , could only continue to be produced for hauling freight trains. Up to 1945, EMD manufactured 1,096 examples. In 1942 the authorities banned the construction of the six-axled Series E express passenger locomotive, that also came from EMD.

Conceptually, the machines clearly deviated from those manufactured in Europe at that time. As well as the so-called A Units, locos with a cab, B Units that had no cab were made to provide additional power; they were controlled from the A Unit. Across the Atlantic at that time, the technology of multiple unit control had matured, while in Germany for example it did not appear until the development of the Series V 200. The slow-running 16-cylinder two-stroke engine drove a direct current generator that powered the axle motors.

The European "nose" locos of Nohab

In principle this concept was adopted by the Europeans, who also copied the distinctive appearance. Technically some alterations had to be planned. The heavy diesel locos could not have just four axles, like their model. In order not to exceed the maximum allowable axle loading of European tracks, all European originated "round noses" have six axles. Also, the cross-section profile of the American loco had to be changed to conform to the European loading gauge. Among other things, the standard UIC profile required a stronger roof curvature. The construction had to be adapted further to allow for the transfer of drawbar loads and pressures through screw couplings and separate buffers, since in North America only centre buffer couplings existed. Also the

Above: The Nohabs of Danish national railways were in service until late 2000.

Left: A heavy freight driven by two Danish My locomotives in double traction.

Opposite page, top: The American Type F 7 diesel loco, here coupled to a B Unit, is the forerunner of all "nose" locos.

Opposite page, top: Locomotives of the same type also operate in Australia.

three-light top signal customary in Europe clearly changed the appearance of the engines. Nevertheless, an unmistakable relationship with the GM locomotives remained.

The most important European licensee was the Swedish company Nydqvist och Holm Aktiebolaget, known as Nohab for short. The locomotive factory was located in Trollhättan and belonged to the mechanical engineering and arms company Bofors. Nohab worked from GM's revised plans for the the Australian B Class, that were in turn derived from the North American F class. Operating conditions in Australia resembled those in Europe, in that an axle load of 26 t (29 tons) was too high. From the second series on, Clyde Engineering of Granville in the Australian state of New South Wales also built locomotives with two cabs.

So far as Nohab was concerned, neither America's B Units nor the twin-locomotive sets would be part of the production. The first client was Danish National Railways, which began by ordering four lowland engines with the wheel arrangement (A1A)'(A1A)'. In the following years, the DSB ordered 54 more locomotives, to whose production the Danish manufacturers Frichs, Thrige and Titan contributed. The last were the Series My locos with 1,433-kW (1,921 hp) engines, appearing on the tracks in 1965. Nohab also developed the Mx series, a lower-performance, lighter machine that could operate on a wider range of tracks withits maximum axle load of 15 t (16½ tons). Externally, these locomotives with a power of 1,047 kW (1,403 hp) are easily recognized with their smaller noses and interrupted line of air intakes. Both series had multiple unit control following US standards. The data was trans-

mitted using 65 volts direct current over a 27-wire connecting cable. Ten Mx and five My locomotives, the latter equipped with heat generators, were fitted with an additional control by the DSB for use with reversing trains. Data transmission for this was carried out using UIC standard cable. Between 1987 and 1993, the DSB withdrew its Mx engines completely. The My series too were being taken out of service, carrying out their final operations at the end of 2000. Latterly they towed freight trains, and worked in shunting and track-maintenance roles. Numbers Mx 1001 and My 1101 became museum locomotives, while Mx 1040 and My 1104 went to the busy GM Tradition Group in Trondheim in Norway. Mx 1035 was mounted as a monument on a plinth in Struer while the My 1112 enriched the railrway museum at Odense. My 1105 finally ended up at the Danish railway club in Holsterbrö.

21 Mx locomotives were sold to Danish private lines, 19 of them being used operationally and two being used as spare part donors. The Privatbane Sönderjylland acquired six more of the My series. The Danish "round noses" also reached Sweden. The buyer was the Inlandsbana, which organizes museum trips on the line of the same name. Ten My locomotives moved to the once-Danish region of Schleswig-Holstein. The North German railway company, a subsidiary of the Vossloh group, painted them as V 170 locos in blue and silver.

"Nose" locos for Norway: the Di 3 series

In parallel with the first engines for the DSB, Nohab built a Co'Co' "nose" locomotive at its own risk. This underwent test runs in Norway from September 1954. From Trondheim at the same time six-axle diesel-hydraulic locos from

Germany were being tested. After the testing programme, the Norwegian national railways ordered the first series. Designated the Series Di 3a, there were 32 examples of these Co'Co' locomotives. Apart from three machines, they were 30 cm (12 in) shorter than their Danish sisters and had slightly different braking equipment. At 105 km/h (65 mph) their maximum speed was about 28 km/h (17 mph) slower. The diesel engine had a power of 1,305 kW (1,749 hp). In addition the NSB also obtained three Series Di 3b locomotives with an axle arrangement of (A1A)'(A1A)' and a top speed of 143 km/h (56 mph). These came about because Nohab had expected an order from the Finnish national railways and had built two broad gauge locos on spec as well as a construction-pattern locomotive. Since the Finns decided differently, Nohab had to look for another customer. The Norwegians were grateful buyers, the gauge being adjusted to standard.

In the 1970s, the NSB removed the entrance ladder and door on the right sides of all the Di 3s and replaced the front aprons with snow ploughs. In addition most of the locomotives were fitted with train heating equipment. For the driver, this meant an additional burden of noise. Since cab number 1 was quieter, the locos were turned at the terminus so as not to use cab number 2. In addition some of the engines were fitted with facilities for automatic train control. Originally, the NSB planned that the Di 3 should be phased out at the end of the 1990s. A replacement was ready in the form of the Siemens Di 6 Siemens 6. However the NSB had to return the new locomotives to the manufacturer because, packed with technology, they were not robust enough to survive the rough business of everyday life. Intended for Norway, the engines

Above: An international convention of "nose" locomotives. Engines from Denmark, Norway, Belgium and Luxembourg meeting in Roskilde for a big parade.

Opposite page: Scheduled use of "nose" locomotives by the NSB came to an end in the latter part of the year 2000. On 3 July 2000, Di 3.633 and its E 477 delight the photographer as it passes Manskogan.

Below: In Norway the Di 3 hauled heavy good trains in double traction.

were unusually arranged for German circumstances, and Siemens had to modify them thoroughly before putting the locos in its own locomotive pool, hiring them to private freight train operators. For passenger train service, the NSB ordered the "Talent" motor coach train.

Nohabs in Hungary: the M 61 series

Hungarian Railways were third-party customers of the Swedish Americans. In 1963/64, Nohab manufactured 20 of the Norwegian Di 3a locomotives with the same 1,433 kW (1,921 hp) engines. The MÁV called it the M 61 series. Although the Nohabs had a train heating system, the Eastern bloc country gave up further deliveries and acquired alternative locomotives that beat the drum from the Soviet Union but were only usable for freight train services. But the "nose" locos were highly regarded, as was shown by the fact that locomotives M 61 014 and 019 were allowed to haul the government trains until the breakdown of the Communist dictatorship. Contrary to widely circulated opinion, there was no contract between the members of the Council of Mutual Economic Aid, regulating the division of the locomotive building between the individual states. However, there were negotiations over a so-called specialization agreement, according to which some governments received advance notice of what was required. Anyway it is debatable whether any satellite country could have avoided the procurement of Soviet locomotives. Eventually, virtually all of the management authority was controlled, arranged and certified by the centralised bureaucracy.

The locomotives that had been imported from the west lasted well into in the nineties. At end of 1999, the MÁV could give up the Nohabs. One engine, M 61 017, became a test vehicle. Numbers M 61 001 and 020 are preserved in the Budapest-Istvántelek railway workshops museum.

Nohabs in Belgium

The Belgian and the Luxembourg national railways also showed interest in the "nose" locomotives. But they did not want to acquire them ready-built

Above and right: The history of the M 61 lives on in Hungary. In the spring of 2000, they were still indomitable on the north shore of the Platten lake. Locomotive M 61 020 is especially handsome, preserved as a museum loco.

Opposite page, top: Nohab V 170 locomotives haul NEG freight trains on German lines, in this case a steel train in the Ruhr.

Opposite page, middle: In Belgium the "nose" locos are known as "potato beetles".

Opposite page, bottom: M 61 013 in Budapest West station, August 1988.

from the Swedish manufacturer. Anglo-Franco-Belge (AFB) offered itself as an alternative. This company obtained licences from both General Motors and Nohab, and as usual there were a number of details that diverged from US standards. Curiously AFB put the cab entrance on the right side, in spite of the fact that SNCB's traffic ran on the left.

The first to be received were the four Luxembourg engines, to which the numbers 1601 to 1604 were assigned. These locomotives had General Motors diesel engines like the Swedish models, developing 1,170 kW (1,568 hp). The 40 locomotives for the SNCB had AFB Dutch diesel engines with outputs of 1,264 and 1,397 kW (1,694 and 1,873 hp). There were three different variations, in spite of the relatively small quantity made. The 202 and 203 were largely identical and had electric rheostatic brakes, in contrast with the Nohabs. The 202 had a steam train heating system, while the 203 could haul only freight trains. Over the years the SNCB removed the steam heater units from the 202s and thereafter designated them 203s. Meanwhile a number of 203s were fitted with steam heater units and thereafter became 202s. So the designations are complicated, but on the basis of factory numbers it is known that a total of 36 examples were produced of both series together.

The SNCB put into service eight of the Series 204, which had a maximum speed of 140 km/h (87 mph) instead of 120 km/h (75 mph). Among other things, these engines without rheostatic braking towed express trains from Brussels to Paris. From 1971, the SNCB designated the "potato beetles" as Series 52 to 54. Then in 1978 they were given a comprehensive overhaul, the characteristic "nose" being lost. Simply for nostalgic reasons, it was decided that locomotive 5404 should keep its original appearance.

While the Belgian machines are still in operation, the four Luxembourg Series 16 had already vanished from scheduled services in 1994. Three machines remain for posterity. Number 1603 runs on the Venn line, while 1604 is the official CFL museum loco. An unusual fate befell number 1602, which came into private ownership. Since no Belgian "potato beetles" any longer existed in their original colour scheme, the very similar Luxembourg loco was painted green and yellow by its owners, and called number 202 020. The two other nostalgia locomotives also appear with it, still in their original Luxembourg livery.

Many railway enthusiasts are unaware that there is also one "round nose" loco with tap switching. Between 1955 and 1961, the Swedish national railways put ten Series Ra express locomotives into service. Their bodywork resembled the Danish My series, but the air inlets under the roof betray them as only distant relatives of the Nohab.

Top: BB 9288, one of the locos SNCF modified for speeds of 200 km/h (124 mph).

Left: The Chambery depot using its BB 7200 in double traction. Goods trains destined for Modane, the border station between France and Italy on the Mont Cenis line, are being coupled. Here are locos 7349 and 7360.

Some experts today doubt whether the French BB 9004 actually reached a speed of 331 km/h (206 mph) on 29 March 1955 as CC 7107 had a few days before. Regardless of this debate the design from these four prototypes became the model for one of the most successful French loco-motives: the BB 9200. A consortium made up of the French manufacturers Schneider-Jeumont, MTE and CEM built the first French series production express locomotive with four axles in 1957. Four conventionally controlled direct current motors transferred their torque to the four driven axles via Cardan shafts. SNCF had bigger plans for its high-performance locomotives, however. In 1966 six locomotives were fitted with high-speed wheel and axle drives as well as Faiveley single-arm pantographs. They were painted in an elegant red/grey livery instead of turquoise for use hauling "Le Capitole", the long-distance express between Paris and Toulouse. While SNCF allowed loco-motives BB 9278, 9281, 9282 and 9288 to travel at a top speed of 200 km/h (124 mph), BB 9291 and 9292 were given transmissions with ratios that made speeds of up to 250 km/h (155 mph) possible.

The "nez cassé" ("broken nose") locomotives: CC 40100 and BB 15000 — two nez cassé pioneers

In 1971 a completely new generation of electric locomotives took to the rails that, with their modular design, were suitable for both the direct current and alternating current systems used in France. With their striking nez cassé ("broken nose") fronts and single-motor bogies, they were based visually and technically on the famous six-axle CC 40100 four-system engine from 1964. The CC 40100s, over 22 m (72 ft) long, were the first electric locomo-tives that could in principle be used with nearly all European overhead wire systems. Two different transmissions that could be switched over when the locomotive was stationary were mounted on the single-motor bogie, allow-ing maximum speeds of either 160 or 240 km/h (99 or 149 mph). Their area of usage also included international TEE trains where they superseded a wide range of locomotives. Initially SNCF put four engines into operation from 1964 but then in 1969 and 1970 another six considerably more powerful loco-motives followed.

The four-axle nez cassé locomotive made its debut in 1971 in the form of the BB 15000 for the 25,000 volt alternating current network. This did not incorporate the speed-change gear that enabled the CC 40100 to be used for both goods and express trains. Nevertheless, following the Swedish example, a thyristor phase control was used for the first time in a French engine to ensure smooth tractive effort across the whole speed range. SNCF set a

maximum speed of 160 km/h (99 mph) in scheduled operation for the engines designed to travel at a top speed of 200 km/h (124 mph). While the first five engines rolled out of the factory halls in the classic SNCF green, the other 60 were painted in the elegant colours symbolic of luxury, with shades of red, silver and orange. The unmistakable feature on the BB 15000 is its one single-arm pantograph.

The BB 7200: the most successful nez cassé

Following the success of the BB 15000, SNCF decided to develop a locomotive with a similar design for the 15,000 volt network. The BB 15007, modified as the BB 7003 direct current locomotive, was used to test the electronic chopper control for the future BB 7200 direct current locomotive of which 239 were built from 1976. Like the BB 15000, the BB 7200 did not have a speed-change gear. Instead the engineers equipped the locomotives with one of two different transmission ratios. On locomotives BB 7201 to 7235, BB 7343 to 7380 and BB 7411 to 7440 the transmissions in the single-motor bogies were designed to travel at a top speed of 100 km/h (62 mph) and to deliver the high traction needed for towing goods trains. Locomotives BB 7236 to 7342 and BB 7381 to 7410 were intended for use with express trains travelling at a top speed of 160 km/h (99 mph). 34 goods engines are stationed in Limoges and 68 in Chambery.

In 1981 the Netherlands took up old traditions again and turned to French locomotive manufacturers. Initially they purchased 48 engines from the 1600 series, which was largely the same as the BB 7200 series. Further deliveries meant the numbering scheme had to be changed and the engines carried on in the number series starting with 17. In addition to the small technical differences required for the Dutch network, the Dutch locomotives can be distinguished from their French counterparts by the three headlamps, the modified roof fittings and not least their canary yellow colour.

BB 22200: the universal nez cassé

The many technical possibilities for the universal nez cassé were not yet exhausted. In 1977 SNCF sent the BB 22200 two-system variant of the nez cassé (designed for use with the two French power systems) out onto the tracks. To create this universal genius the Alsthom engineers combined the transformer system from the BB 15000 with the chopper control from the BB 7200. While most of the engines are licensed for a maximum speed of 160 km/h (99 mph), SNCF allows a top speed of 200 km/h (124 mph) for the eleven BB 22278 and BB 22351 to 22360 locomotives. A special feature on the BB 22200, which is painted grey and orange similar to the BB 7200, is the joints on the two single-arm pantographs pointing in the same direction. From the total of 202 engines, which can run on both French overhead wire systems, 31 locomotives are stationed in Rennes, 93 in Dijon-Perrigny and 78 in Marseille-Blancard. Nine of the dual-system nez cassés were also granted a special honour. To replace the British locomotives that would be delivered too late for use in the Channel Tunnel, SNCF painted the front of the locomotives yellow to meet British regulations . The locomotives were inevitably given the nickname Yellow Submarine.

Above: BB 26014, an example of the SNCF Sybic generation.

Opposite page: The BB 9200s, including 52524 9R seen here on the line to Albertville in April 1998, are also operated on French alternating current routes.

Sybic: the most modern French locomotive

The tried and tested alternating current BB 15000 was used again as a guinea pig after 1981. BB 10004 with an alternating current synchronous motor was created from BB 15055. Unlike the versions with asynchronous motors it did not require a sophisticated semi-conductor control system. The old BB 15007 again had to face tests to compare the asynchronous principle, which is dominant particularly in Germany. SNCF finally chose the synchronous principle with the proven single-motor bogie due to inadequacies in the semi-conductor technology and not least to difficulties with the 120 series German pre-production locomotives. In the next step to a universal super locomotive, the French locomotive manufacturers equipped the two dual-system BB 22379 and BB 22380 locomotives with the latest frequency converter technology in 1985. The synchronous drive motors in the single-motor bogies on the locomotives, now designated BB 20011 and BB 20012, and the ability to operate on two different power systems — "SYnchrone BICourant" in French — led to the catchy abbreviation "Sybic" being applied to the engines. The two original Sybics, which in contrast to the normal nez cassés are painted in elegant blue, yellow and silver, resplendently bear the label "Moteurs Synchrone Autopilotés" (automatic synchronous motors) next to the train number.

Train fans would have probably liked to have seen further nez cassés built, at least with the same look. However, aerodynamic aspects and new guidelines from the international railway association UIC regarding the stability of the front of the trains in collisions meant it had to be changed. The French locomotive industry therefore combined the tried and tested nez cassé chassis with a completely new body design. In 1984 SNCF ordered 88 Sybics of the BB 26000 series. The French had high expectations for the engines. Even on gradients of 1 in 40 the Sybics had to be capable of pulling 750 t (827 tons), the equivalent of 16 express train coaches, at 200 km/h (124 mph). It was some time before the high-performance engines became operational, however.

The French manufacturer GEC Alsthom gave the TGV Atlantique priority first of all. It was not until 1988 that delivery of the universal locomotives, painted in orange and different shades of grey similar to the TGV Sudest, actually started. Once the Sybics overcame their teething troubles at Alsthom in Belfort, the Dijon-Perrigny depot operated the first locomotives on the Dijon-Vallorbe line from March 1990, towing heavy goods trains and fast passenger trains. Success was not long in coming. In the same year SNCF ordered a further 176 BB 26000s with the option of an additional 44 engines. A total of 512 locomotives were acquired.

145

Above: Railcars were often hailed as the saviour of local railways, but they also frequently made the "last run". This was the case with locomotive 798 534 as N 5180 on 27 May 1988 on the line between Oberriedenberg and Oberbach.

Opposite page, top: A three-part 798 rumbles through the spring landscape.

Opposite page, below: There are a not many passengers on board this DR Series 772 railbus.

After the war the Bundesbahn and Reichsbahn tried to continue the prewar tradition of fast "flying" trains. In 1952 the Bundesbahn acquired a total of 29 Series VT 08.5 diesel railcars for its long distance services that could be combined with intermediate coaches and driving trailers to form three- to five-part sets. Between 1953 and 1957 they put into service for high-speed intercity traffic 12 structurally similar VT 12.5s with the appropriate intermediate coaches and driving trailers. The VT 08.5 was used exclusively for first class coaches while the slower local trains had mixed classes. When more modern trains took over the first-class service, the Bundesbahn equipped the VT 08.5s for use on local traffic and renamed it the Series VT 12.6. Both could be combined with each other at will. Because of their rounded fronts they soon became known as egg-heads, like their electric counterparts.

Franz Kruckenberg was highly gratified that many of his ideas were used in the development of the VT 11.5 TEE motor-coach trains . His influence was also clearly visible in the SVT 137 155 and quite unmistakable in the "rail zeppelin". Usually a seven-part TEE consisted of five intermediate trailers and two engine cars that each had a Maybach diesel motor with an output of 810 kW (1,086 hp). By adding more intermediate coaches it was now possible to form eight- and nine-part units. The motors did not allow more.

This is why the DB tried something new in 1971. The diesel engines were replaced by gas turbines produced by the helicopter company Avco-Lycoming. This doubled the power output of the engine cars. The gas turbine trains, now known as Series 602, had an output of 3,240 kW (4,343 hp) and were now able to reach a maximum speed of 160 km/h (99 mph). In the 1970s the DB was still planning the development of a Series 603 gas turbine train with a maximum speed of 200 km/h (124 mph), but the golden age of fast diesel and gas turbine trains seemed to be over after the oil crisis and with the increasing financial difficulties of the Bundesbahn.

In the 1990s the DB reconsidered its concept of long distance traffic, which depended mainly on electrified lines. Besides the ICE-T, the DB also developed a diesel ICE for the lines between Nuremberg and Dresden and between Munich and Zurich. Technically related in many ways to the Series 411 and 415, the four-part Series 605 was developed as the ICE-TD. A total of four diesel engines operated generators that in turn supplied the power for the three-phase motors. The 605, the DB's first diesel-powered vehicle, exceeded the magic 200 km/h (124 mph) mark. It has been in service on the Nuremberg-Dresden route since the 2001 summer timetable. However, the DB will not be purchasing more of these motor-coach trains because their maintenance is too expensive. Experts have calculated that the trains would only be profitable if they ran at 100% capacity.

Between 1963 and 1965 the Reichsbahn acquired eight express power cars with the designation VT 18.16, which they put into service together with the pre-war SVTs. Usually, these pulled trains that consisted of two engine cars and two intermediate coaches. Longer trains could be created by adding one or two more intermediate coaches. The Reichsbahn put into service a total of seven trains, six additional intermediate coaches and two further engine cars as reserve. They ran throughout the DDR and also travelled to Denmark, Austria, Sweden, Hungary and Czechoslovakia. In 1981 the motor-coach trains were taken out of service. However, two survived, one of which is still in working order.

Railbuses for local traffic

After concentrating mainly on larger diesel railcars in the 1920s, Henschel developed the first railbuses in the early 1930s. These were launched with the numbers VT 133 006 to 008 and their origins as road transport were clearly visible. Shortly afterwards the Wismarer railbus, known as the "Schweinschnäuzchen" or "pig's muzzle", made a triumphant debut on small, non-state-owned railways with various track gauges. World War II meant that there was less revenue from passengers and further pioneering developments for local railways were interrupted. It was only in the postwar years that, spurred on by competition from the rise of the motor car, the railways began to develop again.

In 1949 before the creation of the Deutsche Bundesbahn, the Reichsbahn of the three western occupied zones commissioned the Uerdingen coach-manufacturers to develop a light, reasonably-priced railcar for use on local railways. In 1950 the Bundesbahn bought 11 railcars with the designation VT 95 as well as six constructionally similar trailer vehicles of type VB 142. These ancient DB railbuses differ from all their series-produced successors in their characteristic, collar-like projection on the roof as well as the comparatively short wheelbase of 4.5 m (14'9"). At the time it was still thought that vehicles with longer wheelbases would have problems on the often sharp curves of local railway lines. A railbus achieved a speed of 90 km/h (56 mph) powered by a Büssing lorry engine of 81 kW (109 hp) housed under the reinforced floor. In 1951 the DB ordered a longer version of the original railbus so as to increase the number of seats. However, before being put into service it had to obtain an exemption because the wheelbase was now 6 m (19'8"). This measurement was adopted by all railbuses in both West and East Germany.

In 1952, the series production of railbuses began on a grand scale. The absence of the projection on the roof and baroque decorative elements gave the railbus a more modern appearance, with its characteristic transom windows over the driver's cab.

Series 601, 610, 627.0, 628.2				
Wheel arrangement	B'2'	2'(A1)+(1A)(A1)	2'B'	2'B'+2'2'
First delivery	1957	1992	1974	1987
Last delivery	1957	1992	1974	1989
Withdrawn from service	1993	–	–	–
Quantity	19	20	8	150
Length overall	19.94m (65'5")	51.75m (169'9")	22.5m (73'10")	45.15m (148'2")
Total wheelbase	15.45m (50'8")	44.1m (144'8")	17.0m (55'9")	38.55m (126'6")
Bogie wheelbase	1.7m (5'7")	2.45m (8'0")	1.9m (6'3")	1.9m (6'3")
Wheel diameter	0.95/0.90m (3'1"/2'11")	0.89m (2'11")	0.76m (2'6")	0.76m (2'6")
Working weight	211t (232.6 tons)	95.4t (105.2 tons)	33.9t (37.4 tons)	66.9t (73.7 tons)
Maximum speed	140km/h (87mph)	160km/h (99mph)	120km/h (75mph)	120km/h (75mph)
1-hour rating	2058kW (2759hp)	970kW (1300hp)	294kW (394hp)	410kW (550hp)

The railcars soon became known as the saviours of local railways. The original engine often had difficulty struggling up the steep gradients of local railways, but after 61 railcars had been produced, the output of the engine was raised first to 95 kW (127 hp) and then to 110 kW (147 kW). The small, narrow windows at the top of the driver's cab at the front of the train were a rather unfortunate feature from the driver's point of view. When driving into the sun the driver could see almost nothing. At first an attempt was made to solve the problem by painting the windows with white paint but the problem was finally solved only by doing without the windows in the pitch of the roof. In all the Bundesbahn bought 572 single-engine railbuses and 574 matching trailer vehicles. These continued to have the short wheelbase of 4. 5 m (14'9") and retained the little roof windows until the end, to the great delight of the passengers.

In 1953 it was recognized that even railbuses powered by engines with an output of 110 kW (147 hp) were close to their limit, especially when pulling a trailing coach up steep gradients. The solution was an additional engine. After three prototypes of the twin-engined VT 98, which looked no different from the single-engine type, series production began in 1955. Instead of the Scharfenberg coupling of its predecessor, the twin-engined version had normal screw couplings and side buffers, which allowed it also to pull ordinary coaches.

The VT 98 even hauled through coaches on country lines. The Bundesbahn purchased 329 "large railbuses", as these were often called to distinguish them from the less powerful VT 95, together with 320 VB 98 trailer vehicles

Above: Motor-coach trains of Series 628.2/928.2 are used predominantly on local lines, but they are also sometimes used on main line services.

Opposite page: After being removed from the InterCity service, the VT 11.5 series could be seen as travel agent's trains throughout Germany.

and 329 VS 98 driving trailers. In contrast, the single-engined railbus had no driving trailer. In 1958 the DB bought a special version of the VT 98 for the rack railway section between Honau and Liechtenstein through the Swabian alpine pastures. Known as the VT 97, this had a rack-and-pinion traction drive. The DB also bought six driving trailers and a trailer vehicle. After 151 railbuses had been produced, the VT 98 underwent a thorough improvement of its specifications. Instead of a body resting on plain steel springs, the next generation was fitted with a comfortable air suspension. In 1989 the DB converted 47 of the railbuses now known as Series 798 and 998 for one-man operation; these were designated Series 796 and 996.

The last VT 95s and VB 142s, designated as Series 795 and 995 since 1968, disappeared from the Bundesbahn lines in the early 1980s. However the barely younger twin-engined railbuses survived their smaller sibling by almost 20 years. It was only in the summer of the year 2000 that the modern Regio-Shuttles succeeded in driving out the last red "Brummers" from the tracks in the Tübingen area.

Railcars in the DDR

In the DDR the age of the railbus began in 1957. The coach manufacturers Bautzen built a railbus that they named the VT 2.09.0, which was similar to those developed in the West in several respects as well as appearance. Like the VT 95, the prototype of the East German railbuses had a Büssing engine

for its propulsion. In 1963 and 1964 a first series of 68 vehicles with matching VB 2.07.5 trailers was produced with engines made in the DDR. In 1965 Bautzen launched an improved version, nicknamed "Ferkeltaxe", designated VT 2.09.1 and VT 2.09.2. Instead of the original trailer, the East German railbus now had a matching driving trailer. In 1992 the Deutsche Reichsbahn purchased in all 159 railcars, 70 trailer vehicles and 86 driving trailers of the 771/971 and 772.972 series. In contrast to the DB's own railcars, including those on the Chiemgau railway, which retained their red coat throughout their lifetime, the DB painted the "Ferkeltaxe" that had also been red in turquoise and light grey. There are still a few railbuses working in the former East Germany but their days too are numbered. The combination of the arrival of more modern successors as well as the closure of local lines is driving the small "Brummers" off the tracks.

From the 627 to the 612

It is true that the West German railbuses were often seen as saviours of local railways, but the hard daily routine on worn stretches drained its strength. Passengers came to appreciate the austere charm of the red "Brummers" less and less. The railbus was reaching middle age. According to the Bundesbahnzentralamt (BZA — Railways Central Office) the solution to the problem was to introduce modern one- and two-part railcars with traction components derived from trucks.

Above: The one-part 627 often runs during off-peak hours.
Opposite: Gradually all the 628.2s are being repainted in the current colour scheme.

Between 1974 and 1975 the Kiel-based locomotive manufacturers Maschinenfabrik Kiel (MaK) produced eight prototypes of the one-part, four-axle 627 while the coach manufacturers Waggonfabrik Uerdingen produced 12 sets of the two-part 628. Starting from the Braunschweig and Kempten workshops, the DB tested the new vehicles extensively on the demanding stretches in the Harz and Allgäu regions. Nevertheless, the DB did not manage to come to a decision. In addition there were also bitter discussions about the pros and cons of particular line closures. In view of the increasing financial problems of the DB, the twin-engined 628 seemed too expensive and line closures made the smaller 627 as it stood less useful.

However, in 1981 the DB decided to go ahead with the purchase of the two types of railcars. The one-part railcar, now designated 627.1, was then increased to five. For the 628.1, the DB decided to make do without the second drive unit and bought one half of the two-part railcar as driving trailer 928.1. The DB fitted both with traditional screw couplings instead of the trend-setting Scharfenberg coupling. Their more elegant front was reminiscent of modern electric locomotives. But the 628.1 was even less successful than the modest 627.1. As a result the DB only bought three. There was no future for the 627 because of planned further line closures. Only the 628 was

improved so that a third generation was produced. In 1986 the Bundesbahn bought its first vehicle in the new colours of regional railways — mint turquoise and light grey — in the form of the 628.2 together with the matching 928.2 driving trailer. It acquired 150 of them. The stylish 628.2 soon became the embodiment of the new image of German railways on many stretches. As the Reichsbahn and Bundesbahn came closer together, eventually leading to a merger of the two state railways after German reunification, the Bundesbahn ordered another series of the 628 in 1998. The vehicles, now known as the 628.4, had larger doors at the coupling ends and were therefore slightly longer than their predecessors. The main advantage of the new type was the considerably increased output of the engine compared with the rather lame 628.2. However, the heavy 628.4 with its weight of 116 t (127.9 tons) did not have much in common with the proposals for an up-to-date railcar for local railways formulated in 1992 by the Association for German Transport (Verband Deutscher Verkehrsunternehmen).

In the 1960s the Bundesbahn had already dabbled with curve-dependent tilting coaches in the shape of Series 614 and 634. Although the higher speeds possible meant that there were advantages as far as travelling time and comfort were concerned, the railways did not pursue this pioneering technique. It was only in the late 1980s that the railways decided to commission its own series of tilting trains.

For use on stretches east and north-east of Nuremberg it bought 20 Series 610 diesel railcars fitted with the same type of tilting technique used in Italy and Sweden for regional metro lines. As a result, passengers and railwaymen alike called the trains "Pendolini", after the trains on which they were modelled. The influence of the pre-war SVT was quite unmistakable. Two diesel engines transferred their power to a three-phase generator that provided electricity for three three-phase motors. With the 610's successor, the 611, the DB returned to the trusted and reliable diesel hydraulic transmission. The 611 had tilting coaches that were inspired by technology developed for the armaments industry, but they did not survive the tough conditions on the railways. The 612, a development of the 611 that was bought in large numbers by the DB, was also very reminiscent of the "flying" trains of the pre-war years.

New short-distance railcars

In 1992 when the Association of German Transport Companies (VDV, the Verband Deutscher Verkerhsunternehmen) proposed its new guidelines for local railway vehicles, noone suspected the revolution that was about to take place very shortly, which would drastically change the market for railway vehicles. In principle, the VDV only sketched out plans for a modern tramway system using diesel traction that would run on railway tracks. The idea of a vehicle that had recently experienced a revival dates from well before the proposals of the VDV.

In reply to the DB's 627, Orenstein & Koppel (O&K) in Berlin put forward proposals for the future NE 81 railcar family. In 1981 Waggon-Union, which had taken over O&K in 1980, presented the first railcar for non-federal railways — known as NE — which was unimaginatively but logically called the NE-81. Compared to the DB-627 the powerful NE 81 was rather heavy. The number of vehicles bought up to 1992 were therefore not surprisingly quite

Series 605, 642, 644, 646 and 650					
Wheel arrangement	Bo'Bo'	B'(2)B'	B'2'2'B	2'+Bo+2'	B'B'
First delivery	1999	1999	1997	2000	1999
Last delivery	2001	2001	1998	2001	2000
Withdrawn from service	–	–	–	–	–
Quantity	20	150	59	30	47
Length overall	106.7m (350'0")	41.7m (136'10")	52.16m (171'2")	38.66m (126'10")	25.5m (83'8")
Total wheelbase	19.0m (62'4")	33.9m (111'2")	32.0m (105'0")	31.724m (104'1")	18.9m (62'0")
Bogie wheelbase	2.6m (8'6")	1.9m (6'3")	2.5m (8'2")	2.0m (6'7")	1.8m (5'11")
Wheel diameter	0.86m (2'10")	0.77m (2'6")	0.80m (2'7")	0.68/0.86m (2'3"/2'10")	0.77m (2'6")
Working weight	232t (255.7 tons)	68.2t (75.2 tons)	85.3t (94.0 tons)	54.5t (60.1 tons)	56t (61.7 tons)
Maximum speed	200km/h (124mph)	120km/h (75mph)	120km/h (75mph)	120km/h (75mph)	120km/h (75mph)
1-hour rating	1700kW (2279hp)	550kW (737hp)	1000kW (1340hp)	550kW (737hp)	504kW (676hp)

modest. Waggon-Union was only able to sell 26 railcars, 14 driving trailers and 3 trailer vehicles, mainly to south German railways. However, after its take-over of Waggon-Union at the end of 1990, ABB Henschel recognised that the concept of the NE 81 was in fact pointing in the right direction.

It therefore seemed a good idea to develop the idea further. In 1993 Henschel created the concept of the RegioShuttle, inspired by the NE 81 but with many innovations. When in 1994 ABB Henschel obtained an invitation to tender for the construction of vehicles for the Schönbuch railway, south of Stuttgart, nothing any longer stood in the way of the RegioShuttle, which until then still only existed on the drawing board. After the first RS 1 had been tested and passed by the federal railway authorities, the company, now trading under the name ADtranz, began series production of the train in 1996. ADtranz supplied the vehicles with a low floor 55 or 76 cm (21⅝ or 30 in) above the top surface of the rail. The power was supplied by five- and six-cylinder engines of 228 or 257 kW (306 or 344 hp) that were placed respectively under the two drivers' cabs. Besides the Südwestdeutsche Eisenbahngesellschaft, other railway companies such as the Württembergische Eisenbahngesellschaft, the Regentalbahn, the Hohenzollerische Landesbahn, the Süd-Thüringen-Bahn and the Deutsche Bahn all bought the RS 1. But meanwhile, in spite of the success of the RegioShuttles, other models were on the way.

The arrival of the Talents

Spurred on by the ideas of its competitors, the Aachen-based company Talbot developed its own vehicle, based on the guidelines of the VDV, which was not only like a tramway car but could also become a railway vehicle suitable for high-speed travel. Given the name Talent, the fundamental characteristics of this vehicle are the modular construction of its passenger coaches and their conspicuously elegant design. The striking aerodynamic, rounded shape of the front bears the unmistakable signature of Alexander Neumeister, who was also responsible for the design of the ICE trains. The curved sides of the Talent made it possible to fit the trains later with the ContRoll tilting technique developed by Talbot.

The positive response to a 1:20 scale model of the Talent prompted Talbot to translate the concept into reality. Spurred on by the head start of the competition, it only took Talbot seven months to put the prototype of a two-part Talent with a maximum speed of 160 km/h (99 mph) on the tracks. The Talent was originally considered an "outsider" and unlikely to compete. But by allowing the prototype to travel throughout Europe in order to introduce it to potential buyers, it soon became widely known. On 21 July 1996, after a Europe-wide advertising campaign, the DB ordered the first 120 three-part Talents from Talbot.

Forty-five of these vehicles, the Series 644, were fitted with diesel-electric traction powered by two V-12 engines and four doors per vehicle; these were used for urban railway services in the Cologne region. The slightly shorter 643, also three-part, had two doors per body and two six-cylinder in-line diesel engines. The power of the diesel-hydraulic transmission of these trains was slightly lower than that of the 644 with electric traction motors. They were used for regional traffic in North Rhine-Westphalia and the Rhineland-

Palatinate. The DB limited the two versions of the Talent to a maximum speed of 120 km/h (75 mph).

In the autumn of 1997 the Norwegian National Railways ordered 11 two-part Talents with tilting coaches. On 7 January 1998 the DB increased its order for 45 Series 644 Talents by another 14. Meanwhile, private railways also ordered two- and three-part Talents. The Austrian railways run the Talent on electricity for suburban services around Vienna and Salzburg.

When the regionalization of passenger traffic took place, Siemens was ready to produce a successful railcar concept. The Dürener Kreisbahn, the Vogtlandbahn and a Danish private railway company had already ordered the RegioSprinter. From it, Siemens developed the Desiro family that could use diesel or electric power.

Like the other railcars, the Desiro also consisted of modules. Conceptually, the main difference was the carriage unit, every two coaches being linked by unpowered Jakobs bogies. The drive units were situated beneath the raised floor of the front of the end coaches. The diesel vehicles of the Deutsche Bahn, the Vogtlandbahn and the Kahlgrundbahn do not have a hydrodynamic gear system as might be expected but a hydrodynamic-mechanical gear system with torque converter and five gears.

It was not only the Deutsche Bahn that ordered the Desiro in large numbers. On 12 September 2000 Siemens supplied the first of 30 electric Desiros to the Slovenian railways. The latter put into service two-part units with the

designation EMG 312-0 and three-part units with the designation 312-1. The Greek railways ordered 20 five-part electric Desiros, some of the Jakobs bogies of which had their own power. The Danish railways leased four vehicles for the Odense-Svendborg and Helsingör-Gilleleje routes. But Siemens' largest commission came from Great Britain. In mid-2001, the railway company Stagecoach and the leasing company Angel Trains ordered 800 trains, with an option on a further 400 trains. The Desiro can now rightly claim the title of "Europe's Train".

The Stadler alternative

The Swiss motor vehicle manufacturer Stadler developed its own concept. It combined the advantages of a locomotive with those of a railcar, forming a three-part standard unit consisting of a driving trailer, motor-coach and another driving trailer. There were no sitting or standing places in the motor-coach. A narrow side-corridor linked the two driving trailers.

Because the control trailers were not powered and were conveyed by the motor unit in the centre, the entrances and rear passenger area had a very low floor height. According to the customer's preference this floor height could be 585 or 760 mm (23 or 30 in) above the top of the rail. Only at the front, where a conventional bogie had been mounted for cost reasons, was the floor 1 m (39 in) above the upper surface of the rail. For passengers the complete isolation of the motive power brought another advantage: the

Opposite page: Series 610 marked the beginning of the systematic use of tilting coaches in Germany. They were used in the low mountain region of Nuremberg in the direction of Hof. The photograph was taken in the picturesque Pegnitz valley.

Above: Further development of the 610 resulted in the creation of the 611.

Left: The tilting of the coaches can clearly be seen in this picture. This 612 is leaning to one side like a motorcyclist rounding a bend.

noise and vibration of the propulsion system was no more noticeable in the control trailers than in a conventional passenger coach.

The staff in the repair workshop also quickly came to appreciate the advantages of the Stadler concept. All the components for the drive unit and the gear system were situated in the two engine compartments of the motor unit. The traction was diesel-electric and the traction motors rested half on the frame and half on the axles. These nose-suspended motors could easily achieve a top speed of 120 km/h (75 mph).

Technically, there was no problem in replacing the diesel engine by a transformer, thus converting the diesel train into an electric one. Besides the standard units, Stadler also offered vehicles with additional intermediate passenger modules. It was also possible to build motor-coach trains with two motor units. The Schweizerische Mittelthurgaubahn was the first to use Stadler motor-coaches, which ran on the Radolfzell-Stockach route. In 1999 the Hessian Landesbahn bought 18 motor-coaches. The Deutsche

Bahn acquired it in two versions: the 646.0 for use in the Brandenburg region and the 646.1 for its subsidiary, the Usedomer Bäderbahn. Technically these did not differ from each other, but the Usedomer coaches had five seats per row while the Brandenburg coaches had the conventional 2+2 configuration.

Train with flywheel

With the support of the Nahverkehrsgesellschaft Sachsen-Anhalt, the company running local stopping trains in Saxony, Alstom LHB and DB-Fahrzeug Dessau developed an articulated set of coaches for stopping services . Designated Series 618/619 by the DB and known as the "Leichte ("Light") Innovative Regional Express" (Lirex), it consists of six parts all powered individually.

Technically both halves are identical. At first glance, the most striking features are the unusual front and the oval windows at the ends of the half-

Left: The 605s on the stretch between Zurich and Munich have been elevated to EuroCity express status since June 2001.

Above: The DB subsidiary Usedomer Bäderbahn ordered 14 GTW 2/6 railcars.

Right: A DB 646.0 passing the Neoplan-Hochhaus in Berlin-Spandau.

Below: Talbot designed its Talent for a maximum speed of 160 km/h (99 mph).

trains, and the curved sides. It is only on closer inspection that the train's even more unusual features become apparent. It turns out that the Lirex runs on non-bogie tilting axles. Alstom calls this type of construction "Kerf", standing for "Kurvengesteuerte Einzelradfahrwerke" ("curve-controlled tilting axles"). The same hydraulic tilting technique had already been tried out in Denmark.

The other innovation is concealed under the body panels. The two diesel motors together with the generators, converters and a flywheel — the first to be fitted on a slow stopping train — are not housed under the floor of the coach but under the unusually high roof. Naturally this makes the work of the maintenance workshop much easier in that all that is needed to change the drive unit is a crane above the coach.

There were fears that the train might fly off the track because of its unusually high centre of gravity, but these were unfounded. Most steam locomotives had an even higher point of gravity and were perfectly safe. Also, like most modern "light" railcars the Lirex can hardly be considered a fly-weight. The average axle-load is about 17 t (18.7 tons), while Alstom also builds some versions with 21 t (23.1 tons), the maximum permitted. The flywheel stores the energy produced by the electric brakes, which conventional diesel railcars waste by dissipating it in electric resistances. At 25.000 revolutions per minute, the energy stored in the flywheel can drive one of the six traction motors at a maximum speed equivalent to 160 km/h (99 mph). But the train cannot maintain this for long because the flywheel quickly loses its speed.

Inside the prototype it is pure luxury. The comfortable seats and the clear layout may not be in complete harmony with the overall somewhat playful design. But this is not yet relevant because the train must be reduced in cost before it can be produced in series . So far the prototype has not been officially tested, and it is therefore impossible to say whether the DB will decide to order the train. Much testing and price negotiation will have to take place first.

Above: Now a preserved museum piece, loco E 94 279 is still in working order.

Right: An unusual meeting of "crocodiles": the E 93, the SBB crocodile and a Series 1189 crocodile of the ÖBB, on display in Munich.

Bavaria took the lead in Germany so far as electric express locomotives were concerned. In the early 1920s the Gruppenverwaltung Bayern (Bavarian region) of the Deutsche Reichsbahn ordered five modern express locomotives with the 1'Do1' axle arrangement, with the Bavarian designation ES1. While all the mechanical components were produced exclusively by Krauss, all the electrical parts such as the complicated but effective Buchli drive were supplied by BBC. With this concept the Swiss Jakob Buchli had discovered how to fix the traction motors to the frame of the locomotive and transfer their torque to the driving wheels through a complicated lever mechanism on one side. This substantially reduced the unsprung weight of the locomotive, enabled it to run much more smoothly at high speed. In 1926 the Reichsbahn put the first locomotive of the Series E 16 — as it was now designated — into service in Munich. From the start the E 16 was widely admired for its maximum speed of 120 km/h (75 mph). Five more locomotives followed in the same year but these were fitted with the bogie developed by Richard Helmholtz and patented as the Krauss-Helmholtz bogie that enabled the locomotives to negotiate curves more easily. In 1927 the number of locomotives of the E 16 series was increased to 17 by the addition of seven slightly more powerful ones.

When the Reichsbahn planned a standard electric locomotive in 1927, the E 16 was high on the list of possible designs. However, the Reichsbahn decided against the E 16 because of its complicated Buchli drive. Malicious gossip had it that anti-Bavarian feeling in Prussian Berlin had tipped the scales against this successful locomotive series. When the Bavarian region announced that it needed more express locomotives, Krauss built four more E 16s that were about 10% more powerful than the previous ones.

The E 17 marks the arrival of production locomotives

The success of the Kleinow flexible coil-spring transmission that had proved so effective in the E 21.0 prototype built in 1927 resulted in orders being placed for the E 17 in the same year. This was constructed by WASSEG, an amalgamation of AEG and SSW, which used the trend-setting 1'Do1' axle

arrangement with a Krauss-Helmholtz bogie that had been further developed by AEG, instead of the asymmetrical 2'Do1' axle arrangement. Visually the E 17 with its two short ends was influenced by the single-ended nose of the successful E 21.0. The four double motors of the E 17 were also derived from the prototype from the same stable.

By 1930 the Reichsbahn had bought a total of 38 E 17s, which were to serve as a model for a whole generation of express locomotives. At first the Reichsbahn put the locomotives into service only in Saxony. In 1931 they also started using the E 17 on the demanding express service between Stuttgart and Munich, which included the notorious Geislinger mountain section. In Saxony the model were replaced by the lighter E 04, which was constructionally similar in many respects; in principle it was a light E 17.

After World War II, locomotives E 17 123 and 124 remained in the part of the country that became the DDR, while the Bundesbahn took over 26 locomotives. Originally the DB had planned a complete conversion of the locomotives with fittings similar to those of new locomotives. In 1978 the last E 17s now renamed the 117, rolled into the sidings in Augsburg to be scrapped.

The Series E 04

Produced in three series from 1933, visually the E 04 cannot deny the influence of the E 17, in that the silhouette of the E 04 is very reminiscent of the E 17 without one of the middle driving axles. It might at first appear that the E 04 was designed for the Reichsbahn simply as a lighter version of the E 17, but in

fact the main aim of the engineers at AEG and SSW was to simplify the construction of the E 17 as much as possible and perfect its details, while only reducing its slightly performance. The E 04 had a conventional sheet metal frame instead of a complicated fabricated framework. Instead of the twin motors that were expensive to maintain, the E 04 used three single motors for propulsion. Nevertheless, at 2,000 kW (2,681 hp) the E 04 only had 300 kW (402 hp) less than the E 17. However, the E 04's bigger sister could pull heavier loads for short periods. A new type of control system prevented the typical jerking when switching in low voltage at the moment of starting and allowed a smooth transfer of the tractive effort. This conversion with all its innovations also made the construction of a Super-E-17 possible. This took place in 1935 with the launch of the E 18, a greatly improved version of the E 04.

The Reichsbahn initially ordered a first series of locomotives of the E 04 series that were approved for a top speed of 110 km/h (68 mph). The second series of 11 locomotives, also delivered in 1933, had a maximum speed of 130 km/h (81 mph) because it had a different gear transmission ratio, but of course this also meant that the locomotives could not pull so heavy a load. With locomotive E 04 23 the Reichsbahn tested a new type of reversible control that only became widespread after the war, but without which today's railways would be unimaginable. Before World War II the Reichsbahn used the E 04 on lines to Magdeburg, Leipzig and Munich. After the end of the war 14 locomotives remained in East Germany, a few of which ended up in the Soviet Union in 1955 where they were in everyday service. Renamed the

Series 204, they continued in regular service until 1976. After the war the Bundesbahn still had six locomotives. The final locomotives, now renamed Series 104, left the Osnabrück workshops in the late 1970s and were used to pull express trains. The last two locomotives were taken out of service in 1981.

The Series 44: a universal locomotive

After the Reichsbahn had successfully completed its search for an electric express locomotive with the purchase of the E 17, it still needed a universal locomotive for passenger and freight service as well as for light expresses. But the world economic crisis of the early 1930s prevented this, because the Reichsbahn did not have the money for costly experiments. From its point of view it therefore seemed more satisfactory to modernize the steam locomotive that dated back the time of the "Länder Railways". Driven by necessity, locomotive manufacturers which were already working on projects for electric express trains took the initiative. In 1931 the Bergmann-Elektrizitätswerke (BEW), a cooperation between Maffei in Munich and Schwartzkopff in Berlin, Maffei-Schwartzkoffwerke (MSW), as well as Siemens-Schuckert-Werke (SSW) on their initiative each put forward a constructively similar proposal for the future E 44 universal locomotive in the hope of winning the approval of the railway authorities. All three manufacturers proposed a four-axle bogie locomotive without carrying axles in which all the fundamental components made use of modern welding techniques.

It went without saying that all axles were driven, each with its own sturdy

Above: An E 04 and an E 18 of the Deutsche Reichsbahn in perfect order, exhibited in a parade at Riesa.

Below: The E 44 was renamed the Series 244 in the DDR.

nose-suspended traction motor. The unusual aspect of all three E 44 proposals was that the tractive effort in both directions was transferred directly to the bogies, which were coupled to each other. As a result the frame and superstructure were not subjected to excessive stress.

Although the three locomotives were similar in concept, the three manufacturers followed completely different technical approaches. In developing the E 44.0, SSW rather surprisingly borrowed several elements from the two E 15 and 16.5 prototypes that had failed completely four years earlier in the competition for the future standard express locomotive. That the SSW locomotive then became the foundation stone for one of Germany's most successful series of electric locomotives can only be explained by the fact that SSW developed and improved the locomotive in a masterly manner. Visually, with its box-shaped superstructure and striking sun-visors over the front windows the E 44.1 somewhat resembled the plainly longer E 75. Technically it was very much up-to-date. Instead of the antiquated rod drives, the four drive motors transferred their torque directly to the four axles. The third proposal by BEW was similarly inspired by the E 75 of 1927. This was undoubtedly because many of the engineers who worked on the mechanical parts of both the E 44.1 and the E 44.2 came from Schwartzkopff, which later became Berliner Maschinenbau AG (BMAG).

Soon after the series of tests were completed, the Reichsbahn ordered a production of 20 E 44.0s, only a few details of which had been reworked. They remained in service until 1932. The E 44.1 was particularly appreciated by the railway authorities of southern Germany. After the prototype of the small box-shaped electric locomotive had passed the test on the demanding mountain stretch between Freilassing and Berchtesgaden with flying colours, four constructionally similar locomotives were purchased in 1933. Inside, it

Series E 04, E 16, E 17 and E 44, and E 69 05				
Wheel arrangement	1'Co1'	1'Do1'	1'Do1'	Bo'Bo'	Bo
First delivery	1932	1926	1928	1930	1930
Last delivery	1935	1933	1930	1951	1930
Withdrawn from service	1981	1979	1979	1989	1981
Quantity	23	21	38	181	1
Length overall	15.12m (49'7")	16.3m (53'6")	15.95m (52'4")	15.29m (50'2")	8.7m (28'7")
Total wheelbase	11.6m (38'1")	12.6m (41'4")	12.3m (40'4")	9.8m (32'2")	3.8m (12'6")
Bogie wheelbase	1.6m (5'3")	1.6m (5'3")	1.6m (5'3")	1.25m (4'1")	1.0m (3'3")
Wheel diameter	1.0m (3'3")	1.0m (3'3")	1.0m (3'3")	1.0m (3'3")	–
Working weight	92t (101.4 tons)	110.8t (122.1 tons)	111.7t (123.1 tons)	78t (86.0 tons)	32t (35.3 tons)
Maximum speed	130km/h (81mph)	120km/h (75mph)	120km/h (75mph)	90km/h (56mph)	50km/h (31mph)
1-hour rating	2190kW (2936hp)	2944kW (3946hp)	2800kW (3753hp)	2200kW (2949hp)	605kW (811hp)

contained many components of the now very successful E 44.0. In 1934 four more improved E 44.1 completed the fleet of nine locomotives. In 1938, when the Reichsbahn had almost 100 E 44.0s in service, the designations of the E 44.1s were changed to E 44 501 to 509 in order to avoid a conflict in the numbering system.

The Bergmann E 44.2 remained a lone locomotive that lived side by side with the E 44.5. It was not produced in quantity because it failed to impress any potential customers. Its life ended without any ado in 1950 in Freilassing. A total of 174 E 44.0s had been built by 1945. In theory, the number should also include the two test locomotives E 244 11 and E 244 21.

These were built in 1936 for use on the Höllentalbahn which was electrified with a different electric supply of 20,000 volts and 50 cycles. After World War II the Deutsche Reichsbahn of the DDR still had 45 locomotives of the E 44 series. In the 1950s the Bundesbahn built another seven E 44s from available parts, and when the 50-cycle system became obsolete at the beginning of the 1960s, the two Höllental locomotives were brought to line with the other

The local railway line between Murnau and Oberammergau is famous not only among railway fans. As Germany's first standard-gauge track it became electrified as early as 1905. The overhead contact line supplied alternating current with a tension of 5,500 volts and 16 cycles.

On February 1906 the railway put its first electric locomotive into service. Built by Siemens in Katharinenhütte, this could pull 50-t (55-ton) trains on uphill stretches with a gradient of 1 in 33 at a speed of 20 km/h (12½ mph). In 1909 and 1913 Siemens and Krauss supplied two slightly more powerful locomotives. Pulling 85 t (94 tons), these could reach a maximum speed of 23 km/h (14 mph). Siemens also built a curious vehicle in 1919. Using half of a 1901 bogie locomotive built for the Marienfelde-Zossen test track near Berlin, Siemens built an alternating current locomotive. To house the pantograph, Siemens built a roof that projected widely over the superstructure. Locomotive number 4 did not perform well so it was taken out of service in 1929 and modernised at the beginning of the 1930s. At the same time, Siemens also overhauled locomotives 1 to 3. In the meantime the Murnau family acquired a new addition, LAG 5, which was not only the longest and heaviest locomotive but also the most powerful. A few years later, in 1938, the private railway was taken under the wing of the Deutsche Reichsbahn, which gave the locomotive series number E 69. In 1954 the successor to the Reichsbahn, the Bundesbahn, converted the tracks and locomotives to the

standard electric system of central and north-European electric system, with a single-phase current supply of a tension of 15,000 volts and 16.67 cycles. This meant that the Bundesbahn had no use for the five locomotives, and they were therefore used as shunting locomotives abroad. It was only in 1964 that the E 69s returned home. In the 1970s the Bundesbahn began to take the E 69, now known as series 169, out of service, but the five locomotives have all been preserved for posterity.

locomotives in the series. Until the mid-1980s the two German railways were unable to do without the E 44. While the last E 44.5 had already disappeared from the Upper Bavarian tracks, the E 44.0, at least in the form of the 144 and 145 (with electric dynamic rheostatic brakes) could be found in the Würzburg railway repair shop until 1984. In East Germany the E 44s, now given the designation 244, remained in service until 1989.

An elegant express locomotive: the Series E 18

The E 17 and the more recent E 04 had set high standards for the German locomotive industry. The potential of both these types of locomotives was already revealed in 1933 by the E 04 when it succeeded in breaking the 150 km/h 93 mph) mark. In 1933 the quality of these two types encouraged the Deutsche Reichsbahn to order a Super E 17 from AEG combining all the advantages of these locomotives. Consequently, this electric locomotive was given the series number E 18 after the famous express steam locomotives.

From a purely technical point of view, they combined the slightly more powerful motors of the E 04 with a completely welded frame like that used for the E 17. As in these two models the reliable Kleinow spring drive transferred the torque of the traction motors flexibly to the wheel sets. The fine notch speed control first introduced with the E 04 was fitted with an electric drive so that the train driver only needed to move a master control switch up or down to accelerate the locomotive or slow it down.

The E 18 presented in 1935 worked completely differently. Its elegant, parabolically rounded front influenced a whole range of successful express railcars since the 1930s. As well as the visual merits of the streamlined design of the E 18, which still looks modern today, there was a considerable reduction in the wind resistance compared with the rather baroque shape of its predecessors. The locomotives were able to display their technical qualities on test runs between Munich and Stuttgart. The locomotive reached a maximum speed of 165 km/h (203 mph) without difficulty — 10 % faster than had been expected. In addition, their traction motors produced an output that for a short time could exceed the magical 6,000-hp (8,043 kW) barrier.

The amazing performance of the E 18 also impressed the jury at the Paris Exhibition in 1937. After winning three prizes, the locomotive returned to Munich on 17 December. However, by the beginning of 1940 AEG had only built 53 of the 100 locomotives that had been planned, on account of other priorities brought about by the war.

In 1938, after the success of the E 18, the Austrian railway system, at that time the Österreichische Bundesbahnen (BBÖ), ordered locomotives like the E 18 from Austrian locomotive manufacturers. After the annexation of Austria by Hitler's Germany, the Reichsbahn modified the locomotives in the course of being built to meet German requirements. Known as the E 18.2, a reduced gear ratio meant that the locomotives had a maximum speed of only 130 km/h (81 mph). However, the locomotives came into their own on mountain sections, since with their greater tractive effort they performed better there than their German sisters.

After the war the DB in West Germany still had 36 E 18s and the Reichsbahn in East Germany had nine, while Austria had two German E 18s as well as eight E 18.2s. After the war the ÖBB renamed its E 18.2, giving it the designation 1018. The German locomotive E 18 42 became the 1118.01. Locomotive

Top: Series 144 locomotives were mainly used for local services in the 1970s and 1980s.

Above: Loco 144 017 was photographed on 9 April 1979 pulling a local train past Burg Zwingenburg on the Neckartalbahn, on its way to Heidelberg.

Right: This blue locomotive number E 19 045 was photographed in the main station in Stuttgart.

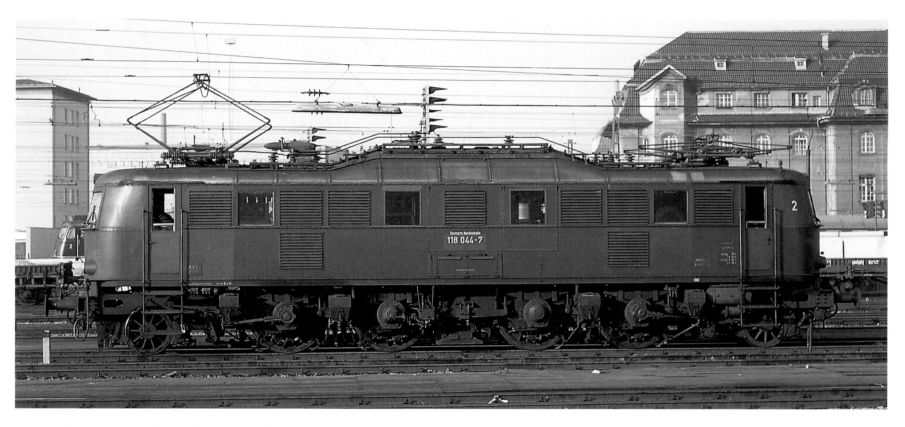

Above: A few E 18s were still painted green even after being given the new designation 118. This photograph was taken in Munich main station.

Below: The blood-orange colour of Austrian trains suited the E 18s very well. Unlike the two German state railways, the ÖBB modernized its E 18s. This is particularly apparent in the front part of the locomotives. Redesignated 1018/1118, these locomotives were in use as express locomotives until the 1990s.

Above: A heavy ballast train travelling from Eschenlohe not far from Garmisch-Partenkirchen, pulled by the classic 194 as it approached the end of its career.

Opposite page: So as to have a stylistically authentic locomotive to pull museum trains, the ÖBB decided to rebuild its locomotive 1020 027 that had been damaged in a fire, and paint it pine green. It is also used on some scheduled services. Here it is hauling the freight train 448 13 from Innsbruck to the Brenner.

E 18 046 was rebuilt with parts of E 18 206 that had been taken out of service and became the oddball Austria-German locomotive 1018.101.

In spite of the growing competition from more modern series the ÖBB did not want to take the reliable 1018 and 1118 out of service. Austria completely modernised all the locomotives at the end of the 1960s so as to prolong their use, which in the case of the 1018 continued until the beginning of the 1990s.

Electric traction had no future in the DDR because of the Soviet decision to use diesel power in East Germany. On 29 March 1946 the Soviet military administration ordered the dismantling of the electrification system. A few weeks later, a large number of electric locomotives, including the first two of five E 18s, started their long trek to the Soviet Union as reparation payments. Four more locomotives that had been damaged were sent to the scrap yard at Velten near Berlin. Between summer 1952 and summer 1953, the five express electric locomotives were returned one by one to the DDR as an official gift from the USSR to the DDR. Because of the lack of spare parts and raw materials of every kind, in autumn 1953 the Reichsbahn exchanged its five E 18s for steam locomotive spare parts and copper for contact wires from the Bundesbahn in West Germany. The contact wire was needed for the renewed electrification of the lines that had now been approved by the Soviets. As electrification expanded on the Reichsbahn tracks, the railway management

recalled the four E 18s that had been withdrawn from service near Berlin. Between May 1958 and January 1961, three of the four E 18 were put back into service as E 18 19, 31 and 40. In the mid-1960s the Reichsbahn painted the undercarriage in the typical brilliant red of Reichsbahn electric locomotives in order to detect possible cracks in the framework. While the main repair workshop in Dessau converted engines E 18 19 and 40 for testing to pull passenger trains a maximum speed of 180 km/h (112 mph), locomotive E 18 31 kept its original transmission ratio. After E 18 40 became involved in a serious accident during the test running at Grosskorbetha, the Reichsbahn decided in the early 1970s to use spare parts from the crashed locomotive to convert locomotive E 18 31 so that it too could reach a maximum speed of 180 km/h (112 mph). Renamed Series 218, the East German E 18s survived reunification and are still on active service.

Unlike the two neighbouring railway companies, the Deutsche Bundesbahn did not display much enthusiasm for experimenting with the E 18s. Admittedly in 1955 it rebuilt locomotives E 18 054 and 055 with spare parts but it left everything else untouched. In the 1960s many of the DB locomotives were fitted with the smaller hooded standard DB lights, disrespectfully known as frog's eyes by railway enthusiasts. At first the locomotives were still all green, but they were painted an elegant cobalt blue in the 1950s.

Series E 18, E 19.0, E 19.1, E 93 and E 94					
Wheel arrangement	1'Do1'	1'Do1'	1'Do1'	Co'Co'	Co'Co'
First delivery	1935	1939	1939	1933	1940
Last delivery	1940	1939	1940	1940	1956
Withdrawn from service	1984	1978	1977	1985	1995
Quantity	53	2	2	18	204
Length overall	16.92m (55'6")	16.92m (55'6")	16.92m (55'6")	17.7m (58'1")	18.6m (61'0")
Total wheelbase	12.8m (42'0")	12.8m (42'0")	12.8m (42'0")	12.8m (42'0")	13.7m (44'11")
Bogie wheelbase	1.6m (5'3")	1.6m (5'3")	1.6m (5'3")	1.25m (4'1")	1.25m (4'1")
Wheel diameter	1.0m (3'3")	1.0m (3'3")	1.0m (3'3")	–	–
Working weight	108.5t (119.6 tons)	113t (124.6 tons)	110.7t (122.0 tons)	117.6t (129.6 tons)	121t (133.4 tons)
Maximum speed	150km/h (93mph)	180km/h (112mph)	180km/h (112mph)	70km/h (43mph)	90km/h (56mph)
1-hour rating	3040kW (4075hp)	4000kW (5362hp)	4080kW (5469hp)	2502kW (3354hp)	4680kW (4496hp)

Later three of the locomotives were painted in the ocean-blue and beige which were typical colours of the 1970s and 1980s.

In 1974 there were still some of these locomotives left in Würzburg although by now the series had been renamed 118. Gradually the E 18s began to be displaced by the younger 111 series. The last E 18s had to bow out in 1984, by which time when were already 200 Series 111 locomotives in service. Today there are only very few E 18s left, some of which are used as museum locomotives to pull special trains.

The E 93: a locomotive with projecting ends

In the early 1930s the Deutsche Reichsbahn only had two series suitable for pulling heavy freight trains. There were 46 Series E 91/91.9 locomotives, with Winterthur oblique rod drive and C'C' axle arrangement. They were used particularly on mountain sections but there were not enough of them. On flat terrain it was the giant Series E 95 powerhouses that dominated the scene. The Stuttgart-Ulm section and its connecting line to the freight station of Kornwestheim had been electrified since 1 July 1933. The journey to Ulm across the famous Geislinger Steige (Geisler mountain stretch) with its uphill climb of 1 in 44 required powerful locomotives that could pull trains of 1,600 t

(over 1,750 tons) to Göppingen and trains of 1,200 tons (over 1,300 tons) to Altenstadt. On the Geisler Steige the train was pushed up the hill. Development of the E 91/91.1 had to be ruled out because of its complicated rod drive. The trend was towards individual control with nose-suspended motors. The new locomotives were conceived as a long-term replacement for the high-maintenance rod-driven locomotives. Instead of a rod drive, they had a Co'Co' axle arrangement. At first only two of these locomotives were ordered from AEG because the volume of traffic had not yet recovered from the world depression of the 1930s.

The E 93 had three bogies, each with three driving axles. The drive was transferred from nose-suspended motors, the various components being fixed on a long, stable, rigid underframe. This rested on three points on each of the two driving bogies. This type of construction resulted in a fairly high axle loading. In order to reduce this weight, all items of equipment that did not need to be accessible during the journey were housed under low projecting sections. This led to the E 93s characteristic appearance, rather reminiscent of the Swiss "crocodile" that also had projecting sections at each end, albeit much longer than those of the E 93. Another feature of the E 93 was the completely welded chassis and engine compartment, only the sheet metal of the sides and the roof being secured by rivets. The bogies too were of riveted construction.

The electrical system had been newly developed and at the same time brought into line with the E 44 electric locomotives. For instance, the fine speed control was largely identical in all three series. In the course of six years the DR acquired 18 locomotives from AEG. The locomotives were popular because of their smooth running, and the wear and tear of the wheel flanges predicted by critics because of the heavy weight of the locomotives was within acceptable limits.

Redesignated 193 in 1968, the series was reduced to pulling pick-up goods trains in the 1970s. From 1976 onwards they were gradually sent to the scrapheap and by 1984 they had been completely taken out of service.

Right: This photograph of locomotive 254 114 of the DR was taken in 1976. It is pulling its full train of tank wagons from Böhlen to Karl-Marx-Stadt, the present-day Chemnitz.

Opposite page: Locomotives of 194 series were often used as pusher locomotives on the mountain stretches of the low German mountain ranges. Two 194s were in service round the clock on the Laufach-Heigenbrücken section.

The E 94 mountain locomotive

From mid-1937 onwards, the need for powerful electric locomotives to haul heavy freight trains increased considerably. Following the takeover of power by the National Socialist party the volume of traffic greatly increased. Passenger train services were speeded up and the lines had to be as free as possible. The new locomotives had be powerful enough to pull heavy express trains at a speed of 90 km/h (56 mph). The E 94, as the planned locomotive was called, had to be able t pull a load of 2,000 t (2,200 tons) on the level at a speed of 85 km/h (53 mph). Pulling 1,600 t (1,760 tons) on an uphill stretch with a gradient of 1 in 100, it had to maintain a speed of at least 40 km/h (25 mph).

The E 94 was actually very similar to the E 93. It too had axle-hung drive motors and projecting sections at each end. Because the locomotives were to be used mainly on the Austrian mountain sections of the Arlberg, Brenner and Tauern, they were fitted with electric rheostatic brakes under pressure from the Austrian authorities. The first orders for the E 94 came in in 1937 but the first deliveries only took place in 1940. A total of 143 locomotives came into service during the war. This was only because the E 94 was categorised as KEL 2, "KEL" standing for "Kriegs-Elektro-Lokomotive", "War Electric Locomotive". (KEL 1 was the E 44). The manufacturers included among others AEG, Krauss-Maffei and SSW. Delivery problems and the interruption of production runs in favour of goods more essential to the war effort resulted in the Vienna-based locomotive manufacturer Floridsdorf and other locomotive manufacturers becoming involved in building the locomotives. On 1 January 1946 there were 67 Series E 94 locomotives in the

West German zone, 29 in the east and 44 in Austria. Railway companies continued buying the E 94 even after the war ended. There followed by a prefabricated phase and a reproduction phase. The first lasted from 1945 to 1953. The shortage of locomotives led to the completion of nine of the E 94s ordered and partly assembled during the Reichsbahn period. In the second phase — 1954 to 1956 — old locomotives were reproduced because new developments were not yet ready for series production and the electrification of further stretches of the network in the late 1940s had led to a growing need for electric locomotives. Forty-three E 94s were produced because its universal quality made it so popular. Twenty-three of these were fitted with a stronger power output. The DB also implemented various constructional changes; for instance, from 1956 the E 94s were fitted with an Indusi system when they came in for a general overhaul.

The original plan had been to take the DB-194 out of service at the end of 1987. But because the delivery of the 120.1 universal locomotive had been delayed, the E 94s remained in service for another five months. The last 194s were finally taken out of service in 1988. But several locomotives such as number 194 579 survived in working order and are now museum pieces. The Reichsbahn in the DDR gave the E 94 series number 254. These were taken out of service in the 1990s.

Series 1020 of the ÖBB

In May 1940 locomotives E 94 001 and the E 94 002 to 006 arrived in Innsbruck where they were stationed at the local depot. Their main role was to

Above: Locomotive 1020 044 in 1994, seen here on the Arlberg section. It has now been painted green again and can be seen in the locomotive museum in Innsbruck.

Left: One of the most beautiful stretches of the Tauernbahn that ran between Mallnitz and Kaponig until November 1999. Today this section with its many bridges has been replaced by a tunnel. The 1020s based in Villach were used for unscheduled journeys on this section until well into the 1990s. This photograph was taken on August 1994.

pull war-related freight trains on the Brenner line. During the war, more E 94s came to Austria. They were stationed in the depots at Innsbruck, Salzburg, Schwarzach-St Veit, Spittal-Millstättersee and Bludenz. All the E 94s still in Austria after the end of the war were to remain there in accordance with a decree of the Allied Control Council. There were 44 E 94s in Austria. Three more locomotives, commissioned by the ÖBB, were built by the Vienna locomotive factory (WLF) and EAG from half-finished parts. In 1953, the ÖBB introduced its new numbering system and the E 94 series was now called 1020. The new numbering system included the locomotives built by Krauss-Maffei and AEG, which were included in the same ÖBB numbering system. From 1952 the Motive Power Department in Villach also had the powerful six-axle locomotive.

The arrival of the ÖBB Series 1010 and 1110 in the mid-1950s signalled the beginning of the end for the 1020s, which were used for both express passenger and freight services. The 1020s were now used mainly to pull freight trains, although there were still some 1020s used in scheduled passenger services. Salzburg, Villach, Innsbruck and Bludenz became strongholds of the 1020 series. But the process of displacement could not be halted. In 1978 the Series 1044 universal locomotive came out and this took over many of the 1020's cross-country runs. From 1983 onwards the locomotives were gradually taken out of service. But this process was temporarily halted in 1990

because there were not enough locomotives available for the "Neue Austro-takt 1991" (NAT) that had been advertised at great expense. In 1990 a repair programme was planned for the 1020s. This was to take place in the Linz main repair shop where the 1020s were painted in a variety of colours. The 1020's career ended in the summer of 1994 when it finished up at the Motive Power Depot in Bludenz. But it still appeared in the rolling stock roster of other locomotives.

While undergoing major repair work, the former E 94s were given the typical features that distinguished it as ÖBB Series 1020. Besides being painted a blood-orange colour, the ÖBB locomotives were given standard headlights and rear lights. Maintenance flaps were installed in the end wall and front roof. At the beginning of the 1960s, independently of the repair programme, all 44 locomotives were fitted with nozzle ventilation grills in the side maintenance doors of the projecting sections and fixed snow-plough blades. The construction of the pantograph was altered in the 1950s, and by 1962 the double collector shoe had become the norm. In 1989 those 10120s that were used by the NAT were painted signal red. The last 1020s were taken out of service on 1 July 1995.

Most of the locomotives were scrapped, but a number of them have ended up in museums or tourist locations (10120 018, the former E 94 001, 037, 041, 044 and 047).

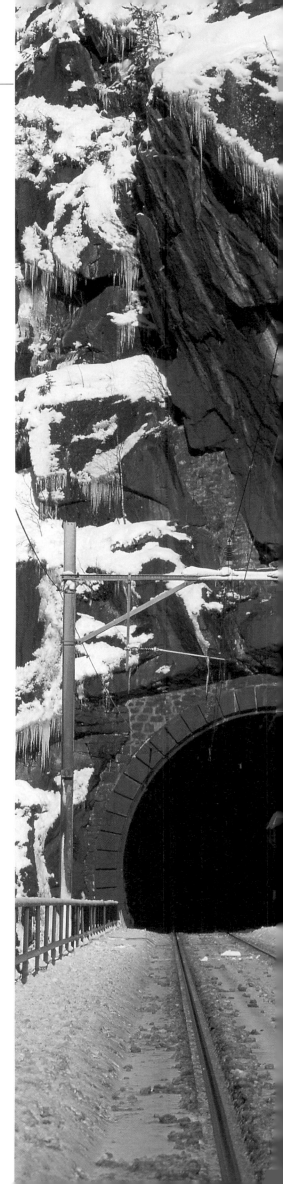

The age of the dinosaur started in the Gotthard in the year 1920. Lithe, dinosaur-like electric locomotive, soon universally known by the name "Crocodile" ("Krokodil"), chased the steam-powered Iron Horse off the famous mountain line between Lucerne and Chiasso. After the success of the Ur-Crocodile Ce 6/8 II — of which a total of 33 were built between 1920 and 1922 — the SBB decided in 1926 to build a second improved Crocodile series totalling 18 locomotives. In order to distinguish them from the previous series these were designated Ce 6/8 III. These locomotives were 60 cm (24 in) longer and their more powerful motors gave them a total 1-hour rating of 1,800 kW (2,413 hp). Constructionally they were still very similar to their predecessors. The centre part with the two drivers' cabs and the main transformer together with the tap changer rested on the two coupled sets of driving wheels without itself transferring any traction forces. The end sections, which were slightly wider than those of the Ce 6/8 II, housed the four traction motors and auxiliary circuits.

The second generation of the Crocodile

One of the innovations in the second generation of the Crocodile was the transmission from the driving motors to the track. There were two driving motors in each group of driving wheels, which were connected to each other by gear wheels. Their torque was passed on to a jack shaft placed between coupled axles 1 and 2, and axles 5 and 6 at the other end. A diagonal rod drive of the Winterthur type then finally transferred the power of the motors to the driving wheels. The new transmission technique was considerably simplified compared to the first generation Crocodiles, which had had complicated triangular connecting rods attached at three points. As a result of its construction with fewer moving parts, the maximum speed of the Ce 6/8 III increased considerably from 65 to 75 km/h (40 to 47 mph) without any constructional changes. The higher top speed gave the locomotive its new name Be 6/8 III.

From the mid-1950s onwards the newly-launched Ae 6/6 increasingly displaced the Crocodile from its ancient stamping ground on the Gotthard line.

Above: Based in the depot at Erstfeld, from time to time this Crocodile number 14253 was drafted to haul a train on the Gotthard line.

Right: With a mighty rumbling this Crocodile emerges from the Leggisteinkehr tunnel and travels across the Meienreuss bridge.

Above: View over the long bonnet of the Crocodile. Compared with modern locomotives, the driver's cab is relatively simply equipped.

Left: The depths of winter on the Gotthard line. The Crocodile heads a long freight train descending towards Wassen.

The mountain dinosaurs found a new home in the lower hills and planes of Switzerland. In 1968 locomotive number 13318 was taken out of service. In 1973 the SBB restricted the top speed of the Crocodile to 65 km/h (40 mph) because of increasing problems, and in 1977 the last Be 6/8, number 13308, was withdrawn from service. Twelve Crocodiles of the original type were converted to shunting locomotives. In the process they lost one of the two pantographs and were later fitted with special platforms for shunting personnel. A few of the converted shunting Crocodiles survived until the early 1980s, outlasting their sister locomotives used for ordinary service. Fortunately, a few Crocodiles of both kinds succeeded in escaping the cutting torches of the scrapyard and can now be seen in transport museums.

The celebrated Rhätische Bahn Crocodile

Smaller Crocodiles were in service for a much longer time in the canton of the Grisons. Until the late 1990s Ge 6/6s were regularly used to pull scheduled trains on the Rhätische Bahn, the Rhaetian Railway. Technically, they were more like the second series of the Crocodile but with a diagonal rod drives. Between 1921 and 1929 the canton railways had 15 locomotives in service and these faced no competition for a very long time. The universal six-axle locomotive

Series Ce 6/8 II, Ce 6/8 III, Ge 6/6 I, Ae 4/7 and Ae 6/8				
Wheel arrangement	(1'C)(C1')	(1'C)(C1')	C'C'	2'D1'	1'Co+Co1'
First delivery	1920	1926	1921	1927	1926
Last delivery	1922	1927	1929	1933	1943
Withdrawn from service	1982	1977	–	1996	1997
Quantity	33	18	15	127	8
Length overall	19.46m (63'10")	20.06m (65'10")	13.3m (43'8")	16.76m (55'0")	20.26m (66'6")
Total wheelbase	16.5m (54'2")	17.0m (55'9")	10.35m (34'0")	12.675m (41'7")	16.6m (54'6")
Bogie wheelbase	1.35m (4'5")	1.35m (4'5")	1.07m (3'6")	1.6m (5'3")	1.35m (4'5")
Wheel diameter	0.95m (3'1")	0.95m (3'1")	–	0.95m (3'1")	0.95m (3'1")
Working weight	128t (141.1 tons)	131t (144.4 tons)	66t (72.8 tons)	123t (135.6 tons)	140t (154.3 tons)
Maximum speed	75km/h (47mph)	75km/h (47mph)	55km/h (34mph)	100km/h (62mph)	100km/h (62mph)
1-hour rating	2700kW (3619hp)	1800kW (2413hp)	790kW (1059hp)	2300kW (3083hp)	4412kW (5914hp)

Series Ae 3/5, Ae 3/6 I, Ae 3/6 II			
Wheel arrangement	1'Co1'	2'Co1'	2'C1'
First delivery	1922	1921	1923
Last delivery	1925	1929	1926
Withdrawn from service	1983	1994	1977
Quantity	26	114	60
Length overall	12.32m (40'5")	14.76m (48'5")	14.15m (46'5")
Total wheelbase	9.3m (30'6")	10.73m (35'2")	10.8m (35'5")
Bogie wheelbase	1.61m (5'3")	1.61m (5'3")	1.61m (5'3")
Wheel diameter	1.0m (3'3")	1.0m (3'3")	1.0m (3'3")
Working weight	81t (89.3 tons)	93t (102.5 tons)	98t (108.0 tons)
Maximum speed	90km/h (56mph)	110km/h (68mph)	100km/h (62mph)
1-hour rating	972kW (1302hp)	1600kW (2145hp)	1470kW (1971hp)

Right: On the Disentis-Chur line, this original RhB Crocodile Ge 6/6 I operates on weekdays hauling goods trains. Here the wagon controller is checking the goods train as it is about to depart, in September 1994.

Opposite page: On the Engadine section of the Rhaetian line (St Moritz-Scuol) rod-drive engines were still hauling goods trains until the 1990s.

pulled light passenger trains as well as heavy goods trains. Neither the Ge 4/4 nor the Ge 6/6 II succeeded in displacing these sturdy rod-driven locomotives, and even the Ge 6/6 IIIs delivered in the 1970s could not displace them. Only the Ge 6/6 401 ended up on the scrap-heap after an accident. It was not until the 1980s when a second series, the Ge 4/4 II, was launched that the Rhaetian Railway had a replacement for the ancient locomotives, now 60 years old, which were slowly but surely taken out of service. The Ge 4/4 III launched in the 1990s finally put an end to the long career of these sturdy machines, which now became occasional part-timers.

Naturally, one example was preserved for posterity. The Rhaetian Railway now organizes some scheduled services and special excursions on trains pulled by its most famous locomotive. A Rhaetian Small Crocodile stands proudly on a pediment in Bergün station, and Ge 6/6 402 is in the Transport Museum in Lucerne. Since June 2001 there has also been a Crocodile in the Deutsche Museum in Munich. Several experts dispute the Ge 6/6 I's claim to to be a Crocodile because it does not have the leading axles. But the moving front parts and the pitching gait entitle it to be part of the family.

Asymmetrical: the Ae 3/6 I and Ae 4/7

In the early 1920s electric traction was gaining ground inexorably in Switzerland. The Crocodile had become firmly established in mountainous areas. But there were still no efficient electric locomotives for flatter areas. The SBB asked three specialist electric locomotive companies Brown, Boveri & Cie (BBC), Maschinenfabrik Oerlikon (MFO) and Aktiengesellschaft Ateliers Sécheron (SAAS) to submit their designs for a new fast locomotive for use on relatively level terrain. The specifications included a maximum speed of 65 km/h (40 mph) while pulling 480 t (530 tons) even on uphill gradients of 1 in 100. BBC was doubly prescient with its proposed design. The Baden-based engineers proposed the first express train locomotive, and they also revealed their pioneering spirit with the new individual axle drive known as the Buchli drive. A lever mechanism, on one side of the locomotive only, transferred the

torque of the three traction motors situated in the frame of the locomotive flexibly to the driving wheels. This made the locomotive longitudinally asymmetric in section, and the heavy transformer of the locomotive also required an asymmetric wheelbase. Nevertheless, the Ae 3/6 performed excellently. The first series of 36 locomotives, purchased between 1921 and 1925, was followed by another 40 whose traction output was increased from 1,450 to 1,600 kW (1,944 to 2,145 hp). Even after launch of its successful successor, the Series Ae 4/7, the SBB still put 38 more Ae 3/6 Is into service between 1927 and 1929. In 1937 the maximum speed had been raised from 100 to 110 km/h (62 to 68 mph) for fast urban trains composed of light steel coaches.

The Ae 3/6 I had become clear favourite among all the locomotives for level conditions. But now a more efficient locomotive for mountain railways was needed. The quickest way to solve this problem was to develop a mountain loco from the successful Ae 3/6 I. In principle all that was needed was to extend the length of the proven, reliable Ae 3/6 I by adding one driving axle to make an Ae 4/7. With an additional traction motor and a larger transformer, the traction output rose first to 2,000 kW (2,681 hp). In later series, as had occurred with its forebear the Ae 3/6 I, the traction output was further increased, in this case to 2,300 kW (3,083 hp). Between 1927 and 1934 a total of 127 locomotives left the workshops of the Schweizerische Lokomotiv- und Maschinenfabrik (SLM) in Winterthur.

By the mid-1950s the modern Ae 6/6 was beginning to displace the Ae 4/7 from the high mountain railways in Switzerland. Now the sturdy Buchli-drive locomotive was set to pulling freight trains instead of expresses, a little like the legendary Ae 8/14 in double traction. It was not until 1998 that the last Ae 4/7 was finally taken out of service by the SBB.

Miscellaneous types: the Ae 3/5 and Ae 3/6 III

For its little Ae 3/5, Sécheron in Geneva decided from the start to use the Westinghouse design of transmission, modified in-house. This transferred the torque of the traction motors located in the frames to a hollow shaft or quill

Opposite page, top: A mixed double in the Basel shunting yards, with an SBB 4/7 leading a DB 144.

Above: At the Erstfeld depot Crocodile number 14253 works beside locomotive Ae 8/14 11801. On a December day in 1998 they are hauling a pick-up goods train to Göschenen.

Opposite page, below: This Ae 4/7 is pulling a short freight train near Uzwil on 20 July 1992.

Left: On 20 June 1988, one of the many Ae 3/6s still hauling regional trains is seen here near Gelfingen.

Series Ae 8/14 11 801, 11851 and 11852			
Wheel arrangement	(1'A)A1A(A1')+(1'A)A1A(A1')		
First delivery	1931	1932	1939
Last delivery	1931	1932	1939
Withdrawn from service	–	1977	1971
Quantity	1	1	1
Length overall	34.0m (111'7")	34.0m (111'7")	34.0m (111'7")
Total wheelbase	29.0m (95'2")	29.0m (95'2")	29.0m (95'2")
Bogie wheelbase	1.61m (5'3")	1.35m (4'5")	1.35m (4'5")
Wheel diameter	0.95m (3'1")	0.95m (3'1")	0.95m (3'1")
Working weight	246t (271.2 tons)	244t (269.0 tons)	236t (260.1 tons)
Maximum speed	100kw/h (62mph)	100kw/h (62mph)	110kw/h (68mph)
1 hour rating	5400kW (7239hp)	6066kW (8131hp)	8161kW (10940hp)

surrounding the axle and from there through intermediate spring links to the wheel centres. In spite of the pioneering technique, which in principle is that used in all modern electric locomotives, the 26 Ae 3/5s were not a particular success. At first glance the small and, above all, short electric locomotive gave a discordant, imbalanced impression with poor running qualities. Admittedly, in 1925 engineers tried to improve the quality of the undercarriage by adding one more carrying axle, thus converting it to an Ae 3/6 III. But even so, compared to very successful Ae 3/6 I, only 11 locomotive of the lengthened version of the Sécheron Ae 3/6 III were produced, and it disappeared from all scheduled service in 1980. The Ae 3/5 survived its younger sister by some three years. Fitted with multiple unit control, the locomotives were used to pull car transporters through the Simplon and Gotthard tunnels until 1983.

The rod-driven Ae 3/6 II

After the success of the Crocodile, Oerlikon (MFO), unlike its competitors, opted for the conservative but proven rod drive for the Ae 3/6 II. This propulsion system transferred the torque of the two motors through a gear drive to a jack shaft and coupling rods to the three driving axles. This solution was unique for a Swiss express locomotive. Originally approved for a maximum speed of 90 km/h (56 mph), later increased to 100 km/h (62 mph), these locomotives fulfilled expectations, although the increasing weight of trains soon necessitated even more powerful locomotives. In spite of their rather unadventurous technical design, the last Ae 3/6 II remained in use until 1976.

While locomotive 10448 found a new home at Classic Rail, number 10439 has been preserved in impeccable order in its original brown colour of the 1920s, and is now the only museum piece in working order at the Olten depot.

Monsters of the line: the three Ae 8/14s

After the success of the one-sided axle drive developed by Jakob Buchli and used in Ae 3/6 I and Ae 4/7 series of locomotives, the Swiss locomotive builders SLM decided to develop a more powerful Gotthard locomotive with this trend-setting transmission. However, instead of building a new, lissom locomotive with Buchli transmission, the engineers turned to existing components. In theory, they merely put together two Ae 4/7s back to back, having removed the driver's cab from one end of each locomotive. The resulting Ae 8/14 had the axles arranged symmetrically and at regular intervals over the two halves of the locomotive. That this created one of the most curious axle arrangements in the world did not seem to worry anyone. The almost indescribable but completely symmetrical axles arrangement of the Ae 8/14 was as follows: (1'A)A1A(A1') + (1'A)A1A(A1').

In 1931, the Super Crocodile Ae 8/14 number 118001 with a power of 4,588 kW (6,150 hp) was set to challenge the clearly weaker ordinary Crocodile on the Gotthard line. The year 1932 saw the delivery of the similarly-constructed sister locomotive 11851, fitted with the more modern SLM universal transmission. In 1939 the prototypes were joined by number 11852, which later became better known under the name of "Landi-Lok". This had a much more modern

Right: The deployment of the legendary Ae 6/8 of the BLS is already a matter of history. The sight of double-headed locomotives hauling freight trains over the Lötschberg was unforgettable. Here just such a team hauls a train from Spiez to Brig over the Finnengraben viaduct on the south side of the Lötschberg in July 1998.

Above: While two double-headed Ae 6/8s have a driver in each loco, the Ae 4/7 is equipped with multiple control. The picture shows a freight train heading to Geneva.
Opposite page: Another view of the picturesque Ae 6/8 team, photographed on the return journey from Brig to Bern. In the valley is the town of Visp.

locomotive body. However, all three locomotives remained outsiders in spite of their excellent performance. Progress in control technology made possible multiple unit working using smaller locomotives on the Gotthard line instead of the giant double locomotives. When in 1952 a six-axle locomotive providing total adhesion was created in the shape of the Ae 6/6, whose output of 4,300 kW (5,764 hp) compared favourably with the Ae 8/14, the dream of the Super Crocodile was finally over. The elegant, streamlined Ae 6/6 became the progenitor of a whole new generation of SBB locomotives.

Soon after the launch of the Ae 6/6 series in the mid-1950s, the Crocodiles were moved from their original habitat, the Gotthard line, and used in the lowlands until they were finally retired. Locomotive Ae 8/14 number 11801 can still be admired in perfect working order in the SBB's transport museum. "Landi-Lok", number 11852, lost its inner workings in a fire but has found a home in the transport museum in Lucerne. Unfortunately the locomotive that had been given the head-shape of the Ae 6/6 driver's cab in 1961 was scrapped in 1977.

A Lötschberg classic: the Ae 6/8

While the Buchli transmission continued its triumphant progress with SBB, the Bern-Lötschberg-Simplon (BLS) line was already looking at the competition in the 1920s. The little railway in the Lötschberg region opted for the flexible transmission developed by Sécheron. In 1926 the BLS put two Be 6/8 locomotives into service on the more demanding steep climbs on both sides of the Lötschberg, and in 1931 they put two more into service. The mechanical parts of the eight-axle locomotives were produced by Breda, which was based in Milan, while the electrical parts and the innovative transmission were supplied by Sécheron. With their 1-hour rating of 3,300 kW (4,424 mph), the four locomotives were then the most powerful in the world. Spurred on by this success,

BLS acquired four more locomotives between 1939 and 1943. Because the top speed had been increased from 75 to 90 km/h (47 to 56 mph) the locomotives were given the designation Ae 6/8. But there were other changes. The locomotives were now assembled at the SLM workshops in Winterthur, and they had new driver's cabs with a rounded head-shape, reminiscent of the German E 18 of 1935. With a power of 3,900 kW (5,228 hp) they were no longer the most powerful locomotives in the world, but they were undoubtedly more elegant than the Ae 8/14 to which they had to hand over that title.

When deliveries of the Ae 6/8 started, the BLS began the technical conversion of the four Be 6/8s to Ae 6/8s. In 1955 the BLS brought the locomotives visually into line with the second series: the elegant head-shape replaced the square driver's cab of the Breda design. After the conversion, only experts could distinguish the four Breda locomotives from the four SLM locomotives. In 1961 the BLS recalled their Ae 6/8s to the workshops once more. They were fitted with the Ae 6/6 traction motors, a new transformer system and up-to-date high tension distribution, which gave the eight Ae 6/8s a traction power of about 4,400 kW. But there were also visual changes: the large ventilator grills replacing the engine room windows on one side of the locomotive provided the transformer and traction motors with the cooling air necessary on mountain lines. In addition, the compact drive unit made it necessary to enlarge the brake resistances, which until now had been fitted along each side of the roof. As a result the Ae 6/8 had to sacrifice one of its twin-arm pantographs. The elegant mountain locomotives were indispensable in the Lötschberg region until the mid-1990s. Only the more modern 465s were able to displace the Ae 6/8 from its traditional home. Today Ae 6/8 number 205 has found a home in a museum where it illustrates one of the high points of Swiss locomotive building. Unfortunately, none of the Breda locomotives has survived.

Above: The prototype E 03 001 in operation. It is always used to pull special trains.

Left: The start of the journey. The driver and conductor discuss important details about the length and the weight of the train. In a few minutes the 103 will leave Cologne's main station with its InterCity train .

Above left: Here locomotive 103 102 with an InterCity train rushes through the spring landscape past Boppard in the Rhineland, 26 April 1988.

the roof of the locomotive when collapsed, and it can be safely used in both directions.

The Bundesbahn acquired 145 production locomotives. The first was delivered on 19 July 1970. Less than four years later, on 26 June 1974, the Bundesbahn took delivery of 103 145. While the 103.1s, the designation of the production locomotives, were used for the important InterCity service, the prototype locomotives were moved to the Central Railway Offices at Minden and Munich, where they were used for trials and experimental testing. It was there that 103 003, fitted with special bogies in 1983, reached a record speed of 283 km/h (176 mph) on 14 June 1984. In addition, they were also used to pull passenger trains of all categories. In 1986 the Bundesbahn took the first locomotive of the series, namely 103 002, out of service. In 1997, the Bundesbahn withdrew its pre-series locomotives. With the exception of the 103 003, which was scrapped, all the other locomotives were preserved for posterity. Will a single locomotive of the production Series 103 series be saved? An enterprising organisation will probably take at least one locomotive, but the DB has made no official statement about this.

Light freight train locomotive: Series 151

At the end of the 1960s the Bundesbahn decided that passenger train services should not be the only sector to enjoy increased speeds. At that time, freight trains were able to reach a maximum speed of 100 km/h (62 mph), but the railway management was actually thinking of direct through trains reaching 140 km/h (87 mph), and the reliable E 50 series was therefore too slow.

Above: With the decline of the 101 in Austria, the 103 took over with its remarkable international capability. These locomotives travel west from Vienna as far as Cologne. Here one is seen between Regensburg and Nuremberg in May 1999.
Left: Having left Vienna barely one hour earlier, locomotive 103 245, the last 103 to be built, approaches the next scheduled stop at Linz with its EuroCity train.
Below: Locomotive103 184 with its InterCity train heads south past Oberwesel.

The next series, the 151, had a maximum speed of 120 km/h (75 mph) and the Bundesbahn optimized the haulage capacity. The electrical part of the locomotive was on the whole very similar to that of the 150. The high tension switchgear had the same thyristor supply breaker as the 103. The motor had been further developed and produced an output of about 100 kW (134 hp). As far as the mechanical side was concerned, Krupp and AEG were inspired by the Series 103 and chose a similar through-bridge frame. The side panels and roof were removable, non-loadbearing parts. This led to a considerable weight reduction. In general, the weight of the locomotive played an important part in dictating the construction. The customer and the manufacturer had agreed that the 151 should be lighter than the 150, and as a result of its lighter constructional approach, the weight of the 151 was reduced to 118 t (130 tons). But to achieve this the Bundesbahn had to give up the idea of mechanical parts being interchangeable between different freight train classes.

The Bundesbahn acquired four sub-series of the Series 151 with a total of 170 locomotives in all. The last locomotives were withdrawn from service on 13 September 1977. The locomotives were stationed in the motive power depot at Hagen-Eckesey and the Nuremberg marshalling yard. Twenty locomotives left the factory with automatic central buffer coupling. Double-headed, they could pull 500 t (551 tons) of heavy mineral wagons from the harbour of Hamburg to Peine and Salzgitter, the region of the Ruhr and Moselle stretch of the Koblenz-Trier line. In 1990, the Bundesbahn fitted 85 locomotives with continuous automatic train control (LZB) so that they could be used on the new stretches of track equipped for this. From the very beginning, the 151s were among the most heavily loaded locomotives of the Deutsche Bundesbahn. Running records of about 20,000 km (12,400 miles)

Above: On the north-south route near Oberrieden, this oriental red 151 makes a striking contrast with the blooming fields of oilseed rape.

Left: Locomotive number 103 220 was painted in a dazzling colour scheme as a tourist train. A set of matching coaches was similarly painted. Of course, the loco was also used with normal trains. Here it is photographed on its way to Basel SBB.

Below: The Series 151 freight train locos will long be indispensable. Gradually they are being painted the new signal red colour and fitted with a single-arm pantograph.

travelled each month reveal the high level of performance of the series, which in northern Germany were used almost exclusively to pull freight trains. South of the line of the river Main , they were also used for pulling regional trains. This made possible a particularly efficient use of rolling stock and personnel. If there was enough rolling stock, the Bundesbahn would attach additional carriages without conductors to the locomotives that had to be moved and use them as express trains. This provided an excellent deal for customers, and it cost the Bundesbahn very little since the locomotives had to make the return journey in any case.

Another express train locomotive: Series 111

Series 111, the latest standard electric locomotive, was ready in 1974. Originally the Bundesbahn had planned another sub-series of the 110. But gradually it requested more and more changes to be made so that the development of a new series appeared to be justified. From a technical point of view, the new locomotive designed by Siemens and Krauss-Maffei was based on the 110. Many of

Above: Still painted green, locomotive 151 008 passes through an arch in the rock not far from Regensburg. Container trains from northern Germany sometimes travel cross-country to Vienna.

Right: Series 181 locos could operate on the French power system as well as the one common in Germany. They therefore mainly came into use in the Saar and Moselle areas on routes to France and Luxembourg. Locomotive 181 210 is seen near Güls.

Series 103, 111, 151 and 181.2				
Wheel arrangement	Co'Co'	Bo'Bo'	Co'Co'	Bo'Bo'
First delivery	1965	1974	1972	1974
Last delivery	1974	1984	1977	1975
Withdrawn from service	–	–	–	–
Quantity	149	227	170	25
Length overall	20.2m (66'3")	16.75m (54'11")	19.49m (63'11")	17.94m (58'10")
Total wheelbase	14.1m (46'3")	11.3m (37'2")	13.66m (44'7")	12.0m (39'4")
Bogie wheelbase	2 x 2.25m (7'5")	3.4m (11'2")	2.45+2.00m (8'2"+6'7")	3.0m (9'10")
Wheel diameter	1.250m (4'1")	1.250m (4'1")	1.250m (4'1")	1.250m (4'1")
Service weight	114t (125.7 tons)	83t (91.5 tons)	118t (130.1 tons)	82.5t (90.0 tons)
Maximum speed	200km/h (124mph)	160km/h (99mph)	120km/h (75mph)	160km/h (99mph)
1-hour rating	7440kW (9973hp)	3850kW (5161hp)	6300kW (8885hp)	3300kW (4424hp)

Above: The idea of transferring ecologically and economically questionable short local flights to rail is not new. In the 1990s German Railways and Lufthansa created the airport express to reduce short range flights. This train is seen between Cologne and Frankfurt. Later the same train was pulled by a 103, replacing the 111 which at only 160 km/h (99 mph) was too slow.

Right: One of the main tasks of the Series 111 today is the operation of high-quality regional express trains.

Opposite page: Until the delivery of the series 101, the 111 was also used for inter-regional trains. Today, the locomotives of the Regio division of German Railways are rarely seen at the head of long-distance trains.

the ideas developed in the series 103 and 151 were not used, such as the removable panels of the engine compartment. As a result, the 111 has always seemed more of a temporary measure than a specially designed express locomotive.

Also, the Bundesbahn did not seem to know exactly what to do with the locomotive. The first two series were used to pull express trains, a use which certainly made sense for a locomotive with a maximum speed of 150 km/h (93 mph). But to the astonishment of many railway engineers, the third series of the Series 111 suddenly found itself pulling the suburban trains of the newly organised Rhein-Ruhr network. The authorities of the Bundesbahn were not put off from their narrow-minded approach, although they themselves were also under some pressure. Because the acquisition of the Series 120 had been delayed by lack of funds, locomotive factories were experiencing financial problems. In order to prevent job losses a further 111 Series 120 locomotives were produced. In the end the Bundesbahn had 227 locomotives of a single class, instead of the 45 they had originally planned to buy. In spite of everything, today these locomotives are considered the mainstay of the passenger train service. Technically simple but extremely versatile, they have mainly been pulling slow stopping trains since the reform of the German railway system. However, because of their high top speed they are also ideally suited for express trains and the InterRegio inter-regional service.

The story of the standard locomotives would be incomplete if it did not include the multi-system locomotives of Series 181 to 184. Extremely ambitious in concept, the 181 was the only series with a significant number of loco-

motives built, namely 25. These were used exclusively on stretches leading to France and Luxembourg. They marked the end of the development of multi-system locomotives for many years. It was only with the 185 series that the German industry again developed an electric locomotive suitable for several systems of currents.

New beginnings in the east

It took the German Democratic Republic some time before its industry was able to develop an electric locomotive for its own use. It is true that LEW, the expropriated AEG factory based in Hennigdorf, resumed production of electric locomotives soon after the end of the war. But these locomotives were sent to the Soviet Union in fulfilment of the reparations agreement. Later, LEW also built locomotives for other friendly Iron Curtain countries. In the second half of the 1950s, LEW developed a type of locomotive similar to the West German E 10/E 40 with changeable gear ratios, which was therefore suitable for both freight and passenger trains. The Reichsbahn believed it would be able to survive without acquiring another type of locomotive, because there was not an enormous speed differential between freight trains, with a maximum speed of 100 km/h (62 mph), and passenger trains, with a maximum speed of 120 km/h (75 mph), although in practice the braking system on the passenger train version was designed to cope with a top speed of 140 km/h (87 mph). However, the locomotives had axle-hung motors, a design unsuited to higher speeds.

LEW delivered the first two E 11s at the end of the 1960s. Like the E 10s of

West Germany, these had four axles with four traction motors, but they only developed an output of 2,600 kW (3,485 hp) instead of 3,620 kW (4,853 hp). This was an aspect that clearly reflected the technical under-development of the DDR. From locomotive E 11 008, the continuous power output increased to at least 2,740 kW (3,673 hp). The low-tension control mechanism seemed anything but modern and up-to-date. Nonetheless, from the start the locomotives were extremely busy and they provided a solid technical basis for the planned large-scale electrification of the network. Series production of the E 11 started in 1962. The following year LEW interrupted the production of the passenger train version at number 042 because freight train locomotives were more urgently needed.

Then in 1966 the Politbüro made a momentous decision that had serious consequences. Henceforth steam locomotives were to be replaced not by electric locomotives but by diesel ones. The fuel would be provided cheaply by the Soviet Union and most of the locomotives would be manufactured in the Ukraine. Electric traction fell out of favour.

As a result, the Reichsbahn needed fewer locomotives. Admittedly production continued but not at the rate originally intended. On 24 November 1976 the Reichsbahn took delivery of the last of the 292 freight locomotives. Two months later the last passenger train locomotive, 211 096, was ready. Since 1970, when the Reichsbahn also introduced computerised numbering, these locomotives have been known as 211 and 242. As a matter of fact, these were both universal locomotives. The 242 was usually employed pulling slow stopping trains, for instance on the suburban train network of Saxony-Anhalt. That the 211 was also able to pull freight trains is demonstrated by four locomotives numbered 4-1314 to 4-1317. These were former Reichsbahn E 11s that were assigned for use in the Bitterfeld lignite mines, where they operated on the Delitzsch connecting railway. The E 42 would in fact have been better suited to this, but the Reichsbahn wanted to keep these for its own purposes.

After German reunification, the star of these locomotives, nicknamed "wooden scooters", quickly waned. Because of the decline in the volume of transport services provided, East Germany's Reichsbahn had a large surplus of locomotives. The new Germany's Bundesbahn was not interested in old locomotives and preferred to use the more modern 243. In addition the E 11s and the E 42s were, like all the other Reichsbahn locomotives, much too slow for the newly unified country. The universal locomotives were converted into specialist ones, which in the case of the "wooden scooter" noone really needed. The E 11 became the Series 109 in 1992, and was already removed from service in 1994. Four of the locomotives were later put back into service for a short while, but in May 1998 they ended up in a storage hangar. Twelve 242s, renamed 142 in 1992, ended up in Switzerland where they found refuge in private railways. Their DB sisters went into holding sidings in 1999. Locomotives E 11 001 and E 42 001 were preserved for posterity.

Series 109, 112, 142, 143, 155					
Wheel arrangement	Bo'Bo'	Bo'Bo'	Bo'Bo'	Bo'Bo'	Co'Co'
First delivery	1960	1982	1963	1982	1974
Last delivery	1977	1994	1976	1989	1984
Withdrawn from service	1998	–	1999	–	–
Quantity	96	130	292	646	273
Length overall	16.26m (53'4")	16.64m (54'0")	16.26m (53'4")	16.64m (54'0")	19.60m (64'4")
Total wheelbase	11.3m (37'2")	11.8m (38'9")	11.3m (37'2")	11.8m (38'9")	14.5m (47'7")
Bogie wheelbase	3.5m (11'6")	3.3m (10'10")	3.5m (11'6")	3.3m (10'10")	2.5+ 2.0m (8'2"+6'7")
Wheel diameter	1.35m (4'5")	1.25m (4'1")	1.35m (4'5")	1.25m (4'1")	1.25m (4'1")
Service weight	83t (91.5 tons)	82t (90.4 tons)	83t (91.5 tons)	82t (90.4 tons)	123t (135.6 tons)
Maximum speed	120km/h (75mph)	160 km/h (99 mph)	100km/h (62mph)	125km/h (78mph)	120km/h (75mph)
1-hour rating	2920kW (3914hp)	4220kW (5657hp)	2920kW (3914hp)	3720kW (4987hp)	5400kW (7239hp)

Above: Here locomotive 155 037 is hauling a heavy coal train as well as a sister locomotive .

Left: The Series 112 is used in the travel and tourism division of German Railways, so it is often seen at the head of long-distance trains. Here 112 107 pulls an InterRegio train between Weimar and Erfurt.

Below: Locomotive 155 150 pulling a freight train at Gensungen-Felsberg on 18 October 1997.

Above: The Series 155 is largely based in Mannheim, so the Rhine route is one of the main areas in which it is used. Here 155 203 is just leaving the Lorelei tunnel.

Right: A 155 at Eichstädt pulling a heavy load towards Munich.

Series 250 six-axle universal locomotive

Will the "Stromcontainer" ("electricity box") ever be honoured as a traditional locomotive? In the German Democratic Republic it was undoubtedly seen as a universal locomotive in that it could pull heavy passenger trains at a speed of 120 km/h (75 mph) and freight trains at up to 100 km/h (62 mph). The 250 series was quite conventional from a technical point of view. A high-tension control mechanism, thyristor discs and series-wound motors — the locomotives certainly did not reflect the "world level" so often proclaimed by the DDR leadership. At 5,400 kW (7,239 hp), their 1-hour power rating was lower than that of the roughly contemporary West German Series 151. This too reflected the technical backwardness of East Germany.

In all the Reichsbahn acquired 273 Series 250 locomotives, a substantial number considering the size of the country. They could cope with the heavy freight trains which could only be pulled by Series 254 and 242 locomotives run in double-header formation. In addition, they were ideally suited to steep mountain stretches because of their efficient dynamic braking. Because of the newly developed LEW conical ring spring transmission system they did not overload the track bed in spite of the six driving axles. It would have been technically possible to increase the maximum speed to 125 km/h (78 mph), but this was not required by the Reichsbahn.

Since 1992 the locomotives, now renamed the Series 155, have pulled freight trains in the united Germany. It used to be rare to see them heading other types of trains. In 1994, German Railways moved a few locomotives to suburban train services in the Berlin area. At the end of the 1990s they were used to pull intercity night trains between Berlin and Munich. They also did some useful work along the Rhine and the slopes of the Franconian Forest. For instance, they moved freight trains from the interchange station in Venlo in the Netherlands to Basel and from Mannheim to Seddin. How long they will remain in service is uncertain. On the one hand, DB Cargo has given some of the locomotives a general overhaul. On the other hand, the Freight Train Service has purchased a number of new locomotives that only replaced the less efficient Series 150. In the long term it can be assumed that DB Cargo will only keep the Series 145, 151, 152, 182 (Taurus) and 185.

Above left: 112 114 on 11 October 1993, still carrying the DR designation.
Left: In 1997, 171 014 was still employed to pull passenger trains on the Rübelandbahn. The photograph shows the locomotive on the bridge at Neuwerk.
Above right: 143 001, better known as the "White Lady", being used experimentally as an advertising support for ADtranz.

The everyday locomotives of Series 143

Another rival has disappeared, although not as a result of being taken out of service. Following the railway reform of 1994, the Series 143 universal locomotive was transferred to slow stopping suburban services, only rarely pulling freight trains. The Reichsbahn's concept of the desirability of approximately similar speeds is highlighted in their purchase of this series of locomotive. However, the LEW engineers who designed the locomotive originally had a genuine express train in mind.

The 212 001, presented at the Leipzig Spring Fair, officially reached a speed of 140 km/h (87 mph), although technically it was able to reach a maximum speed of 160 km/h (99 mph). Indeed unofficial reports hold that it was requested that the pre-series locomotive should also be tested at a speed of 160 km/h (99 mph), but the Reichsbahn head office and the Ministry of Transport decided that 120 km/h (75 mph) was sufficient for the DDR. The Council of Ministers had taken a similar decision. It seemed that the State and Party leaders did not believe in the possibility of exports.

Each new locomotive series was dismantled by the Reichsbahn during the initial phase as part of its trials. This was not to so much to give the workers extra practice but rather to find out more about the locomotive with a view to making future maintenance easier. This often also led to changes in the design. The Reichsbahn used the dismantling test of the 212 001 to change the gearing. As a result of the different gear ratio, the locomotive reached a maximum speed of 120 km/h (75 mph). It was therefore renamed 243 001.

At home everywhere: Series 243 "Schienentrabi"

The slow version of the series developed into a real everyday locomotive. Soon locomotives of the 243 series could be seen all over the DDR wherever there were overhead power wires. They pulled express and slow trains, non-stop trains and pick-up goods trains, and they were also used in urban railway service. The Reichsbahn bought no fewer than 646 Series 243 locomotives.

After German reunification they were used in the west where they were known as Series 143. Whether on the Freiburg-Titisee Höllentalbahn, the Nuremberg urban railway network or slow stopping services around Stuttgart, the unpretentious locomotives were everywhere, demonstrating that they had become thoroughly westernized. The railway authorities decided that when acquiring the express train version the maximum speed should be 160 km/h (99 mph).

The Reichsbahn had already started planning the improvement of the most important stretches of line in the run-up to reunification . In 1990 it took delivery of four locomotives of the 243 series, with a top speed of 160 km/h (99 mph). Meanwhile the Bundesbahn, encouraged by the performance of the 143, expressed its interest in the "Schienentrabis" or "rail trotter". Jointly with the Reichsbahn it ordered 90 locomotives that had been slightly improved from a technical point of view, designated the 112.1 sub-series. The little signal lights meeting western standards were the most striking feature of their appearance.

It is impossible to imagine either part of Germany without these plain, simple locomotives. It is true that from a technical point of view they did not reflect what would have been possible in the Bundesrepublik in the early 1980s. Although the 143/112 were thyristor locomotives, they still had traditional series-wound motors. The only real construction fault was in a self-induction coil designed to protect the power circuit contactor. This was made from aluminium because of materials shortages in the DDR. Several locomotives actually caught fire as a result of defective self-induction coils, and the part was subsequently replaced. Nevertheless many old railwaymen disliked the "Schienentrabi", which can still be seen all over in the country.

After the 212/243 the Reichsbahn bought a small number of locomotives of three further series. One series consisted of dual-current locomotives, produced by Skoda, intended for use on lines to the Czech Republic, Slovakia and Poland. Another was a six-axle freight locomotive based on 212/243. The four prototype locomotives of Series 252 (156) are still in use today, as is the Series 230 (180) dual-current locomotive. The third in the trio were the Series 251 six-axle locomotives to be used on the Rübeland line in the Harz region. The power supply on that stretch is alternating current with a tension of 25,000 volts and a frequency of 25 cycles. Named the Series 171, these locomotives were used for freight transport, and since 2000 they have no longer been allowed to pull passenger trains. As far as freight transport is concerned, they are in danger of being replaced by diesel locomotives.

The first of the postwar Belgian electric locomotives was the 122 series in 1954. In tune with the style of the times, the Belgian locomotive industry built an elegant and aerodynamic direct current locomotive with four axles that anticipated the visual design elements of the later German electric locomotives, which had a uniform appearance. As early as 1955 an improved version of the 122 series was produced with the 123 series. The additional regenerative braking made the 123 much heavier than its predecessor: it weighed 93.3 t (103 tons), possibly a record-breaking weight for a four-axle locomotive. While both the 122 series and the 123 001 to 082 worked using an axle-hung motor, SNCB examined the use of an ACEC spring drive in what was initially called 124 001. This made it possible to suspend the driving motors fully, while with the axle-hung motor half of the weight was put on the axle without any cushioning. Later the Belgian State Railway renamed the one-of-a-kind locomotive 123 083.

The Belgian 22 and 23: mass and class

The machines of both series began their careers with the state railway SNCB/NMBS in the uniform green paint with a light green décor-stripe on the side that ran forward to the front into a V shape. Locomotives 2355, 2376, and 2380 had to serve as test objects for a new paint job in different shades of green and yellow starting in 1976. In 1978 SNCB decided to do it differently: canary yellow and different shades of blue were chosen as the new colours for the Belgian electric locomotives. This is the paint they have when two of them pull heavy ore trains.

The Belgian 16: little known European locomotive

Belgian electric locomotives reach their national borders quickly. In the relatively small railway system of the kingdom, the electric locomotives soon reach the limits of both the country and the electrical system. In order to avoid the complicated, double change of locomotives, for example on the fast trains on the Paris-Brussels-Amsterdam route, the Belgian state railway SNCB decided quite early to build multi-system locomotives that could also travel in neighbouring countries. As a further development of the 150 Series (later 15), the similar, but more elegantly designed 160 series was produced as of 1966 which could also accept electricity from the German 15,000 volt contact line. A transformer with a rectifier bridge of silicon diodes converted the power from the French, Luxembourg, and German alternating-current systems for the conventional direct current operation of the locomotive. While Siemens was responsible for the electrical parts for locomotives 160 001 to 160 004 (as of 1970 1601 to 1604), the inner workings of locomotives 160 021 to 160 024 (as of 1970 1605 to 1608) came from the Belgian producer ACEC. On the roof of the machines over driver's cabin 1 there is the one-leg pantograph for the German system with a broad pallet and, with a jog inwards, the straps for the two direct current systems. Over driver's cabin 2 there is a current collector with a narrow rocker for operation under 25,000 volt contact lines and for travelling in Switzerland. The locomotives with their home base in Brussels were initially painted blue, but as of 1978 they were subject to several colour versions in canary yellow and blue until a more classic paint scheme was introduced in the 1980s with a base colour in the

Page 204, top: The 13 Series of SNCB is based on the Sybic family. It is used mostly with high quality fast trains. This picture is from 25 April 2000. The picture was taken near Trooz.

Top: The 5540 pulls a passenger train near Vielsalm.

Left: The Belgian 16 Series is a constant guest on German railways. Before the Thalys took away the high quality traffic, the multi-system locomotives (they have three current collectors on the roof) moved all the high quality trains from the main Cologne train station towards Belgium.

original blue and a canary yellow décor stripe running along under the windows. Movement in the colours came again for the 16 series in 1995 — now stationed in Ostend — when the model railroad manufacturer Märklin sponsored the repainting of the 1602 in the elegant silver, red, blue, and yellow tones of the Eurocity "Memling". The 1601 received support from Märklin a year later as the second locomotive to receive the Memling paint, but this time combined with other colours. Nowadays the Thalys type high speed trains have almost completely replaced the Belgian 16 on the DB tracks between Aachen and Cologne.

The Belgian Series 205

In the 1960s the Belgian state railways continued to pursue a change of power systems and ordered a large number of diesel locomotives. In addition to the "potato beetles" of the 202 and 203 series, they bought 42 similar machines of the 204 series. They were delivered in 1961 and 1962 and stationed in Kinkempois, Montzen, and Ronet. They mostly pulled passenger trains, including international trains to Cologne and Luxembourg. The machines received a special peak signal for use on German rails. However, the robust six-axle locomotives were often used to pull freight trains as well. They were used, for example, for traffic on the Athus-Meuse line in conjunction with the potato beetles of the 52 and 53 series.

At this point they were already called Series 55. At the beginning of the 1970s SNCB replaced the six digit numbers with four digit ones. The first two digits described the series while digits three and four were then used for the serial number. No one ever really understood the advantages of the new system.

Starting in 1975 SNCB had to rebuild several locomotives. By that time electric heating for passenger coaches on trains had become standard. The

Left: The 23 series of SNCB is strong, compact and indestructible. Used mainly with heavy freight trains, the locomotives will not be replaced in the foreseeable future. Here the 2316 and the 2374 are working near Villers-La-Ville, hauling a train of empty mineral ore cars.
Below: The 62 series is also used with passenger trains.

55 series, on the other hand, was only equipped with steam heating. SNCB first rebuilt the 5540 in 1975. The name stayed the same. In order to differentiate the machine from its steam sisters, it received an orange décor stripe that was later replaced by a blue one. Later, six other locomotives of the 55 series received the new equipment so that the series could still be used to pull high quality trains. On occasion the 55s with electric heating also pulled freight trains. Nowadays the locomotives have had to surrender some services since after electrification of various routes the roaring diesel locomotives are no longer as welcome as they used to be. They are far from retirement, however.

The Dutch 1200

Even while Alsthom was supplying the 1100 Series to Nederlandse Spoorwegen, the state railway was looking for an alternative to promote the domestic locomotive industry. First they too a look over the Atlantic and designed one of the most successful European locomotives in 1951. With licences from the US producers Baldwin and Westinghouse, but also with entire modules supplied from overseas — the modern cast steel bogies were supplied by Baldwin, electrical components came from Westinghouse — the 1200 series with its completely un-European look was built at Werkspoor in Amsterdam.

Although they were actually designed for maximum speeds of up to 150 km/h (93 mph), NS only allowed them to travel at the 135 km/h (84 mph) that was typical in the Netherlands. In spite of the simple axle-hung drive, the machines were a great design. At the beginning the machines were painted in a light, turquoise blue while later they were painted Berlin blue. The 1215 also travelled over the rails in an elegant mahogany for a while. Since 1971 the locomotives have given up the old blue for a new colour scheme in gray with yellow contrast surfaces. Even in the 1980s when modern alternating-current locomotives became popular, NS could not do without the Americans.

As with the 1100 series, NS rebuilt them starting in 1979. The renovated locomotives can be recognized from the outside by their double lights, similar to the German uniform electric locomotives. On 28 March 1998 the last of the nine locomotives of the 1200 series ended its successful career. On their last day in service they once again pulled InterRegio trains between Bad Bentheim and Amsterdam and between Haarlem and Maastricht in the morning; in the afternoon they took part in a parade in Geldermalsen for a final goodbye from their fans.

Just a short time later the first locomotive returned to everyday service under the operation of a private railway.

Top: Locomotive 2355 hauling a freight train

Middle: The 18 series was used in Germany for many years as well. This is loco 1801.

Bottom: Two locomotives of the 53 Series are pulling a mixed freight train not far from Bertrix.

Opposite page, top: Near Zaltbommel, locomotive 1255 with a passenger train is reflected in the Rhine-Meuse delta on 1 May 1997.

Opposite page, bottom: Locomotive 1208 is under way with an InterRegio made up of DB cars on 26 September 1997 near Apeldoorn.

Above: The Ae 4/4 of the BLS is still in regular use today.

Right: The similarly brown-painted Re 4/4 pulling historic carriages is sometimes mistaken for an Ae 4/4.. On the contrary, the brown body contains modern technology. This is the Lötschberg EuroCity train on the Luogelkinn viaduct.

The Ae 4/4 is the ancestor of all modern electric locomotives. There is no word that better describes the legendary electric locomotives of the Berne-Lötschberg-Simplon Railway (BLS). These set the standards that are still valid today in the locomotive building industry: axles grouped in pairs in bogies, with each axle driven by its own motor. Non-driving axles became a thing of the past.

Four-axle bogie locomotive were not a new invention. As early as 1912 the Königlich Bayerische Staatsbahnen (Royal Bavarian State Railways) had experimented with an electric locomotive with the then-unusual Bo'Bo' axle arrangement, a four-axle two-bogie locomotive with individual axle drive. However, the little EG 4 x 1/1 was only approved for a speed of 50 km/h (31 mph). In the 1930s the Deutsche Reichsbahn broke the 100 km/h (62 mph) speed barrier for the first time with a locomotive with all-driving axles, when testing its new E 44. In Germany the war prevented the E 44 being developed further to become the first bogie locomotive for express trains.

In 1944 the innovative BLS, which had already attracted attention in the past with its trend-setting designs, decided to opt for the fast Ae 4/4 bogie locomotive. It commissioned Swiss Locomotive and Machine Works (SLM) to develop the mechanical part of the locomotive, while Brown, Boveri Co. (BBC) was responsible for the electrical part. Although the BBC engineers had long favoured the complicated Buchli drive, they decided for the first time to use the newly-developed disc drive, which structurally resembled the well-tested Sécheron drive. The torque of the motor fixed in the bogie is transferred elastically to the sprung axles. In this way the engineers prevented the traction motor from resting more or less unsprung on the axles (as is the case with nose-suspended motors), thus reducing damage to the rails at high speed. In spite of an overall weight of a mere 80 t (88.2 tons), the Ae 4/4 was still capable of producing a tractive force of around 3,000 kW (4,000 hp) on the rails. A multiple-unit control system made it possible to use two locomotives double-headed to pull particularly heavy trains. Between 1944 and 1955 the BLS

Above: With the Ae 8/8 twin locomotive, the BLS hoped to avoid the inconvenience of running trains double-headed. The five Ae 8/8s did not disappoint in this respect.

Opposite page: The Re 4/4 I was a light universal locomotive, but its career went downhill . From the TEE in its early years, it was reduced to pulling mail trains in the 1990s.

Below: This Re 4/4s of the BLS are often seen double-headed pulling long freight trains. At the Lötschberg they can pull trains of 1,200 t (over 1,300 tons) uphill with ease.

Series Ae 4/4 (BLS), Ae 8/8, Re 4/4 I and Ae 6/6				
Wheel arrangement	Bo'Bo'	Bo'Bo'+Bo'Bo'	Bo'Bo'	Co'Co'
First delivery	1944	1959	1946	1952
Last delivery	1955	1966	1951	1966
Withdrawn from service	–	–	1997	–
Quantity	8	5	50	120
Length overall	20.26m (66'6")	30.23m (99'2")	14.9m (48'11")	18.4m (60'4")
Total wheelbase	11.5m (37'9")	26.13m (85'9")	10.8m (35'5")	13.0m (42'8")
Bogie wheelbase	3.25m (10'8")	3.25m (10'8")	3.00m (9'10")	4.30m (14'1")
Wheel diameter	1.25m (4'1")	1.25m (4'1")	1.33m (4'4")	1.26m (4'2")
Service weight	80t (88.2 tons)	160t (176.4 tons)	57t (62.8 tons)	124t (136.7 tons)
Maximum speed	125km/h (78mph)	125km/h (78mph)	125km/h (78mph)	125km/h (78mph)
1-hour rating	2940kW (3941hp)	6480kW (8686hp)	1900kW (2547hp)	4300kW (5764hp)

acquired eight Ae 4/4s in all. At the end of the 1950s the locomotives, like the Ae 6/8s, lost their second twin-arm pantograph when the BLS strengthened the rheostatic brakes of its locomotives and therefore needed more space on the roof for the brake resistance.

Because the Ae 4/4 often reached its limits when pulling heavy freight even when double-headed, the BLS perfected the principle by taking it further. In 1959, it ordered two Ae 8/8 double locomotives. In essence these were two Ae 4/4s coupled back to back, the main difference being that the two driver's cabs at the back of each locomotive were removed. This allowed the tractive force of the double unit to be increased to almost 6,500 kW (8,700 hp). The Ae 8/8 was a great success. In the mid-1960s when the new Re 4/4 began to compete with the Ae 4/4, the BLS simply decided in 1966 to convert four of its Ae 4/4s into two Ae 8/8s. The two converted locomotives did not differ technically or visually from the three original Ae 8/8s built in 1959. While three of these five powerful locomotives have now been retired, the odd Ae 4/4 can still occasionally be seen on its old stamping ground in the Simmental.

Re 4/4 (BLS): A universal locomotive

The Ae 4/4 was very advanced for its time, but when the BLS began to think of a successor in the early 1960s, the former star locomotive was reaching middle age. By now electric locomotives could have motors of up to 1,000 kW (1,340 hp) per axle. The great progress made in semiconductor techniques caused conventional series-wound motors powered by alternating current to become obsolete. Once again the BLS proved extremely enterprising and innovative. For its new locomotive, which was originally designated Ae 4/4 II, the BLS opted to use semiconductor technology. A conventional tap-changer control mechanism on the high voltage side of the transformer supplied the compact but efficient undulating-current motors through a Greatz bridge silicon diode rectifier. By removing the bulky alternating current motors, the driving force of the five prototypes of 1964 rose to a respectable 5,000 kW, about 6,700 hp. In 1968 the BLS tested a thyristor contactless phase angle control system on the locomotive with series number 261 instead of the mechanical high voltage tap-changer control mechanism. The thyristor-controlled locomotive was indeed remarkably successful. But the technique of semiconductors tended to interfere with the signalling system on the SBB sections of track. Series production of electronic locomotive control was therefore dropped.

The BLS also experimented in another field with the Swiss locomotive manufacturer. Because of their favourable size, the new motors made it possible to get the most out of the bogies and therefore the running performance

of the locomotives. Instead of a speed of 125 km/h (78 mph) as was the case with the Ae 4/4 I and the prototypes, the series-produced locomotives built from 1970 onward could reach a maximum speed of 140 km/h (87 mph). As a result the BLS named the locomotives Re 4/4 and modified the pre-series to the higher speed. Visually the there was hardly any difference between the Re 4/4 and their Ae 4/4 predecessors of some 20 years earlier. Only experts could tell them apart, on the basis of the side ventilator grills. Up to 1983 the lines belonging to the BLS acquired a total of 35 Re 4/4 locomotives, which today bear the series number 425. While the locomotives grew 37 cm (nearly 15 in) in length in 1972 onwards, the 190 built in 1982 was the first to be fitted with the now standard single-arm pantograph instead of the previous twin-arm pantograph. Meanwhile the former stars of the BLS were losing out to the much more powerful 465.

SBB light mixed traffic locomotive: Re 4/4 I

Lightweight construction was common in Switzerland in the 1930s. After the success of the so-called "lightweight steel coach", the SBB decided in the early 1940s to build a matching locomotive. In contrast to the BLS's powerful Ae 4/4 of 1944, the SBB produced the Re 4/4 I. This was also a locomotive providing total adhesion, but it was lighter, less powerful and quicker round curves. In the period 1946 to 1948, the Swiss locomotive factories SLM, MFO, BBC and SAAS delivered the first series of the Re 4/4 to the SBB. The doors at each end and multiple unit control made it possible to put the locomotive anywhere in the train, and with its regenerative braking, energy was returned to the network when braking. In the second series produced in 1950 and 1951, the SBB dropped all these fittings and used the weight thus saved to produce more efficient traction motors. Because of its rounder forms and characteristic sides turning inwards at the bottom, this locomotive became known to railwaymen and others as the "bath tub". Well-known as locomotives hauling city express trains, the Re 4/4 of the second series was entrusted from 30 May 1965 with pulling the Trans-Europ-Express "Rheingold" between Basel and Geneva. In 1971, the Re 4/4s of the second series were also assigned to the TEE "Bavaria" between Lindau and Zürich. As a result, four of the locomotives were allowed to display the red and beige colours of the TEE. Meanwhile, Re 4/4 IIs were being produced in increasingly large numbers, and they gradually displaced the Re 4/4 I locomotives, replacing them in short-distance traffic and for postal services.

Until the 1990s the lightweight locomotive had proved indispensable on level terrain, but on 27 September 1997, these popular locomotives were removed from the SBB rail network. Six locomotives were given a reprieve and

Above: An Ae 6/6 with stylish chrome trim. Only the first 25 locomotives were given this.

Right: A traditional load on the Gotthard line. Until the 1980s, heavy freight trains were pulled over the mountain pass by double-headed Ae 6/6s.

used as shunting engines in the train-washing sidings in Basel. At the end of the 1990s a small scandal broke out when some Re 4/4 Is appeared on the Mittelthurgaubahn as a result of a middleman's dealings. The SBB was desperate to prevent its competitors from using locomotives that it had decided to scrap. But there was nothing it could do as it watched the "condemned" locomotives giving excellent service for the post office on the Mittelthurgaubahn.

The Gotthard classics: Ae 6/6

Streamlined electric locomotives were not a German invention. The SBB's Ae 6/6s dating from 1952 already displayed the elegant, arrow-shaped front that influenced a whole generation of locomotives. Admittedly, the increasing tonnage hauled across the Gotthard in the postwar years did not demand a streamlined front, but it required efficient, modern electric locomotives sooner than this need arose in Germany. A good example for the new Gotthard locomotive to follow was the BLS's successful Ae 4/4, a locomotive providing total adhesion. But the load to be carried was much beyond it, so a new six-axle locomotive was specified, capable of pulling 650 t (717 tons) at a speed of 75 km/h (47 mph) up gradients of 1 in 37. In addition, the SBB expected these locomotives to go round curves at higher speeds than the Re 4/4. The SBB's future mountain locomotive would therefore be an Re 6/6.

In 1952 and 1953 SLM and BBC launched two prototypes that met all requirements as far as performance was concerned. However, there were problems from the beginning with the three-axle bogies, which seriously affected the permanent way. Admittedly, technical experts tried to minimize the wear and tear on the rails and wheel flanges of the production locomotives, which were 4 t (4.4 tons) lighter, by fitting axles with lateral play. But the achievement of higher speeds round curves remained a dream even after further improvements. The new Gotthard locomotive was actually slightly slower than the Ae 6/6 round curves. In 1954 and 1956 the SBB ordered 24 locomotives in two series, and in 1960 they ordered 24 more locomotives. The first 25 locomotives had applied, ornamental chrome strips along the sides, and three

pairs of chrome strips arranged in a distinctive "moustache" shape at the front. Each of the 25 Swiss cantons adopted a locomotive as its own, and the locomotives were named accordingly. The locomotives of subsequent series were no longer adorned with the distinctive chrome strips, and they were named after the main cities and locations in the cantons. When these ran out, they were named after the best-known Swiss railway stations. By 1966, the number of these powerful universal locomotives had grown to 120 in all.

But at the beginning of the 1970s, the Ae 6/6s were displaced by the four-axle Re 4/4 II and III on the express train service across the Gotthard. In 1977 the extraordinarily powerful Re 6/6 production locomotives also took over the Ae 6/6's speciality, namely the freight train service. The former mountain queen of the Gotthard was now given the task of pulling heavy goods trains on the level. The locomotives are still operational today in almost the whole of Switzerland. Even the two prototypes are still in use.

The musclemen of the Re 6/6 series

What could be better than a Co'Co'? This is the question Swiss Railways asked itself when it decided to acquire a new six-axle electric locomotive in the early

Opposite page: The work on the Gotthard is shared between the Re 6/6 and the 460. Above: Here an Re 6/6 pulls an express train at Gubiasco, on the upward slope towards Monte Ceneri. Now the Ae 6/6s have migrated to the lowland. Here a locomotive hauls a good train from Landquart to the Zurich shunting yard.

Above: On the line from Chiasso, locomotive Re 6/6 11616 heads a non-stop EuroCity train passing Brunnen station.

Left: Two Re 6/6s pulling an express train is a rare sight. It usually only occurs when the load demands it, because a single Re 6/6 today can haul 800 t (882 tons) The second engine will probably pick up a non-scheduled train in Chiasso. A trip on the Gotthard line is a thrilling experience; here the train crosses the lower Meienreus bridge over the Wassen bridge.

1970s. It is true that the locomotives of the Re 6/6 series had proved their worth. However, the three-axle bogies had two disadvantages. First, the locomotives were forced to reduce their speed when negotiating curves. Secondly, the wheel flanges and rails wore out more quickly on the sharp curves of the mountain lines than the SBB would have liked.

Technical experts had a simple solution to cure these problems. As they put it, Bo'Bo'Bo' would be even better than Co'Co'. These descriptions of the wheel arrangements distinguished the two different ways of arranging six driven axles: a locomotive with three bogies, each with two driven axles (designated Bo'Bo'Bo'), and a locomotive with two bogies, each with three axles (Co'Co').

In 1972, the SBB put four pre-production locomotives of the Bo'Bo'Bo' Re 6/6 series into service. Two of them had a body divided vertically with a horizontal hinge in the centre. The SBB believed this would be an advantage on a track with an uneven profile. In an ideal situation, the weight of the locomotive would be distributed evenly over the two bogies. But this proved a false hope. It became apparent in test runs that the expensive construction had no particular advantages. All that was necessary was to fit the central bogie more loosely.

Otherwise, SBB carried out few experiments with new technology, such as the thyristor-controlled locomotive. Admittedly, the latter had already proved its value and efficiency in Sweden and Austria. But the surface current generated by the thyristors interfered with the signalling and telephone lines along the track, and these had to be altered before thyristor locomotives could be introduced. In Switzerland this work lasted until the late 1970s.

Consequently the SBB bought an ultra-conventional locomotive whose main distinction was its unusual axle arrangement. Another substantial distinction was its 1-hour output of 7,900 kW (10,590 hp). Even the up-to-date 465 of the BLS could not compete with this. Only a few Swiss locomotives such as the legendary "Landi-lok" surpassed the Re 6/6 by 250 kW (335 hp).

Because of its top speed 140 km/h (87 mph), the Re 6/6 was able to pull both freight and passenger trains. It was used mainly on the Gotthard section. Often it would pull a heavy goods train across the mountain with the assistance of a locomotive of the Re 4/4 II series. Railwaymen jokingly called this combination the Re 10/10. Strangely enough, no one ever spoke of a Bo'Bo'Bo' + Bo'Bo' locomotive.

Right: A powerful package, consisting of a Re 4/4 III and a Re 6/6 on the line to the Gotthard. Incidentally, at the head of the train is one of the prototype locomotives, with the body divided in the centre. In the background is the Zugersee.

Series Re 4/4 (BLS), Re 4/4 II, Re 4/4 III, Re 6/6 and Re 4/4 IV					
Wheel arrangement	Bo'Bo'	Bo'Bo'	Bo'Bo'	Bo'Bo'Bo'	Bo'Bo'
First delivery	1964	1964	1971	1972	1982
Last delivery	1983	1985	1971	1980	1982
Withdrawn from service	–	–	–	–	–
Quantity	35	283	20	89	4
Length overall	15.1m (49'6")	15.41m (50'7")	15.41m (50'7")	19.31m (63'4")	15.8m (51'10")
Total wheelbase	10.8m (35'5")	10.7m (35'1")	10.7m (35'1")	14.3m (46'11")	10.8m (35'5")
Bogie wheelbase	2.8m (9'2")	2.8m (9'2")	2.8m (9'2")	2.9m (9'6")	2.9m (9'6")
Wheel diameter	1.25m (4'1")	1.26m (4'2")	1.26m (4'2")	1.2m (3'11")	1.26m (4'2")
Service weight	80t (88.2 tons)	80t (88.2 tons)	80t (88.2 tons)	120t (132.3 tons)	80t (88.2 tons)
Maximum speed	140km/h (87mph)	140km/h (87mph)	125km/h (78mph)	140km/h (87mph)	160km/h (99mph)
1-hour rating	4990kW (6689hp)	4700kW (6300hp)	4700kW (6300hp)	7900kW (10590hp)	5050kW (6769hp)

Above: Many international express trains travelling from Zürich to the border station of Buchs are pulled by an Re 4/4 II.

Left: Once again, an Re 10/10, this time seen near San Nazzaro, on the shore of Lake Maggiore. The train of mixed freight traffic will be transferred to the Italian railway system at the frontier station of Luino.

Re 4/4 II — the universal genius

"There is nothing that it cannot do." This was a comment about the universally applicable Re 4/4 II. In the early 1960s the SBB decided to acquire a universal locomotive to replace the elderly prewar locomotives. With its multiple unit control it would be suitable for pulling the heaviest trains, and in spite of an axle load of 20 t (22 tons), it would also be able to operate on fast, winding sections. As a result, it was allowed to bear the abbreviation R in the construction specifications. Like the Ae 6/6, it was strongly modelled on the BLS's well-tested, reliable Ae 4/4. Indeed, the SBB itself still did not have an equally efficient locomotive of the same type. In 1964, a consortium made up of SLM, BBC and MFO proposed six prototypes of the new Re 4/4 II using comparatively conservative technology. In 1969, these prototypes were followed by a first series of 49 locomotives. The second series, about 50 cm (20 in) longer, now had two single-arm pantographs instead of one double pantograph frame. In addition, it was fitted with a contact strip in order to meet the standards of German and Austrian railways for journeys across the frontier. Like its smaller sister, the Re 4/4 I, a few Re 4/4 IIs

were also allowed to display the elegant TEE colours. In fact, locomotives 11158 to 11161 and 11249 to 11253 left the workshop already painted in red and beige.

In the early 1980s, it was intended that the new Re 4/4 IV with thyristor control should take over from the universal genius. But this did not happen. After only four prototypes, launched in 1982, the SBB decided in favour of a future three-phase locomotive instead of a thyristor one. The short-term need for efficient electric locomotives led to a series of 20 quickly converted Re 4/4 IIIs for use on the Gotthard, followed by a fourth series of 27 Re 4/4 IIs between 1984 and 1986. The locomotives were still supplied with the rectangular headlamps — disparagingly described as lorry headlamps — that survived in the older series during various overhauls. Several private railway companies bought the universal locomotive as well as the SBB. The Südostbahn (SOB) bought one Re 4/4 III of the first 1985 series from the SBB, and also locomotives 11351 to 11353 from the second series. At the end of 1994 the SOB seized a unique opportunity and exchanged its four Re 4/4 IIs for four of the SBB's Re 4/4 IV thyristor locomotives.

An unpopular container locomotive: Re 4/4 IV

It took the SBB a long time before it decided to buy an electric thyristor loco-motive with phase angle control. It was only in 1982, when Germany and France were already using locomotives with single-phase/three-phase con-verter sets, that Swiss locomotive factories delivered the first thyristor loco-motives to the SBB. The new Re 4/4 IV — whose name "Lok 2000" reflected the hopes of Swiss Railways — was technically inspired by the Austrian 1044. In addition to a maximum speed of 160 km/h (99 mph), the specifications of the new locomotive required a multiple unit control system also suitable for conventional locomotives, in order to be able to pull multiple-unit "piggy-back" or container trains across the Gotthard. The angular silhouette of the locomotive with its distinctive sharp nose and "crimped" side walls (the cause of its nickname "tin can") was not the result of trying to achieve minimum air resistance. It was actually to minimise pressure waves when trains passed each other. Their successors were used by the SBB for intercity trains in the Rhonetal where the SBB permitted speeds of 160 km/h (99 mph) on certain sections. But a decrease in freight transport prevented them being bought in large numbers. In 1992, when the Re 460 emerged as a particular successful machine, the thyristor locomotives lost their "Lok 2000" label. Although the locomotives were still in excellent working order, SBB disposed of the remain-ing locomotives and exchanged them with the Südostbahn (SOB) for four conventional locomotives of the Re 4/4 III series.

The SOB proudly marketed its new "showpiece" Series 446 locomotive as an advertising medium. The first in the series of "advertising" locomotives was the 446 446. Painted blue, this advertised the Seedamm Centre in the town of Rapperswil. Locomotive 446 447 conveyed a completely different kind of message. Apparently constructed of parts from the long-established Märklin metal construction set, it has been a milestone in Märklin history since it was first shown on 8 June 1996. In 1997, to celebrate the 150th anniversary of Swiss Railways, this locomotive shed its sheet metal "dress". The ceremony took place on 16 August 1997 in Frutigen where locomotive 446 447, adorned with pictures of many Swiss personalities, wished "Happy Birthday" to Swiss Railways.

Number 446, originally painted white to advertise Swiss Telecom, is now painted blue and white to advertise its successor, Swisscom. Environmentally-friendly kitchen manufacturers Alno is advertised by locomotive 446 445 with a green and white theme.

Above: Photographed in April 1991, this colourfully painted Re 4/4 IV is in service with SBB. It is mainly used on the Lötschberg and Simplon lines.

Right: When the SOB acquired its four Re 460 locomotives, it turned them into colourful, eye-catching advertising mediums. Seen here is the Swisscom locomotive. On the opposite page, below, is the Märklin-Metallbaukasten locomotive

Opposite page, top: With its multiple control, Re 4/4 IIs can be used economically in double header configuration. They are often seen hauling freight trains, as here at St Triphon in Wallis.

Above: Only about 20 of the E 424 series were still in service with the FS at the end of the year 2000. They are used for light passenger service.

Opposite page: The 300 existing E 636s will continue to be used to haul freight for several years to come. This mixed freight train is at Laives in September 2000.

At the start of electrification, Italy's state railway company the Ferrovie dello Stato (FS) favoured a three-phase alternating current supply. However this system did not prove satisfactory since it required two wires to be suspended over each line of track. In crowded areas, this necessitated extremely expensive cable installations. Therefore, the FS changed to 3,000-volt direct current, the power supply that is still used today.

For the expanding electric network, the FS acquired two series of technically similar, brown-painted locomotives, E 636 and E 424. The latter was also known as the "Two-thirds E 636".

The E 636 was derived from the E 626 acquired in 1931. Unlike the railways of Germany, Austria and Switzerland, the FS liked did not adopt the successful "crocodile" principle but went its own way. It developed a locomotive with three bogies, each with two axles, thus following the Bo'Bo'Bo' arrangement of the E 626. This axle arrangement improved the performance of the locomotive round curves. The electric part of the E 626 was used without modification in its successor. Alfredo d'Arbela, the engineer who was responsible for the design, revised the mechanical parts. The loco body was divided in the middle and connected with joints. The tripartite fronts gave the sturdy locomotives an appearance that was at that time modern and aerodynamic .

Series production of the E 636 started immediately after the presentation of the design in 1940 and a total of 108 locomotives had been made by 1942. Breda was the manufacturer, a company that among other things had made history with the Ae 6/8s of the BLS Lötschbergbahn, and Savigliano. With a maximum speed of 110 km/h (68 mph), the E 636 was soon hauling express passenger and freight trains on all the direct current sections of the network.

The locomotives proved themselves so well that the FS continued to order more of them after World War II. Procurement of the E 636 ended only in 1962, by which time a remarkable 459 examples had been acquired. There were no external differences between the various series, with the exception of

Opposite page, top: A Turin-based E 636 hauls a regional train from Savonna to Turin.

Opposite page, below: This Milan-based E 645 014 is hauling a freight train from Tirano to Milan.

Left: The E 656 hauls many stopping trains in the Mont Cenis region and the Alpine pass to Turin. This photograph was taken at Chiomonte.

the locomotives destined for mountainous areas, which were equipped with large, yellow and black snow ploughs . These were solidly mounted on the locomotives and remained in position throughout the year.

Engine number E 636 082 was fitted experimentally with regenerative braking, in which the momentum of the train generates electricity with its motors that is fed back into the network. This locomotive therefore had altered roof arrangements and ventilation equipment. After an accident, number E 636 284 was fitted with the angular cab of the E 656 series. It was painted red in front with grey sides. Number E 636 080 had a green and beige colour scheme.

The rest of the locomotives still preserve their brown paint today. They have of course in the meantime stopped working on the most important services, but they are still encountered all over the country, even though the FS has scrapped quite a number that had become seriously damaged. Mainly they haul freight trains, but the FS still uses some of these old locomotives for short and long distance traffic.

High performance successor

From 1959, the FS acquired a successor series, the E 645, which also had three bogies with two axles each. This time the mechanical part was adopted unchanged while the electric part was modified. The single motor of the E 636s were replaced the twin motors. Consequently the performance of the 98 examples of the E 645 was double that of its predecessor. The 33rd locomotive of the series was the first to have a different body with a straight front and two windows.

The first series of the E 645 is still operating today largely unchanged . On the other hand, over the years many locomotives of the second series have been fitted with reversible control for use in the local traffic. The locomotives based at Milan and Turin have the grey, red and orange FS colours for local traffic. Five ES 645s were fitted on a trial basis with a transmission gear ratio giving a maximum speed of 140 km/h (87 mph). The FS designated these the Series E 646. According to the building records, this group of five was numbered E 645 101 to 105.

Electric loco with luggage compartment

The first ES 424, the "Two-thirds E 636", was built in 1943 and 158 machines were delivered in the course of six years. Their fronts admittedly resembled the E 636, but otherwise they clearly differed substantially from the sister-series. They were almost 3 m (10 ft) shorter and the body did not need to be divided. Since the drive equipment did not use all the space in the machine compartment, the FS fitted a roll-up door in one side to give access to a luggage compartment with a volume of 9 m³ (318 cu ft). Railway enthusiasts therefore called the E 424 a motor luggage van, but this did not unduly worry the railway management in Rome.

Conceptually, the ES 636 and the E 424 were similar. The transformation

Series E 424, E 636 and E 645			
Wheel arrangement	Bo'Bo'	Bo'Bo'Bo'	Bo'Bo'Bo'
First delivery	1943	1940	1959
Last delivery	1948	1962	1965
Withdrawn from service	–	–	–
Quantity	158	459	98
Length overall	15.5m (50'10")	18.25m (59'11")	18.25m (59'11")
Total wheelbase	8.72m (28'7")	13.55m (44'5")	13.25m (13'3")
Bogie wheelbase	2.01m (6'7")	3.15m (10'4")	2.85m (9'4")
Wheel diameter	1.03m (3'5")	1.25m (4'1")	1.25m (4'1")
Working weight	72.4t (81.8 tons)	101t (111.3 tons)	112t (123.5 tons)
Maximum speed	105km/h (65 mph)	110km/h (68 mph)	120km/h (75mph)
1-hour rating	1550kW (2078hp)	2100kW (2815hp)	4320kW (5791hp)

was successful, but it would appear that economy was avoided as much as possible. For instance, the ES 636 had wheels 1.25 m (4ft 11 in) in diameter. What could be simpler than to use the same wheels on the E 424? The FS did no such thing — it fitted 1.03 m (3 ft 4½ in) wheels instead.

With modernization some of the E 424's luggage space was lost. For use on difficult, steep gradients anti-slip equipment was fitted. In appearance, the most obvious feature of these locomotives are the additional red side lights made necessary by their reversing capability. The FS designated these modernised locomotives sub-Series E 424.2. They operate in all parts of the country. In the north, the locomotives haul local traffic as far as the Brenner pass. The unmodernized engines operate mainly in southern Italy and around the important junction of Alessandria.

Cautious progress without too much risk

In the 1970s the FS management became aware that the future development of rail traffic could not be carried out with essentially prewar rolling stock. In 1976 the Series E 656 was technically still able to hold its own, except that it used conventional switched speed control technology. The FS ordered its first electronically controlled locomotives on 20 December 1976.

The state railway company did not want to appear to be taking too many risks with the new design. Therefore, the direct current motor remained as it was. Only the thyristor chopper phase control technique was new. In itself, this allowed the use of 2,000-volt motors instead of the 1,500-volts ones used until then. The FS decided to change the single-axle final drive that had been used earlier. Instead the three motors each drove both axles of each bogie. The result was a B'B'B' locomotive, contrary to the trend to four-axled locomotives. For express train services, a maximum speed of 160 km/h (99 mph) was achieved, while for universal service 130 km/h was enough. The step so cautiously taken by the FS admittedly led in the right direction; to have truly

up-to-date locomotives they would have had to have been less averse to risk.

In 1979, the FS put the first locomotive of the slower version, the E 633 series, into service. Three more batches followed in 1980, as well as the first of the faster E 632 series. The specification required that the locomotive should haul an express train of 1,000 t (1,100 tons) at its maximum speed on the level. It also had to reach a maximum speed of 100 km/h (62 mph) hauling a train of 800 t (882 tons) up of a gradient of 1 in 100 to 1 in 67.

Italian Railways attached great importance to an up-to-date, generously proportioned driver's cab. Initially, reversible and multiple unit controls were not envisaged. However, locomotives E 632 002 to 066 had 78-way cabling installed so that these locos could be used for reversible operation. The E 633 series began with 106 locomotives equipped with reversible control equipment as standard. The multiple unit control important for heavy freight traffic was fitted to the first of the second series, which the FS designated sub-Series E 633.2.

Both the E 632 and the E 633 sub-series operated mainly in northern Italy, hauling trains of all types. On the Brenner pass, the FS mainly ran the E 633.2 in double traction, while one engine was enough on the valley section to Verona. The maximum weight of the trains was 1,200 t (1,323 tons). The drawbar did not allow a greater weight to be pulled, so many trains had to be hauled by the E 652.

Only in 1989 did the FS take the step to full electronic control. In that year, the E 652, developed from the E 632, was put in service. The FS had already been testing the technical equipment in locomotive number E 632 043 since 1985. Until 1991, the FS subjected the six prototype locomotives to extensive trials before it finally came to a decision to commit to series production. The last locomotive was completed in 1994 with the delivery of the 126th engine. Beside the Brenner, the powerful locomotives also haul freight traffic on the Mont Cenis line and the Venice-Udine-Tarvisio route.

Opposite page: A modernized E 424.2 pulling a regional train in the direction of Verona.

Above: Two E 412s under multiple control have picked up a mixed train at Brenner and are hauling it to Verona.

Left: These two E 633s are also under multiple control as they haul a complete train from France to Italy over the Mont Cenis section with its many bridges, seen above Chiomonte.

Series E 412, E 632, E 633 and E 652			
Wheel arrangement	Bo'Bo'	B'B'B'	B'B'B'	B'B'B'
First delivery	1997	1980	1979	1989
Last delivery	1999	1987	1988	1994
Withdrawn from service	–	–	–	–
Quantity	20	65	146	126
Length overall	19.4m (63'8")	17.8m (58'4")	17.8m (58'4")	17.8m (58'4")
Total wheelbase	12.65m (41'6")	12.65m (41'6")	12.65m (41'6")	12.65m (41'6")
Bogie wheelbase	2.03m (6'8")	2.15m (7'2")	2.15m (7'2")	2.15m (7'2")
Wheel diameter	1.1m (3'7")	1.04m (3'5")	1.04m (3'5")	1.04m (3'5")
Working weight	88t (97.0 tons)	103t (113.6 tons)	103t (113.6 tons)	106t (116.8 tons)
Maximum speed	200km/h (124 mph)	160km/h (99mph)	130km/h (81mph)	160km/h (99mph)
1-hour rating	1550kW (2078hp)	4200kW (5630hp)	4200kW (5630hp)	5100kW (6836hp)

Three in one

On the Brenner pass section, it was not only the capability of the locos that caused headaches for the train planners of the region. An even greater problem was the power supply. While the FS had originally used three-phase current, and then a 3,000-volt direct current supply, the Austrian Federal Railways had electrified its section of the route with the north European standard of 15,000-volt single phase alternating current with a frequency of 16.67 cycles. Locomotives therefore had to be changed at the Brenner, a procedure that was archaic in the age of the high-performance electronics. Therefore on 14 April 1997, the FS and ADtranz together launched a dual-voltage loco, the Series E 412. Its electrical technology was derived from the Swiss locos of the 460 series, while the mechanical parts largely corresponded to those of the German Eco-2000 101 series . As the third party cooperating in creating the E 412, an Italian designer created the body.

Nevertheless, the locomotive still looks like a locomotive. This not always the case when designers become involved with trains. The body is typical of a loco with its roof crowded with equipment, its ventilator grills and its running gear. There could be argument over the choice and arrangement of the colours, which made the locomotive look somewhat plain and inconspicuous. Perhaps Poland made a better job of this part of the operation. In place of the anthracite grey front, Poland decided in favour of an agreeable red. The Polish locomotives are now working for an Italian private railway company, since the Polish National Railways could not pay for them.

To be precise, the E 412 is actually a triple-voltage locomotive, because it can also operate on direct current of 1,500 volts, as is used on some French lines for example. However, in this mode the performance of the locomotive is much diminished, so in practical terms it is a dual-voltage locomotive. Despite the large area in which the locomotive could be used, the FS only ordered 20 examples equipped with all the Italian, Austrian and German safety facilities. The safety technology for Switzerland is lacking, in spite of the fact that the FS had agreed to close cooperation over freight traffic with the SBB. On top of this, bureaucracy managed to play an evil practical joke on the rail planners. It was decided to electrify newly built tracks with alternating current of 25,000 volts and 50 cycles — precisely the combination that the E 412 is not equipped to handle.

Right: A train hauled by an E 652 on the descent from Brenner to Bologna in the valley near Bressanone. The loco is painted in the current livery of the FS.

Electric locomotives – no thank you. That was the basic Austrian policy in the early years of the 20th century. Before World War I there were a few electric-powered narrow gauge railways, for example the Maria-zellerbahn, which was successfully electrified in 1911. However, strategic considerations and a strong coal lobby held up the rapid electrification of the entire network, although the industry would have been perfectly capable of building the necessary tracks and locomotives. After 1920 the Austrian locomotive makers built a number of electric locomotives that had to prove themselves on the steepest, most winding sections of the Austrian railway network. The engineers had to battle with weight and control problems. These difficulties were largely solved through the reduction of axle weight and the progress made in propulsion technology. In 1927 the 1170 series with Bo'Bo' wheel arrangement and Sécheron drive was launched, and this had constructional elements that were considerably lighter than those used in nose-suspended propulsion. However the real breakthrough of electric traction only came at the beginning of the 1950s.

Series 1040: a light universal locomotive

After World War II the ÖBB (Austrian Federal Railways) decided not to build any more of the old prewar types of locomotives. As early as October 1950 it received a newly built locomotive, the 1040, in which the technical achievements of the prewar years were further developed . The precursor of the 1040 was the 1245, whose operational areas it also took over. Compared to the last series of the 1245, the locomotives of the 1040 series were fitted with more efficient motors and transformers. The electro-pneumatic direct current contactor had 21 drive steps, three times more than the 1245. The locomotive was still fitted with the very reliable Sécheron spring transmission drive, which remained unchanged. The running quality was improved by a reduction of the thrust force of the guiding bogie. This was achieved by a triangular coupling placed between the bogies and ensuring the transmission of traction power.

From 1950 to 1953, the ÖBB acquired a total of 16 locomotives. The first 1040s were based at the Salzburg locomotive depot. From here they were put into service on the Tauern mountain railway. Ten locomotives ended up in Vienna West, after the electrification of the Attnang-Puchheim-Vienna

section of the line. During the 1960s this line was mainly used for freight transport.

Unfortunately, the 1040 suffered many breakdowns. The reason was the shortage of raw materials. The Sécheron spring transmission drive was made from low-grade steel and broke down frequently. For the same reason, the cabling of the locomotive had to be completely renewed after about ten years. In addition, to avoid overloading the motors, the top speed had to be restricted to 80 km/h (50 mph). When these 1040s underwent their main overhaul, they lost their angular shape but did not acquire the rounded sides of their final six siblings.

After the launch of the 1042 series, the 1040s were transferred in the 1960s to Amstetten and Mürzzuschlag. There they were used for regional and freight transport, and also as assisting locomotives on the Semmering line. Today they are used to pull freight trains and carry out marshalling operations in Selztal and its surroundings. The remaining 1040s are still based in the Selztal locomotive depot.

Series 1041/1141: Expresses for the Westbahn

The ÖBB expressed its desire for a new type of locomotive even before the 1040s had all been delivered. It is true that the electrical installations remained unchanged in the 1041 series, but from a mechanical point of view, the run was smoother and greater adhesive power was achieved. Swiss Railways had already carried out useful experiments in this field when building rolling stock and the ÖBB was able to make use of the findings. The changes in the construction consisted in the fact that the traction and transmission gear that was formerly attached to the bogies in the 1040s were now part of the main frame, which was itself supported in a cradle by the bogies. Power transmission was by the existing Kleinow quill spring drive that had already been used in the 1018 series in the late 1930s. The 1041 was in service from 1952 to 1954 and 25 locomotives were produced in all. In 1955 they were replaced by the more powerful 1141, of which 30 were produced. The abolition of the maximum speed limit of 100 km/h (62 mph) encouraged further developments. The 1041 had reached a speed of 90 km/h (56 mph) and the objective was to develop a faster version. The ÖBB was relying on a traction technique that until then had only been used on a prototype by the DB in West Germany. This propulsion technique was the Siemens rubber ring spring drive, which was fitted to all the 30 locomotives of the 1141 series. This system did not disappoint its supporters and it remained the standard transmission for Austrian electric locomotives for many years.

What was new on the 1141 was the transverse coupling. This helped to reduce wear and tear on the wheel flanges on tightly curved sections of track. In order to keep the weight of the locomotive at the recommended 80 t (88.2 tons), the electric rheostatic braking of the 1041 was dropped. In appearance the 1141 differed from the 1041 in its rounded transition from the front part to the sides. Few other changes were made to the 1141. Some electrical components were changed and in the course of improvement work, one driver's door was replaced by a window. More significant changes were made to the 1041. In 1990 the electric rheostatic braking was removed. With four locomotives, the top speed was increased from 90 to

110 km/h (56 to 68 mph) after the gear unit was redesigned, so they were now as fast as the 1141. The designation of this locomotive was 1041.200. The opportunity to see the 1041 and 1141 series in action at Selzthal or Attnang-Puchheim should be taken as soon as possible before they are withdrawn. The 1141 also runs on the Pyhrn line from Linz to Selzthal.

Series 1010/1110.5: a stronger six-axle loco

The story now returns to the 1950s. In 1952 the Westbahn was electrified between Vienna and Salzburg. However, there were not enough electric locomotives to provide express services on this main line. There were the prewar Series 1018, 1118, 1670.1 and 1245 locomotives, as well as the 1040 that had been delivered two years earlier and the first 1041s. This is the reason why freight train locomotives of the 1020 series with a maximum speed of a mere 90 km/h (56 mph) were used to help out the express service by increasing the number of locomotives available, although the freight service itself could barely spare them. In addition, it happened that the electrification of the Südbahn (from Semmering to Klagenfurt) had been brought forward, so new express locomotives were also needed on that line. Having looked at neighbouring Switzerland, where the SBB was very happy with its new Ae 6/6 Gotthard locomotive, the ÖBB decided to look into six-axle locomotives. It also toyed with the idea of simply developing the 1018 further, or just building another Bo'Bo' locomotive.

Above: Here a 1041 and an 1141 haul a goods train from Liezen to Selzthal.

Opposite page: This Series 1040 locomotive is in operation around Selzthal. It will probably be withdrawn from service in 2002.

Below: A meeting between a prewar and a postwar locomotive. On the right, the 1245 is pulling a goods train, while its descendant, the 1041, is at the head of a regional train. This conjunction took place in May 1994 at Steeg-Gosau station in the Salzkammergut.

Series 1040, 1041, 1141, 1042 and 1043					
Wheel arrangement	Bo'Bo'	Bo'Bo'	Bo'Bo'	Bo'Bo'	Bo'Bo'
First delivery	1950	1952	1955	1963	1971
Last delivery	1953	1954	1955	1977	1973
Withdrawn from service	–	–	–	–	–
Quantity	16	25	30	257	10
Length overall	12.92m (42'5")	15.32m (50'3")	15.26m (50'3")	16.20m (53'2")	15.58m (51'1")
Total wheelbase	9.04m (29'8")	10.70m (35'1")	10.70m (35'1")	11.20m (36'9")	10.40m (34'1")
Bogie wheelbase	3.1m (10'2")	3.2m (10'6")	3.2m (10'6")	3.4m (11'2")	2.7m (8'10")
Wheel diameter	1.35m (4'5")	1.35m (4'5")	1.30m (4'3")	1.25m (4'1")	1.30m (4'3")
Service weight	81t (89.3 tons)	83t (91.5 tons)	80t (88.2 tons)	84t (92.6 tons)	83t (91.5 tons)
Maximum speed	90km/h (56mph)	110km/h (68mph)	110km/h (68mph)	130km/h (81mph)	135km/h (84mph)
1-hour rating	2360kW (3164hp)	2290kW (3070hp)	2400kW (3217hp)	3600kW (4826hp)	4000kW (5362hp)

At first the new locomotive was planned as a universal locomotive; fast on the flat and powerful on the steep Arlberg and Semmering mountain lines. However, these requirements proved to conflict too much with each other to be carried out. Instead, two versions of the same series of locomotive were developed. The 1010 could reach a maximum speed of 130 km/h (81 mph) while the 1110 had a maximum speed of only 110 km/h (68 mph).

Different versions

The first eight locomotives were commissioned by the ÖBB in 1952, and they were delivered in 1955. This included two locomotives, 1010.01 and 1010.02, with a new type of bogie. This did not have the normal bogie pivot arrangement connecting it to the body. Instead the body of the locomotive was supported on two rocker beams, which rested at both ends on leaf springs. The rocker beams were placed at a right angles to the bogie between the two axles. Side buffers allowed the bogies to be pushed back into its base position. The push and pull forces were transferred by drawbars in a fairly high position, at a height of 825 mm (32½ in). In unfavourable conditions this caused the bogie to tilt, resulting in a reduction of the load on the axle. These experiences caused the ÖBB to change its mind and return to the traditional bogies with bogie pivots for locomotives 1010.03 to 1010.20. In this design the traction force occurred at a height of 255 mm (10 in). However, there was a problem of space with the central axle in the symmetrical, three-axle driving bogie because of the proximity of the traction motor and the bogie pivot. But this problem was solved by the installation of an additional support for the bogie pivot under the relevant motor.

In 1956 the first slower locomotives of the 1110 series were delivered to the ÖBB. Numbers 01 to 04 and 06 to 10 were fitted with the low-mounted bogie pivots, as described above. Only locomotive 1110.05 was designed without bogie pivots. This was a further development of the design that had been unsuccessfully tested on the experimental locomotives of the 1010 series. It worked much better, so 20 locomotives of the second 1110 series were fitted with this type of bogie design. These locomotives had long additional front skirts to solve the problem of drifting snow that had become all too evident. Gradually the other locomotives were fitted with this special protective device when they were overhauled.

Left: An 1110 at the head of a colourful container train rumbles past the monastery of Melk in lower Austria, travelling north from Linz.

Top: Locomotive 1010.09 has been restored to its original dark green colour. When the 1010/1110 locomotives have been withdrawn from service, this will survive as a museum locomotive recalling this successful series.

Above: Two 1042s at Selzthal station struggling to pull a heavy ore train.

Opposite page: One of the Bludenzer 1110.5s and a 1044 travelling past the west face of the Arlberg at the start of the Schmiedtobel viaduct. The resistances of the rheostatic braking system are under the housings on the roof.

All the 1010s and 1110s were equipped with spring-supported transverse couplings placed between the bogies in order to reduce wear on the wheel flanges and to prevent the lurching of the locomotive.

Various changes were made in 1972. That year saw the beginning of the process of fitting direct current rheostatic brakes to ten locomotives of the 1110 series, whose general overhaul was due in any case. The brake resistances were mounted on the roof of the locomotive and the crossed-arm pantographs collecting the electric current were replaced by single-arm pantographs. The new locomotives were now able to use their braking power of 2,460 kW (3,298 hp) to great effect on steep stretches. These locomotives were able to bring a train of 450 t (496 tons) to a halt on a 1 in 40 gradient. By the end of 1974 the ÖBB had fitted all ten locomotives with electric rheostatic brakes under the designation 1110.5.

The next phase of modernisation started at the beginning of the 1990s. The ÖBB upgraded 17 locomotives of the 1010 and 1110 series during their general overhaul. External changes included the addition of small standard indicator lights on the front and a new colour scheme, red with agate-grey ornamental stripes.

The 1110s were stationed for many years at Bludenz and Innsbruck.

Because of their great weight they were moved from their original stamping ground to Salzburg, Linz and Villach. From these stations, they serviced the Giselabahn and Westbahn as well as the Tauern and Ennstal lines. Since 1998, they have operated almost exclusively in the region of Salzburg and Linz, and again in Bludenz. A few locomotives have recently been withdrawn from service. Two of these were 1010.006 and 1110.13, both victims of accidents, as well as 1010.018, which was downgraded to become a source of spare parts. The year 2002 marks the end of the six-axle locomotive.

Series 1042: Austria's first high-performance loco

The ÖBB had become convinced of the advantages of the six-axle express locomotive with its smaller axle loading resulting from the Co'Co' wheel arrangement. But it was all too apparent that on sections with many curves, for instance on the Semmeringbahn, wear and tear on the wheel flanges was very marked. What was needed on winding mountain lines such as these was a more agile locomotive. The industry was therefore commissioned to build a four-axle locomotive. This type of construction was technically more advanced and it therefore seemed to be an attractive alternative to the six-axle locomotive.

The new locomotives of Series 1042 left the factory in 1963. Components such as the rubber-ring spring-drive, the high voltage control switching and the tranverse-coupled bogies with low-mounted bogie pivots were preserved and used again in this series. A pneumatic axle load equalizer made the pulling of heavy trains easier.

The motors fitted to the first 40 locomotives had a power of 890 kW (1,193 hp) and they nearly all had commutator problems. The second series was fitted with different motors, similar to those used on the Swiss Gotthard Ae 6/6 locomotives. Motors of 1,000 kW (1,340 hp) were fitted to locomotives that were built later .

In 1966 another version was produced, designated 1042.5. These locomotives were adapted to the maximum speed allowed on the Austrian railways, and they could now also be used on DB stretches in West Germany. Their top speed was now 150 km/h (93 mph) instead of 130 km/h (81 mph). The first 20 of these locomotives were fitted with a combination of regenerative and rheostatic brakes with a power of 800 kW (1,072 hp). In contrast, locomotives starting from number 531 were fitted with thyristor-controlled direct current rheostatic brakes with a power of 2,400 kW (3,217 hp). Because of the space required by the brake resistances on the roof, the single-arm pantographs were rotated by 180°.

In 1990, a few alterations were made to the 1042. The round corner window disappeared and was replaced by plain sheet metal. This change was partly dictated by a concern for safety. Another change involved the rear lights, which were moved from above the advance signal light to below it. In 1955 the ÖBB began to weld the driver's cabin doors shut, which was not such a good idea because the lack of a second escape route for the driver is now being criticised as a serious safety fault.

The colour of the 1042 was changed from the original ÖBB green to red. The 1042.510 that came out in 1968 was the first red locomotive in its series. From the mid-1990s onwards, locomotives being repainted during routine repair work were given the new colours, which were red with pale grey stripes.

Above: On the north side of the Semmeringbahn, the 1142 and a 1042 make a double header. The gradient of this section is 1 in 40.

Left: At only moderate speed, these two 1142s are travelling uphill on the Krauselklause viaduct on the Semmeringbahn.

Below: Gradually all the locomotives of the 4010 series have been modernised and painted in the current colour scheme of the ÖBB. Here 4010 020 is on the line from Vienna South.

In 1996 reversible trains were used on the regional railways of the ÖBB. Sixty-seven locomotives of the 1042.5 series, which were already equipped with high performance brakes, were now fitted with reversible controls in the main workshop in Linz. This involved mounting two more leads on the 13-wire UIC cable to carry out data exchange between the locomotive and the driver's cabin. It also required the installation of equipment for controlling the opening and closing of the doors, the lighting of the train, the train's automatic heating system, and overall operational monitoring. The ÖBB also fitted fire alarms, and an anti-slip device in order to be able to control unmanned locomotives as well.

Nowadays, the 1142 is also mainly used to pull reversible trains or to pull freight trains as one of a tandem. The 1042s, on the other hand, are used mainly for freight and excursion trains on the main lines. The 1042, 1042.5 and 1142 series are all stationed at Linz. In addition, they are also in service in Innsbruck, Vienna West, Vienna South, Graz and Villach. There are also a few 1142s based in Graz and Vienna South. Locomotive 1042.044 has been repainted in its original green colour.

Series 4010: elegant motor coach trains

As far as electric motor coach trains are concerned, the ÖBB still used a few prewar models in the first ten years after the war. It was only in 1956 that the ÖBB began to commission new electric motor coach sets.

At first, the 4030 universal electric locomotive was supplied with a maximum speed of 100 km/h (62 mph). However, the ÖBB introduced four express locomotives of the 4130 series with a maximum speed of 130 km/h (81 mph) for the 1958 summer timetable of the "Transalpine" Vienna-Basel express. The 4130s were 4030s that had been further developed. A second intermediate carriage was added to increase the seating capacity. But soon even the capacity of the 4130 was not enough. Control problems and an increasing demand for comfort prompted the ÖBB to commission six-car motor coach trains.

The first new electric motor coach trains were delivered between December 1964 and May 1965. The 4010.01 consisted of the following units: driving unit with driver's compartment and baggage compartment (4010), driving trailer with luggage compartment, driver's compartment and two large compartments (6010), dining car with air-conditioned restaurant and a large 2nd class compartment (7310 0), large capacity 2nd class compartment coach (7010 100), 2nd class compartment coach (7110 100), and a 1st and 2nd class compartment coach (7110 200). The driving unit had no seating accommodation because of the lack of comfort.

After only a short period of testing, the 4010 was used in the 1965 summer timetable of the "Transalpine" express. Because a high level of use was not initially expected, these trains had no 7110 100 compartment coaches. This series is distinguished by a number of small differences. The driving unit was 110 mm (4¼ in) longer, which resulted in a larger driver's cabin. The number of seating places in the restaurant was reduced in favour of seats in

Right: With its traditional look, when the 4010 still ran as the Transalpine Express, this five-car set in intercity livery is travelling on the line from Linz to Graz at Windischgarsten on the Phyrn line.

the large capacity coach. The side walls and width of the seats also underwent some changes so that the passenger windows could be completely lowered. In all, 14 motor coach trains of this second series were produced. The last two again consisted of six units because they were intended for the "Johann Strauss" express. In the years to 1971 a fourth intermediate coach was built for the rest of the trains. Three more 4010s were delivered in 1976. The final series was delivered in 1978 and consisted of nine sets, so that there were now a total of 29 trains available in all.

The distinctive feature of the 4010s was the elegantly shaped driver's compartment, which was made of fibreglass components. However, the industry's lack of experience of combining fibreglass with a steel structure was to lead to problems. For this reason the front parts in the second series were made from steel. In locomotives 4010.01 to 4010.03 the fibreglass components were gradually replaced by steel ones. In the first three of the series, there were no rear lights under the top warning light. These were added later.

The power output of the 4010 was 2,500 kW (3,351 hp). The front of the driving unit and the driving trailer had traditional push/pull couplings, while the coaches were attached to each other with Scharfenberg couplings. The driving unit rested on two bogies connected by a spring-supported transverse coupling. The bogies contained four motors that conveyed their power through BBC spring drives. One of the two pantographs on the roof had a small collector shoe so that the 4010 could also work on Swiss overhead contact lines. The motors were controlled by a

Above: Locomotive 1043 002 and an 1110 together haul freight train 44815 from Lienz in the east Tyrol to the border station of Innichen in the south Tyrol.

Left: In September 1992 locomotive 1043 003 still had its "Swedish look", as seen here on the Weidmoser viaduct on the north side of the Tauernbahn.

Below: The 1044 is at home anywhere in Austria where there are overhead wires. At Spittal station on the Pyhrn line, this train is waiting at a junction. On single-track sections, it is an everyday rule that freight trains give priority to passenger ones.

Above: The colourful livery of locomotive 1044 282 quickly made it a popular subject with photographers. Here it is near Strasswalchen pulling a train to Salzburg.
Right: To save a second driver, most 1044s are "tandem capable", meaning that two locomotives can be controlled by one man.

BBC low-voltage controller mechanism with 28 steps. The train driver could reach the driver's cabin through a door situated on the right hand side, facing the direction of the destination.

Passenger numbers rose considerably over the years and soon the 4010 trains were no longer large enough. More coaches had to be added, and the enlarged train was pushed from behind by an extra locomotive. This laborious solution led in 1972 to the first 4010s being equipped with a multiple control system. The rest of the motor coach trains were gradually fitted with the same multiple control system, making it possible to use the 4010s in double traction.

The colour scheme of the 4010 originally consisted of sapphire blue and ivory. Bright red areas framed the two lower warning lights and created a pleasant contrast with the other colours. In September 1975 the ÖBB tried new colours. Train 4010.12 had creamy-white areas instead of ivory and ultramarine instead of sapphire blue. This ultramarine was also used for the new driving units and the contrasting areas were now painted in blood-orange. The first red and umber-grey locomotive was first presented in May 1990. However, the improvements also included other changes. For instance, the corner windows on the driving unit and the driving trailer both

disappeared, and the hinged folding doors were replaced by automatic closing doors.

The main areas in which the 4010s were used were on lines towards Switzerland and on internal Austrian city links. Today the trains are stationed in Vienna South. They operate on the Südbahn and between Salzburg/Linz and Graz.

Series 1043: a Swede in Austria

In 1970 a Swedish Series Rc locomotive came as a visitor to Austria's railways. Its fully electronic control system impressed the ÖBB and it ordered ten locomotives of this type. In Sweden the success story of this series of locomotive had started in the mid-1960s, when the Swedish electronic group ASEA successfully tested thyristor phase-chopper control switches on a Swedish Railways (SJ) locomotive. In 1967 the SJ acquired 300 locomotives of the Rc series. It was a representative of the prototype series Rc that was tested by the ÖBB.

The ten locomotives ordered by the ÖBB arrived between 1971 and 1973. They revealed their Swedish origin with their unusual ornamental stripes and the construction of the front lights. Instead of the traditional double pantographs, ÖBB type IV single-arm pantographs were fitted on the locomotives. The bogies were lowered following the designs of ASEA but their performance was improved with hydraulic shock absorbers. The ÖBB also ordered the installation of another main switch, and block brakes in addition to disc brakes.

Although only ten locomotives of the 1043 series came to the ÖBB, there were several variations on the design. While numbers 1043.01 to 1043.04 had four motors each with a power of 900 kW (1,206 hp), the power of the motors fitted to numbers 1043. 05 to 1043.10 was increased to 1,000 kW (1,340 hp). This was because the ten locomotives supplied to the ÖBB were produced in two different series, which differed from those intended for

Series 1010, 1110, 1110.5, 4010 and 1044					
Wheel arrangement	Co'Co'	Co'Co'	Co'Co'	Bo'Bo'	Bo'Bo'
First delivery	1955	1956	1992	1964	1974
Last delivery	1955	1962	1997	1978	1992
Withdrawn from service	–	–	–	–	–
Quantity	20	30	10	29	217
Length overall	17.86m (58'7")	17.86m (58'7")	17.86m (58'7")	16.82m (55'2")	16.06m (52'8")
Total wheelbase	12.7m (41'8")	12.7m (41'8")	12.7m (41'8")	11.2m (36'9")	10.9m (35'9")
Bogie wheelbase	2 x 2.05m (6'9")	2 x 2.05m (6'9")	2 x 2.05m (6'9")	3.1m (10'2")	2.9m (9'6")
Wheel diameter	1.3m (4'3")	1.3m (4'3")	1.3m (4'3")	1.145m (3'9")	1.3m (4'3")
Service weight	110t (121.3 tons)	110t (121.3 tons)	111t (122.4 tons)	73t (80.5 tons)	84t (92.6 tons)
Maximum speed	130km/h (81mph)	110km/h (68mph)	110km/h (68mph)	150km/h (93mph)	160km/h (99mph)
1-hour rating	4000kW (5362hp)	4000kW (5362hp)	4000kW (5362hp)	2500kW (3351hp)	5400kW (7239hp)

Swedish Railways. An electrical rheostatic braking system was fitted on locomotives 1043.04 to 1043.10.

The 1043s were first based in Villach. Without the slightest difficulty they pulled freight trains on the Tauern line and between Villach and Tarvisio. However, the traction power control had to be perfected by the ÖBB. This was in order to prevent twisting oscillations of one side of the axle, which was the result of occasional uneven wheel slippage. A pressure-operated anti-slip device provided the solution.

By fitting two 1043s with automatic central buffer couplings, it became possible to use these locomotives for the Mallnitz-Obervellach-Böckstein autorail service. The other locomotives were used for heavy freight transport between Villach and Tarvisio.

It might well be asked why the ÖBB did not order more of this successful series of locomotives. The reason is the reaction of the Austrian locomotive industry, which was also involved in the development of thyristor controlled locomotives. The result was an even more efficient type of locomotive, the 1044, that was delivered to the ÖBB in 1974.

Series 1044: at home everywhere

The 1044 was produced between 1974 and 1992, during which period 217 were built. The Austrian industry presented its plan for the 1044 series of thyristor-controlled locomotives at about the same time that the second series of the 1043 was being delivered.

Like the 1043, the machinery compartment of the 1044 had oval windows and flanged sides. However, the fronts and the position of the access doors were different. But there were even greater differences inside the 1044. The 1043 reflected the technology current in 1966, while the 1044 revealed the technological progress of the 1970s. The two types of locomotives — both with four motors — differed above all in their performance and in their respective maximum speeds. The 1043 had a top speed of 135 km/h

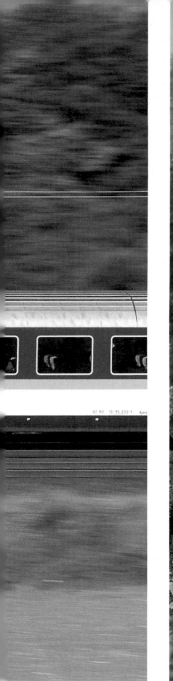

Above: Until the late 1990s this was a familiar picture: Series 120 locomotives at the head of express freight treains. Here is number 120 136 near Eichenberg in November 1989.

Left: In November 1998 the 70th birthday of the most famous mouse in the world was celebrated. For this occasion Märklin created a special locomotive in cooperation with Walt Disney and the DB. Number 120 119 became one of the most famous of all engines. The picture shows it shortly after it was launched in Cologne.

Opposite page: This 120 series pulls train EC 171 at full speed on the North-South line near Oberrieden on 19 August 1989.

to negotiate the longer tunnels. But otherwise the basic concept remained unchanged.

This meant that the series-produced locomotives were already technically overtaken by the time they were put into service. On 27 August 1987 the DB took delivery of the first locomotive, and the last one was delivered on 8 December 1989. In order to distinguish the production locomotives from the pre-series ones, numbering started with 120 101. In 1989 the DB designated locomotives number 120 001 to 005, which had been used only for testing, as the Series 752.

So the concept of the universal locomotive was put to the test. Series 120.1 pulled InterCity trains at speeds of up to 200 km/h (124 mph). It was also used for freight transport as well as local trains. The original plan to use them for pulling passenger trains during the day and freight trains at night was never really carried out in a consistent manner. Critics of the series believed that the higher costs of building a universal locomotive were not justified. This was to have certain consequences.

The death of an idea: the unbuilt Series 121

In the early 1990s the Bundesbahn had to think seriously about replacing its electric locomotives from the 1950s and 1960s. From an economic point of view, the Bundesbahn needed 100 new locomotives per year from 1990 onwards. There was no question of buying more of the Series 120 because semi-conductor techniques had developed so quickly. Known internally as the 121, the successor series was taking shape on the drawing board. It too had been conceived as a universal locomotive. However, in the debates on the implementation of railway reforms, the supporters of splitting up the railway system won the argument. They advocated separate companies for local passenger services, long distance passenger services and freight transport. This naturally heralded the demise of the universal locomotive, and the plans for Series 121 were filed away.

Instead the Bundesbahn launched a "beauty contest". AEG, ABB and the consortium of Siemens and Krauss-Maffei presented proposals of their concepts for a new generation of locomotives. Electric locomotive pioneer Siemens presented its proposal in the shape of a new prototype locomotive with the descriptive name "EuroSprinter". The name of the AEG model had a more technical sound: 12 X. ABB's proposal consisted of the insertion of a few

Right: In the reform of German railways, all the DB's engines were assigned to specific divisions. The 120 series went to the Travel and Tourist division, therefore hauling passenger trains almost exclusively. This freight train was a rare exception.

Series 120.1, 101, 152, 145 and 146					
Wheel arrangement	Bo'Bo'	Bo'Bo'	Bo'Bo'	Bo'Bo'	Bo'Bo'
First delivery	1987	1996	1997	1997	2001
Last delivery	1989	1999	2001	2000	2001
Withdrawn from service	–	–	–	–	–
Quantity	65	145	170	80	31
Length overall	19.2m (63'0")	19.1m (62'8")	19.58m (64'3")	18.9m (62'0")	18.9m (62'0")
Total wheelbase	13.0m (42'8")	13.6m (44'7")	12.9m (42'4")	13.0m (42'8")	13.0m (42'8")
Bogie wheelbase	2.8m (9'2")	2.65m (8'8")	3.0m (9'10")	2.6m (8'6")	2.6m (8'6")
Wheel diameter	1.25m (4'1")	1.25m (4'1")	1.25m (4'1")	1.25m (4'1")	1.25m (4'1")
Working weight	84t (92.6 tons)	84t (92.6 tons)	86t (94.8 tons)	80t (88.2 tons)	80t (88.2 tons)
Maximum speed	200km/h (124mph)	220km/h (137mph)	140km/h (87mph)	140km/h (87mph)	160km/h (99mph)
1-hour rating	5600kW (7507hp)	6400kW (8589hp)	6400kW (8589hp)	4200kW (5630hp)	4200kW (5630hp)

Above: Number 101 096 as an advertising engine for Bayer, seen in Cologne.

Right: Among the most successful advertising locomotives, nearly all the 101 series appeared in more or less showy designs, such as Aspirin's 101 097 here.

individual components of the "Eco 2000" concept into locomotives 120 004 and 005. It was this solution that satisfied the Bundesbahn authorities, and ABB was commissioned to develop a successor to the aged Series 103. The Deutsche Bahn did not require or wait for a prototype locomotive. Instead, on 28 July 1995 it commissioned over 145 locomotives. In fact, the Bundesbahn had purchased a similar number of Series 103 production locomotives 25 years earlier. Interestingly, the six-axle 103 was clearly more powerful than its four-axle successor. The 103.1 had 7,440 kW (9,973 hp) while the 101 had 6,440 kW (8,633 hp). The 101's starting tractive effort of 300 kN (67,440 lbf), the 101 was also inferior to that of the 103.1, which achieved 312 kN (70,138 lbf). This is why the 114-t (126-ton) 103.1 was able to pull a load 30 t (33 tons) greater than its successor.

The Series 101 universal locomotive

On 1 July 1996 ADtranz and Deutsche Bahn presented locomotive 101 001 to the public in Kassel. The ADtranz company had developed from ABB, which in the meantime had fused with AEG. The Kassel-based manufacturers delivered all the locomotives by 1999. For a time as many as 11 locomotives a month were produced because the DB needed them so urgently. The 101s were already pulling scheduled trains as early as summer 1997, barely four months after approval. Of the 16 locomotives delivered, ten were already destined for a scheduled service. A year later there were five services, which regulated the use of 96 locomotives. At the head of InterCity and EuroCity trains, the locomotives stationed in Hamburg reached all destinations in Germany. But more was required of them. They were scheduled to travel as far as the German-Danish interchange station of Padborg and also Venlo on the Dutch border. To the south, they reached Basel, where they were detached from the carriages because they could not operate in Switzerland because the overhead contact wire was arranged slightly differently. Locomotives expected to operate in Germany and Switzerland had to have two different pantographs. Meanwhile, the 101 was also approved in Austria and travelled to and from Vienna several times a day.

Above: This 101 series is performing a solid task hauling an InterRegio train on the Black Forest line from Offenburg to Constance.

Right: The same applies to this Munich-Würzburg InterRegio train. Locomotive 101 001 is in the advertising livery of the Football World Cup 2006.

Minor teething troubles

Naturally, the 101 also had a few minor teething problems. For instance, the pantograph contact strip was not completely reliable. The computer diagnosed a fracture in the contact strip and the locomotive was sent back to the workshop. Another problem was interference with the radio links between stations, which could have had serious consequences. However, the problem was soon identified. The transformer was given better screening and the radio links between stations behaved perfectly when a 101 passed by. In addition, the locomotives did not always operate properly with the driving trailer. The reason was that the railways had only used short trains when testing the locomotives, and the problem of transferring commands arose when using long trains. The lack of a diagnostic display in the driving trailer aggravated the problem. Why the railways decided against is a mystery.

Apart from these teething troubles, the 101 was extremely reliable and safe to operate. Its reliability convinced the other divisions of German Railways and 101s were used both for freight transport and for local passenger services. In 1998 and 1999, for instance, the 101 was used to pull city express trains on the Freiburg-Titisee line of the Höllentalbahn. It also caused a stir when it was used to pull a direct freight train between Mannheim and Munich. The freight transport division sometimes had to hire express locomotives: at the beginning of the year 2000 the Deutsche Post initiated its Parcel-Intercity service, which could travel at a top speed of 160 km/h (99 mph). But DB Cargo did not own a locomotive that could travel at that speed.

Series 101 locomotives could easily cope with the demands made on them. Strictly speaking, it was a universal locomotive, a type of locomotive that

Above: There is only one timetable slot for the 101 to haul a freight train from Mannheim to Munich, which includes the steeply graded Geislinger section. A second engine at the rear (not in the picture) helps it over the mountain.

Left: Number 101 050 pulling a Stuttgart-Munich EuroCity train near Geislingen.

had officially been reviled by the railways. It combined a high maximum speed with an enormous haulage capacity at lower speeds. Its starting tractive effort was the same as that of Series 152, the second new model of Deutsche Bahn. The tractive effort at 140 km/h (87 mph), the maximum speed of the 152, was 164 kN (36,867 lbf).

Another concept: the Series 152

It is true that ABB had won the competition launched at the beginning of the 1990s with its Eco-2000 concept. But this did not mean that the company would build all the new locomotives; their competitors were asked to build the same as well. A similar situation had arisen in the 1950s with the standard electric locomotives of the 110, 139, 140, 141 and 150 series.

However, this time Siemens and Krauss-Maffei succeeded in obtaining the commission to build the project they had submitted in the competition. As a result, the 101 and 152 series were both grouped in numerous sub-series. This was sometimes inconvenient. For instance, the controls of both locomotives were micro-processor controlled, but Siemens and ADtranz used different systems. For the railways, this meant that they had to stock a double set of many expensive spare parts. The strict separation between divisions only confused the situation further.

Unlike the Series 101, the Series 152 was not a universal locomotive. Naturally, it was equipped with various components for use when pulling passenger trains. Among other features, the locomotives were fitted with reversible train control equipment and door release controls. At the same time, the concept of pure freight train locomotives was now also emerging, which would reveal the maximum speeds of which they were capable.

For the Bundesbahn and its successor the Deutsche Bahn, the cost of the locomotives was extremely important. The price of the 152 was about 10% less per locomotive than the 101. This amounted to a substantial saving on the 195 Series 152 locomotives purchased by the Bahn. It was an impressive sum, so long as the additional costs of abandoning the idea of a standard design of new locomotives were neither calculated nor taken into account. In reality, having to equip the network for both types of locomotives can hardly have been an economical approach.

A slower high-performance locomotive

The 152 saw a return to the axle-hung or nose-suspended motor, meaning that the motor was supported half on the bogie frame and half suspended on the axle. This simple design was inexpensive and quick to build. But the disadvantage was obvious: the wheel sets transferred half the weight of the

motors and their oscillations to the track, causing wear to the permanent way and the wheel flanges. For this reason the 100-km/h (62-mph) locomotives of the E 50 series did not have axle-hung motors at the beginning of the 1960s. It is true that the motors of the time were much heavier than the three-phase motors of the 152. But experts were divided about the suitability of the axle-hung motor for a high-performance locomotive reaching 140 km/h (87 mph).

There was no doubt that the Series 152 was a high-performance locomotive. With 6,400 kW (8,579 hp) it had the same power as the Series 101 locomotives, and at 7,720 kW (10,348 hp) its transformer capacity was about 120 kW (161 hp) greater than that of the 101, although the latter figure is of relatively little importance in an age of high-performance electronics. Today the maximum performance of a locomotive is determined by the type of construction and the capacity of the phase inverter. For this reason it is hardly possible to overload the transformers and motors, however briefly. Nor is there any longer much difference between continuous output and the 1-hour rating. As a result the higher duty of the transformer in the Series 152 hardly affected the performance.

On 10 December 1996 the manufacturer and German Railways together presented the first locomotive. Four more locomotives followed during 1997. At the start of the following year, deliveries started in larger quantities. The

Above: Number 127 001, the "EuroSprinter", the test locomotive for the new series.

Left: Freight train 54362 on schedule hauled by locomotives of the 152 and 101 series, seen in Mannheim on 22 August 2000.

Opposite page: An unscheduled auto train headed by two 152s travelling from Ingolstadt Nord to Munich North on 2 May 2001. On arrival the newly-built Audis will be distributed to international freight trains for delivery.

DB took delivery of another 152 practically every two weeks, delivery being completed by the end of 2001. In the meantime the DB relinquished the option on a further 100 locomotives, but instead it ordered multi-system locomotives. These were inspired by the "EuroSprinter" and similar to the Austrian "Taurus".

Nevertheless, other locomotives of the 152 series were produced. Siemens built two locomotives on its own account to increase its stock of locomotives for chartering. Painted silver and yellow, these are chartered to private railway companies to haul freight trains throughout Germany. This resulted in further competition for the Deutsche Bahn, but there was nothing it could do to prevent it. The development of the 152 had been carried out almost entirely by Siemens and Krauss-Maffei, so the Bahn was unable to stop Siemens building more 152s for its own use.

The DB's red 152 locomotives are also seen pulling heavy freight trains throughout Germany, as well as the chartered engines. From the start DB Cargo preferred to used the 152 to pull its fast freight trains. But these were rarely able to show off their top speed because most goods wagons are only approved for a speed of 100 km/h (62 mph).

Series 145: the middle-range locomotive

A maximum speed of 140 km/h (87 mph) was also achieved by a third new type, Series 145 freight locomotive. Once again, it was descended from the "Eco 2000" family and was built by ADtranz. Originally the commission had gone to AEG, although it had not built any locomotives after the 12 X concept model. German Railways needed a middle-range locomotive, for which a continuous output of 4,200 kW (5,630 hp) was enough. In 1997—98 a first run of ten Series 145 locomotives was produced. When the production of the Series 101 was discontinued at the beginning of 1999, ADtranz began working on the 145. From a technical point of view, it was very much like a slimmed-down 101. DB Cargo also opted for the supposedly more efficient axle-hung transmission, but the forces were transferred from the bogie to the locomotive frame by means of torque rods as in the 101. In the 152, this task was carried out by the bogie pivot. ADtranz also adopted a few components from the Siemens locomotive. For instance, the driver's automatic brake valve was similar to that fitted on the 152.

Although conceived as a freight train locomotive, the 145 was naturally also suitable for local trains, and for this reason DB Cargo fitted 22 locomotives with local train control equipment. Externally, it could be identified by the destination indicator in the left window of the driver's cabin. The first test runs were completed in Rheinland-Pfalz. For Expo 2000 they pulled reversible trains consisting of double-deck coaches in the area of Hanover. Up to September 2000 DB Regio had ordered 31 locomotives of the 146 series, derived from the 145, for use in Rheinland-Pfalz and North Rhine-Westphalia. The Bahn insisted that the locomotives should have a high-performance, suspended transmission, namely the Gealaif transmission developed by AEG. It was approved for speeds of up to 250 km/h (155 mph). For the Series 146, the Bahn was happy with a top speed of 160 km/h (99 mph), which was indeed enough for the fast regional traffic. Because both locomotives had the same tractive effort at a speed of 140 km/h (97 mph), the bogies would be exchangeable. Even an upgrade of the 145 was comparatively inexpensive.

Above: Locomotive 152 005 near Dollnstein hauling a mixed freight train north.

Left: It is not only DB Cargo that has the services of the 152. As number 152 902 of the Siemens fleet of charter locomotives, the 152 is also used by private companies. After access to the DB network was given to third parties, several private railway operators have become established.

Below: A series 145 heads a freight train through the Ruhr.

Above: With the Series 185 multi-system locomotive, DB Cargo intends to become strongly involved in international freight, securing long-term traffic with the neighbouring countries in Europe.

Left: In addition to its work for DB Cargo, the 145 is used for high quality regional services.

Externally, the 146 differed from the local service 145 locomotives in the position of the destination indicator: on the 146 it was displayed in both windows. In addition, the 146 was also prepared for one-man train operation. However, it is questionable whether the Bahn will be able to implement its plan to dispense with guards on local trains.

Series 185: the dual-voltage variation

The delivery of 80 locomotives of Series 145 was completed by early 2001. In addition, ADtranz also produced ten locomotives for private railway companies in Germany and Switzerland. Production of the 146 started immediately afterwards. The plan was to deliver all 31 engines in the course of 2001.

After that, what remained was the most important item on the programme: the Series 185. It too was derived from the Series 145 and had a top speed of 140 km/h (87 mph). Unlike its elder sister, it could also be used in France, Luxembourg, Denmark, the Czech Republic and Hungary. In these countries the current used is 25,000 volts at 50 cycles, while in Germany, Austria, Norway, Sweden and Switzerland the power supply is 15,000 volts at 16.7 cycles. As a result two sets of some of the components are needed, and the locomotives are about 4 t (4.4 tons) heavier than the single-voltage equivalent. Externally, they can be identified by the lower roof where the pantographs are situated, caused by the loading gauge being lower in France than in Germany. But in spite of its versatility, the 400 series 185 locomotives are not able to travel from Scandinavia to Hungary. All the railways of Europe have in the past developed their own train protection systems, so a true pan-European locomotive has to include several different safety systems. These raise the weight to about 90 tons, giving an axle load of 22. 5 t (24.8 tons), which is higher than the railway systems in some countries can support.

Above: At rest in Bludenz station. After the pusher locomotive has been uncoupled, the train continues to the marshalling yard at Wohlfurt.

Opposite page: In the Arlberg forest, locomotive 1016 022 hauls the "Transalpin" EuroCity express from the west slope uphill towards St Anton on 13 May 2001.

There are places in Arlberg that railway photographers love to visit because they know they are likely to have good views of their favourite trains and locomotives. Since summer 2000 this Alpine railway in the west of Austria has had a further attraction. The newest locomotive of the Österreichische Bundesbahn (Austrian Railways) has come into service there: the Series 1016, the "Taurus".

The story of this noble "racer" started in 1996 with the Europe-wide announcement of a new type of locomotive. The last large-scale order had taken place several decades earlier. Manufacture of the 1044 thyristor locomotive, a universal locomotive, began in 1974 and continued until 1995 with a total of 217 locomotives. However the tried and tested concept of the 1044 was no longer at the forefront of technology. The ÖBB wanted to purchase an electric locomotive that would be more up-to-date and faster than the 1044 with its 5,400 kW (7239 hp). In addition, it should be less expensive than the 1012 of 6,400 kW (8579 hp), of which only three prototypes existed. What was required was a fast locomotive with an output of 6,400 kW (8579 hp) and a maximum speed of 230 km/h (143 mph). In addition, the new universal locomotive was to be equipped with continuous automatic train-running control as well as reversible facilities for passenger trains and tandem heavy freight transport on winding mountain stretches.

Cost reduction through teamwork

In July 1997 it became clear where the new locomotives would be manufactured. The EuroSprinter product range by Siemens and Krauss-Maffei had won the race. The advantages vis-à-vis the other contenders, ADtranz (which built the 101) and Alsthom/Elin (SNCF BB 36000) lay in the concept of the locomotive frame and the willingness of the manufacturer to reduce production costs by using the ÖBB's own workshops for assembly work. Siemens and Krauss-Maffei supplied the components and the final assembly was carried out in the ÖBB's own workshops in Linz. The concept of the locomotive frame made it

274

Left, top: This Taurus is travelling towards Stuttgart, pulling the coaches of EuroCity express EC 18 from Munich. It will return with express EC 65. Taken near Uhingen in May 2001.

Left, bottom: The Taurus will mainly be used for heavy freight duties. Up inclined stretches it can pull loads 100 t (110 tons) heavier than slower locomotives such as the Series 1044. So the Taurus can pull 650 t (717 tons) up the Arlberg incline. The 1044 series requires a second locomotive (either as a double-header or pusher) for loads above about 550 t (600 tons).

Series 1016, 1116 and 182			
Wheel arrangement	Bo'Bo'	Bo'Bo'	Bo'Bo'
First delivery	1999	1999	2001
Last delivery	2001	2004	2002
Withdrawn from service	–	–	–
Quantity	50	350	25
Length overall	19.28m (63'3")	19.28m (63'3")	19.28m (63'3")
Total wheelbase	12.9m (42'4")	12.9m (42'4")	12.9m (42'4")
Bogie wheelbase	3.0m (9'10")	3.0m (9'10")	3.0m (9'10")
Wheel diameter	1.15m (3'9")	1.15m (3'9")	1.15m (3'9")
Working weight	86t (94.8 tons)	86t (94.8 tons)	86t (94.8 tons)
Maximum speed	230km/h (143mph)	230km/h (143mph)	230km/h (143mph)
1-hour rating	6400kW (8579hp)	6400kW (8579hp)	6400kW (8579hp)

possible for the manufacturers to meet the particular wishes of the client without difficulty. Reliable, well-tested, existing production modules were adopted from the Sprinter concept at favourable cost. The ÖBB placed its orders in three stages: in 1997 it ordered 50 single-voltage locomotives, Series 1016, and 25 dual-voltage locomotives, Series 1116. In 1999 it ordered 100 more Series 1116 locomotives, and a further 225 dual-current locomotives in July 2000. The fleet of 1116s was to make the ÖBB a leading contender in freight transport with Austria's neighbouring countries the Czech Republic, Slovakia and Hungary.

Tests of motive power and controls

On 12 July 1999 locomotive 1016.001 left the Munich Siemens workshop to be presented to the public for the first time. Test runs took place in autumn of the same year on the Wegberg-Wildenrath test section and on the Austrian sections where it would be used in the future. On 4 January 2000 the first 1016 was delivered on schedule to the ÖBB. The 30-day service trial took place near the Linz assembly workshop. The first scheduled applications started on 28 May 2000. These included pulling the "Transalpin" EuroCity express (between Vienna West and Buchs SG), and the EN 467/468 "Wiener Walzer" service, as well as hauling two pairs of goods trains to Munich South.

One of the requirements for building the 1016 was a reduction in cost. This meant that there could be no complex curved surfaces panel-beaten or pressed from sheet metal. As a result the steel part at the front of the train only went up to the lower edge of the window. The compound-curved roof and the curved corners housing the headlights were made of synthetic material reinforced with glass fibre. The constructional principle of the body of the 1016/1116 locomotive was similar to that of the DB-152: lightweight steel construction combined with aluminium and synthetic components. For example, the two-part snow-plough of the 1016/1116 was made from aluminium. The rounded front of the Taurus was inspired by the streamlined front of the

modern DB driving trailer. So far as colour was concerned, the bull-headed locomotive was painted a brilliant red. The Taurus also included a few features that were typical of ÖBB locomotives, such as the pneumatic hinged rear-view mirror and the repositioning of the engine compartment entrance doors. In the event of a rear-end collision at a speed of up to 40 km/h (25 mph), the locomotive was designed so that the body, the transformer and the bogies would suffer relatively little damage. Instead of the traditional replaceable buffer beams, the individual buffers were built with deformation elements that would be pushed inwards on impact to a depth of 65 cm (26 in), absorbing a large part of the energy of the collision in doing so.

A suspension easy on the tracks

While the DB-152 had axle-hung motors, the Taurus has a modern, high performance transmission with separate brake shaft. In this type of construction the traction motor, the hollow drive shafts to the wheel axle and the braking equipment are all mounted in the sprung bogie frame. Two pinions act on the large gearwheel of the hollow shaft, one pinion belonging to the traction motor and the other to the shaft on the outside of the brake discs. Both driving and decelerating torque is transferred to and from the hollow shaft by a cardan (universally jointed) coupling. The unsprung weight affecting the track is reduced by 68% compared to the axle-hung motor of the 152. The body of the locomotive is supported on the bogie frame by a pair of coil springs. Forces created by pulling or braking are transferred to the body of the locomotive through the bogie pivot and rubber-lined friction plates.

Computer control with voice warnings

For the electronics of the Taurus, it was decided to use reliable, proven components from the basic EuroSprinter programme. This type of modular construction made it possible to adapt the single-voltage locomotive to operate on 25,000 volt/50 cycle power supplies at a later date.

As soon as the driver enters the cabin and puts the locomotive into operation, the on-board computer switches on. There is an auto-check at the start of each journey, however short. All the systems are displayed on the monitor and diagnostic checks are made. If anything is wrong, a pleasant but firm woman's voice can be heard. It is the recorded voice of the Austrian radio presenter Chris Lohner.

The driving and transmission controls are activated by the SIBAS 32 control system. The data transfer of the multiple-unit running and reversibility is conveyed by means of a second separate bus system.

was now given the more impressive name of InterCityExperimental, or ICE. First the two driving units of the ICE were produced in 1985 by a number of rail vehicle manufacturers, and the intermediate trailers were completed shortly afterwards. On 20 September 1985, very soon after it was first coupled together, the five-part ICE undertook its first test run on the Munich Nordring. No time was wasted and on 26 November the ICE made a record-breaking run by crossing the 300 km/h (186 mph) mark. Unofficially, it had already achieved a speed of 324 km/h (201 mph) on 19 November.

Public and experts alike were fired with enthusiasm when the Bundesbahn presented the super-train at the 150th Jubilee of Railways in Germany. The ICE continued to break new speed records. The most spectacular run took place on 1 May 1988. Shortly after emerging from the Einmalberg tunnel on the newly built Würzburg-Fulda line, the train reached a breathtaking speed of 406.9 km/h (253 mph). This was a world record. It appeared that nothing would stand in the way of a series production of the ICE.

But the Bahn thought differently. Engineers adapted the record-breaking prototype and produced a series version with a maximum speed of 280 km/h (174 mph), which was much cheaper to build than the expensive prototype. The intermediate coaches were lengthened again to the standard measurement of 26.4 m (87 ft) and carried on not particularly comfortable bogies of the kind normally used with ordinary InterCity coaches. The elaborate linking corridors between coaches were accordion-shaped, reminiscent of the pioneering days of the railways.

In spite of being a step backwards in many respects the InterCityExpress (ICE) was a success. Heralding the age of high-speed travel, the first of 60 InterCity Express trains were ready to be included in the 1991 timetable as

ICE 1, ICE 2, ICE 3 (403) and ICE T (411)				
Wheel arrangement	Bo'Bo'; ICE 3, ICE T with powered drive trailers			
First delivery	1990	1996	1999	1998
Last delivery	1995	1998	2004	2004
Withdrawn from service	–	–	–	–
Quantity	60	46	50	60
Length overall	358m (1,175'6")	205.4m (673'11")	200.8m (658'10")	185m (606'11")
Total wheelbase	14.46m (47'5")	14.46m (47'5")	17.375m (57'0")	19.00m (62'4")
Bogie wheelbase	3.0m (9'10")	3.0m (9'10")	2.5m (8'2")	2.85m (9'4")
Wheel diameter	1.04m (3'5")	1.04m (3'5")	0.89m (2'11")	0.89m (2'11")
Working weight	782t (862.0 tons)	410t (452.0 tons)	409t (450.8 tons)	350t (385.8 tons)
Maximum speed	280km/h (174mph)	280km/h (174mph)	330km/h (205mph)	230km/h (143mph)
1-hour rating	9600kW (12869hp)	4800kW (6434hp)	8000kW (10724hp)	4000kW (5362hp)

planned. They were used on the Hamburg-Frankfurt-Stuttgart-Munich line as well as on the new stretch between Mannheim and Stuttgart, and between Würzburg and Hanover. Success was immediate. The numbers of passengers on high-speed stretches rose even faster than expected.

Nevertheless, no more Series 401 ICE sets were purchased for future new and renovated stretches. In order to be able to use its trains as flexibly as possible and in line with demand on the growing high-speed network, the DB developed the so-called "half-train" concept. Two half-trains, each consisting of a 402 driving unit, up to six intermediate coaches and a driving trailer, would start its journey nose to nose as a twin unit, from Munich for instance. The two sets of through coaches would subsequently separate to reach their respective destinations of Hamburg and Bremen. DB ordered 44 of these ICE-half trains with a top speed of 280 km/h (174 mph), which have now been running since 1996. At first only "full trains" ran because the driving trailer was only delivered later. There is no doubt that the 402 with its pneumatically suspended bogies is much superior to its older brother, the 401, which can still

sometimes be heard noisily tearing along the high-speed tracks. Nevertheless, no more Series 402s are to be built beyond the existing 44 sets. Its successor, the ICE 3, already existed on the design computer screens when the 402 undertook its first tentative test run.

The third generation

After the successes of ICE 1 and ICE 2, DB wanted to tread entirely new ground with its third generation of high-speed classics. Instead of the heavy driving units the driving power would in future be distributed over the whole train. With its maximum speed of 330 km/h (205 mph), new braking systems would provide a reliable means of slowing the ICE 3 on the inclines of the newly built Frankfurt-Cologne section. On 5 November 1997, the DB and the "Arbeitsgemeinschaft ICE 2" consortium, which consisted of Siemens and ADtranz, presented the ICE-S, the test train for the new components, to the public. The "S" of the designation stood for "Schnellfahrt", meaning "high-speed travel". The five-part test train consisted of two ICE 2 driving units and three ICE 2 intermediate coaches bought from the consortium. Visually, the ICE-S had an unusual decorative stripe distinguishing it from previous ICE types. The testing and recording coach without a driving unit was to test the wear-resistant eddy-current brakes. They had already been tested in the InterCityExperimental but they had to prove that their suitability to everyday service was comparable with electric magnetic rail brakes. The other two Arbeitsgemeinschaft ICE 2 intermediate coaches were motorized, with a power of 2,000 kW (2,681 hp) each. In them the various systems for the transmission of the torque to the driving wheels were tested. Together with the two driving units with an output each of 4,800 kW (6,434 hp), the ICE-S had a total power output of 13,600 kW (18,230 hp), enabling it to reach a speed of 400 km/h (285 mph) with ease, as a result of having more power and a higher gear ratio than the original ICE 2 train. Theoretically the ICE-S

Above: The modern instrument panel of the ICE traction unit.
Opposite age: The ICE is reliable even in extreme conditions. Here it is climbing the Geislinger mountain section at -20 °C (-4 °F).

could reach even higher speeds, and a new track speed record is therefore now well within the realm of possibilities.

But the DB had also been pursuing an entirely different concept that did not originally fit into the ICE family. Even away from the new sections of track, it was argued that new five- to seven-part trains should be able to speed up long distance traffic on existing lines. An effective way of raising speeds and shortening travelling times was the use of tilting coaches. Since the end of the 1980s the so-called "Pendolini" had been a great success. These trains tilted on curves, like motorbikes cornering, thus reducing the unpleasant effect of lateral acceleration on passengers. The Deutsche Bahn notched up its first success using this technique in 1992 with the German Pendolino Series 160, which considerably speeded up local traffic on sections east of Nuremberg. The great demand for using the tilting technique in long distance trains prompted the DB to develop the IC-T trains. As had previously been done in the legendary Series 403 of 1973, the engineers distributed the drive over the whole train. It is still not known whether the "T" in IC-T stands "Triebwagen" (railcar) or "tilting" train.

Denmark produced a very individual railcar, known as the "Flexliner". This was one of the first trains to be built in modules. Constructed by ABB Scandia, it was available with electric or diesel propulsion according to choice. The Flexliner can be used as three-part IC 3 with a top speed of 180 km/h (112 mph) but also as two-part regional railcar. At 20 m (65'7") the coaches are comparatively short but pleasantly wide, with a width of 3.10 m (9'11"). The most striking feature of the "Flexliner" are the rubber beads on the front parts. When two trains coupled together are running as a unit, the staff can remove the fronts of the driver's cabs. As a result it is possible to have a communicating passage between the two parts of the train, unlike the German ICE that can only form a set of through coaches. Up to five units can be coupled together to form a long train, and even mixed operation of electric and diesel units is possible. The whole train is built of light aluminium, and the engineers were able to reduce the weight further by the use of Jacobs bogies. The unladen weight of the IC3 is 620 kg (0.7 tons) per seat, while in comparison the German ICE 1 is 1,180 kg (1.3 tons) per seat. As a result two diesel engines of 294 kW (394 hp) each are enough to accelerate the train. The "Flexliner" concept convinced

The Danish Flexliner has a somewhat unusual appearance.

not only the Danes but also the Swedish, Spanish and Israeli railways, all of which ordered trains. However ABB, which became ADtranz in 1996, was unable to convince the German railways of the advantages of this concept.

Whatever the answer to this riddle may be, there is no doubt that conceptually the IC-T trains have been influenced by earlier ICE generations. The DB put the first of these IC-T trains with a top speed of 230 km/h (143 mph) into service on the Stuttgart-Zürich line in 1999. The DB changed the designation of the train to ICE-T . Gradually the five-part 415 and seven-part 411 acquired all the characteristics of offspring of the ICE-family. While the five-part 415 shared its territory between Stuttgart and Zurich with the Series ETR 480 Cisalpino railcar, the 411 became the undisputed star of ICE line 8 from Munich to Berlin as well as line 9 between Dresden and Saarbrücken. But no further developments of the comfortable ICEs with tilting coaches are to be expected. Accountants have pointed out that the maintenance of the train is very expensive and that in order to be profitable the trains should always be filled to capacity, which of course is easier said than done. The DB is currently looking for more economical alternatives.

ICN: the Swiss version of the tilting technique

The hot favourite to succeed using the tilting coach technique is the Swiss ICN. This too is an electric railcar with tilting coaches but with comparatively spartan fittings. Since the timetable change on 28 May 2000, the train has been running on the Jura-Südfuss line between Geneva, Biel, Zurich and St Gallen. Initially Swiss Railways used the railcar for some trains only in existing timetables because there were not enough vehicles to provide a full service. Indeed, passengers had to make do without a restaurant car.

At first Schweizerischen Bundesbahnen ordered 24 railcars. But after ADtranz announced that it was closing down its factory in Switzerland, the SBB was forced to look for alternatives. Moreover, ADtranz did not want to depend on just one customer, so it developed the ICN into a European train with tilting coaches. The manufacturers offered the 200 km/h (124 mph) "Crusaris ECN" as a single or dual-voltage traction unit with an output of up to 5,200 kW (6,971 hp).

The ICE 3

A year after the première of the ICE-T, the ICE 3 made its debut. As a tribute to the innovative InterCity railcars of the early 1970s it was given the series number 403. The ICE-T trains were already much more elegant than the earlier ICE generations, and the ICE 3 was even more streamlined. Its elegant, flattened nose is now synonymous with the high-speed image of the ICE 3. Technically, the trains are capable of reaching 330 km/h (205 mph), but on their everyday journeys on the new line between Frankfurt and Cologne they travel at 300 km/h (186 mph). As with the ICE-T trains, the ICE 3 has no separate locomotive to obstruct the passengers' view of the track. The first and second class passengers sit on slightly raised seats in special lounges, as if in a cinema, enjoying a panoramic view of the track above the shoulders of the driver. The eight-part units consist of two three-part traction units and two intermediate coaches without drives. The traction units consist of the motorized end-coach, the transformer coach without drive and then the motorized phase converter coach. The high degree of motorization with half the axles being driven means that the ICE 3 is capable of reaching a speed of 330 km/h (205 mph) on the new steep stretch between Frankfurt and Cologne.

The DB now has 37 Series 403 trains that are mostly used as a twin units. As well as the trains suited only to the 15,000 volt system, the DB ha also acquired 13 multi-voltage trains, which in principle could be used on all European overhead contact lines. Four structurally similar trains are also used by the Dutch railways. They only differ from their DB counterparts in having the blue Dutch double-arrow logo as well as different wording on the restaurant car. The ICE 3 provided special train services to the Hanover Expo 2000, passing this acid test and increasingly replacing the remaining locomotive-hauled InterCity trains . While the ICE-T and ICE 3 are the latest generations of ICE trains, the fourth ICE generation is currently being created in the design offices of the main train constructors.

France's TGV-family

Originally the Deutsche Bahn and the SNCF (French Railways) wanted to cooperate. The aim was to build a train that would be a cross between the ICE and the TGV, the French high speed train, the first generation of which appeared in 1981.

Fifteen years earlier the SNCF had proposed a programme studying the "possibilities of the technical renovation of the railways with a new infrastructure". The aim was to develop a new network of high speed trains consisting of new and modernized stretches spreading from Paris out into the whole country. This project clearly reflected the political and administrative structure in France. The geography of the country is such that all roads lead to Paris in any case, unlike the German situation where it was necessary to

Above: The DB has put its most modern train, the ICE-3, into service on the line connecting Berlin to Munich. The journey is very pleasant, especially in first class.

Left: The Swiss tilting train design is the ICN. It travels fast on winding stretches without causing any discomfort to the passengers.

Above: In the winter months a Eurostar train takes winter sports enthusiasts from London via Brussels to Bourg St Maurice in the French Alps. The train only travels on Saturdays.

Opposite page: A TGV Duplex carrying holidaymakers from London to the French Alps. This photograph was taken in Albertville in April 1999.

Below: The Eurostar's usual routes connect London with Brussels and Paris through the Channel Tunnel.

create a dense high-speed train network linking numerous cities of various sizes. In 1967 a prototype gas turbine-powered vehicle for test purposes was produced. Technically the concept was very convincing, but it was less so financially because gas turbines consumed too much fuel. When oil prices began to rise in the mid-1970s the SNCF finally filed the turbine propulsion proposal away. It was evident that the future lay with electric locomotives, particularly since the power needed would largely come from nuclear power stations to which the French government was strongly committed. Electricity was therefore relatively inexpensive.

The first "Train à Grande Vitesse" (TGV) or "High-speed train" undertook its trial run in 1972. The articulated train with Jacobs bogies performed extremely well. The aerodynamics were improved considerably when the coaches were attached very closely to each other, which also improved the riding stability. The traction motors were fixed to the frame and cardan shafts transferred the power across to the four driving axles of the driving unit. A high-voltage line housed on the roof supplied the other driving unit with current.

The TGV breaks the world record

In 1976 the SNCF ordered two prototypes of the TGV from Alsthom Atlantique and Francorail MTE. These were ready for trial runs in 1978. It was at about the same time that the building of the Paris-Lyons high-speed line began, a line that was to be used exclusively for passenger trains. This allowed uphill gradients of up to 1 in 28.6. The stretch was electrified with 25,000-volt alternating current with a frequency of 50 cycles. The manufacturer also equipped the first generation of TGVs to run on direct current of 1,500 volts, the power supply used elsewhere in France. Because a few trains were to travel from Lyons to Lausanne, eight of them were also fitted with special components for the central European supply of 15,000-volt alternating current with a frequency of 16.67 cycles.

In 1981 the SNCF inaugurated the high-speed line with the TGV PSE. "PSE" stood for "Paris-Sud-Est", "Paris-South-East". Customers greeted the scheme with enthusiasm. In the first year the number of passengers rose from 14,000 a day to 55,000 a day. The SNCF gradually expanded its high-speed network. In 1989, the second generation was launched in the shape of the TGV "Atlantique", its name indicating the destination of the train. The maximum speed rose from 270 to 300 km/h (168 to 186 mph) and the output was doubled to 8800 kW (11,796 hp). This enabled the number of intermediate coaches to be increased from eight to ten. The train was now fitted with GTO-thyristor control. The new air-suspension greatly increased the passengers' comfort. The SNCF carried out trials with the specially adapted TGV A 325, which first reached a top speed of 482 km/h (299 mph) and later the breathtaking speed of 515 km/h (320 mph) — a world record.

In 1992 the SNCF inaugurated the Paris-Lille line. Because one part of the train was to travel to Brussels, 30 trains were fitted with equipment to operate on the Belgian supply, 3,000-volt direct current. In 1993 a new TGV, the 20-part "Eurostar", attracted wide interest. Because it was designed to operate on the English side of the Channel, it was also equipped to run on a direct current supply of 750 volts, which was prevalent in England. It also fitted within the narrower British loading gauge. Initially it was fitted with Alsthom asynchronous motors, together producing an output of 12,240 kW (16,408 hp).

Four countries were accessible to the "Thalys" train, launched in 1996; from Paris it travelled via Brussels to Amsterdam and Cologne. Eighteen of them were produced. The driving units produced 8,800 kW (11,796 hp). The SNCF ordered 30 sets of the TGV "Duplex" train. This did not indicate that it

Above: The TGV EuroCity express on the Milan-Paris section, photographed on the Mont Cenis.

Right: A leading light of the railways: the Thalys connects Paris and Cologne.

was twice as long as its predecessor — it is in fact the same length. It was given this name because of its double-deck intermediate coaches, which increased the number of seats by about 40%.

The trains of the TGV family travel not only on high-speed stretches but also on lines with lower speeds, for instance, as far as the ski-ing areas in the Alps, Italy and Switzerland. The SBB has its own motor-coach train in the shape of the TGV PSE 112.

The SNCF is planning to increase the TGV's top speed even further. With three-phase asynchronous current the TGV is expected to reach a maximum speed of 360 km/h (224 hp). There is even talk of a maximum speed of 400 km/h (248 mph) but it is not yet clear when this will come into effect.

The original "Pendolini"

The French "Thalys" runs regularly to Cologne as does the Danish IC3, while the Dutch railways have bought several dual-voltage ICE trains specially to run its trains into the Ruhr region and to Berlin. Stuttgart too has access to the world of modern railways with the Italian-Swiss "Cisalpino". This tilting train provides a service to Zurich and on to Milan and is a descendant of the celebrated "Pendolino" family.

The active hydraulically tilting body was developed by Fiat Ferroviaria, part of the enterprise that owns the famous car manufacturer. This division now belongs to the French group Alsthom. In 1988, after lengthy trials, the Italian State Railways put the first motor-coach trains of the ETR 450 series into service.

The ETR 450 consists of four two-part traction units and a non-motor-ized restaurant car. Because the drive is distributed over the whole train,

TGV PSE, Atlantique, Eurostar, Thalys and Duplex					
Wheel arrangement	Driving unit Bo'Bo'; PSE with front and rear driving trailers				
First delivery	1978	1989	1993	1996	1996
Last delivery	1985	1992	1994	1997	1998
Withdrawn from service	–	–	–	–	–
Quantity	109	105	16	16	30
Length overall	200.19m (656'9")	237.59m (779'6")	393.72m (1219'9")	200.19m (656'9")	200.19m (656'9")
Total wheelbase	Driving unit: 17m (55'9"); Driving trailer: 21.7m (71'2")				
Bogie wheelbase	both 0.920 m (3'0")				
Working weight	418t (460.8 tons)	484t (533.5 tons)	816t (899.5 tons)	424t (467.4 tons)	424t (467.4 tons)
Maximum speed	270km/h (168mph)	300km/h (186mph)	300km/h (186mph)	300km/h (186mph)	300km/h (186mph)
1-hour rating	6450kW (8646hp)	8800kW (11796hp)	12240kW (16408hp)	8800kW (11796hp)	8800kW (11796hp)

Above: The elegant CIS seen rounding a bend, making its way up Monte Ceneri.

Right: A pair of CIS trains links Milan to Stuttgart via the Gotthard on a daily basis.

the axle-loading remains low, which is a prerequisite for tilting trains. Trains reach a maximum speed of 250 km/h (155 mph) between Rome and Florence on the newly built "Dirittissima" line. Even on older lines, the trains are able to reach higher speeds than before thanks to the tilting technique which prevents the passengers suffering any discomfort to . This is in fact the only advantage of the tilting technique. The forces affecting the train in curves are not compensated for by the tilting technique; on the contrary, using the tilting technique, the lateral acceleration is up to 2 m/s^2 (6.56 ft/s^2) higher than in conventional trains where it is 1 m/s^2 (3.28 ft/s^2). The limit beyond which there is a danger of derailing the train is 2.5 m/s^2 (8.2 ft/s^2).

In 1974 Fiat delivered the first Pendolino with a further developed and improved tilting system, the ETR 460. This too reached a maximum speed of 250 km/h (155 mph). Three of the ten nine-part units were equipped as dual-voltage trains. These were designed to run a service connecting Turin, where the trains operate on 3,000 volts direct current, to Lyons, where the voltage is half as much. On 29 September 1996 they ran on the Mont Cenis line. Travelling time was 3 hours and 40 minutes, which meant a reduction of half an hour. Because a top speed of 250 km/h (155 mph) was not required on mountain stretches the gear ratio was changed so that the 460 twin-voltage traction unit has a maximum speed of 200 km/h (124 mph).

The nine nine-part sets of the ETR 470 ordered by the Italian-Swiss company Cisalpino have the same top speed. At first this train ran as a shuttle between Milan and Geneva and between Milan and Zurich, until the line to Stuttgart was adapted for tilting trains. Instead of being equipped for the French electricity system, it has components that make it compatible with the central European system. The transformer for this purpose is placed under the non-motorized restaurant car. Like the Pendolino it had regenerative braking, able to redirect the energy created by the electric braking effort back into the network. In addition it also had electro-magnetic rail brakes. Fiat has also sold tilting trains abroad to customers including the Finnish and Czech railway systems.

The star of Italian Railways did not need a tilting system. For the Diritissima line the FS bought 30 Series ETR 500 motor-coach trains, which could reach a top speed of 300 km/h (186 mph). These were only compatible with the existing Italian electricity supply system. In addition, the FS has put 30 dual-voltage ETR-500s with two driving units and eleven intermediate coaches into service. This is because in the future, Italy is planning to build new sections of track with 25,000-volt alternating current and a frequency of 50 cycles.

Above: In the observation car travelling through the wild Rhine gorge.
Opposite page: The climax of the journey in the Glacier Express is the Landwasser viaduct and the Landwasser tunnel that follows it.

The railways of Switzerland boast "the slowest express train in the world", with an average speed of only about 35 km/h (22 mph). This is the famous Glacier Express, a run of 285 km (177 miles) on metre-gauge (3' 3") track that lasts almost eight hours. It begins in St Moritz in the Upper Engadine and finishes in Zermatt at the foot of the Matterhorn. The route consists of three sections belonging to very different railway companies: the Rhätischen Bahn (RhB), the Furka-Oberalpbahn (FO) and the Brig-Visp-Zermatt Bahn (BVZ). The Glacier Express is the result of close cooperation between these three companies. The coaches are unchanged throughout, but the locomotive must be changed where the FO meets the RhB. This is necessitated and justified by the different technical characteristics of the different section of the route s. The RhB has a maximum gradient of 1 in 28.6 and uses pure adhesion throughout. But the other two lines have sections with gradients of up to 1 in 9 (FO) and 1 in 8 (BVZ). These have Abt system rack sections and therefore require appropriately equipped locomotives.

A modern concept: the Ge 4/4 IIIs

The locomotive used in the RhB section is the Ge 4/4 III. Since 1989, 15 examples of this series have been ordered. This dates back to the KTU design created by SLM and BBC, which developed a "2000" locomotive for private lines. "KTU" stands for "Konzessionierte Transport-Unternehmungen", meaning "licensed transport undertakings". Originally, the KTU locos were built to run on standard gauge tracks, but interest from narrow gauge lines such as the RhB and the MOB (Montreux-Berner-Oberlandbahn) led to narrow gauge variations. Since the locos were modular in construction this was no problem, and the RhB narrow gauge variants also catered for different electrical supplies. Between 1973 and 1985 the RhB had already acquired 23 Ge 4/4 IIs, but with the constant development of technology these were no longer up-to-date. The management therefore decided to order a modern locomotive with efficient electronics immediately. Among other things, these were intended

for the new line through the Vereina tunnel. The RhB locomotive has a compact, futuristic appearance with its square lights and its striking, box-like body 15.4 m (50' 5") long. The powerful, red-painted locomotive proved ideal for carrying advertising messages, which have been painted or pasted on its large, smooth sides since 1995. Among the most attractive designs is one for a Graubünden cement plant that includes graceful ibexes, the animals of the coat of arms of the canton. Another loco carries an advertisement promoting RhB's own Heidiland-Bernina Express. But all Ge 4/4 IIIs have one thing in common: each one is resplendent with the name and the coat of arms of a Graubünden commune, as was already the tradition with the Ge 4/4 IIs and Ge 6/6 IIs.

Ge 4/4 II universal loco

As with the younger Ge 4/4 III, the Ge 4/4 IIs of the 1970s from which it was descended were universal locos, used by the RhB for freight traffic as well as passenger duties. The four-axle locos were built by SLM and BBC. The first ten Ge 4/4 IIs were delivered in 1973. Since the RhB was anxious to replace the original rod-driven Ge 6/6 Is, a further 13 locos followed in the 1980s. The locomotives of the first delivery series were painted green. The Ge 4/4 II was the first time that a locomotive of the RhB was fitted with a coupling between the locomotive body and the bogies. The power was transmitted by a traction gear on the body of the locomotive. Electropneumatic cable traction made it possible to balance the axle load in the bogie. The motors operated through a BBC quill drive. A further characteristic of the Ge 4/4 II was its electric rheostatic braking.

The Ge 6/6 II: good for curves

Delivery of the Series Ge 6/6 II began at the end of the 1950s. The locomotive had three bogies with two axles each. This Bo'Bo'Bo' axle arrangement had proved to be an advantage on winding stretches. Furthermore, the Ge 6/6 II has a body divided in the middle and connected through a joint, thus also allowing some vertical movement. The locomotive weight was evenly distributed over the axles, with the flexible centre part rested on the middle bogie, enabling the locomotive to negotiate tight curves easily. The series of locomotives was built by SLM, BBC and MFO and included seven other examples in all. Two prototypes had appeared 1958. A further series of five locos was delivered to the RhB seven years later in 1965. Unlike the two prototypes, the series-produced locomotives had no doors at the front. Consequently, the tripartite front window arrangement was replaced with two front windscreens. In the interests of standardization, the front doors of the two prototype locos were welded shut after delivery of the first series-produced engines. Altogether the six-axle locomotives have proved themselves throughout the RhB network, and still today they are dependable temporary workers when required for either passenger of freight train traffic. So it is not surprising that the Ge 6/6 II can even occasionally be spotted at the head of the Glacier Express.

The HGe 4/4 II mountain-climbing locomotive

Relatively old electric locomotives and railcars were still giving good service on the Furka-Oberalp Bahn (FO) in the 1980s. Some of these dated from the

Above: Locomotive Ge 4/4 II 622 with its observation cars will soon reach Filisur. At weekends and holidays in the high season the Glacier Express becomes a special train, pulling only observation cars over the Rheichenau directly from St Moritz.

Right: Autumn in the Albula valley. Although the days are becoming shorter, the autumn colours of the larches give this wild, romantic valley a special appeal.

Opposite page: This view from the Stulsertobel with its viaducts is only recommended to hikers who have a confident foothold and no tendency to dizziness. Here a Ge 6/6 II of the Rhätische line is seen heading towards the Engadine.

Series Ge 4/4 I, II, III, Ge 6/6 II and HGe 4/4 II				
Wheel arrangement	Bo'Bo'	Bo'Bo'	Bo'Bo'	Bo'Bo'Bo'	Bo'Bo'
First delivery	1947	1973	1993	1958	1985
Last delivery	1953	1980	1999	1965	1990
Withdrawn from service	–	–	–	–	–
Quantity	10	25	19	7	21
Length overall	12.1m (39'8")	12.96m (42'6")	16.1m (52'10")	14.5m (47'7")	14.776m (48'6")
Total wheelbase	6.2m (20'4")	6.2m (20'4")	11.4m (37'5")	11.1m (36'5")	10.34m (33'11")
Bogie wheelbase	2.5m (8'2")	2.3m (7'7")	2.4m (7'10")	2.5m (8'2")	2.98m (9'9")
Wheel diameter	1.07m (3'6")	1.07m (3'6")	1.07m (3'6")	1.07m (3'6")	0.943m (3'1")
Working weight	47t (51.8 tons)	50t (55.1 tons)	72t (79.4 tons)	65t (71.7 tons)	64t (70.6 tons)
Maximum speed	80km/h (50mph)	90km/h (56mph)	120km/h (75mph)	80km/h (50mph)	90/35km/h (56/22mph)
1-hour rating	1176kW (1576hp)	1700kW (2279hp)	2400kW (3217hp)	1764kW (2365hp)	1935kW (2594hp)

early days of the line's electrification. The FO was operated by steam locomotives until 1940, but electric traction has been used since 1941. In fact, it
was not so much the age of the original electric locomotives as their low maximum speed that caused difficulties for the FO. It wanted to acquire faster,
more modern locomotives for its high-profile trains such as the Glacier
Express, thus bringing the route across the Alps up-to-date.

The FO made the same choice as the SBB, which was also ordering new
locos for its narrow-gauge Brünigbahn. Two Series HGe 4/4 II prototypes,
produced by ABB and SLM arrived at the FO in 1985. There were two reasons
for the common procurement of the locomotives by SBB and FO. First, the
unit price could be reduced for the larger quantity. Secondly, the Swiss National Traffic Bureau (BAV), in its role as subsidy provider, had strongly pressed for
a trend towards standardizing the locomotive types of the many Swiss lines.
A third railway company, the BVZ (Brig-Visp-Zermattbahn), also joined in the
purchase. Altogether eight vehicles arrived at the FO, including two from the
Brünig line. These two SBB prototype were handed over to the FO at the end
of 1990. The SBB acquired eight further Series HGe 4/4 II locomotives for the
Brünigbahn, while the BVZ received five locomotives.

Technically the locomotive combines adhesion and rack drive, through an
SLM differential transmission. This drive design puts less wear on the rack, in
that the normal power of adhesion is used as much as possible; in rack sections of the line, one-third of the traction power is transferred to the wheels.
The maximum speed of the HGe 4/4 II is 90 km/h (56 mph) in adhesion sections and 35 km/h (22 mph) in the rack parts. Other characteristics of the
locomotive include the combined traction and speed control, which makes the
driver's task easier, as do the automatic vacuum brakes. There is a single
overhead pantograph and regenerative braking. The locomotive also has an
emergency braking system used on rack sections, which will even bring the
train to a halt if the power is completely cut off. The compressed air and vacuum pumps are powered by the locomotive's battery.

Externally, the locomotives of the different companies have substantially
similar paint schemes. The basic colour is red. The corresponding logo of

Right: One of the most attractive advertising locomotives is this Ge 4/4 III with its ibex
livery, from Wappentier in the canton of Graubünden. It is hauling the
Glacier Express through Schanfig towards Filisur.

Above: At Fiesch in the Obergoms, the landscape becomes more tranquil again. A busy Glacier Express travels downhill towards Brig.

Right: A rack is needed to climb the steep gradient of the Oberalppass. Here an HGe 4/4 II loco advertising Sion's bid for the Winter Olympics is heading downhill.

each railway company appears on the sides. A common identification feature of the series is that all the locomotives have two front windscreens of unequal size.

RhB lines: the Albula valley and the Rhine gorge

The Glacier Express connects Zermatt in the Wallis with St Moritz in the canton of Graubünden. A train of this name was already running in the 1930s. It was in the tradition of the luxury trains of the 1920s, to which the Orient Express belonged. In its present form the Glacier Express has been in operation since 1982. The creation of the railway in the canton of Graubünden was owed not to a a native of Switzerland, but to a Dutch merchant Willem Jan Holsboer, 1834—98, during the golden age of railways. Holsboer had settled in Davos with his wife, whom he had brought there in the hope of easing her tuberculosis. In view of the difficulty of reaching the town, it quickly became apparent to him that a railway link from Landquart through Klosters to Davos would be a great advantage for the Swiss inhabitants as well as for visitors. Holsboer, who had also established the Davos sanitarium, campaigned for the railroad with great commitment and success. After the route of the Landquart-Davos railway (LD) had been completed in 1890, Holsboer fought for the expansion of the Graubünden railway. In the same year, the LD became the concessionaire for the Landquart-Chur-Thusis line, and this was opened on 29 August 1896. Meanwhile, the LD company was reconstituted in

1894 and renamed itself the Rhätische Bahn, RhB. The RhB built the technically interesting St Moritz-Albulapass-Thusis section in the years 1898 to 1904. The Reichenau-Tamins-Ilanz line was opened in 1903, and its extension from Disentis was inaugurated in 1912.

The Glacier Express leaves St Moritz in the early morning. A supplement is charged and reservation is compulsory. Several trains of this category start consecutively, with different kinds of coaches. Since 1993 there have been modern 1st class coaches, with large panoramic windows. Another detail to be noted is the sections of the route on which dining cars will be available. Similar arrangements apply in the reverse direction, leaving from Zermatt. After leaving St Moritz, the train vanishes into two tunnels immediately following one another. The train passes through a wall of rock to emerge into a high wide valley, where the track follows the course of the young river Inn. The next significant stop is Samedan. At an altitude of 1,705 m (5,594 ft) above sea level the line descends towards the Lower Engadine and Pontresina to the Berninabahn.

After Bever, the climb to the Albula tunnel begins. The line turns towards the west in a narrow left curve. Up to the station of Spinas, 1,814 m (5,951 ft), the track runs through the car-free Val Bever for about 3.5 km (2 miles). Immediately behind Spinas, it travels along the right side of the valley to the entrance of the Albula tunnel, 5,864 m (6,413 yards) long. Emerging once more into the daylight, the line enters the Albula valley. Here, the railway

At the Oberalppass - with the FO on the way

The history of the FO began in 1910 with the foundation of the Compagnie suisse de Chemin de fer de la Furka, with a majority of French shareholders. The construction of the line was carried out to French standards which caused some concern, so it came as no surprise that the Swiss Federal Government had eventually to intervene. During World War I, work came to a halt completely and the company went bankrupt. A new company, AG Furka-Oberalp-Bahn, was established in 1925 and work could continue. By 1926, it the OB had succeeded in completing the whole route from Disentis over the Oberalppass to Brig in the Rhône valley, and in that year RhB coaches began running between St Moritz and Brig.

The trip over the 2,033-m (6,670-ft) high Oberalppass exceeds all that has gone previously. The first rack section is immediately behind Disentis. One of the most beautiful viaducts in the FO network is the stone-built Val Bugnei viaduct 106 m (348 ft) long in front of Bugnei station. After this comes Sedrun, 1,441 m (4,728 ft) high. Here there is the opportunity of taking the car transporter to Andermatt. Shortly before the Tschamut-Selva interchange station, the last stop for automobile traffic in the winter, is the start of the longest rack section of the FO line, 6.1-km (4-mile) long. The surrounding landscape is treeless, formed of bare green meadows. Soon the train arrives at the highest point of the Glacier Express route, Oberalppass station at an altitude of 2,033 m (6,670 ft) high. It lies amid a desolate rocky, grassy landscape by a reservoir.

In its first years of business, FO trains operated only during the summer months. When winter working was planned, several sections had to be fitted with protective constructions, such as the avalanche galleries at the Oberalpsee.

Still at a height of about 2,000 m (6,500 ft), the track proceeds gently down from Passhöhe to the station at Nätschen, 1,843 m (6,047 ft). The next dramatic valley is soon reached, and this is the most exciting section of the FO line. The steep descent takes place in three tight bends after Andermatt. Again, the locomotive latches itself onto the rack. Slowly it descends as the valley widens below, with the gleaming roofs of Andermatt. Arriving at the bottom of the valley, the track follows the line of the Furkareuss which it crosses several times on the way to Realp. Then the line vanishes into the long Furka-Basis tunnel, which is 15,442 m (16,888 yards) long. The train emerges into the daylight again shortly before Oberwald. The tunnel has been open since 1982, having taken nine years to build. With car transporter facilities in Realp and Oberwald, this complements the similar facilities of the BLS-Lötschberg tunnel. Either tunnel can be used to reach the Rhône valley.

The Furka tunnel handles traffic throughout the year, and its opening marked the end of operations for the cost-intensive Furka mountain railway, which — in summer only — reached a height of 2,160 m (7,087 ft). Since 1993 this wonderful section has been under restoration by the Furka Mountain Railway Steam Society. This was founded in 1983 by a number of active railway enthusiasts, and has energetically given much help in repairing the old rack section.

The FO line follows the young river Rhône from Oberwald. Immediately

provides a spectacular drama along the Albula river: a combination of winding tunnels and hairpin bends, repeatedly revealing new views and thoroughly confusing the passenger's sense of direction. The train only finishes its gyroscopic course at Bergün.

The station of Filisur is reached after a journey of about one hour. Here the Albula line and the line from Davos meet. Shortly after leaving the station in the direction of Thusis, the train dives into a tunnel. The tunnel exit connects directly to the Landwasser viaduct, an elegant construction 130 m (427 ft) long and 65 m (213 ft) high. A little later, it is followed by the Schmittentobel viaduct 137 m (449 ft) long. Both viaducts are built of stonework. Passing Alvaneu and Tiefencastel, the line follows the Albula river through the Schin valley and further on to Thusis. The Rhb's tallest construction is shortly beyond Tiefencastel. It is the Solis bridge, 164 m (538 ft) long, spanning the Schin valley at a height of 85 m (279 ft). At Thusis, the Albula runs into the Hinterrhein, which accompanies the line to Reichenau-Tamins.

From Reichenau-Tamins, the line follows the Rhine gorge, Switzerland's "Grand Canyon". After a few more minutes the Felsental is reached, where the river and the line are framed by the rock. As the train progresses the rock formations become increasingly bizarre. The unique river landscape about 15 km (9 miles) long loses its wild quality shortly before Ilanz. About 30 minutes later, the train arrives at Disentis. At this station, the "draught horses" are changed, the RhB engine being exchanged for an FO rack locomotive. This is because the FO section that follows has gradients that are too steep to be handled by an adhesion locomotive.

after the end of the tunnel, the track crosses a bridge 59 m (65 yards) long over a mountain stream. This has its source in the Rhône glacier, which can be admired from the old Furka line. The train manages the easy descent to the health resort of Fiesch almost entirely without needing the rack. There is just a short rack section to provide assistance between Bellwald and Fiesch. After the next station, Lax, 1,045 m (3,428 ft), there are two further rack sections, with gradients of 1 in 10 and 1 in 15, and a curved tunnel before the station of Grengiols. The train arrives at the little town of Brig in the canton of Wallis after a descent of about 400 m (1,300 ft).

The BVZ line to Zermatt

The railway station area at Brig is a very interesting place. The standard-gauge tracks of the SBB-Simplonbahn and the BLS as well as the metre-gauge tracks of both the FO and the BVZ all meet here. The platforms for the two mountain-climbers are located on the railway station forecourt while the standard-gauge trains are behind the reception building.

A trip to Zermatt on the BVZ line has been possible since 1930, while the Visp-Zermatt connection had been in existence since 1891. In 1886 a banker from Lausanne had requested the concession for a railway line from Visp to Zermatt. He wanted to cater for the increasing number of tourists who had heard about one of the most beautiful summits of the Switzerland, the Matterhorn, 4,478 m (14,692 ft) high. The line was intended to allow them to experience the sight of it from close at hand. Work started on the line in 1888. Three years later the railway to Zermatt was ready. The construction of the additional section from Visp to Brig, which by then was the only gap in the line between Zermatt and St Moritz, began in the 1920s and it was opened in 1930.

The train encounters six rack sections on its trip of 27 km (17 miles). The FO locomotive is changed for a BVZ one at the station. This now pulls the coaches over Visp through the sunny Vispertal. After 25 minutes, the train arrives at the first Abt rack section, in the vicinity of Stalden station. The terrain becomes visibly narrower as the train begins its trip through the Kipfen valley. The river bed of the young Vispa and the track cling closely together,

seeking a way through the rocky landscape. Often, however, the track cannot follow the same route as the water, and in this situation tunnels follow one another frequently. Shortly before Kalpetran the line crosses a deeply-cut ravine on an elegant, concrete bridge 67 m (73 yards) long. The line crosses the river Vispa several times on its way to Zermatt. Through the panoramic windows of the Glacier Express there are magnificent views on both sides of the track, including many mountain peaks of 4,000 m (13,000 ft) and more. After the small stations of St Niklaus, Herbriggen and Randa comes the larger station of Täsch, which can be reached by car. An enormous parking area means that it is possible to leave the car here and continue to the car-free town of Zermatt by rail.

This last section of the line is protected by avalanche galleries, so the view to the left of the train into the valley below is hardly possible any more. However, Zermatt is reached in a mere 11 minutes, and the magnificent journey of the Glacier Express ends in its dark station hall. The avalanche protection was constructed in the 1980s. It is undeniably ugly but of course it provides essential protection for the permanent way and the trains from devastating falls of snow.

The final stage of the journey can be enjoyed by leaving the concourse of the station and walking to the inconspicuous station building of the Gorner-gratbahn that is located nearby. This is a rack railway 9 km (6 miles) long, opened in 1898. Within three-quarters of an hour, the brown railcars climb to an altitude of 3,089 m (10,135 ft).

The Glacier Express sets off on its return journey to St Moritz early in the morning of the next day.

Right: Near Hospental, an HGe 4/4 II of the FO hauls the Glacier Express towards the Furka tunnel.

Above: The powerful, modern HGe 4/4 II is also in service with the BVZ.

Opposite page: Not far from Disentis, this HGe 4/4 II 102 of the FO has passed the first rack section and is now tackling a less severe gradient. The picture was taken on 3 October 1998.

Above: Only one pair of passenger trains runs daily through Alaska. Its route is between Anchorage and Fairbanks.

Right: This heavy freight train hauls itself along the tracks through the unique panorama of Alsaka's wild landscape.

Alaska's rail traffic is shaped by the government-owned Alaska Railroad, 850 km (528 miles) long. This railroad was not the first to be constructed in the largest state of the United States, but it has turned out to be the most influential and reliable.

In the year 1867, the United States purchased the country from Russia for the sum of 7.2 million gold dollars. The area of Alaska is 1.5 million km^2 (580,000 square miles), but its population is only 546,000. In the short summers the nights are light while during the long winters the sun barely manages to rise above the horizon. More than half of all the glaciers in the world are in Alaska, and there are many wide valleys that never lose their snow and ice. Many species of animal have found a habitat in this apparently inhospitable wilderness and the country is also rich in mineral resources, as the famous gold rush at the end of the 19th century demonstrated. Soon after, efforts were made to extract timber from the vast forests. Both were frustrated by the fact that no means of transport yet existed.

The way to the gold diggers' city

What was wanted was line connecting the cities of the Pacific coast with the gold diggers' city of Fairbanks. So it came about that the Alaska Railroad Commission was established in 1912 and charged with the task of designing a railroad route. The Commission recommended a line with two branches starting from Cordova and Seward, merging into one at Fairbanks. Funds for the construction of the line were approved by Congress in 1914 after passionate debates, the payment finally agreed amounting to US$35 million. The President of the United States Woodrow Wilson appointed three experienced men to the Commission. Travelling on horseback, on foot or by canoe, they explored and surveyed the country. The three pioneers were William Edes, who had already taken part in railroad construction in the American west,

Frederick Mears, who had been involved in the construction of the Panama Canal, and Thomas Riggs Junior, later governor of Alaska.

After a year, their dangerous reconnaissance survey was finished. Immediately they made several proposals. As the starting point they recommended the coastal city of Cordova. Here, a line to the Kennecott copper mine already existed. However the owners of the Copper River & Northwestern Railroad were involved in a political scandal, so the US government of the time decided that it would be imprudent to acquire this line. It therefore limited itself to buying the 72-km (45-miles) long Tanana Valley Railway near Fairbanks.

Seward was proclaimed as the starting point. Here, a railway station building established by merchants from Seattle had already stood since 1904. From it some railroad tracks led into the interior. Also with the goal of reaching Fairbanks, the Alaska Northern Railway had already built 114 km (71 miles) of track from Seward as far as Kern Bay on the Turnagain Arm. The Federal Government began construction of its line at the end of April 1915.

Camps for thousands

Hosts of workers came to Alaska to earn money working on constructing the railroad. The city of Anchorage developed from the first camp that was set up for the workers. Two years after building began, there were already 4,500 people toiling to construct the Alaska railroad. Log cabins, locomotive supply depots, sawmills and hospitals sprang up along the route.

The toughest part of the railroad to build was the section 48 km (30 miles) long at Turnagain Arm, between Kern and Potter. Wooden bridges had to be erected over the Susitna and Tanana rivers. The most spectacular construction consisted of the great curves between Grandview, the highest point of the line through the Kenai mountains, and the tunnel at mile 51 (82 km). This involved building five wooden bridges and a heated tunnel. The maintenance of this section was very expensive and it only remained open until 1951 as a result of new management of the railroad. The Alaska Railroad reached its final point on 23 July 1923 when the tracks reached the station at Nenana reaches. The greatest enemies of the railroad builders were the rigours of nature: ice-cold winters and damp summers in which mosquitoes flourished. Often construction took place during the frosty winter months so long as the glaciers were quiet.

The railroad as an institution

As a state enterprise, the US Government subsidized the Alaska Railroad and charged it with important duties in the public interest. The railway workers were to be guaranteed essential care and agriculture was to be supported. So, the Alaska Railroad owned its own dairy and other food businesses. In addition, it had to handle the sale of state properties, and build power stations and schools. It was also charged with encouraging the

Left: A mixed freight train hauled by four diesel locomotives crossing a steel girder bridge near Portage.

Above: At marker post 358.1, the "Denali Express" reaches the station at Hedy. The train is on its way to Fairbanks.

Opposite page: Tanker wagons are the daily bread of the Alaska Railroad. These come from Prudhoe Bay and are travelling across the Broad Pass.

opening up of the country to tourists. Brochures were published promoting visits to the Denali National Parks or the recreation areas of the Talkeetna Mountains.

During World War II, the Alaska Railroad transported materials and troops from Anchorage and Fairbanks. Alaska was the most important base for the US Army in the Pacific. During the war, a line 19 km (12 miles) long was built from Portage to the ice-free harbour of Whittier where the army set up a petroleum depot. Today, this is an important harbour for passenger and freight traffic. Freight wagons arrive in Whittier from Seattle and Prince Rupert. They belong to the various railroad companies, so many foreign wagons are to be found on the stretches of the Alaska Railroad. After Whittier there is no road connection; everything and everyone travels by the railroad that runs along two valleys and two tunnels through the Chugach Mountains. After end of war, the track beyond Whittier was taken up, but during the Cold War it experienced a renaissance. The United States government restored and reopened it at a cost of $100 million. Today, the route is the most-used line of the Alaska Railroad.

Panorama on polar-nights

The show train of the Alaska Railroad is the "Denali Express." This runs daily and covers the distance between Anchorage and Fairbanks in nine hours.

The locomotives and the coaches are painted in dark blue and yellow colours. On leaving Anchorage, the view is at first fairly monotonous. Then the installations the Elmendorf Air Force Base spread out along the tracks. About 64 km (40 miles) further on the line reaches Manatuska, a centre of fruit and vegetable growing. At mile 159.8 (257 km) the view becomes spectacular as the train passes by a branch of Cook Inlet. Then it passes the village of Wasilla, the home of several celebrated dog sleigh teams. After this, the train glides through extensive forests where cedars, firs and gigantic Sitka spruces line the track. The surface of the tundra appears frequently along the track, changing in the short arctic summer into colourful carpets of flowers.

At Nancy, the landscape is marked with several lakes. The loudspeakers announce that the most beautiful view is soon approaching, at mile 224.3 (139 km). In clear weather the snow-covered peaks of Denali, 6,193 m (20,318 ft), Hunter, 4,530 m (14,862 ft), Foraker, 5,151 m (16,900 ft), Russel, 3,515 m (8,251 ft), and Dall, 2,720 m (8,924 ft) can be seen and marvelled at. The panorama is unique above all on summer nights, when the sun in these polar regions never completely sets. The giant mountains are very likely to form their own clouds during the day, thus preventing a clear view, but during the night they are cloud-free. The white man named Denali Mount McKinley, but today once more it bears its Indian name Denali ("the tall one).

A station in a ghost town

An astonishing view greets the traveller through the compartment window on entering Talkeetna station. The town still looks exactly as it did in the time of the pioneers. The "Fairview Inn" is an early example of a railway hotel and restaurant. Today, the log cabins of Talkeetna are popular base stations for mountain climbers from all over the world. At mile 248 (154 km) lies the ghost town of Curry. In earlier times the trip to Fairbanks still lasted two days, so the passengers would make an overnight stop at the railway hotel. Beyond Curry is the Hurricane ravine, which the train crosses on a steel truss viaduct 90 m (295 ft) high and 280 m (919 ft) long. At mile 304 (489 km) the terrain becomes a tree-less plateau. That "Denali Express" drives over the Broad Pass, the lowest passage across the Rocky Mountain chain. About 16 km (10 miles) further on, at Summit, is the continental watershed. The water of the Summit lake flows on one side to the Pacific and on the other to the Bering Sea. The next remarkable construction is the steel truss bridge over the Riley. Then it is not far to the Denali National Park, the largest magnet for tourism in Alaska. Buses transport tourists along gravel tracks within the 24,394 km^2 (9,419 sq miles) of the great wilderness where black bears, grizzly bears, wolves, elks and other rare animals are native. In the summer, the trains stop daily at the Denali National Park station. The journey to Fairbanks is a further 200 km (124 miles) through a wild, enchanting landscape.

Anyone looking for the remains of former Alaska railways should go to the Wrangell-Saint Elias National Park. The only road that leads into the nature reserve is actually the line of the former Copper River & Northwest Railroad.

After the closure of the route end of 1939, the lines themselves were simply removed. A layer of gravel now covers the sleepers or ties in some places, but in many places the old sleepers lie exposed. In the middle of the wilderness are the well-preserved remains of the Gilahina wooden bridge 260 m (284 yards) long, built in 1911.

Elk highway

The operation of the Alaska Railroad is not always an easy matter. In the summer the problem is the luxuriant vegetation, which grows indiscriminately over sleepers and rails, while in winter avalanches and frosted points sometimes cause interruptions to the service. Animals represent another problem, because in winter when everywhere is covered with snow they use the railroad tracks as a highway, and do not always run out the way quickly enough when the danger of a train approaches. Consequently many elks are run over, even though the Alaska Railroad provides the route with a number of feeding stations intended to keep the animals away from the track.

Today it is no longer gold fever that lures people into the arctic wilderness. Since 1968, the world has been aware of Alaska's lavish oil deposits, now often known as "black gold". However, the transport of oil can threaten nature itself, as the tanker accident off Alaska's coast has shown.

Also clearance has started in the most northern jungle on earth, the Tongass National Forest. The felled giant trees are sold mainly as lumber to Japan. Admittedly the wood economy brings new traffic to the railroad, but it also raises the question of interference with the ecosystem of the Arctic.

Above: A Canadian Pacific freight train hauled by four diesel locomotives, all controlled from the leading engine.

Opposite page: The "Rocky Mountaineer" arriving punctually at a crossing point. Before the journey can continue, an obliging freight train must pass.

Someone wrote in the year 1871 that the need for a transcontinental railroad in Canada had been very clearly expressed. Because of its geographical position as the most western province of Canada, British Columbia made a railway connection with the east of the country a condition of it joining the Canadian confederation in 1867. At that time, the inhabitants of British Columbia threatened to join the United States of America instead if the desired railway connection should not occur. In order to hold the country together, the Canadian government therefore ordered the fastest possible construction of a transcontinental line from Montreal to Vancouver, the main city of British Columbia. The track operators would enjoy customs and tax privileges. In addition, the Canadian government transferred to them about 100,000 km² (38,600 sq miles) of land as well as the line itself, a fact that provided excellent starting conditions for the subsequent development of the railroad company, including entry into foreign railroad enterprises.

A city is born

Work on the line began in 1878. The builders worked outwards from Winnipeg in both directions at once. In the year that the Canadian Pacific Railway was founded, 1881, the surveyors finally succeeded in finding a passage for the railroad through the apparently insurmountable Rocky Mountains. A year later, armies of navvies worked on the line through the pass. This section through the Rockies left many workers dead and injured many others. Success was only achieved at the expense of infinite toil and deprivation. The laborious achievements are still commemorated today in some of

the names along the route, such as Calamity Tunnel, Suicide Rapids and Hell's Gate.

On 23 May 1887 the first passenger train set out to travel over the entire route, a journey that took almost six days. In the course of the ceremonies, the small lumberjack settlement at the western extremity of the line was given a venerable name by the then president of the Canadian Pacific: Vancouver. This referred to the English captain George Vancouver, who in 1792 was the first European to discover the bay in which the city named after him would later be fouded. Captain Vancouver had put the bay together with the offshore island and hinterland under British control. As a result of the new railroad the small setlement blossomed immediately. The little trapper and lumberjack villagebecame transformed into a trading centre, since the railroad enabled the timber wood and mineral resources of western Canada's to be transported away to markets elsewhere that welcomed them.

Downward enormous trains

The route by which the transcontinental railroad first crossed the Rocky Mountains is impressive. The line between Golden and Banff goes through Kicking Horse Pass, until 1908 the steepest route in North America. This section was consequently also known as "Big Hill". Trains heading to the east were pushed up the climb by four steam locomotives, often facing problems with the quantity of rolling stock in the narrow passes and long obstructions of the single-track route as a result. But worse problems faced the trains driving westwards. Their journey often proved to be a descent into hell. The first test train on this route was derailed and fell in the Columbia River. As a result, three escape sections were installed, in which the "runaway trains" could be brought to a halt. However, these escape sections quickly turned Big Hill into a scrap metal area full of wrecked trains.

It was therefore time to think of another solution. This came from Switzerland. There, similar problems on the Gotthard line had been solved by using spiral-shaped tunnels. So, the railroad-engineer J. E. Schwitzer designed two such curved tunnels for the Kicking Horse Pass. The new line had a figure-of-eight shape and extended the route to such an extent that the gradient could be reduced by about the half. The construction of this less-demanding route through the pass took 20 months and it was handed over for traffic in 1908. Several avalanche-protection galleries were also erected at the same the time to provide as much protection as possible against the wilder forces of nature on the mountain sections. A visitor terrace was built opposite the Lower Spiral Tunnel in the Yoho National Park. From there is a dramatic spectacle is to be seen if a long freight train happens to be winding down from the heights of the Kicking Horse Pass. From this viewpoint both ends of the tunnel are in sight, and the double-headed locos become visible at one end while its boxcars are still vanishing into the tunnel entrance to the inside of the mountain at the other.

The original Big Hill section later came to form part of the Trans-Canada Highway, on which today gigantic trucks thunder up and down, still with some element of risk.

The railroad companies: CP, CN and VIA

The government established the state-owned Canadian National Railways (CN) as a competitive counterpart to the privately-owned Canadian Pacific Railway (CP). This was because the government did not want to see all the transcontinental traffic in the hand of the mighty Canadian Pacific alone. The track network of the CN increased to 38,454 km (23,895 miles) by 1981 through the incorporation of smaller lines. At this time the Canadian Pacific network amounted to about 27,000 km (16,800 miles). It had long developed into a gigantic concern of which the railroad formed only one part; the company also owned shipping lines, airlines, hotels and other enterprises.

Another railway company was founded in 1977, VIA Rail Canada, whose locomotives are a brightly identified by their canary yellow fronts. Like AMTRAK in the United States, VIA is intended to operate the whole of the country's long distance traffic.

Concurrent trains

Returning to the Rocky Mountains, over many decades the "Canadian" and the "Super Continental" were the star trains of the CP and the CN, dominating the transcontinental line. In the 1990s, trains of the Great Canadian Railtour Company with their blue and white locos flourished on the scenically impressive stretches from Vancouver to Banff and Calgary. The trains running in the summer months carry the proud name "Rocky

Right: The "Rocky Mountaineer" is the only passenger train that passes through the Banff National Park. It runs from the end of May to until October. The journey lasts two days, stopping overnight stops in hotels.

Mountaineer." The Great Canadian Railtour of Company was established in 1990 by businessmen from Vancouver. Also, VIA has been offering attractive trips on the Vancouver-Toronto line since 1992. VIA has revived the famous "Canadian" again. However, for reasons of cost it does not take the CP line over Big Hill but follows theCN line Vancouver-Edmonton-Saskatoon-Winnipeg-Toronto . The rolling stock of the "Canadian" consists of genuine restored original Streamliners. The silver-coloured coaches with their corrugated exteriors date from the 1950s. There are ordinary compartments and the "Silver & Blue Class", the latter standing for maximum comfort.

On the 4,424 km (2,749 miles) of the route, the traveller can enjoy the view from one of the Dome cars. These are special coaches with an elevated seating platform and a glass dome roof. From them the spectacular view of the landscape panorama can be enjoyed unhindered. The comfortable Streamliner coaches are of Art Deco design with their own sleeping and day compartments, and an exclusive dining car is included. The trip from Vancouver to Toronto lasts 65 hours 55 minutes. Even the starting points of the journey have an air of exclusivity: Union Station in Vancouver and its counterpart of the same name in Toronto date from the early days time of the great railway companies. In Toronto, the citizens were responsible for the purchase and restoration of their railway station. The railway station in Vancouver is just as impressive. Today the two buildings dating from the 1920s are protected monuments. Consequently, the traveller today can still admire the magnificent foyers and share in the luxurious ambience of the "Canadians". At Vancouver the "Canadian" coming from Toronto is shunted over a triangle of track before arriving at the railway station, so that it enters backwards before coming to a standstill in the arrival hall. This is a service for the "Silver & Blue" class, whose travellers can step straight out onto the concourse.

Unfortunately, only few of the fashionable Streamliner coaches exist. Consequently, the "Canadian" has a only a limited number of places available, and in summer and early autumn the trips of the star train are always fully booked, so reservation well in advance is recommended. For the railway enthusiast planning a tour that also includes parts of the United States, there is the possibility of proceeding from Vancouver by AMTRAK trains. A pair of trains of the US rail company runs daily to Seattle and further into the interior of the country.

Freight traffic and nostalgia trips

So far as freight traffic is concerned, this is divided between Canadian Pacific, Canadian National Railways and the state railway of the province of British Columbia (BC Rail) among others. On its network 2,000 km (1,250 miles) long, the BC transports timber and coal from the north of the province mainly to Vancouver. There is also a passenger service on the scenically attractive route through the coastal mountain range to Prince George. In the summer months, BC Rail runs nostalgia trips with steam-hauled trains on this line.

Left: This Canadian Pacific freight train is hauling a load of grain wagons and container trucks through the spectacular mountain landscape above it.

Above: A Canadian Pacific container train travelling between Red Pass and Yellowhead.

Opposite page: Two Canadian National locomotives hauling their long freight train along the bank of the Thompson River towards Lytton.

In North Vancouver, the beautifully maintained Royal Hudson steam locomotives numbered 2860 and 3716 stand ready to haul one of BC Rail's special trains. The length of the steam train route amounts to 64 km (40 miles) and after Squamish arrives at Howe Sound, which is well worth seeing in itself.

All the railroad companies have one thing in common: apart from the small number of nostalgic steam trains, they exclusively use diesel-electric locomotives on all their lines.

The Canadian Pacific uses the Series DRF-30, with over 2,200 kW (3,000 hp), for example. In contrast to the situation in Europe, freight trains on the North American continent are very long, often reaching a length of over 2 km (1¼ miles), therefore requiring the use of several such diesel locomotives together. VIA uses even more powerful locomotives of 2,600 kW (3,500 hp). The "Canadian" is hauled by two of these yellow-fronted locomotives in double-header formation. In total, over 30% of Canada's freight is transported by rail today.

Rival routes

Curiously, the lines of the CN and CP railways run beside each other from Vancouver to Kamloops. They follow the course of the Fraser River, whose river valley is initially very wide. From the town of Hope onwards the Fraser valley narrows however. Consequently, both lines now squeeze together through the mountains, each on its side of the river, and so they remain for 460 km (286 miles) until Kamloops comes into view. The lines finally separate after Kamloops. The Canadian National route branches off northwards. It follows the course of the North Thompson River and over the Yellowhead Pass reaches the railway station of Jasper. This is in the large national park of the same name, which has an area of 10,800 km² (4,170 sq miles). CN has a small locomotive depot at Jasper. Beyond this, the line descends on the east side of the Rockies towards Edmonton and from there towards the east.

The Canadian Pacific route continues in an eastern direction from Kamloops. Today it is mainly used by freight trains. In Revelstoke there is a small railroad museum, containing CP tender locomotive number 5468, among other exhibits. Beyond Revelstoke the line negotiates the Roger Pass, and shortly before the town of Golden the line crosses the Columbia River. Then comes the steep uphill gradient of the Kicking Horse Pass with its spiral tunnels. The subsequent descent passes through Banff and its National Park to Calgary, the city celebrated for its cowboy rodeos. On the rest of the journey to the east, the train glides for a time through almost unending corn fields that cover the landscape of the Great Plains extending northwards from the USA. The terrain changes its character again as it enters the area of lakes towards Winnipeg.

The crossing of the Rocky Mountains is undoubtedly the most spectacular section of the Canadian transcontinental railways, and the CP was quick to identify tourism as a source of revenue from its early days. The track opened up a huge potential of natural beauty. Therefore, the railroad company built hotels at the foot of the Rockies such as the "Banff Springs" and the "Chateau Lake Louise" that were quickly recognized as among the most elegant and celebrated in the country.

The Northlander

Toronto is also the starting point of a no less interesting track in the north of the country. Since the end of the 1990s a special train leaves Union Station daily including Saturdays, the "Northlander." Its trip to Cochrane 750 km (466 miles) away takes ten hours. The "Northlander" is operated by the province's own railroad, the Ontario Northland Railway (ONR). But since this train makes a loss its future is by no means rosy. Passenger services in Canada and the United States are dominated by the automobile and aeroplane. Many tracks and star trains have had to give way before this reality and have now vanished.

The route of the "Northlander" proceeds through dense forests and reaches the small town of Huntsville with 16,000 inhabitants after two hours and 47 minutes. The area around Huntsville clearly shows why the province deserves its name Ontario, which is Indian for "glittering water". The town lies amid an extensive lakeland region and attracts many tourists, especially in the summer, increasing the number of "Northlander" passengers at this time of year. In the winter months, the train's passengers are mostly Canadians who prefer to relax in a comfortable seat in a coach compartment than to struggle through the icy roads in a car at a temperature of -30 °C (-22 °F).

Above: Union Station in Toronto. On 12 January1997 a VIA train sets off on its journey in the bitter cold of the morning.

Opposite page, top and bottom: The "Northlander" on its journey from Toronto to North Bay. The FP 7, more than 40 years old, has a new engine compartment. Although the train has only three coaches, a driving trailer is coupled behind the locomotive to provide extra power.

The management of the ONR is in North Bay. Once, this city, which today has about 55,000 inhabitants, was one of the bases from which the mineral resources of the northern hinterland were opened up. Once it had been mined, the ore would be transported to the cities of the south by railroad, and the Ontario Northland Railway was established for this purpose by the state government in 1902.

From the T-Trains to the FP 7

There is one period in the history of the ONR that is of particular interest to Europeans. From 1977, the Northlander line used former Trans-Europ-Express trains that between 1957 and 1974 had operated through the Netherlands, Germany and Switzerland. The TEE trains with their distinctive driving units with prominent noses exchanged their red and white colour scheme for that of the ONR. These trains had been bought by the Canadian Urban Transportation Development Corporation, which acquired four of the former luxury trains from the Netherlands Railway (NS) and the Swiss Federal Railways (SBB). leasing them on to the ONR.

The sets were received from Europe in good condition, painted and equipped to Canadian standards with bell, multi-toned horn and number boxes. These elegant trains were given the name "Northlander", but they were designated internally as "T-Trains" by the ONR management. The former TEE trains acquitted themselves quite well, although the Canadian railway workers had first to get used to their unusual drive technology with quill-driven motors, since they were only familiar with robust axle-hung motors. However the T-Trains had to struggle in winter against the extremely severe cold, far beyond anything they had encountered in Europe. Air and water pipes had to be relocated or better insulated. In addition, the motors were slowly wearing out. Therefore in the early 1980s, as the driving units became older they were replaced with robust diesel-electric locomotives of the FP 7 series. The passenger coaches were still in use until 1992. For use after this the ONR acquired coaches previously used for suburban traffic in Toronto. But the new equipment did not approach the levels of comfort of the T-Trains.

In the 1990s, the FP 7 locomotives with a power of 1,566kW (2100hp) were fitted with a new engine room and modern control facilities by the ONR. Up to 1960, General Motors had delivered 7,617 examples of this locomotive to 50 different railway companies. However the ONR has only recently brought them into operation. Two Swiss sets of the old T-Trains became known as "TEE-Classics" and efforts are being made to bring about their restoration.

The luxury trains of the "Golden Twenties" did not run only through the countries of Europe. The great transcontinental trains of the United States were also extremely glamorous, with names that have in some cases lasted until the present day.

As an example, the famous "Empire Builder" may be quoted. A train of this name has run from Lake Michigan to the Pacific coast since 1929. Today the route of about 3,550 km (2,206 miles) would take 43 hours at an average speed of 82.6 km/h (51 mph). The journey begins in Chicago and passes through Milwaukee, Minneapolis, St Paul and Spokane on its way to Seattle, following the line built as the Great Northern Railway. The most impressive part consists of the climbing sections of the Maria Pass between Browning and Whitefish.

The search for the "Lost Pass"

When a suitable pass through the north of the Rocky Mountains was being sought, the records of the explorer Lewis were researched. The Blackfoot American Indians had informed him in about 1805 that there was a pass that could be comfortably negotiated . But decades later the Native Americans could not or would not remember this Pass any no longer. Probably therefore, they too named it the "Lost Pass." In the event the mountain pass 1,590 m (5,216 ft) high was rediscovered in 1889 by the railroad engineer John F. Steven. He gave it the name "Maria Pass." The Great Northern Railway had already advanced through the broad plains up to the Rocky Mountains. Now at last it had found the way to continue over the mountain range that had obstructed the way to the Pacific. On 6 January 1893 the Great Northern opened its mountain route.

The Great Northern Railway

A few years after opening its transcontinental route, the Great Northern Railway consolidated its position as the greatest American railroad company. As its logo it had its snow goat "Rocky", which became a very well-known

Above: The station sign of Bison is riddled with bullet holes.
Right: A long freight train of the Northern Burlington railroad winds uphill over the Maria Pass.

symbol. The Great Northern owed its success to the railroad magnate James Hill, who understood the activities of the railroad and extended the company's activities into non-railroad areas. He increased the company by steadily buying up other railroad companies and adding them to his empire.

The Great Northern transported agricultural goods, such as wheat, and it also ran an individual agriculture department, advising farmers and cattlemen on the foundation and the expansion of their farms.

As a tribute to the brilliant businessman James Hill, the Great Northern named its show train the "Empire builder".

The era of amalgamations

As result of the great competition between the individual railroad companies, the period from 1957 until the 1990s became one of amalgamations. In the history of the US railroads, this is known as the "Merger Era" . So in 1970 the Great Northern joined together with other lines to form the Burlington Northern Railroad.

The Burlington Northern (BN) concentrated on freight traffic. Each day, the freight company moved an average of 1,300 trains. The largest share of transport volume in the year 2000 consisted of coal transport (25%), inter-modal traffic between different carriers (42%), and timber, chemical and petroleum transport (22%).

Until the merger with the Santa Fe (SF) railroad at the end of the 1990s, the diesel engines of the Burlington Northern has a grass-green ("cascade green") livery. Since then, the new short name BNSF adorns the sides of many locos, while the new colour scheme takes up elements of the Santa Fe livery: orange-red and yellow.

Another merger attempt was thwarted, however. In December 1999, the BNSF announced that it would amalgamate with the Canadian National. The result would have been an extensive rail network of some 80,000 km (50,000 miles), but this was prevented because it would have meant that it had a monopoly position in North America. Then in January 2001, CN announced its takeover of the Wisconsin Central Transportation Corporation (WCTC). The amalgamation with WCTC widened the CN network, whose most important assets until now had consisted of its east-west transcontinental connection through Canada and a branch from Chicago as far south as New Orleans.

The US government handed over the merger request of the two giant railroad companies, BNSF and CS, to the Surface Transportation Board, the STB. Because of the negative consequences that had emerged after the amalgamation of the South Pacific and the Union Pacific in 1997, a higher level of vigilance was in force at the STB.

In March 2000 the STB arranged a 15-month moratorium on any amalgamation. It was working on the preparation of principles that were intended to be helpful in the resolution of future amalgamation proposals. The guiding principles of the STB include concepts such as safety and the ability of railroad companies to fulfil their responsibilities. In the face of the moratorium, the merger plans of the BNSF and CN in July 2000 were rejected again.

Left: Forming over 40% of freight traffic, containers dominate the railroads of the United States. A Union Pacific freight train on its way near Creston.

Above: An Amtrak passenger train hauled by two FS 40 PHs leaving Salt Lake City.
Opposite page, top: A BN mixed freight train on its way to the Maria Pass.
Opposite page, bottom: Amtrak passenger train in Portland, September 1998.

Coaches and locos of the "Empire Builder"

In the field of US passenger transport, this had been dominated by the semi-governmental passenger train company Amtrak since its foundation in 1971. It serves about 530 stations in 45 federal states. Apart from the Alaska Railroad, there is no other railway company besides Amtrak operating passenger trains independently. However many cities own local traffic systems with tied tracks.

As its passenger coaches today, the "Empire Builder" has double-deck Superliner coaches about 4.80 m (15 ft 9 in) high. The side walls of the silver-grey coaches and the loco are drawn together and embellished with red, white and blue bands, the colours of Amtrak.

Normally, the train is headed by two Series F 40 PHS locomotives. These passenger train locomotives manufactured by EMD have enclosed bodies as well as train heating and power supply equipment. Their maximum speed is 166 km/h (103 mph). Altogether 405 examples of the FS 40 PHS and FS 40 PH-2S were built. Of this total, 200 went to Amtrak. The company has been operating these locos on the transcontinental lines for over 20 years.

While the gauge throughout North America is 4 ft 8½ in (1,435 mm) like most European countries, locomotive standards are very different. Most US types are for example much heavier than European ones, since the permanent way tolerates higher axle loads. So, the Series F 40 PHS diesel loco is 18.03 m (59 ft 2 in) long, measured over the couplings , and has a service weight of 118 t (130.1 tons) on the scales. The maximum axle load is declared at 30 t (33.1 tons). So far as performance is concerned, these locomotives with Bo'Bo' axle arrangement develop a power of 2,500 k (3,351 hp).

On the way to "Big Sky Country"

The journey from Chicago to Seattle is particularly fascinating for European passengers. On the trip through the states of Wisconsin, Minnesota, North Dakota and Montana the unending expanse of the country can be enthusiastically enjoyed. There are prairies of grain as far as the eye can see, and also bare, hilly grassland from which giant rocks jut out.

While the train drives through Montana, it remains close to the Canadian border. The Rocky Mountains are a breathtaking panorama, and it is not for nothing that Montana is known as "Big Sky Country". With the sight of the mountain ridges, the "Empire Builder" enters the Glacier National Park, one of the most beautiful parks of the USA. It has 50 glaciers and 200 lakes as well as many animal species threatened with extinction. From the East Glacier Park railway station the line begins a continuous uphill gradient to the highest point at the Maria Pass. The reception building of the East Glacier Park welcomes its visitors warmly and appropriately. It takes the form of a traditional log cabin. As it continues, parts of the track is protected by avalanche galleries and roofs giving protection from the snow, because here in the Rockies, the winter snow falls can reach a height of up to 6m (20 ft).

One of the most remarkable man-made constructions is located at the Flathead River. Here the train crosses the river valley on a huge steel truss bridge. In the railway station of Essex, several diesel locomotives are stationed for use double-heading or pushing. They wait there until they are needed to provide extra power for long and heavy freight trains on the gradient to the Maria Pass. The mountain route next travels for over 100 km (62 miles) through the National Park to the next stop: West Glacier. Here, the passengers can transfer to old red buses that drive along the "Going-to-the-Sun-Road" through the park. However, this road is open only in the summer. Near the railway station of West Glacier there is a crystal-clear mountain lake, Lake McDonald. It is worth interrupting the train trip for a stay by this scenic jewel. There is plenty of accommodation available round the lake.

To the west :the Union Pacific

The North American railroad company Union Pacific Railroad can look back on a long history full of change. In the year 1862, while the American Civil War was being fought in the south, the Federal Government of the United States arranged for the foundation of a railroad company with a particular purpose. This was to be the creation of a line running from Omaha, Nebraska, through the Rocky Mountains and across to Utah, there to join the line of the Central Pacific Railroad; the latter had struggled eastward through the mountains from Sacramento. In this way the Union Pacific Railroad (UP) came to be founded.

The engineers of the Union of Pacific needed three years to find a route for the line. The country was undeveloped and financial resources were scarce. Therefore, the construction works had to be as economical as possible. Where the line passed through even terrain, the sleepers were simply laid on the ground and light rails were simply spiked to them. The track builders managed over 10 km (6 miles) per day with this method. Tunnels were not used, so the route was formed of steep gradients and tight curves. The bridges that could not be avoided were erected using wood. The sections of the Union Pacific and the Central Pacific met on 10 May 1869 at Promontory, to the north of the Great Salt Lake. The way to the Pacific was clear and North America's first transcontinental line of was created.

In its early years the Union Pacific had to struggle with several difficulties. At this stage the company's debts were huge and the financial framework

proved to be very constricted. Nevertheless, in 1880 the UP acquired several other railroad companies, through which it could extend its network into the Rocky Mountains. Further purchases took place in the year 1897, including the Southern Pacific among others. However, the decision of the US monopolies commission in 1912 broke off the merger of the Union Pacific and Southern Pacific. What remained was operational cooperation. With great persistence, the UP strove for a connection to Chicago where all the most important railway lines joined together. It succeeded in achieving this link in 1982 through an additional purchase of further lines in Missouri and Illinois.

Consequently, the Union Pacific continued to prosper. The private railroad company has been substantially profitable and could also afford the restoration of its famous museum locomotives, such as the largest operational steam locomotive in the world, the Challenger 3985.

The transportation crisis

On 11 September 1996 the Union Pacific and the Southern Pacific joined together to form the largest railroad company in North America. The new giant wanted to dominate the nation's rail freight transport. The SP locomotives were quickly repainted in UP's bright yellow livery, using the colour known as "armour yellow". But the enterprise immediately faced problems. The reasons lay partly in the ailing locos of the SP and partly in the incompatible information systems of UP and SP, as well as in the UP's efforts to centralize all operations. So the SP despatcher centre in Denver, Colorado, was given up and the UP Central took over its functions in Omaha, many of the SP

employees being replaced with UP people. The wrong decisions were made, bringing about a serious shortage of capacity a year later. To help overcome the crisis, the "Surface Transportation board" or STB, the US government authority that had been in existence since 1980, became involved. This body was responsible for safety matters and the control of competition. In October 1997 the STB forced the UP to open up parts of its network to third parties in order to counteract the capacity shortages. Among other things, the Burlington Northern Santa Fe (BNSP) profited from this arrangement. In addition, inspectors were sent out in order to check that the UP was carrying out these events properly. The UP was given one month to put right the worst of the problems. In this it was largely successful through the reactivation of locomotives that had been withdrawn from service and also the hiring of new staff. There is now close cooperation between the UP and the BNSF, that expresses itself in the common business of sections and despatcher centres.

Famous rolling stock

The Union Pacific is still the largest railroad company in the United States, and over the years its prestige has been enhanced by its famous rolling stock. In 1969 the UP celebrated its 100 years of existence by acquiring from General Motors 47 examples of the biggest and strongest diesel locomotive in the world: the DD A 40-X with Do'Do' wheel arrangement and a power of 2 x 2,750 kW (2 x 3,686 hp). But today these are no longer in use, and they have not been so for some time. The UP is also the owner of two famous steam locomotives that still operate on the track, magnificently hauling special trains on the track.

Above: A Union Pacific container train in the barren landscape near Cable, California, taken in June 1998.

Opposite page: Some locos already carry the BNSF logo, while others still operate in the classic Sante Fe livery, at Klingmann, Arizona, 15 August 1998.

Below: "Big Boy" is the largest steam locomotive in the world. It can be seen in the railroad museum at Denver, Colorado.

The Challenger 3985 and "Big Boy"

The Challenger 3985 is still the largest operational steam locomotive in the world. It was manufactured in 1943 by the American Locomotive Company (Alco). A total of 104 further Challenger steam locomotives were built for Union Pacific between 1936 and 1943. The axle arrangement is 4-6-6-4: four carrying wheels, two ranks each of six coupled driving wheels, and four trailing wheels. This corresponds to the continental description of (2'C)C2'. The Challenger series was developed for heavy freight train services in the Rocky Mountains.

Challenger locomotive number 3985 hauled scheduled heavy freight trains through certain Rocky Mountains sections until 1957. In 1962, it escaped being scrapped and found shelter in the loco depot at Cheyenne, Wyoming, until 1975. There it stood as a deserted monument in the proximity of the Cheyenne railway workshops, until in 1981 co-workers of the UP itself assumed responsibility for it and restored it to operational condition. Since then, it has been hauling special trains in the west of the USA. In 1990, it was converted from coal to oil firing. The maximum speed of the Challenger 3985 is 70 mph, a little over 110 km/h. With its tender, the loco is 37.2 m (122 ft) long, compared for instance to the length of the German Series 01 steam locomotive of 23.75 m (77 ft 11 in). In 1997, the UP prescribed a longer out-of-service interval for the Challenger in order to give it a substantial overhaul.

Another UP engine is the world's largest steam locomotive ever built, "Big Boy." From 1941 to 1944, 25 examples of the Series 4000 loco with a six-wheeled separate tender were manufactured, also by Alco. This giant of the tracks has a 4-8-8-4 axle arrangement, a total weight of 508 t (560 tons) and brought an axle load of 35 t (38.6 tons) on the track. The indexed performance amounted to about 6,000 kW (over 8,000 hp). Unfortunately today there are no "Big Boy" locomotives in working condition. A non-operating example can be admired in the railroad museum of Denver, Colorado.

Full of symbolism: the 844 "Northern"

The second of Union Pacific's operational star steam locomotives is an express passenger loco. It is number 844, a 4-8-4 ("Northern") loco built by the American Locomotive Company. Between 1937 and 1944, as well as number 884 the Union Pacific bought 44 more Northern locos of the 800 series. With a length of 30 m (98 ft 5 in), these locos were among the most modern and most handsome steam locos in the world at that time. For this reason the UP restored number 844 as a fully operational example.

To avoid confusion with the diesel locomotive numbering system, the loco was renumbered 8444 in 1962. Thereafter, the steam locomotive served until the 1970s as an advertising medium for Union Pacific. The locomotive with its distinctive whistle — it sounded like a steamship — became the symbol for the rising railroad company. At the head of special trains it was a wonderful spectacle admired by all. From 1991 to 1996, the loco was given a

Left: The two giants of the railroad, the Challenger number 3985 and the Northern number 844. They are hauling a special Union Pacific train on the way to an exhibition in California.

complete general overhaul. Since then, it has displayed its original number 844 again.

Elegance on wheels - the "Daylight"

In the United States, long distance passenger traffic plays a subordinate role today when freight trains dominate the main lines. It was many decades ago that the passenger express was in its prime. Each railway company created its own show train. These offered travel through scenically attractive stretches of line, luxuriously comfortable trains or especially fast connections. At the end of the 1930s one particular train stood out from the offerings of the large luxury trains. The Southern Pacific railroad company owned a coastal route from San Francisco through Sacramento and Portland to Seattle.

The SP introduced its "Daylight" trains onto this line in the late 1930s. These trains were distinguished by their integrated appearance. Locomotives and coaches were painted in matching colours, forming a non-stop red and orange-coloured stripe over the whole length of the train as the sides of the coaches pass by.

After the amalgamation of SP with UP, this elegant train continued to be used for special trips. Some of the old coaches with their solid construction and traditional atmosphere had survived, and a matching steam locomotive was found in a scrap yard. This "Daylight" locomotive had been built in 1941 as the last in a production series of 30. Engine number SP 4449 is a powerful steam locomotive with a 4-8-4 "Northern" wheel arrangement.

Above: "Daylight" locomotive number SP 4449 on long journey.
Opposite page: An intermediate stop at Rawlings, where the giants pause.
Below: The elegant "Daylight" locomotive steaming powerfully round the curve.

Above: Chatting round the locomotive in Durango.
Right: A sublime landscape in the Rockies with a museum freight train.

Narrow gauge through the Rockies

Once, several narrow gauge lines used to run through the Rocky Mountains. These served the many small mining centres where gold, silver and mineral ore were extracted. Gradually small towns and railroad support facilities developed from the settlements that originally consisted simply of the huts of the gold prospectors.

As a common characteristic, all these lines had a gauge of 36 inches (914 mm). This standard became generally accepted because of its economy. It allowed narrower curves and required less expensive locos and coaches. Most of the narrow gauge mountain tracks had admittedly been shut down by the 1950s, but some still exist today and flourish very successfully as museum lines.

The Durango & Silverton narrow gauge railroad

The starting point of this spectacular museum railroad lies at the heart of the Rocky Mountains, in southern Colorado near the border with New Mexico. Steam-hauled trains run on the dare-devil line between Durango and Silverton as they did years ago.

The line was once a part of the extensive narrow-gauge network of the Denver & Rio Grande Western Railroad. This railroad company was established in 1879 at Durango. After it became connected to the Denver & Rio Grande Western Railroad in August 1881, further work began in the autumn of the same year to extend it towards Silverton. The route is about 70 km (43½ miles) long was already operating in July 1882, after a construction period of only 11 months. It ran passenger trains and freight trains carrying silver and gold ore from the San Juan mountains.

On 25 March 1981, about 100 years after the building of the line, the Durango & Silverton Narrow Gauge (D&SNG) railroad company acquired the line together with the rolling stock, railway stations and warehouse. The founding principle of the new company was never to start a diesel

Above: Locomotive number 482 hauling its special train along the steep rock face at Rockwood. The Animas River flows along the bottom of the valley.
Opposite page: Between the trips the steam locomotives have to be maintained and looked after.

engine. It undertook the obligation to restore the historic track so that it would be as true to the original as possible. The efforts of the D&SNG have been rewarded by the visits of thousands of railroad enthusiasts who arrive each year in order to take a trip by steam train to Silverton.

In addition, the D&SNG has a narrow gauge railway museum. The interesting collection includes old steam locos, coaches and many more items that once formed part of the everyday life of a railroad in the Rockies.

The vehicles used by the D&SNG on the route from Durango to Silverton include two locomotives with separate tenders and several old passenger coaches that date from the original period of the line. The coaches are in excellent condition, considering their age, and the two steam locos are lovingly cared for. Locomotive number 482 belongs to the K 36 series built by the Baldwin locomotive works in the 1920s. The second engine, number 476, is a Class 28 steam loco. The trains run in winter as well as in summer, since the historic passenger coaches can be heated. Tickets should be bought at the latest on the day before the journey, since the popular steam trains quickly become fully booked.

High above the river valley

The journey from Durango, 2,000 m (over 6,500 ft) high, to Silverton is rich in dramatic spectacles. The first few kilometres are not spectacular, but the line becomes more exciting from Hermosa, where the engine receives the assistance of a second locomotive that is needed for the climb of 10 km (6 miles) to Rockwood. This is the steepest section of the line on the way to Silverton, leading through a narrow valley past Shalona Lake. After the railway station of Rockwood, the train continues its journey along a steep rock face. The line is perched on a narrow ledge with an abyss about 30 m (100 ft) deep immediately outside the window.

The route follows the course of the Animas river through the San Juan National Forest, a nature reserve that is accessible only by railroad, since there are no roads for cars. The train crosses to the other side of the river by the Steel Truss Bridge. After the passing point at Tacoma, it heads into a siding to pick up water. Also the second loco uncouples here, since the steepest sections are now past. The next stops Needleton and Elk Park are starting points for mountain walkers. Shortly before Silverton, tunnel entrances can

The line has 25 Baldwin Series 75 locomotives and most of the 50 Henschel Series 75H locomotives . The huge fleet made possible the line's survival until the 1990s with little investment. Defective locomotives served as donors of spare parts for the operational locomotives. So, over the years the locomotive graveyard at El Maiten has acquired 38 locomotives.

The route begins in Ingeniero Jacobacci, at a height of 876 m (2,874 ft). Initially the line follows the three-rail track of the main line after Barriloche. From Empalme, the line climbs a gradient of 1 in 67 to reach its highest point at Ojos de Agua, an altitude of 1,214 m (3,983 ft). The track descends about 1,000 m (3,300 ft) and then climbs again for 98 km (61 miles), reaching a height of 1,132 m (3,714 ft). Cerro Mesa is only 871 m (2,858 ft) high. A header locomotive is always waiting in a small locomotive shed there. The train continues along the part of the route that was constructionally the most demanding, with a deep cutting, a viaduct 105 m (345 ft) long, said to be the longest steel truss bridge in South America, and the line's only tunnel. Then the line climbs once again to 1,208 m (3,963 ft) and reaches the plateau of Chacay Huarruca. From here, the first view of the Andes mountain range can be seen. The line continues in wide curves down to Norquinco. El Maite is reached shortly after crossing the Rio Chubut. The line's workshop facilities have been at El Maite since the 1950s, and the locomotives are always changed here. The Baldwin engines normally pull the train from Ingeniero Jacobacci, while on the section to Esquel the train uses Henschel locomotives. Now the track follows the Andes in wide curves until the Nahuel Pan pass is reached. The final stage is the steep descent to the little town of Esquel at an altitude of 600 m (1,969 ft).

The private railway companies were nationalized and brought under government control in 1948. However, the old railway companies had already

Above: The "Patagonian Express" always pulls some freight wagons and usually some tankers as well as the passenger coaches.

Opposite page, top and bottom: On leaving Salta, the "Train to the Clouds" passes through the breathtaking wilderness and crosses some daredevil bridges, such as this one at Polvorillo.

Below: The station of El Maiten.

Above: With some tanker wagons at the summit of the El Maiten line.

Left: The "Patagonian Express" makes its journey through the wildly romantic landscape once a week.

withdrawn much of their investment in anticipation of nationalization. Of the total of about 4,000 steam locomotives, 1,200 were out of action and damaged. Nevertheless, in 1948 new steam locomotives were still being ordered from England, including a 4-8-0 locomotive from the Vulcan Foundry that was delivered to the General Roca line. This loco survives in working order and pulls museum trains in Buenos Aires today.

The old steam locomotives came mainly from England and France. Only the state-owned metre gauge lines acquired further new steam-powered engines. After nationalization came into effect, diesel engines increasingly replaced the outdated stock of steam locomotives. The American locomotive factories of the United States quickly became the main suppliers.

That "Train to the Clouds"

In 1948 the second line crossing the Andes was finally completed, the metre gauge line between Salta and Antofagasta via Socompa. For many years this line was the main area in which the powerful 2'D1' (4-8-2) locomotives delivered by Henschel and Skoda to Argentina from 1939 were used. The celebrated "Train to the Clouds" climbs the Andes to a height of 4,475 m (14,682 ft). The "Tren a las Nubes", to give it its Spanish name, is above all a tourist train and there are many sensational views in the trip. In the course of the journey the train passes through 21 tunnels and crosses 13 large viaducts. The train runs from March until late November every Saturday. The long journey begins at 7 a.m. in Salta. During the lowland part of the route, the train negotiates two hairpin bends. After this the General Motors Type GT22-CU locomotive, with a power of 1,807 kW (2,422 hp), hauls the train uphill along countless curves clinging to the steep hillside. At about lunchtime, the train drives through the summit tunnel of Abra Munano at a height of over 3,500 m (11,500 ft). Here begins the Puna and there is a view of the peak of Mount Acay, 5,950 m (19,521 ft) high. At about 4,200 m (13,800 ft) above mean sea level, the train reaches the highest point of the route shortly beyond San Antonio de las Cobres. Shortly afterwards, the train drives through Mina Concordia, about 215 km (133 miles) from Salta. Here is the climax of the trip, the

Above: At the Rio Gallegos locomotive depot.
Below: The fireman cleans a salmon caught in the Rio Turbio in the loco's feed water.

La Polvorilla viaduct. At an altitude of over 4,000 m, this is 224 m (735 ft) long and 63 m (207 ft) high. This is the final point of the "Train to the Clouds". After about 20 minutes, the train returns to Salta.

Coal line in the south

In 1951, another remarkable line opened in Argentina. The coal line 200 km (124 miles) long from Rio Gallegos to Rio Turbio in southern Patagonia is recognized as the southernmost railway in the world. It has a number of unusual features. It is built with a gauge of 750 mm (29½-in). The reason for this uncommon measurement lay in the fact that there were already stocks of materials in the Chubut province for a line from Esquel to the Atlantic that was never built. First, eight Henschel 1'D1' (2-8-2) locomotives arrived at Rio Gallegos, the same type as was already well-known from the Ingeniero Jacobacci-Esquel line. But since these locomotives were not nearly powerful enough to pull the heavy coal trains, Argentina ordered a number of modern 2-10-2 steam locomotives from Mitsubishi. Altogether 20 locomotives came to Patagonia in two batches, the first being delivered in 1956 and the second in 1963. The line's chief engineer L. D. Porta fundamentally modernized these engines and among other things fitted them with a "gas producer" firebox. In this, the air supply underneath is restricted and additional air is blown in above it. This causes the gaseous components of the coal to be given off and burnt as gas. The locomotive performance increased considerably as a result of this modification. The narrow gauge locos virtually equalled the traction of the German Series 50. The locomotives weighed some 86 t (94.8 tons) and developed about 875 kW (1,173 hp) after modification. They could tow trains that normally consisted of 50 wagons weighing a total of about 1,200 t (1,323 tons).

From 1997, after the denationalization of the former state-owned coal company, the line acquired five Bo'Bo' diesel locomotives. These were built by Henschel from a Bulgarian design. Equipped with new Caterpillar engines developing 736 kW (987 hp), these have hauled the Patagonian coal trains since then. The steam locos were gradually withdrawn from service and many were scrapped. In 2001, a group of railway enthusiasts restored one of the locomotives.

The Argentinian national state railways suffered from chronic lack of capital and an enormous volume of debt. Therefore a process of privatization began in 1991, starting with the five large regional freight networks. In 1991, the first private company took over a network of 5,287 km (3,285 miles) between Rosario and Bahia Blanca, and others followed until 1994. In proportion to their size, they received the outdated diesel stock of the national railways, with the result that numerous repaired Alco, General Electric and EMD locomotives from the 1960s are still hauling trains throughout Argentina

Above: A fully-laden coal train on the journey to Rio Gallegos. The sky is free of clouds on only a few days a year, and the wind always blows unpleasantly in this region of coal fields.

Left: Waiting for the countermove. At the crossing points away from settlements, the engine crew drink tea while they wait for the other train.

today. There are also some Type D 500 locomotives, an export Alco variant of the well-known United States series of locomotives.

As a result of the dissolution of the national railway system, most of the passenger services ended. The passenger trains that still exist are operated under provincial management. So, the wealthy province of Buenos Aires runs quite a dense network with trains to the largest cities. The most important is the line to Mar del Plata with ten pairs of trains a day. Also belonging to this category is the Rio Negro province, which for financial reasons shortened the route from Barriloche to Buenos Aires so that it runs only from Barriloche to Viedma.

With the denationalization campaign of President Menem, dark clouds also gathered for the Ingeniero Jacobacci-Esquel line. In 1993 the state decided 1993 to discontinue all subsidized passenger trains. This included the "Trochita" ("little helter-skelter"), as the track is lovingly called in Argentina, as well as the express trains from Buenos Aires that stopped at Ingeniero Jacobacci after Bariloche. After being brought to a halt at the end of 1993, the two provinces involved decided to revive the business. Eventually the Rio Negro province withdrew, however, and handed over the business on its section between El Maiten and Ingeniero Jacobacci. So today the little train still puffs its way as a tourist attraction from Esquel to El Maiten. Furthermore, a train drives between Esquel and Nahuel Pan. There is also something else positive to report: 1994 saw the reconstruction of a route long 8 km (5 miles) in Ushuaia for the tourism enabled. This uses restored steam locomotives, including a Garratt articulated locomotive among others.

Above: A coal train of about 1,000 t (1,100 tons) coming from the Rio Turbio near Bela Vista on the way to Rio Gallegos.

Opposite page, top: The RFIRT locomotive no. 118 comes from the second series of ten 2-10-0 locos, built by Mitsubishi in 1962. With its 44 coal wagons, it still has a journey of several hours before it reaches Rio Gallegos.

Below: The fireman prepares the coal before setting off. A semi-automatic stoker pushes the coal towards him.

Opposite page, bottom left: The coal loading installation at Rio Turbio.

Opposite page, bottom right: The view from the cab of the infinite wilderness of the coal fields. To the right of the picture is the Turbio river.

The southernmost country in the Andes is Chile, taking up more than half of the west coast of South America with a length of about 4,900 km (over 3,000 miles) in total. The main crests of the Andes form the country's eastern border. Mount Anconcagua rises skywards to an imposing height of 6,972 m (22,874 ft) . The mountain passes in central and northern Chile climb to heights of over 4,000 m (13,000 ft). But it is not just the high altitudes that make transport in the Andes difficult; it is the structure of the Andean valleys as well. These are often sliced through by ravines or canyons, so it is no surprise that the first railways in Chile were built alongside the Andean ridges.

Chile started to build its rail network with greater energy than other South American countries. The first one-metre (3 ft 3 in) gauge train ran in 1853, from the port of Caldera to the inland mining centre at Copiapo. The first locomotive, a 4-4-0 (2'B) type made by Norris, has been preserved and, after

travelling 118,643 km (73,723 miles), today stands in the National Museum of Chile. The mountain section 184 km (114 miles) long between Valparaiso and Santiago was completed between 1857 and 1863 in 5 ft 6 in (1,676 mm) gauge. Locomotives purchased from Hawthorn and Avonside in England were run on this line. The Southern Railroad had been established as early as 1855 with the purpose of building a line from Santiago to Talca. President Montt opened the first section to San Bernardo with a length of 16 km (10 miles) on 17 September 1857. By 1868 the Southern Railroad had built 185 km (115 miles) of track and reached Curico. The largest structure created on the railway was the Bio-Bio bridge, 500 m (1,640 ft) long. At that time 30 passenger engines and 37 goods locomotives were in use on the Southern Railroad , all of which were built in the USA.

By 1873 the Chilean network was 1,254 km (779 miles). The Southern Railroad extended to San Rosendo. In this year the government decided to built a main trunk line through the central valley down to Puerto Montt. The biggest ports on the Pacific were to be linked to the largest towns in the Andean foothills via branch lines. Even today this railway line is of major importance to the country's supply system, linking up central Chile and also connecting with the southern farming regions. The agricultural areas in the south form a continuous plateau, making it an obvious site for a railway. The important Southern Railroad was therefore rapidly built out and extended in several sections via Talcan, Chillian to Valdivia. Various 2-9-0, 4-6-0, 2-6-2 and 2-6-0 (1'D, 2'C, 1'C1' and 1'C) locomotives from Borsig, Baldwin, Henschel and North British were operated. A couple of these engines survive today as museum exhibits.

Highest point

Northern Chile, in contrast, is dry and barren. Hills and mountains are dotted randomly through the landscape while other parts are just featureless deserts. Nevertheless, the desert areas in the Atacama, Chile's northern provinces, are particularly rich in mineral deposits. This led to the construction of several private pit and mining railways. The majority of these were British-owned. The most important of these, the Antofagasta & Bolivia railway, still exists today and was constructed from 1873 onwards in 750 mm (29½ in) gauge. From 1889 it ran from the port of Antofagasta to Uyuni and from 1892 to Oruro. By 1928 the network had been converted to one-metre (3 ft 3 in) gauge. The line is 924 km (574 miles) long, of which 366 km (227 miles) lie in Chile and the rest are on Bolivian territory. The line climbs through the Andes at heights of over 4,000 m (13,000 ft). A branch line used solely for connection purposes reaches 4,826 m (15,833 ft) above sea level at Collahuasi, making it the highest point in the global rail network.

During the mining crisis at the end of the 19th century, the Chilean government nationalised numerous railways that had been built in the north to exploit the rich ore deposits. These included Chile's first railway, which was 281 km (175 miles) long at the time it was taken over. The company was given the first concession to build a Trans-Andean railway between Chile and Argentina. Although route surveys were performed in 1868 and 1874, financial difficulties prevented the start of building work. The line later became part of the Northern Railroad, as did the Coquimbo line established in 1895. After fighting Bolivia and Peru in the Saltpetre War, Chile gained large areas of land to its north in 1884, north of Copiapo, and simultaneously several lines that had been built purely as mining railways. Chile thereby strengthened its position as an important supplier of raw materials.

The saltpetre and mining railways in existence around 1890 had different track gauges. There were lines of 24 in (600 mm) gauge, one metre (3 ft 3 in) gauge, and Cape gauge, 3 ft 6 in (1,067 mm). The fleets of locomotives were likewise varied and irregular. Of the northern saltpetre railways, only the two most important are named here. The standard gauge nitrate railway ran from Iquique to Pisagua, a distance of 389 km (242 miles). In the south the line extended to Lagunas. The route followed an extremely tortuous course, from the port of Pisagua and from Iquigue, with inclines of up to 1 in 20 and several sharp bends. Until 1920 many Fairlie articulated locomotives were deployed here. and the railway was one of the main users of the type anywhere in the world. Iquique was a centre of the saltpetre trade at the end of the 19th Century, and the nitrate railway, which linked several pits, was of corresponding importance. Once the pits were exhausted, the railway lost its significance.

Another saltpetre railway, the Tocopilla-Taco line, built between 1888 and 1890, starts from the port of Tocopilla situated north of Antofagasta. It cuts through extremely mountainous country and climbs to a height of 1,495 m (4,905 ft). The uphill stretch 39 km (24 miles) long was electrified in 1927. The railway acquired six Bo'Bo' locomotives with 438 kW (587 hp) output made by General Electric for this purpose. In contrast to the nitrate railway, it is still in operation today.

It was thus in 1895 that work began in Chile on the first Trans-Andean railway. The first kilometres from Los Andes via Juncal to Salto del Soldado had

Above: The daily goods train from Iquique pulled by a diesel engine built by General Motors. Locomotive 13030 still has many hours to run through a hot desert landscape before reaching its destination in Copiapo.

Opposite page, top: Locomotive 3511 is one of a mass-produced series of one-metre gauge steam engines built by Baldwin for the desert stretches. As the last representative of its construction class, it is still occasionally put into service.

Opposite page, bottom: A 2-8-0 (1′D) locomotive of the 800 class, built by Mitsubishi in 1952, stands in the unique railway park in Santiago. More than 30 witnesses to Chilean rail history are preserved and cared for here.

already been completed. On 25 May 1910 the struggle to build a line across the Andes was brought to a successful conclusion with the inauguration of the stretch. Financial problems had continually interrupted the work. The construction work itself involved huge difficulties. Building materials and provisions for the workmen had to be transported with difficulty through the inaccessible terrain on the backs of mules. In many places supply paths first had to be carved out of the cliff walls. The numerous tunnels, including the Scheitel tunnel 3,039 m (9,970 ft) long on the Chilean side, also held up the construction work. Lastly, the line reached inclines of up to 1 in 12.5, which did nothing to speed traffic along even once the individual sections of track had been completed. The high construction costs and the high operating expenditure of the rack-and-pinion system were always going to be a problem for the line. As the first trans-continental railway in South America, its effect at the time was more of a stimulus than one of carrying traffic. The difficulties also included the very harsh winters with extreme snow storms over mountain passes 3,205 m (10,515 ft) high. For this reason the railway needed its own design of engine from the start. Two 1′C1′ (2-6-2) rack-and-pinion tank locomotives weighing 40 t (44 tons) each from Borsig were used at first, although these were only able to pull 70 t (77 tons) over the ramp. These were joined later by a similar 1′C2′ (2-6-4) locomotive from Borsig. Between 1907 and 1912 the railway acquired D'+C' (0-8-0+0-6-0) locomotives in rack-and-pinion design from Meyer-Kitson in England, which at around 90 t (99 tons) in weight, were then able to pull 150 t (165 tons) over the mountains. Engines for international passenger trains consisting of six carriages weighed around 120 t (132 tons). Two of these powerful locomotives have been preserved. One of them was even given a major overhaul in the mid-1970s with aim of using it in snow clearing service. However, it was never deployed again and has stood in the sheds at Los Andes for some time now. The second is exhibited in the Quinta Normal museum park.

Above and opposite page: Winter brings a great deal of snow to southern Chile, too. Locomotive 714, built in 1919 by Alco, travels the line to Lonquimay once planned as the Trans-Andean railway. An Andes crossing to Argentina is still being considered today.

Transit railway to Argentina

A line was built from 1905 onwards between the Pacific port of Arica in northern Chile and the Bolivian capital La Paz. The railway was a result of the Pacific War, in which Bolivia lost its access to the ocean. In the peace treaty Chile granted the Bolivian state the right to operate a railway on its territory. This created the Arica-La-Paz railway 460 km (286 miles) long, which was completed in 1913. Due to the difficult terrain — the line rises to an altitude of 4,256 m (13,963 ft) — the railway had rack-and-pinion sections with inclines of up to 1 in 16½. In the 1930s 40 locomotives were in use, and added to these were eight rack-and-pinion engines. Maschinenfabrik Esslingen later supplied several 1'D1' (2-8-2) rack-and-pinion locomotives to the railway, the last series of which was delivered to Chile as late as 1950. In the meantime, type U 13 C diesel locomotives from General Electric with an output of 1,036 kW (1,389 hp) were in use here. These had to be subjected to a dedicated safety check each time before the downward run.

By 1909 there were 5,295 km (3,290 miles) of track in operation, of which almost 70% were wider gauge lines in the south of the country. The 1,269 km (789 miles) of the Southern Railroad, starting from Valparaiso via Osorno through to Puerto Montt, was finally opened in 1912. This part of the route includes the most impressive railway structure in Chile, the Malleco viaduct 350 m (1,148 ft) long and 105 m (344 ft) high. At this time the government of

Chile decided to electrify about 1,200 km (750 miles) of track. This included the uphill section of the Chilean Trans-Andean railway. In addition, there were plans to create a Northern Railroad, similar to the Southern Railroad, although in narrow gauge, which was to connect the numerous pit and mining railways in the north.

In 1913 the state merged its lines in northern Chile with the Los Vilos Railway and the Huasco Railway. This finally created the Northern Railroad. In 1917 this company operated 1,726 km (1,073 miles) of track, the Southern Railroad 2,748 km (1,708 miles). Work on the northern longitudinal line in Pueblo Hundido had already been started in 1909. The line reached its terminus in Iquique in 1929. The planned extension to Arica was never executed. Baldwin supplied a series of more than 60 2-8-2 (1'D1') locomotives for daily operations. The last engines of this W class still stand today in the sheds at Baquedano, but only one locomotive is still in working condition.

On account of the operating difficulties of the Trans-Andean railway, the idea of a second Andean crossing situated further south had already been proposed in 1895, which was intended to connect the wider-gauge network directly over more friendly terrain. A branch line was therefore built in Chile towards the Andes from Pua to Curacautin. In 1922 Chile and Argentina signed a treaty concerning the construction of the planned railway.

Over the course of the years the route was then surveyed. The only actual

work performed on the southern Trans-Andean railway was in Chile. After a tunnel 4,528 m (14,856 ft) long had been completed in 1938, the line reached its provisional terminal in Lonquimay. Another 145 km (90 miles) of track were still needed to reach Zapala. Over the years, ever new agreements were made to finally finish the line. The pressure on politicians from the now private rail operators to do something tangible has been growing in recent times.

Operational bottlenecks during World War I brought a wide-ranging programme of electrification in their wake. By 1924 the main line from Valparaiso to Santiago and the branch line from Las Vegas to Los Andes had been provided with overhead cables carrying 3,000 volt direct current. Baldwin and Westinghouse delivered 15 C+C goods locomotives of 1,314 kW (1,761 hp) output and six 1'C+C'1 express locomotives with of 1,752 kW (2,349 hp) outputs for daily operations. The large-scale investment was completed with 11 passenger train locomotives of 1,198 kW (1,606 hp) and seven shunting locomotives of 467 kW (626 hp) output, each B+B types. Delivery was later taken of another three powerful 2'C+C2' locomotives of 3,613 kW (4,843 hp) weighing 210 t (231 tons). The engines were nicknamed "serpientes", meaning "snakes", on account of their long, stretched snake-like front end. One of these engines still stands in Santiago today.

By the 1930s Chile had the most extensive and modern railway system in South America. A total of 1,307 locomotives were in use at that time. The first section of the Trans-Andean railway from Juncal to the country's border had been electrified in 1927. SLM and BBC supplied three 1'C+C'1 locomotives for this purpose. The last is still in service today on the remaining run to Rio Blanco. In 1935 German locomotive builders shipped a series of powerful 1'D1' (2-8-2) locomotives to Chile for the non-electrified sections of the Southern Railroad. Krupp, Henschel and even Maschinenfabrik Esslingen participated in this order for the 70 class. Before this the Southern Railroad took delivery of the first 80 class locomotives, 2'D1' (4-8-2) locomotives. The first were supplied by Baldwin and the last by Mitsubishi. A range of locomotives was used until the end of steam power operation, a number still existing today.

The second Trans-Andean railway

After long discussions, a second Trans-Andean railway was finally opened in 1948. The line ran from Antofagasta via the Socompa Pass to Salta. This stretch created an extensive, uniform one-metre (3 ft 3 in) gauge network between Chile, Bolivia, northern Argentina and, via the Corumba link, to Brazil. By 1954 Chile had a total of 9,600 km (5,965 miles) of track in operation. In subsequent years investments primarily aimed to further electrify the Southern Railroad towards Chillan. For this purpose GAI and Breda in Italy supplied electric "nose" locomotives of 3,328 and 2,219 kW (4,461 hp and 2,975 hp). The E-30 class were 98-t (108-ton) Bo'Bo' locomotives, while the E-32 class were 136-t (150-ton) Co'Co' locomotives. When buying diesel locomotives, Chile, like Argentina, tended to look to the products of US manufacturers. Thus several Alco DL 541 RSD 20s operate in Chile. These are joined by more modern machines from General Electric and GMD.

The slow end to the Trans-Andean railway finally came in 1979. The last regular passenger service ran that year, a small railcar supplied by Schindler in the 1960s. Parts of the line in Chile were damaged by rainfall in 1984. When the

Above: E 3009 waits in Santiago for its next run. The loco, built in 1956 by Westinghouse, is reminiscent of the electric engines on the USA Pennsylvania Railroad.
Opposite page: Locomotive 604 waits with its soda-laden carriages at Quillagua junction for a train coming in the opposite direction. Of the eight electric locomotives originally delivered, six are still in service today.

state subsidies were withdrawn, no-one at the national railways was interested in maintaining the line anymore. Only the section to Rio Blanco is still in operation for goods trains. As a rule these are drawn by Alco type DL 537 diesel locomotives. Since that time, traffic with Argentina threads tortuously along a pass through the Andes with a seemingly never-ending series of hairpin bends.

The first diesel locomotives in Chile were deployed on the Northern Railroad. Two small Bo'Bo' engines of 292 kW (391 hp) were supplied by General Electric in 1945. These served as shunting engines in the Gavilolen tunnel, which did not have an adequate steam extraction system and was therefore extremely problematic for steam traction. Then in 1951 and 1952 type GE 756 diesel locomotives of 876 kW (1,174 hp), likewise built by General Electric as A1A+A1A engines for passenger trains, arrived on the Northern Railroad. They were de-commissioned in 1972 when passenger services were terminated. From 1957 General Electric then supplied Chile with locomotives of types U 9 C and U 12 C, Alco DL 535 and General Motors GR 12. These made the steam engines superfluous, despite the increased volume in traffic.

Numerous steam engines were still in use up to the start of the 1980s on the non-electrified southern network around Temoco. The Quinta Normal museum park was created at this time in Santiago with an impressive number of preserved steam engines. The exhibits include a Kitson-Meyer locomotive from the Trans-Andean Railway and also the largest Southern Railway engine, the massive 110 class 2'D1' locomotive made by Alco, weighing 220 t (242 tons).

Passenger services on the line from Valparaiso to Santiago were stopped in 1989. Due to the difficult route through the chain of mountains along the coast, the line built in the 19th century traces a large arc. Today the road follows the more direct route. Therefore, once the state subsidies had been withdrawn, Southern Railroad decided to stop operations. The privatization of the Northern Railroad, which now goes under the name of Ferronor, was completed in the same year. A new goods traffic company was created for the Southern Railroad as a further step towards privatization. Fepasa was partly privatized in 1995. The Chilean state retaining a 49% stake. The infrastructure remained with the national railway. A dedicated company has now likewise been created for passenger services.

Peru has always been known for its mineral wealth. It is therefore no surprise that numerous railways were built to exploit these natural resources. The geographic lie of the land, however, does not exactly lend itself to building railways. For this reason, the first rail lines, as in other South American countries, connected existing ports to their hinterlands. Typical of this was the Peruvian line from Lima to the port of Callao. The inaugural train ran on this 14-km (9-mile) stretch as early as 1851, making it the first railway in South America. It was followed in 1854 by the line from Tacna to the port of Arica.

Construction work progressed with vigour under President Balta, who recognised the great importance of the railways for his country. The completion of the first part section of the Central Railroad from Lima to Chosica and the Southern Railroad from Mollendo to Arequipa represented significant advances. The rail system was expanded energetically from around 1869 onwards. 1,852 km (1,151 miles) of track were already in operation or under

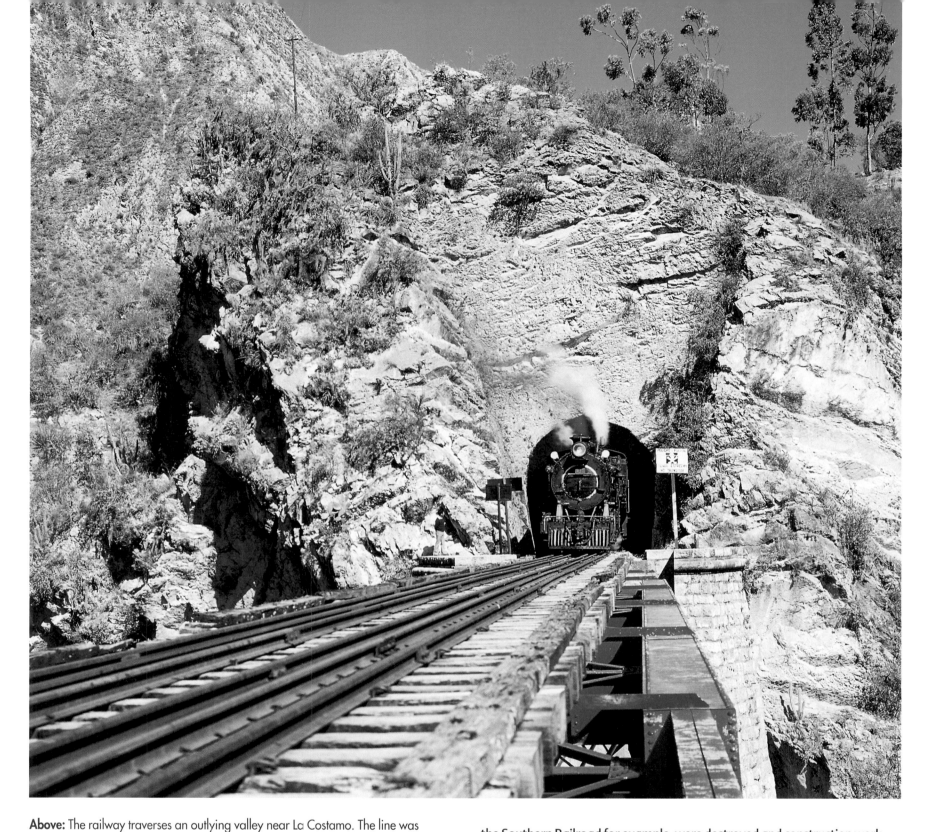

Above: The railway traverses an outlying valley near La Costamo. The line was intended to run from Huancayo to Ayacucho, but after an initial section had been completed, the plans were changed and the line was re-routed to Huancavelica.

Opposite page, top: Stopping for water in Aguas Calientes, this 2-8-0 (1'D) loco was built in 1936 by Hunslet, supplementing the ageing fleet of old Baldwin locomotives.

Opposite page, bottom: Double locomotive 503 and 504, a model made by Alco for export, awaiting departure in Sicuani with a goods train to Cuzco. The Southern Railroad from Mollendo via Arequipa, Puno to Cuzco was the workplace of the two "nose" locomotives for many years.

construction by 1880. Apart from the Central Railroad and the Southern Railroad, this included lines starting from Eten, Pisco, Paita and Chiclayo. In the south this included the Ilo-Moquegua railway.

Then came the Saltpetre War, in which Peru not only lost its southern province to Chile, but also various rail lines. Sections of a number of railways,

the Southern Railroad for example, were destroyed and construction work came to a standstill throughout the country. The war and the subsequent revolution worsened the country's financial situation dramatically. The government swapped its external debt in a deal with the Peruvian Corporation in exchange for a number of railways, mines, extensive land holdings and navigation rights on Lake Titicaca.

The Central Railroad finally reached Oroya in 1893 and at the second major attempt, the Southern Railroad extended to Puno. Both routes are among the most impressive railway construction works in South America. The first line crosses the Andes at Galera at a height of 4,782 m (15,689 ft), the second in Crucero Alto at 4,482 m (14,705 ft) above sea level. In contrast to other South American countries, the track built was in standard gauge. The Central Railroad has justly become famous on account of the spectacular course it follows. In the Verrugas viaduct it has one of the highest bridges in the

Top: The two Henschel locomotives 0996 and 0995 started running from Cuzco to Macchu Picchu, a section of track important for tourism, in 1985. Locomotive 0995, built in 1928, was scrapped a couple of years later. Number 0996 today stands at the entry to the town of Cuzco as a memorial engine.

world. The first viaduct was destroyed in 1889 after heavy mountain storms. The second viaduct was no longer able to bear the trains as they became heavier and it was replaced by the third bridge in 1937. The railway features one of the first spiral tunnels in the world. The Infiernillo bridge directly connects two tunnels between the vertical cliff faces here. Countless "zig-zags" had to be built to take the track up to this great altitude at anything like an acceptable incline — in the upper section it is 1 in 23. Five zig-zags were created around Chicla and more were built at Casapalca and Chinchanpais, a total of 15. The line has 65 tunnels and 67 large bridges. The remarkable setting of the line has attracted adventurous travellers from the start. A trip on the Central Railroad was always an absolute "must" for visitors to Peru.

Varied fleet of locomotives

Several small railroads had been built in the north of Peru in the meantime, which mainly served to transport agricultural products to the nearest sea port. Added to these were various regional lines in the Lima area. All owned a really quite varied fleet of locomotives of British and US manufacture. The majority of these railroads no longer exist today. More important, in contrast, was the opening of the mining railway from La Oroya to Cerro de Pasco in 1904, and its extension three years later to Gollarisquisca. Likewise in 1907, the Central Railroad constructed what then became the highest point of a railway used regularly by trains, at 4,817 m (15,804 ft) through the Ticlio Pass

on a branch line near Anticona. The main line of the Central Railroad had reached Huari in the meantime, and the Southern Railroad extended to Secuani. Thus by 1908 a very respectable 2,367 km (1,471 miles) of track were in operation. The state financed the new construction work at that time with its revenue from the tobacco monopoly.

It had already been decided in 1904 to extend the railway from Huancayo, the terminal of the Central Railroad, through to Ayacucho. Work on the route began in 1907, but by 1910 just 20 km (12½ miles) had been finished. The government only took over the initiative in 1918. The original plans were altered and the route was redirected over 77 km (48 miles) to La Mejorada. Lines were to be constructed from there to Ayacucho and Huancavelica. The Ayacucho line was never built and work on the branch line initially only got as far as 18 km (11 miles). At that time three Baldwin 2-6-0 (1'C) locomotives were deployed on the railway, one of which was still in service through to the 1980s. It was 1926 before the line finally reached Huancavelica.

There were 3,200 km (1,988 miles) of track in operation by 1922. The Central Railroad ended in Huancayo and the Southern Railroad in Cuzco. Steam ships started operating ferry services on Lake Titicaca. The first section of the Santa Ana Railroad starting out from Cuzco was built as a 3-ft (914 mm) narrow gauge line and completed in 1922. It ran initially from Cuzco to Puente Ruinas below the Inca city of Macchu Picchu only discovered a few years previously. The railway leaves the cauldron of Cuzco at a gradient of 1 in 26 through

PUNTO FERROVIARIO
MAS ALTO DEL MUNDO
4.818 METROS - 15 805 PIES

Below: Locals in Izuchaca wait for the train from Cuzco to Quilla-bamba. An engine built by Bombardier is used. This was converted from standard gauge to the narrow gauge of 3 ft (914 mm) at the beginning of the 1980s, thereby completing the traction change.

Left: At a height of 4,818 m (15,807 ft), the highest point reached by a publicly operated rail line anywhere in the world. A branch line of the Peruvian Central Railroad climbs to this imposing height.

Top left: The route taken by the Quillabamba railway out of Cuzco is highly impressive. The track climbs out of the narrow amphitheatre around Cuzco through many zig-zag bends. The 1'D (2-8-0) locomotive delivered to Peru in the 1950s worked at full capacity on the difficult stretches of line.

three zig-zags and three large loops. Travellers enjoy imposing views over the historic old town of Cuzco. The line traverses the pass at El Arco at a height of 3,720 m (12,205 ft). The route then winds down in loops through the agricultural highlands. After Poroy the line begins the steep descent into the Urubamba valley. To date the stretch is 113 km (70 miles) long.

The locomotives which ran on the Central Railroad from the 1920s onwards were made by Rogers, North British, Alco, Baldwin and Beyer Pea-cock. The 21 2-8-0 (1'D) types from North British and Rogers were the most common series models. These were developed to create the legendary, so-called "Andes" types, examples of which also ran on the Cerro-de-Pasco line on the Southern Railroad. Just one specimen has survived the course of the years, locomotive no. 206, which still occasionally gets a run out in special service. Oil-fired engines, incidentally, had already been introduced in Peru by 1910, mainly because the oil extracted in the country was cheaper than coal. Coal-fired engines nevertheless ensured that firemen had no easy job. Loco-motives always carried two firemen, one for direct stoking and the other to provide back-up supplies from the fuel bunker. The lack of oxygen at high alti-tude was a great discomfort for railway personnel and travellers alike. Pas-senger trains always carried oxygen to combat altitude sickness.

By 1930 the Peruvian rail network consisted of 4,522 km (2,810 miles) of track. The lines were operated by no less than 32 companies. Most of these railroads served the hinterlands of the Pacific harbours. Other attempts to build this or that railway in the Andes ended in dismal failure. This was due to the limited financial resources of the small private companies, although also to the difficult geographic circumstances of the country. Parts of the Pacasmayo railway were destroyed no less than four times by heavy rain storms and earth-quakes. Moreover, an extension of the line from the terminal in Chilete to Caja-marca, an important market centre in the north of Peru, would have required 17 zig-zags. It would have meant negotiating an altitude difference of over 2,900 m (9,500 ft) over a distance of some 40 km (25 miles). It was therefore decided not to connect the northern Andean provinces to the rail network, a decision that later led to considerable political problems. The massive earth-quake of 1970 destroyed parts of various railroads in the north of Peru. As they were of only minor regional significance, they were never started up again.

Diesel power on the march

The fleet of locomotives only started to be modernised relatively late in the day, perhaps because locomotives of the Andes type still represented extremely powerful traction engines for service in the mountains. Added to this, initial test runs with diesel locomotives had not been a great success. Though more powerful than steam locomotives on paper, they were hardly able to pull their own weight at such high altitudes. It was only after an atmospheric compensation mechanism had been fitted that locomotives made by Alco were deployed in 1964. The robustness of these DL 560 locomotives,

Above: Engine change in Chosicá. The small town east of Lima, situated at the foot of the Andes, is where locomotives are changed. Due to the high altitudes negotiated, the mountain locomotives have different engine settings to level line locomotives. The Alco DL 560 is also reversed, so that the driver's cabin always looks forward. This gives the engine driver a better view over the tricky route ahead.

Left: Tamboraque features one of the numerous zig-zag ascents. In order to build a normal gauge rail line over the Andes at a reasonable expenditure, the engineers decided to use these to negotiate the steepest ascents.

Opposite page: Each of the many Andean railways has its own character amongst the impressive mountain scenery of South America. Anyone who has the opportunity of travelling by train here will never forget the experience.

with a then remarkable 1,900 kW (2,545 hp) output, made them an extraordinary success. Some engines are still in service today on the Central Railroad. The locomotives used on the level Callao-Lima-Chosicá line are different from those operated in the mountains. Among those in service here, and similarly between La Oroya and Hunacayo, are DL 543s made by Alco.

In contrast, the first diesel locomotives had already been introduced onto the Southern Railroad network in 1956. These were Alco "nose" locomotives of type DL 500 C — also known as FD 7. These were later joined by other Alcos, primarily engines of type DL 532 B and DL 535. The Cerro-de-Pasco Railway began running diesel locomotives in 1965. Diesels of type GR 12 W with 956 kW (1,282 hp) outputs supplied by EMD were deployed here.

New stretches of track are built

Railways were still being built in Peru during the 1960s. Southern Peru Copper started operating its works line of 187 km (116 miles) between Toquepala, an ore mine situated 3,300 m (10,827 ft) high in the Andes, and the Pacific port of Ilo in 1960. At least one 2,000-t (2,205-ton) train leaves the heights of the Andes each day to make the descent to the copper works in Ilo. An additional 30-km (19-mile) branch line to Cuajone started operating in 1976. This branch line consists almost entirely of numerous tunnels ranging from 1 to 14.7 km (⅝ to 9 miles). Here, too, one train per day travels the line, pulled by three of the 38 diesel locomotives. These are primarily GM GP 9s of 1,277 kW (1,712 hp) and GM GP 28s of 1,314 kW (1,761 hp).

The Cuzco-Santa-Ana Railroad was similarly extended by some 30 km (19 miles) to Chaullay in 1962, the line finally reached the agricultural centre in Quillabamba in 1978. The total length of the railway thus measured 171 km (106 miles). The damage caused by "El Niño" in the Winter of 1997—98 has interrupted the stretch between Puente Ruinas and Chaullay. Two observation railcars supplied by Ferrostal in Dortmund were brought onto the line in 1966. After a long time in the sidings, they have started being used again for tourism since 2001. After 2-8-2 (1'D1') locomotives from Baldwin and Henschel had pulled the

trains here over the years, from 1972 onwards the baton was taken up by DE 483 diesel locomotives of 876 kW (1,174 hp) made by MLW in Canada and converted to narrow gauge. Despite the importance for tourism, steam engines no longer operate here. Modern railcars made in Spain transport visitors to the fabled Inca city of Macchu-Picchu .

In 1973, after the concessions of the Peruvian Corporation had finally expired, the state-owned Peruvian Railway ENAFER took over running operations on the Central and Southern Railroads. When privatisation started in 1996, 85 diesel and 10 steam locomotives were running on ENAFER's network. Among these were the two steam engines which still survive today in Huancayo - no. 104, a Henschel 1'D1' (2-8-2) locomotive from 1951, and no. 107, a Hunslet 2-8-0 (1'D) locomotive from 1936. However, many of the locomotives could only be put to limited use, making the railways very unreliable. As in the other countries, the state rail operator suffered financial difficulties. ENAFER nevertheless tried to modernise its fleet of engines. The latest acquisitions were GM diesel type GT 26 CW locomotive of 2,200 kW (2,949 hp), and before that five 2,410 kilowatt of type GT 26 CW 2B diesel locomotives of 2,410 kW (3,230 hp) had been purchased from Villares. Privatization created two large companies, Peruvian Andean Railways with the old Central Railroad and the Cerro de Pasco network, and Peruvian Railways with the Southern Railroad network and the Cuzco-Santa-Ana Railroad. The lines from Huncayo to Hunacavelica and from Tacna to Arica remain with state-owned ENAFER until 2001.

It is possible to imagine Peru going down a completely different path to other countries in Latin America. Greater emphasis is being placed on the railways here, particularly within the framework of a rail-oriented tourism concept. The Central Railroad is once again offering passenger services, and the last standard gauge steam locomotive has been repaired for excursion trains. ENAFER is thinking about repairing steam locomotives for both its stretches of track. The new Peruvian rail operators have made tangible improvements in train services with regard to both quality and quantity.

The "Queenslander" only makes the Brisbane-Cairns run once a week. The Cape gauge express takes 31½ hours for the journey of 1,681 km (1,045 miles). Cars can be taken along, too, at the end of the train. The engine on 21 May 2001 at Gordonvale was a 1,472-kW (1,973-hp) locomotive of the QR 2100 class.

In view of the general developments on the fifth continent, it should come as no great surprise that the history of the railways in Australia is tied up closely with the mother country, Great Britain. The first steam-operated railway line ran between Melbourne and the port at the mouth of the Yarra River in September 1854. The track gauge selected was influenced by the plans of the Sydney Railroad Company in neighbouring New South Wales, and thus the state of Victoria chose the track gauge commonly used in Ireland 5 ft 3 in (1,600 mm). When the Irish chief engineer was replaced by a Scot the Sydney-Paramatta line was built in the standard gauge of 4 ft 8½ in (1 435 mm), thus heralding the start of almost 150 years of on-going problems for a railway system based on several centres with different gauges.

Once it became clear that none of the private rail companies could survive financially, the individual states took charge of expanding the rail networks. While the New South Wales Government Railway (NSWGR) steadfastly used the standard gauge, the Victoria Railway (VR), having made its decision for the broad gauge, kept to it and built an extensive network around the Melbourne economic hub. Together with the South Australia Railway (SAR) around Adelaide, whose tracks were likewise built in 5 ft 3 in (1,600 mm) gauge, an expansive broad gauge network was created in the south of the continent. For a long time this was the only rail link between two provincial capitals that did not require a change of gauge. While the NSWGR and

VR at least stuck consistently to a uniform gauge, SAR started to build some narrow gauge lines in the so-called Cape gauge of 3 ft 6 in (1,067 mm) from 1870 onwards for reasons of costs. The rail pioneers in the remaining colonies and today's federal states finally settled on the Cape gauge, too, likewise for reasons of cost. The Queensland Government Railway (QGR) was built around Brisbane, the Western Australia Government Railway (WAGR) around Perth and the Tasmanian Government Railway (TGR) centred on Hobart.

In addition to the individual railways operated by the states, the federal government established the interstate Commonwealth Railway (CR). The primary goal of this was to build interstate lines across the continent, which could hardly be financed by one state alone. As the first large-scale project, the almost 1,700-km (1,050-mile) "Trans-Australia" route from Pt Augusta (SA) through the endless expanse of the Nullarbor Plain and endless desert sand to Kalgoorlie (WA) was created between 1912 and 1917. Linking two Cape gauge networks with a standard gauge line might, at first glance, seem to be yet another episode in the track gauge chaos. But in fact it turned out to be a far-sighted move as it started the standardization of gauges. It would be several decades, however, before rail traffic could roll freely right across the continent.

A second rail project important for the Northern Territory (NT), under financially-dependent administration, was to connect Darwin to the Australian network. Although CR took over SAR's "Great Northern" narrow gauge line completed as early as 1891 from Pt Augusta via the Pichi Richi Pass to Oodnadatta on the border with the NT, and also the Darwin-Pine Creek line built from the north in 1911, the anticipated interconnection never took place. The southern section was extended to the economic centre of Alice Springs while in the north the line ended in Birdum. The northern stretch closed in 1976, while standard gauge trains were able to run between Alice Springs and Pt Augusta from 1980 onwards. The new route ran to the "Trans-Australia" via Tarcoola. Adelaide was the last provincial capital to be linked to the normal gauge tracks via Pt Pirie in 1982.

Several more gauge conversion and new construction projects helped the standard gauge to prevail and thus to the completion of the long-awaited Sydney-Perth transcontinental link. It started with the Sydney-Brisbane stretch opened in 1930. A standard gauge track was laid between Albury (NSW) and Melbourne parallel to the broad gauge line in 1962. The gauge conversion work on the Broken Hill (NSW)-Pt Augusta (SA) and Kalgoorlie - Perth (WA) lines were completed in 1970. The last gap between the important provincial capitals and economic centres was closed when the Melbourne-Adelaide standard gauge line was opened in 1995.

While the former confusion of track gauges was slowly but surely being untangled, efforts to establish interstate railway management largely came to nothing. A minor success in this direction was the merger of CR, SAR and TGR in 1976 to become Australian National (AN). Then in the 1990s the long settled world Australian railways went through a massive shake-up. The state railroads have now largely been replaced by privately operated, and in several places competing, rail lines. This brought a comprehensive modernisation of the vehicle fleet in its wake.

A further milestone in Australian rail history came in 1993 when the National Rail Corporation (NRC) was established to manage interstate container goods traffic between the major economic centres. The founding members included the Commonwealth Railway and the states of NSW and Victoria. In contrast to AN, NRC has been able to survive in the open market. As well as other goods trains used to transport trailers and steel products, NRC has in the meantime also taken over the world-famous "Ghan", "Indian Pacific" and "Overland" tourist trains under commission from Great Southern Railway (GSR). In the first instance the locomotives used had to come from those railways involved in NRC. Then between the end of 1996 and mid-1997 General Electric and Goninan supplied 120 NR class diesel locomotives of 2,920 kW (3,914 hp). These run in most states of Australia. It is not impossible that NRC will also be privatized some time in the future. The number of competitors on the Australian standard gauge network is growing constantly.

Broad gauge railways in Victoria

V/Line, the successor to VR, today has a broad gauge network consisting of nearly 5,900 km (3,666 miles) of track. After privatisation in 1999, its goods division was taken over by Rail America, an American company. The goods traffic scene in south-east Australia is nowadays dominated by the dark green locomotives of Freight Victoria and Freight Australia. V/Line's

Above: The West Coast Railway operates its service from Melbourne's Spencer Street station via Geelong to Warrnambool with, among others, locomotives of the S class built by General Motors and taken over from V/Line. Alongside it on 19 April 2001, a diesel traction car belonging to V/Line waits for its next task.

Below: The "Puffing Billy" Railway is without doubt one of the most lovable and scenically attractive museum railways in Australia. The tourist railway is operated on a 25-km (15½-mile) section of 30-in (762 mm) gauge track between Belgrave and Gembrook in the Dandenong Ranges. This photograph taken on 2 May 2001 shows the celebrated trestlework bridge at Belgrave.

passenger services from Melbourne were divided into different areas, while uneconomic stretches of track were closed down. The French Connex Group, for example, operates not only Sydney's well-known monorail system, but also a third of the metro network in the Melbourne metropolis of several million inhabitants. A British company, National Express, took over a large part of local passenger services from V/Line Passenger and also parts of the metro and tram systems. Passenger trains still depart from

Melbourne's Spencer Street station every day for South Geelong, Ballerat, Warragul/Traralgon and Seymore, with more irregular services to Swan Hill and to Echuca. An XPT paired train to Sydney, the "Overland" express to Adelaide, which departs several times a week, and not least private operators, such as West Coast Railway (WCR) with its passenger service to Warrnambool, have brought a great deal more colour to Victoria's tracks over the last ten years. The massive S class locomotives, built by EMD in the USA,which were surplus to V/Line's requirements, are among the most popular photo subjects for railway enthusiasts. The steam trips offered at weekends from Melbourne to Warrnambool or Bendigo/Echuca with a powerful R 711 WCR locomotive are another attraction.

The tram system, which links to all attractions, is a comfortable yet inexpensive means of travelling around the centre of Melbourne. Flinders Street station is indisputably one of the city's most pleasing buildings. It is a hub for a number of tram lines and also the suburban metro network. Among the highlights of a stay in Melbourne, although admittedly not cheap, is without doubt a trip right through the city on a Colonial Tramcar Restaurant featuring a gourmet menu.

The range of museum railways is also refreshingly varied: Steamrail Victoria in Ballerat, the Victorian Goldfields Railway in Castlemain, the Mornington Tourist Railway on Mornington Peninsula south of Frankston or the South Gippsland Railway around Korumburra offer, among other things, steam driven museum trains on broad-gauge tracks. The partly rebuilt Bellarine Peninsula Railway south-east of Geelong is a true El Dorado for Cape gauge

Above: SAR's type 106 diesel traction car.

fans. On Sundays and on many public holidays various locomotives make the trip between Queenscliff and Drysdale.

A trip on the Puffing Billy Railway is a must when staying in Melbourne. Through the rain forest situated some 40 km (25 miles) east of Melbourne in the scenic Dandenong Range, it runs from Belgrave to Lakeside or Gembrook over several trestle bridges. It is impossible to overlook the considerable support given by the state to this famous railway built with a 30-inch (762-mm) gauge and operating daily train services. The star of the varied fleet of steam and diesel locomotives is a newly renovated steam engine of the Climax class. Noticeable features are the often very long trains and the extremely steep gradients on the stretch. The oldest museum railway in Australia and at the same time the last surviving narrow-gauge line in Victoria can easily be reached by the metro.

Development in New South Wales

Starting from Sydney, but also including Canberra, NSWGR constructed a relatively tightly-knit network. The main trunk lines run between Albury (-Melbourne), via the Blue Mountains to Broken Hill (-Pt.Augusta/Adelaide/Perth) and in a northerly direction to Brisbane. The main freight transported in NSW is coal with 75% of total volume, followed by grains and cereals.

State Rail, established in 1980 as the successor to NSWGR, was split up into three separate divisions in 1988. CityRail operates the suburban system in Greater Sydney on numerous lines, mostly starting from Sydney Terminal. Its total track length is about 900 km (560 miles) and extends out into the Blue Mountains. Since 1993 it has exclusively deployed double-decker electric traction trains of different construction models.

Countrylink runs the long-distance passenger services to Canberra, Griffith, Moree and Armidale with newly purchased two to four part diesel traction cars of the Xplorer series. Using XPT traction cars imported from Britain (HST there), it operates a paired train in the respective directions Melbourne, Dubbo and Brisbane/Murwillumbah, sometimes with sleeping cars.

FreightRail (today FreightCorp) is responsible for goods traffic services on some 7,500 km 94,660 miles) of track in NSW, although since the 1996 rail reform it has faced increasing competition from the neighbouring states and private companies. One of its main competitors is Silverton, a company that recently started running non-stop trains from Sydney to Perth pulled by diesel locomotives discarded by FreightRail, of the 442 class, for example.

As well as railcar sets, numerous new locomotives have been purchased in recent years — the blue/yellow six-axle 82 and 90 class in 1994, for example — and older machines have been put in the sidings. Electric railcars, incidentally, are being used less and less frequently. In place of the Mitsubishi electric engines of the 85 or 86 class, diesel locomotives often pull trains under overhead cables, for instance in the Blue Mountains. One of the most interesting industrial railways is owned by Australia's second-largest steel works in Pt Kembla south of Wollongong. FreightCorp and the BHP Industrial Rail-

Opposite page and above: The famous "Kingston Flyer" is an especially interesting steam train that gives pleasure to up to 20,000 fans a year with its design in the style of the 1920s. Locomotive 778 is evidently very well maintained.

station. This section of the route takes four hours to cover 234 km (145 miles). After a break of one hour, the "Tranzalpine" returns to Christchurch on the same route.

The way to the ferry harbour of Picton

A third train completes the group of famous trains on the southern island, the "Coastal Pacific", which travels along the Pacific coast as its name suggests. Its goal is Picton, which is the northernmost point on South Island where ferries with passengers and railway coaches aboard head towards Wellington. The route of the "Coastal Pacific" first passes through hilly pastures to wind its way down to the coast. The blue ocean and the Seaward Kaikoura Range, which is up to 2,000 m (6,600 ft) high, form a contrasting backdrop. It is said that travellers sometimes even see dolphins.

After Wharanui, the "Coastal Pacific" leaves the coast and crosses an area of rough grassland. The train climbs down into the largest wine growing region in New Zealand in the Marlborough region after passing Lake Grassmere and crossing over Weld's Pass. Just before reaching the harbour city of Picton, the "Coastal Pacific" crosses the raging Wairau River on a low flood bridge. In the Picton ferry harbour the passenger trains and freight wagons wait for shipment to Wellington. Of the three ferries that travel across the Cook Strait to the northern island, one is used for train traffic.

Travelling on North Island

The main line on North Island, which connects the two largest cities, Wellington and Auckland, was opened in 1908. This is where the "North-

lander" and the "Overlander" are to be found. The first is the only night train in New Zealand. The latter travels the same route by day and requires about ten hours for the trip. A no less spectacular landscape rich in contrasts awaits train travellers on this journey. Again, it is a coast route that the train travels along at first, this time towards the Tasmanian Sea whose high waves are very popular with surfers. A few kilometres after the town of Paekakariki the electric wires of the public transport system of Wellington come to an end.

After a bit more than two hours of travel time, the "Overlander" reaches Palmerston North, the last large city before crossing the mountains. With the aid of the Raurimu Spiral, a height difference of 635 m (2,083 ft) is overcome in only 6 km (4 miles) between Raurimu and National Park. The Raurimu Spiral consists of one complete circle, three horseshoe curves and two tunnels.

The three volcanoes Tongariro, Ngauruahoe, and Ruapehu, all still active, dominate the surrounding landscape. As the journey continues, ancient forests, giant valleys and raging rivers pass by the windows. The end of the journey is signalled by a view of the harbour and skyline of Auckland. The city is famous for the yachts from all over the world that congregate in the harbour.

Nostalgia steam loco — the "Kingston Flyer"

Gold was found in the Southern Alps near the city of Queenstown in the twenties. This discovery was the reason for the construction of a train line from Invercargill to Queenstown. Unfortunately, the line only exists in part today.

The remaining 14 km (9 miles) of track lies in a climatically unfavourable region of South Island distinguished by rapid changes in the weather. Nevertheless, the landscape is wonderful. Furthermore this route, which begins and ends in the small town of Kingston and runs to the former settlement of Fairlight, is still travelled by a steam locomotive. Two pairs of steam trains travel the route every day. In Fairlight there is still a reversing triangle to enable the steam locomotive to turn round. It bears the suggestive name "Kingston Flyer".

The towing locomotives are two Pacific, numbers 778 and 795. They belong to Ab class. Once 125 similar locomotives travelled the railways of New Zealand Rail (NZR). Steam locomotive 778 was produced in 1925 by the Addington company in Christchurch. Locomotive 795 was built two years later in the Hillside steam locomotive works in Dunedin. Both are therefore original New Zealand products. The nostalgia train, which is made up of the locomotives described above and passenger coaches from the 1920s, has been in use since 1971. The true steam locomotive operates from October to April and attracts scores of railway fans and tourists year after year.

From 1902 to 1937 an express train with the name "Kingstone Flayer" travelled between Gore and Kingstone. Along with the steam boat that was used on Lake Wakatipu, it created the link to Queenstown. The newer "Kingston Flyer" fits seamlessly into this tradition. On Lake Wakatipu the steamboat "T.S.S. Earnslaw" is still reviving the era of the golden twenties in today's mundane world.

Above: The fireman first needs to get the fire going properly before the steam special can set off on the great journey.
Right: The best known railway bridge in South Africa must be the Kaaiman's River Bridge on the section from George to Knysna near Wilderness.

The African continent began to be opened up with the help of railways at the end of the 1850s. They were built by the colonial powers, who wanted to use the railways to increase their influence in their sovereign territories in Africa. As the largest colonial power, Britain played a correspondingly important role in developing the African rail network. It mainly focussed on two places: Egypt and South Africa.

The first railway in Africa was the Cairo-Alexandria line opened in 1856. In the south of the continent, short lines first appeared in the densely populated areas on the coast around Cape Town and Durban. The Durban line was inaugurated on 26 October 1860, and that starting from Cape Town on 13 March 1862. Britain was keen on expanding the rail systems in its Cape Colony and in neighbouring Natal, which likewise came under its rule. Railways were built into the interior from the ports on the Indian Ocean, Port Elizabeth, East London and Durban. The line beginning in Durban in Natal ran through the provincial capital Pietermaritzburg northwards to Charlestown.

Diamonds, gold and coal

The pace of development was slower in the neighbouring Boer republics, the Orange Free State and Transvaal (South African Republic). Railways were not built enthusiastically here until the discovery of diamonds around Kimberley in 1868 and of gold in Transvaal in 1886. Johannesburg became an industrial centre, connected by rail to several ports in the south and south-east. The lines from the Indian Ocean ran through the Orange Free State capital of Bloemfontein and on northwards.

The full line through to Johannesburg and on to Pretoria, the administrative centre of the South African Republic, was ready on 1 January 1893. The Cape Town-Beaufort West-De Aar-Kimberley line, which remains the

Above: One of the indestructible locomotives of the 25 NC class hauling a short goods train.

Opposite page: Two engines of the 25 NC class pull a goods train from Kimberley to Bloemfontein over the Modder River near Perdeberg in July 1988.

most important to this day, was opened on 28 November 1885. The period from 1874 to 1900 can be seen as the railway boom phase. Main lines were constructed and branch lines built to connect to the coal mines. Of this network, a few industrial railways remain in the coal fields of north-east Natal. They usually run through majestic countryside and, every so often, steam engines are still put into use today.

The founding of South African Railways

Towards the end of the 19th Century, other countries were likewise building major trunk lines in their sovereign territories. A line 89 km (55 miles) long was built in Mozambique between 1887 and 1890, which connected the Portuguese port of Lorenzo Marques with the settlement at Komati Poort, situated on the border with the Republic of South Africa. The connecting line 475 km (295 miles) long through the Republic of South Africa to Pretoria was completed five years later. The construction of this railway is regarded as a milestone in the development of the railway network in southern Africa. There was now a transverse rail line linking the major trading centres.

Britain constructed further lines in its other possessions in southern and central Africa. The Uganda Railroad from Mombasa via Nairobi to Lake Victoria, for example, was opened in 1901. The Boer states looked upon this British predominance with suspicion. Using British rail companies as a

front, British influence in these countries had been multiplied. The Boers' defensive attitudes provoked a string of military skirmishes with the British Army from 1899 to 1902. After the defeat of the Boers in 1902, their states came under British sovereignty. The four British colonies became united as the Union of South Africa in 1910. All the railways were now also placed under a uniform management. SAR, South African Railways, was founded. At the end of 1910 its overall network amounted to 15,781 km (9,806 miles).

Britain built the Prieska-Kalkfontein rail line during World War I. It connected the network of the Union of South Africa with that of German South West Africa, which became a British mandatory territory after the war. The link to the railroads in Zimbabwe (the country known as Rhodesia until 1980) was established in 1974 with the completion of the section 110 km (68 miles) long between Rutenga and Beitbridge.

Expansion of the main lines

By 1914 so many coal trains were running on the main line through Natal down to Durban that the decision was taken to electrify it. Work, however, did not start until 1922, after World War I, and it took until 1938 to complete. The Johannesburg-Pretoria run had been fully electrified the preceding year. Overhead cables had been installed over the section between Cape Town and Simonstown as early as 1928. The cables at that

Above: A condensation tender is coupled to locomotive 3511. Water is reclaimed from the exhaust steam, which can be seen from the small, white clouds of vapour around the tender.

Opposite page: The potential transport capacity of the narrow 3 ft 6 in (1,067 mm) Cape gauge of is really quite amazing.

time carried 3,000 volts. Some 50 years later this was converted to 25,000 volts and 50 cycles. Overhead cables were gradually erected over more and more main lines. The gauge most commonly used in Africa is the 3 ft 6 in (1,067 mm) gauge, the so-called "Cape gauge". There are, however, some railways with gauges even narrower than this.

Apart from the dense suburban traffic around the large cities, passenger traffic in South Africa is still generally confined to the main lines. Goods trains have retained their importance. As one of the world's leading mining countries, South Africa relies on a properly functioning infrastructure to enable it to export its mineral wealth. For this reason the country's state-owned railway company is not restricted to managing rail traffic only; it also has other systems of transport at its disposal.

On account of its colonial past, SAR, South Africa's nationalized railway company, found itself in possession of steam engines of the most varied construction classes. SAR was privatized in 1989 and re-named South African Transport Services (SATS). A year later it was again renamed, this time as "Transnet". The company's finances are monitored by the minister for public enterprises.

Travelling by Cape gauge: South African steam

At the end of the age of steam, Transnet, with the help of railway enthusiasts, endeavoured to preserve at least one representative of each class of steam engine. This means that today the rail operator has a relatively large number of steam engines in working condition, a fact that makes the country a magnet for railway enthusiasts. In 1970 the three main rail repair shops at Bloemfontein, Kroonstad and Bethlehem between them still deployed over 400 heavy steam engines, but naturally this number shrunk drastically during the 1980s. Line closures took their inevitable toll. Other reasons were the electrification of the main goods lines and the general change to diesel traction.

Transnet's fleet of steam engines today consists of the following main types. There are large engines of SAR classes 1 to 26. Similar engines with minor constructional differences were placed in the same class and differentiated solely by a letter (e.g. 19 D). Some boilers of older classes have been replaced with new ones during the 1930s. These machines were designated with the letter "R" for re-boilered. "M" for main line or "B" for branch line, referring to the field of use of particular locomotives. An "S" signified a shunting engine.

Steam engines running on the stretches through the parched Karoo plains needed to use as little water as possible. SAR therefore acquired 90 4-8-4 (2'D2') locomotives of the 25 class equipped with condensation tenders manufactured by Henschel and North British. Instead of having a blast pipe, locomotives of the 25 class were fitted with a steam turbine. The

Above: The two Star locomotives Red Devil and Blue Devil together haul a heavy goods train near Perdeberg

Opposite page: The Garrett GMAM pulling an excursion train on its way through the Montagu Pass, accelerating under an eye-catching cloud of steam.

exhaust steam from the cylinders was fed over to the condensation tender, which was provided with cooling fins and fans, where the hot exhaust steam was converted back to feed water. The easiest way of recognising these locomotives was the lack of smoke rings. Instead these steam engines emitted a whining noise. The condensation tenders reduced water consumption by 60%.

In addition 50 steam engines were delivered without condensation tenders. They are designated 25 NC (non condensing). Of these models, 39 were produced by Henschel, while North British made the other 11 examples.

The condensation equipment began to be removed once the Tousriver-De Aar line had been converted to diesel. From then on these engines, now likewise called 25 NC, were identifiable by their peculiarly shaped, dismantled tenders, which resemble overturned bath tubs.

The Malletts and Garratts, both special construction models widely used throughout South Africa, were categorised as MA to MJ class

(Mallett engines) and GA to GO class (for Garratt engines). The prefix NG identifies narrow gauge locomotives.

The Blue and Red Devils

Locomotive 26 3450 was converted in 1981. With its complete bodywork painted red, it soon became known everywhere simply as the Red Devil. This steam engine of 4,000 hp (2,984 kW) lost virtually all its red livery in repair work after an accident, only carrying red smoke deflector plates thereafter. The Red Devil was a one-off example created from an engine of the 25 class. The Kimberley-Bloemfontein run was among the routes it travelled.

SAR also created a Blue Devil with blue smoke deflector plates. This one-off example 25 NC 3454 has a chimney system that was altered in 1987. What makes this engine remarkable is its two chimneys installed next to each other. When the Blue and Red Devils jointly pull a heavy goods train, they generate a massive combined power of 7,000 hp (5,222 kW).

Famous eccentrics: the Garratt steam engines

South Africa is renowned for its famous Garratt steam engines. These special models are articulated locomotives based on a design patented by an

English engineer, Herbert Garratt (1864—1913). Garratt initially built its locomotives in 1909 for Tasmania, where they were able to demonstrate their enormous abilities. Garratt locomotives are articulated steam engines with two tenders. The steam boiler and the driver's cabin are situated in the middle. They rest on a connecting frame carried on the inner ends of the two motor trucks. The rear motor truck carries a water tank and coal bunker, and the front one just a water tank.

Garratts still survive mainly on private industrial railways. The Coronation coal mine in Natal, for example, runs Garratt engines painted grass green. Other private narrow gauge railways likewise deploy Garratts, such as the Alfred County Railway on its 24-in (600-mm) gauge line from Port Shepstone to Harding. This runs through the hilly, sub-tropical part of Natal's southern coast. Its starting point, Port Shepstone, lies 150 km (93 miles) south of Durban.

SAR closed a section 122 km (76 miles) long in October 1986, fearing competition from a newly constructed trunk road. Two railway enthusiasts nevertheless managed to take it over and revitalize it. The private railway today earns its keep through goods traffic, which primarily involves transporting wood and sugar cane, and also through tourism. Rail enthusiasts can travel through the richly varied scenery of the coastal region on the "Banana Express".

Transnet's nostalgia trains

Transnet profits from the tourist value of its locomotives and track with its nostalgia trains, which hark back to the tradition of the stately carriages which traversed the South African countryside at the start of the 20th century. The best known of these luxury trains were those belonging to SAR's travel companies, Union Limited and Union Express, which were introduced in 1923. Trains with evocative names are running again, such as the Blue Train, which has operated between Pretoria, Johannesburg and Cape Town since 1972. Nevertheless, steam engine fans in particular prefer the trains of United Limited Steam Railtours, a subsidiary of Transnet. This company deploys steam engines whenever possible. These pull de luxe carriages from the early period of luxury trains, which have been restored to their original state and adapted to meet the needs of today.

Panoramic routes under steam power

The section 67 km (42 miles) long between George-Knysna is the last railway in South Africa that still operates a regular steam service. The line was opened on 17 October 1928 and was known at that time as the most expensive railway line in the world because of the high cost of building its many large bridges. The gauge is the Cape standard of 3 ft 6 in (1,067 mm). Steam trains run here daily, except Sundays, along a magnificent route that time and again opens up to give views out over the waves of the Indian Ocean. One of the steam trains is the "Outeniqua-Choo-Tjoe" with its nostalgic carriage fittings. The railway leaves George

Right: Overlooking the Indian Ocean, Victoria Bay provides some very impressive photo backdrops. An excursion train is on its way to Knysna on 3 June 1997.

Above: The "Banana Express" is a popular tourist attraction. The train is pulled by a green-painted Garratt articulated locomotive.

Opposite page: The distinctive form of Garratt locomotives has always drawn admiring glances from steam engine enthusiasts.

to take the renowned Garden Route running through the Wilderness Tourist Centre and the nature reserve of the same name eastwards. Shortly before reaching Wilderness, the train crosses the most famous structure on the line, the Kaaiman´s River Bridge. This majestic bridge over the river's estuary into the Indian Ocean was built between 1926 and 1928 and is 210 m (689 ft) long. The most central of the 15 bridge piers had to be sunk 21 m (69 ft) deep into the river bed before finally reaching a firm base of solid rock.

On its journey to Knysna, the train traverses a number of so-called low trestle bridges spanned over water. Travellers feel as if they are gliding over the water in the train on these crossings. These bridges were very difficult to construct, either because they had to be continually re-propped onto their anchorages with the help of rocks, or — as in the case of the two lagoon bridges near Knysna, with a total length of 2.4 k m (1½ miles) — they had to be supported on wooden poles sunk deep into the ground. The town of Knysna, a former base of the Dutch East Indies Company, was formerly an important harbour, well protected by a fairly narrow exit to the high seas. The town is situated picturesquely at the foot of the Outeniqua mountains and is now a popular tourist resort.

Steam enthusiasts will find opportunities for many special excursions

Above: A steam engine parade at Coronation. This private coal railway also uses Garratts formerly belonging to the state railways.

Below: Traversing one of the two lagoon bridges near Knysna. Together they are 2.4 km (1½ miles) long.

Opposite page, top: Locomotive 16 D 860 at the head of an excursion train from Swellendam to Ashton on 28 May 1997.

Opposite page, below: Leaving a trail of black smoke in its wake, a 25 NC pulls a coal train to De Aar (1988).

in South Africa. There is usually the chance to stop en-route to take pictures of the line. Such photograph stops are known in South Africa as photo run-bys.

A particularly impressive train journey runs through the Montagu Pass. This stage is also operated by "Union Limited Outeniqua". It takes rail tourists from Mossel Bay out via George to Topping and from there up into the Outeniqua mountains. Running over the Montagu Pass, a high plateau 24 km (15 miles) long, it heads towards the leading ostrich breeding centre in the world, the town of Oudtshoorn. From there it continues

into the plains of Small Karoo, frequently with a Garratt locomotive at the head. The return journey again runs via George and then on once more to Cape Town.

Starting from Cape Town, special excursion trains also set off for the fruit-farming areas east of the metropolis. This highly appealing route runs through the famous Sir Lowry's Pass between Steenbras and Elgin.

A no less popular line starts out from the Indian Ocean, in Port Elizabeth. This is the narrow gauge line to Thornhill/Loerie, on which a nostalgic steam train known as the "Apple Express" runs.

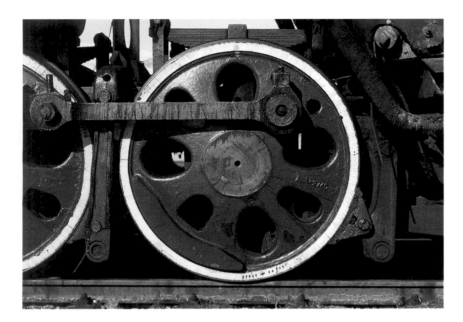

About: View of the driving wheels of the Type QJ freight locomotive.

Right: Sadly, today the fascination of scheduled main-line steam can only be enjoyed in Inner Mongolia.

The era of steam locomotives actually ended long ago. They are only a few "oases" where steam traction is established, for example in Inner Mongolia, an autonomous region of China. Here on 1 December 1995 a railway line from Jining Nan to Tongliao was opened.

In the context of Chinese railway history, there is nothing particularly unusual about the creation of this new line, known as the Ji-Tong line. It is simply another contribution helping to improve the infrastructure of an impassable region.

After the foundation of the People's Republic of China in the year 1949, the standardization and extension of the railway network formed part of successive Five-Year Plans. The plan in force since 1996 requires an extensive replacement of steam locomotives with electric and diesel ones. From this standpoint, it is therefore all the more astonishing that the Ji-Tong line is operated exclusively with steam locomotives, which are vanishing from the rest of China's railways.

Tough beginning

In China, the introduction of railway transport was not a swift triumphal march as it was in Europe and America. On the one hand, this was because of the suspicious attitude of the native rulers who were opposed to the fire-breathing steam locos, which in their eyes resembled fabulous, unpredictable animals. As well as this, there was considerable antagonism towards strangers, the odious colonials, chiefly Englishmen, who were continually pushing for railway construction in China. This enthusiasm was not without ulterior motives, since their own territory would be easier to control with the help of railways. The combination of the fear of unknown technology and suspicion towards foreigners significantly restricted public discussion of the subject of railways in China.

The first technical reports of the development of steam locomotives began to reach the country in about 1840. Even then, the guiding intellectual forces

Above: Semaphore signal on the Jingpeng pass. In this position no train is allowed to pass. It has to wait for the signal to change.

Above: In this position the driver is allowed to proceed to the signal at the end of the next section.

Right: A train controller awaits the passage of a goods train, whose wagon formation he is watching carefully. If there is any sign of irregularity he will halt the train.

Left: The whole line is single track so the continually increasing number of trains have to make use of frequent passing loops. It also provides a short rest for the locomotive and its crew.

Below: These halts are often used for replenishing the locomotive's water. While the fireman looks after this, the driver checks the engine's valve gear.

of China recognized the potential significance of the railway for the country and its economy. However, these opinions were ignored, since the country was already fully occupied with internal disputes and problems of foreign policy. In spite of this, an English company built a test track 500 m (550 yd) in front of the gates of Beijing in 1865. The Chinese ruling house deplored it.

China's first railway line was opened at Shanghai in July 1876. The route was 8 km (5 miles) long and it was the product of cooperation between a British company and Chinese merchants. Despite the native population voicing its approval of the line, it was removed after two years, having become state property. The rolling stock was destroyed. Nevertheless, this did not succeed in keeping railways out of China. A route 10 km (6 miles) long, which would later become part of the main line between Beijing and Tianjin, was opened in June 1881. By 1894 a total of about 400 km (250 miles) of track had been laid. To put this in perspective, by this time the amount of permanent way in Germany alone was about one hundred times as long.

Above: Two QJs working in tandem hauling a heavy wood train. As well as the gradients, the very low temperature demands the most of the engines.

Opposite page: The bitter cold naturally causes a magnificent development of steam. A thin sprinkling of cold and the clear light makes it easy to take extremely beautiful photographs. The best month for a visit is February because the days are getting longer and there is still enough frost to ensure the creation of copious amounts of steam.

Different gauges

At the end the 19th century, railway construction received a new impulse. The high reparations demanded by the Japanese after China's defeat in the Sino-Japanese war of 1894—95 caused great economic difficulties and put China heavily in debt to the colonial powers, such as Britain, Russia and Germany. The foreigners immediately began building railways in order to increase their influence in particular regions. Alternatively they acquired influence through bonds issued to finance the construction of sections of the country's railways.

The building boom had only one snag. The different countries used their own gauges in building the new tracks, so there was no uniform gauge throughout the system. The existing Chinese stretches were united in 1912 as a result of the country's substantial foreign debts and it was constantly

extended until 1927, so that by then about 21,000 km (13,000 miles) existed. But the decision to standardize the track gauge was only taken after the foundation of the People's Republic in 1949.

In the extension of the main lines and the repair of damaged sections, the forces of railway engineers were supplemented by military units. By 1990, the network of the Chinese National Railway had increased to about 80,000 km (50,000 miles).

Four main steam locomotive types

As well as a uniform gauge, the People's Republic of China also strove to standardize the steam locomotives. Instead of a multiplicity of locos from all the different regions, it was decided that only few types robust and reliable steam

Top: The ever-hungry firebox of the QJ.

Above: A meeting between trains seen from the crew's viewpoint. Although it is really warm in the driver's cab, the crew still put their faith in substantial fur hats.

Right: In spite of the hard work, the crew of this locomotive laugh cheerfully with photographers from every part of the world.

Left: Passing loops on entering sections of the single-track line are of course essential. They provide an opportunity to enjoy the thrilling sight of up to four steam locomotives working at once.

locomotives should run on Chinese tracks. Existing locos were standardized and modernized.

From 1952, the production of the four main types was carried out in the country itself. Their names were derived from the key concepts of the Cultural Revolution. QJ comes from "Qianjin", meaning "advance". JF stands for "Jiefang" ("liberation"); in the 1950s these locos with a 1´D 1´ (2-8-2) wheel arrangement were the most widespread steam loco in China. The JS series, from "Jianshe" ("construction") came out 1957 as a development of the JF. Ultimately they were usually used as shunting locomotives. Lastly, the SY series, "Shangyou" ("high goal"), originated in 1960 and is therefore the youngest Chinese steam locomotive type. The SY series, relatively smaller than the other main types, were often put to work in industrial railways, among other duties.

The QJ freight locomotives

The QJs are freight locomotives with a 1´E 1´ (2-10-0) wheel arrangement. The robust steam colossuses with prominent smoke deflectors typified the

appearance of the Chinese railroad during the age of steam. The model for this loco was the Soviet Series LV, whose main measurements were adopted. The prototype was built in 1956 with Soviet help and first carried the designation HP for "heping" ("peace"). Subsequently, the Chinese engineers began to develop the engine and improve it. In order to achieve a higher level of thermal efficiency, they installed a new firebox with a larger heating surface. To increase the forced, draught a flat chimney was installed, designed by the Austrian engineer Giesl-Gieslingen. The measures described helped to reduce the coal consumption by up to 15%. Furthermore, in order to increase the adhesive weight for a short time, the Chinese steam locomotives could transfer weight from the running wheels to the large driving wheels, whose diameter was 1.5 m (4'11") in each case.

The two cylinders together had a capacity of 2,650 cm^3 (161.7 cu in). The service weight was 133.8 t (147.5 tons) plus 87.6 t (96.6 tons) for the four-axle bogie tender, including 14.5 t (16 tons) of coal and 39.5 m^3 (8,700 gal/10,400 US gal) of water. The locomotives with service numbers from 6000 onwards had a six-axle tender with a service weight of 116 t (127.9

The pictures on this double spread express the extremes of joy and agony. The low sun makes for some superb images of the steam locomotives on their spectacular journey, while the drivers and firemen toil away ceaselessly in the cab. Several tons of coal have to be heaved into the firebox of the hungry locomotive in the course of its mountain journey. Nothing would be worse than if the loco should run out of steam and come to an undignified halt.

tons) with 21.5 t 23.7 tons) of coal and 50 m³ (11,000 gal/13,200 US gal) of water. In either case the locomotive and tender weighed of the order of 250 t (275 tons) on the rails, so these often had to be relaid to carry the load. As to the performance of these steam locos, their power was about 3,000 hp.

The imposing QJs were built until 1988 in the Chinese Locomotive Factory of Datong. Altogether, the works delivered about 4,700 locomotives to the Chinese National Railway.

The Ji-Tong line

Returning to the line from Jining Nan to Tongliao, this has existed since 1995 and is run by a private railway company. It is commonly known as the Ji-Tong line after the initial syllables of the names of its terminuses.

The line is about 1,000 km (6,200 miles) long and it was built as a high capacity freight relief route. QJ steam locomotives formerly from the Chinese National Railway are used to haul the trains. They are stationed in the Daban locomotive depot. Altogether, about 120 steam locomotives are in operation.

The traffic on the Ji-Tong line mainly consists of high volume freight. Up to eight trains run in each direction daily. The passenger service is limited to only one train each way. It is probably the last regular scheduled steam service in the world. From early in 2001, both trains unfortunately pass the most beautiful section of the Ji-Tong line during the hours of darkness, so that the impressive crossing of the Da-Hinggang mountains cannot be seen from the compartment window.

Roughly in the middle of the journey is a section about 50 km (31 miles) long that crosses mainly barren steppes, in which the trains must struggle over the Jingpeng pass. More and more railway enthusiasts spare no efforts to take a trip on this unique line and experience the magnificent drama of the Jingpeng pass. Since the local authorities and the railway are comparatively well prepared for the kind of tourism that the steam locomotives have attracted, a the trip on the Ji-Tong line is not an incalculable adventure. People making the journey should simply remember that in the hard winter months the temperature can fall to -30° C (-22° F) degrees, and the only protection is suitable clothing.

The Jingpeng pass

From high points that can be reached by taxi, bus or not too long a walk, for example from the city of Reshui, it is possible to watch a train climbing the gradients for as long as an hour. The mountain section is punctuated with

Left: Because of the long, steep climbs and the difficult conditions of the gradients of the Jingpeng pass trains are nearly always hauled by two steam locomotives. Exceptionally, this long train of empty boxcars needs only one QJ to pull it.

long curves, bridges and tunnels . Here, the QJs hauling freight trains are usually double-headed. The engines that operate on the Ji-Tong line are equipped with radio control facilities and run at a maximum of 80 km/h (50 mph). They were built adopting the newer technology of the 1980s and are therefore quite modern representatives of steam traction. They have semi-automatic mechanical stoking, but this has to be supplemented in winter by hand stoking, since the pieces of coal sometimes freeze together.

In general, the cold winters are quite damaging to the Ji-Tong line. The extremely low temperatures cause problems to the rails, and the permanent way also suffers from the extremely heavy weight of the QJ locomotives. As a result of this, track maintenance gangs are often seen at work, repairing the damage by hand.

Previous double spread: A mixed freight train headed by two QJ locomotives struggles through the snowy landscape. The picture was taken in February 2001.

Above: Tunnel exits are spectacular. After a clearly audible staccato, reinforced by the narrow tube of the tunnel, the steam bursts out of the tunnel mouth and hangs around in the air for some time.

Opposite page: The landscape around the Jingpeng pass might be somewhat monotonous without the thin covering of winter snow.

Above left: Icicles on the cab of a QJ locomotive.

Right: There is often an unpleasant wind whistling through the Jingpen pass, as is shown by the way the clouds of steam are blown downwind.

Above right: The viaduct crossing the valley is supported by a number of elegant concrete piers.

Opposite page: Railway enthusiasts have become a familiar sight to the local village children. Far right, Japanese locomotive enthusiasts, well protected from the cold.

421

Above: The driver's view of the line towards the concrete viaduct across the valley, which will be reached in a few minutes (**right**).

Previous double spread: A wonderful back-lit view of a freight train being hauled up the gradient by two QJ locomotives.

Journey to the steam locomotive reserve

Anyone interested in seeing the steam locomotives of the Ji-Tong line can turn to the various specialist organizations offering group trips of railway interest. The trip can also be carried out independently, if certain precautions are observed. It is essential to apply for a visa from the embassy or consulate of the People's Republic of China, or to arrange for one through a travel agent. Staying in the country can also be arranged through the Chinese state travel agency (CITS). There are also Chinese tour guides who can accommodate the interests of railway enthusiasts.

After arrival at the airport of Beijing, the journey continues by train to Chifeng. Normally, the taxi drivers at Chifeng railway station will know exactly where to go, as soon as the name "Jingpeng" is mentioned. After a trip of about four hours the town of Reshui is reached. This is to the east of the pass in the mountainous section. Here there are some hotels where railway enthusiasts can find accommodation. The railway station of Reshui is called Galadesitai. To the west of the town there is an observation point with a fascinating view of the broad curves of the line and the wide turn it makes as it runs over a bridge.

The peak of the line is reached at Shangdian. The pass is named after Jingpeng, which is on the western slope on the other side of the mountain pass. The trains pass a few little villages as they travel along the pass, where sheer mountainsides and rocky summits form a wildly romantic scenery. Alternatively the trains are found to the west and east of the highest point at the railway stations of Xiakengzi and Liudigou respectively.

Especially in winter, the steam locomotives at Jingpeng are a real treat for the eye, with plumes of smoke and steam visible from far away, rising from the hissing, clattering monsters as they toil up the pass.

R ussia's geography has several superlatives to offer. It is hardly surprising that the longest railway line in the world is found in this country, the Trans-Siberian Railway, or "Transsib" for short. Before its construction, crossing Siberia was considered a great adventure. There was only one rough track, the "Moskovsko Sibirski Trakt", which tortured countless teams of horses. In those distant times there was no talk of exploiting the natural riches of Siberia, such as wood, coal, or precious metals. The lack of infrastructure also went against the strategic interests of the Imperial Court. Nevertheless, it took some time for railways to become established in Russia.

First, an excursion railway line

In 1834 an Austrian, Franz Anton von Gerstner, travelled to the court of the Russian tsars. He wanted to persuade Tsar Nicholas I to build a railway line from St Petersburg to Moscow. The Tsar was initially against this plan. However, he did allow the construction of 28 km (17 miles) of track from St Petersburg to his summer residence, the imperial palace Zarskoye Syelo. This first Russian railway line was opened on 30 October 1837. A year later the line had been extended a further 25 km (16 miles) to the excursion town of Pavlovsk. The St Petersburg-Pavlovsk line was run at weekends with four steam locomotives imported from England and Belgium, but on weekdays it was run as a horse train. It had no economic significance, but Tsar Nicholas I was eventually convinced of the strategic and economic importance of railway trans-

port. So the first major railway line, 650 km (404 miles) long between St Petersburg and Moscow, was built between 1843 and 1851. In St Petersburg the Putilov plant was built with the support of American companies and advisors. This is where the first Russian steam locomotives were built, and it soon became one of the largest industrial companies in Russia. Henceforth Russia pursued railway construction with considerable enthusiasm. New lines were planned to transport grain from distant regions to Moscow and St Petersburg and to make access to the country's ports and naval bases on the Baltic Sea and Black Sea easier.

In contrast to the European standard gauge of 4 ft 8½ in (1,435 mm), the Russians used a broad gauge standard of 5 ft 0 in (1,524 mm).

Beginning from both ends

The enormous distances between European Russia and the eastern parts of the country on the Pacific coast had always caused problems for the country's rulers. Therefore interest in a Trans-Siberian railway line was soon aroused. The first projects were presented between 1857 and 1869. At first there was only talk of a partial line. The first transcontinental railway line in North America in 1869 provided encouragement, and the east-west line in Canada was also making good progress. Tsar Alexander III, who was very open to the Trans-Siberian project, was now the ruler in Russia. He decreed the construction of a "Siberian railway" on 17 March 1891. On 19 May the foundation stone was laid by

Opposite page: The electric locomotives of the TschS 2 series can be seen heading passenger trains.

Above: The locomotive is changed frequently on the Trans-Siberian railway. This is usually done at the borders of the different administrative areas. On some sections travel also takes place on non-electrified rails.

Left: The WL 80 series with its blue and green livery is the most common electric locomotive seen on the Trans-Siberian line. It is used to pull the famous "Rossiya" passenger train that travels between Moscow and Vladivostok.

the Tsarevitch, who later became Tsar Nicholas II. He also became chairman of the committee for the construction of the Siberian railway on 10 February 1893.

The construction of the line was undertaken from two directions; in the west it began in Tscheljabinsk at the eastern edge of the Urals in 1892. At this moment work had already begun in Vladivostok. The entire project was divided into several sections: the west Siberian railway from Chelyabinsk to the Ob, the middle Siberian from the Ob to Irkutsk, the Lake Baikal detour line from Irkutsk to the southern tip of the lake near Murinskaya, the Murinskaya-Sretensk railway across Baikal, the Amur railway from Sretensk to Chabarovsk, and the Chabarovsk-Vladivostok Ussuri railway. The work on nearly all sections was done in parallel, under terrible conditions. As soon as sections were completed they were put into use.

Train ferries across Lake Baikal

By 1900 the Siberian railway had reached Lake Baikal from the west. In the east the line from Vladivostok along the Usuri river to Chabraovsk and the line from Sretensk to Lake Baikal were completed by 1897. The link between Sretensk and Chabarovsk (the Amur railway) was only available after 1916. Until then the trains from Chita had to go through Chinese Manchuria through Harbin to Vladivostok. The legal basis for this shortcut was a treaty between Russia and China made in 1896. This line was used until Russia's loss of the Russian-Japanese war. As a

result of its partial destruction and due to strategic considerations, Russia decided to build the difficult connection from Sretensk to Chabarovsk, which went along the Amur exclusively over Russian territory.

But what happened at Lake Baikal? The detour line turned out to be the greatest challenge because of the mountainous territory. Its construction seemed impossible. In view of this, two ferries were built in Glasgow in 1893, which carried the trains across the lake. The larger of the two ships was called "Baikal", which with its length of 88 m (289 ft) could transport 25 railway carriages, 200 people, and 750 t (827 tons) of cargo . While this flagship was not survived, the smaller "Angara" can still be visited in Irkutsk.

The ferry connection was not viewed as a permanent solution. The bottleneck on the Trans-Siberian line still existed and needed to be removed. Thus between 1902 and 1905 the Baikal detour line between Irkutsk and Sljudyanka was finally built.

Steam, diesel and electricity

In contrast to other countries, the Soviet Union began the development of large diesel locomotive as early as 1920. They were intended to replace steam locomotives in the regions of central Asia where water was scarce. Thus diesel locomotives were used on the Transsib from the mid-1920s. There were experiments with electric operation in the Urals in the 1930s, and as a consequence, electrification progressed steadily.

By 1961 the overhead wires reached from Moscow to Irkutsk, and today the whole line is electrified.

The expansion to double tracks began in the first few years. By 1905 there was a second track between the Urals and Irkutsk. In the 1930s the extension of the second track was pursued until it reached the end of the line on the Pacific. As far as the locomotives are concerned, the current Transsib is characterized by electric locomotives of Russian and Czech manufacture. About 1,000 steam locomotives were stationed along the line until about 1990, mostly Class L, but nowadays there are very few of them left. They are used on special excursions as nostalgia trains.

Through seven time zones

Counting the kilometres on the Transsib starts in Moscow, or to be precise in the Yaroslavler train station; it ends in Vladivostok at kilometre 9,297, a distance of 5,758 miles. A total of seven time zones are crossed in the course of the journey. However, as a train passenger there is no problem with jet-lag. The time on a passenger's watch only has to be changed bit by bit. The express trains stop only in the major cities, the most important of which are listed here.

After leaving Moscow, the train stops for the first time at kilometre 280 (equivalent to mile 174) in Yaroslawl. The city with its historic centre is technically a traffic hub between Transsib and shipping on the Volga. The next station is Kirov at kilometre 957 (mile 595). Afterwards

Opposite page: Inspection tour before departure. The locomotive is a WL 60.

Above: Because of the Russia's economic decline, freight traffic on the Trans-Siberian is also diminishing. For this reason there is not always enough for many locomotives to do. Here a group of four WL 80's are waiting for work.

Below: The engineer of the TschS 7 goes about his work in a cheerful mood.

Top: These passengers are taking plenty of heavy luggage with them.

Above: A double locomotive hauls a fast train.

Below: A diesel locomotive heads the Orient Express on the old Baikal route.

it does not stop again until it reaches the Ural mountains. Perm is reached at kilometre 1,434 (mile 891). In the 1960s major oil refineries were built here which gave the city an economic boom. About 340 km (211 miles) further on, the traveller should look out for a light stone obelisk, 4 m (13 ft) high. This marks km 1,777(mile 1,104) which is the border between Europe and Asia or Siberia.

The train then goes to Tyumen, reached via Yekaterinenburg at kilometre 2,144 (mile 1,332). Parallel to the construction of the railway line, the previously unimportant town grew into a Siberian commercial centre where fur and leather goods were produced and sold. Originally the city was untouched by the Transsib. However, the course of the line was changed in order to link this prospering town with markets further afield.

Omsk is almost 600 km (373 miles) further on. Here the Transsib crosses the Irtysh. A large harbour makes freight traffic to the south towards Kazakhstan possible. The following section of the line, 624 km (388 miles) long from Omsk to Novosibirsk is one of the most heavily travelled freight lines in the world.

The city of Novosibirsk was built on the banks of the Ob with the construction of the Trans-Siberian railway in 1893. Novosibirsk is the largest city in Siberia with 1.45 million inhabitants and it is an economic and cultural centre. Like other Siberian cities, its rapid growth is due to its position on one of the largest waterways in the country as well as being on the Transsib.

At kilometre 4,104 (mile 2,550) Krasnoyarsk is reached. The city lies in the middle of a hilly area with the Yenissei on either side, which is an impressive 2 km (1¼ miles) wide here. There are 11 colleges and universities in Krasnoyarsk, as well as a number of scientific research centres and numerous industrial plants producing all sorts of goods, especially machines and ships, wood products, chemicals and textiles.

On Lake Baikal

It is a good 1,000 km (620 miles) to the next centre, Irkutsk. The city with 600,000 inhabitants is the oldest city in eastern Siberia. Irkutsk is the 26th stop made by the Trans-Siberian Express "Rossiya" from Moscow, after 73 hours of travel time. There are just 4,106 km (2,551 miles) more to Vladivostok, or another 70 hours of travel time.

Thanks to its position on the Angara River that flows in Lake Baikal, Irkutsk rapidly grew into a trading centre for furs and goods from Mongolia and China. The Trans-Siberian railway gave the city an economic boost, encouraging industry to settle in the city whose population increased steadily. An excursion by speedboat from Irkutsk to Listvyanka on the shore of Lake Baikal is recommended. Lake Baikal is the deepest lake on Earth, up to 1,620 m (5,315 ft) deep, 80 km (50 miles) wide and 636 km(395 miles) long. The flora and fauna of the Baikal area is unusual. There is a rare type of seal that lives on the banks of the lake and is adapted to fresh water. Another option to approach Lake Baikal is to travel from Irkutsk to Slyudyanka at the southwest corner of the lake. From here it is possible to travel north-east towards the old Baikal line to the mouth of the Angara. This branch line ends in Port Baikal. It

runs along the stony banks of Lake Baikal and has very attractive views of the landscape and down to the lake.

Back in Slyudyanka the trip to the east can be continued. After making a detour around the south shore of Lake Baikal, Ulan-Ude, the capital of the Buryatic Republic is reached at kilometre 5,647 (mile 3,509). Here the railway line branches out. To the south the Trans-Mongolian railway heads for China, while the Transsib continues to the east. Chita at kilometre 6,204 (mile 3,855) is the next large city. Originally a little town in the Yablonovy mountains, it increased in size and importance with the Trans-Siberian railway. It became famous as a gold-mining centre.

By way of Sretensk, the Transsib route reaches Chabarovsk, with a population of 614,000 at kilometre 8,531 (mile 5,301). The city is named after the Siberian explorer Chabarov and it spreads out on the hilly banks of the Amur River, which forms the border with China. The Ussuri flows into the Amur at Chabarovsk. The Transsib follows the banks of the river on the final stage of its journey to Vladivostok. This section, called the Ussuri railway, was the first section of the Transsib to be opened. Vladivostok greets the traveller with its splendid, renovated train station from imperial days. Apart from the railway, the city is economically important for shipbuilding, fishing, and the food industry.

The Trans-Siberian trains

Group Transsib tours to Vladivostok or to the Chinese capital are offered by several tour companies. The coaches used are usually quite comfortable, and steam locomotives are sometimes employed. The advantage of tour packages is that the necessary visas are taken care of by the tour organizer, and accommodation, trips and transfers are arranged in advance. Individual travel is also possible. Nowadays there is plenty of relevant literature enabling a route to be identified and planned.

As well as the famous Trans-Siberian Express "Rossiya", there are other scheduled express trains that head for Vladivostok or Beijing. The carriages of the Trans-Siberian Express were built by VEB Waggonbau-Ammendorf in the former East Germany, as were those of most other Russian express trains.

Above left: A double locomotive of the WL 80 Series is waiting for more work.
Above right: Sunrise, somewhere in the expanses of Siberia. An oncoming train will soon encounter the Orient Express.

In addition, there are express trains nearly every day from Moscow to Ulan-Ude, Ulan-Bator, Chita and Chabarovsk. The "Baikal", one of the best trains in the country, goes as far as Irkutsk. There are also Chinese trains from Beijing to Moscow. In addition, there is a Russian Orient Express whose cars were renovated in 1990. This "hotel train" stands out with its friendly staff, its teak paneling and its ornate dining and saloon cars. However, when travelling to Beijing passengers have to leave this luxury train at the border train station in Erlian and change to the former government guest train. The line as far as the Beijing is also electrified.

The first Asian country to embrace railways was India. The Great Indian Peninsula railway was opened on 18 November 1852, running from Bombay to Thana and about 35 km (22 miles) long. Railways were then built thick and fast. While the scribes were only able to record a mere 7,683 km (4,774 miles) of track in operation at the end of 1870, this had increased to 14,977 km (9,307 miles) of operational lines by the end of 1880. Although relatively unimportant compared to today's main lines, on which the work is shared by diesel and electric locomotives, the narrow gauge Darjeeling Himalayan Railway is still the best known railway in India. Today the line's ancient, plucky little steam engines of British manufacture can still be seen struggling upwards in the clouds of the Himalayas.

Mountain climbing with the Queen

Snorting impatiently, the "Queen of the Hills" waits for the British and Austrian delegations to arrive. After all, the engine is to pull the celebratory train of the Indian Darjeeling Himalayan Railway (DHR). The special excursion on the narrow gauge railway from New Jalpaiguri to Darjeeling, built between 1879 and 1891, is the highlight of the celebrations as well as being a memorable experience in itself.

Not long ago the closure of this unique mountain railway was being debated. With motorised road traffic and the damage caused to the rail bed each year as a result of the monsoon rains, the prospects for the 88 km (55 miles) of this little railway looked bleak indeed. Its importance declined steadily, while its steam locomotives and carriages were scrapped one after the other.

The efforts to preserve the line, more than a hundred years old, therefore intensified over recent years. The Anglo and Indian DHR Societies, in particular, did everything possible to stop the British-built railroad sinking into oblivion. Fate came to the rescue literally at the last moment with inspiration from an unexpected quarter. In far-off Austria, the "Alliance for Nature" (AFN), a nature and environmental protection organisation, had succeeded in persuading UNESCO to declare the Semmeringbahn a World Heritage Site, the first railway in the world so nominated. Since then its has been under the protection of the community of states. Taking the AFN "World Cultural Heritage Semmeringbahn" initiative as its example, an Anglo-Indian alliance applied to have the DHR likewise recognized as a vitally important heritage. The Champagne corks n popped in December 1999when UNESCO included the Darjeeling Himalayan Railway in the elite list of World Heritage Sites. It thus stands alongside such important monuments and ensembles as Venice and its lagoons, the Pyramids at Giseh, Cologne Cathedral and the Great Wall of China.

The "Queen of the Hills" greets travellers from all over the globe and, of course, local passengers, with whistles of welcome. Fully laden with coal, the Queen can hardly wait to set out on the journey that lasts a good ten hours. Not without reason is the engine called the "Queen of the Hills"; the line climbs over 2,000 m (6,600 ft) to reach the highest railway station in Asia at Ghum, which has an altitude of 2,257 m (7,405 ft).

At the start of the journey the train passes the first tea plantations and schoolchildren in uniform waving. The first station is Siliguri, at 121 m (397 ft).

But after just a few miles an accident occurs. The "Queen" hits a motorcyclist, who luckily manages to jump off in the nick of time. His vehicle has been carried a couple of yards down the line, but it still seems to be more or less intact. Perhaps the old engine was just throwing her weight around a bit. Looking at the engine now it is strange but not unimaginable to see her as a "human heritage", on a par with Big Ben in London or the Statue of Liberty in New York, or perhaps even Mount Everest. As nothing serious has happened the journey can continue, but from Sukna at 162 m (531 ft). the track starts to rise sharply. The engine now really has to pull out all the stops and the tropical forest reverberates with the panting sound so characteristic of steam locomotives. The luminous red and brilliant yellow blossoms of plants and trees growing close to the line pass by the window. But the higher the train climbs, the more the dense, tropical vegetation gives way to a more spacious mountain scenery. The views keep getting better and before long you find yourself gazing down upon deep rifts and valleys.

Trains caught up traffic jams

Sometimes trains wait in frustration to the left and to the right of the road like snakes stranded up and down the mountainside. In places where there is no space between the high rock walls on the one side and the solid ground on other, the rails have been laid down the middle of the asphalt ribbon of the road. It is not surprising, then, that trains sometimes get caught up in traffic jams and can often only be seen in the long queue of motor vehicles with their smoke rising in frustration. The DHR trains have to negotiate gradients of up to 1 in 22½ and a total of 554 bridges, 873 tight curves, three (formerly four) full loops and six zig-zags between the stations in the valley and in the mountains.

A derailed carriage

Travellers occasionally find that a journey on the DHR is a real adventure: The derailment of a carriage is no rare occurrence, apparently happening once or twice each time up the mountain, or at least so they say. As no-one really knows when the carriage is going to be put back on the rails, travellers are often better advised to continue their journey on foot. Sooner or later the engines and carriages will reach DHR's workshop in Tindharia, where they are taken apart completely, repaired and put back together again in working order. After several intermediate stops to take on water and coal, the train gradually approaches Darjeeling.

At the Batasia loop

The scenery around the Batasia loop between the highest outlying station of Ghum and the terminal in Darjeeling is majestic. Whilst Kanchenjunga, at 8,598 m (28,209 ft) is the third highest peak in the world, and other Himalayan peaks rise glittering white towards the blue sky in the background, trains snake up the mountain almost at walking pace. A memorial in the middle of the Batasia loop looks back to British colonial times,but it is thanks to international efforts that this unique railway line has been saved. Reflecting the confident mood, the "Queen of the Hills" thanks her saviours with a whistle salute. Everyone hopes that she will still run snorting and steaming along the Darjeeling Himalayan Railway for many years to come.

Top: The station at Ghum, where it seems that a blind eye is turned to coal theft.
Middle: The route to Darjeeling provides some wonderful views.
Opposite page: On the Batasia loop. On steep sections, the men on the engine have to spread sand in front of the wheels to give the locomotive more traction.
Bottom: The terminal in Darjeeling.

Originally the railways of the Far East served mainly to exploit natural resources. Railway technology came in the from of engineers from Europe, Britain being the leading country in this respect. Thus for instance the Thai railway network was developed under foreign supervision, and most of the lines of the Far East were built between 1919 and 1924.

Traveling in colonial style

One of the most beautiful railway lines in Asia connects the capitals of Bangkok, Kuala Lumpur, and Singapore. The line is just over 2,000 km (1,240 miles) long and is travelled by a special train, the Eastern & Oriental Express (E&O). The luxury train needs a good 41 hours to cover this distance. It has existed since 1993 and represents the oriental counterpart to the VSOE (Venice Simplon Orient Express). Both trains belong to the American James B. Sherwood. When fully booked, the E&O travels with 22 carriages. They were built in 1972 and were once used in New Zealand. They were restored and refitted in colonial style over a period of six years . Each carriage received a four-digit number — but the Chinese unlucky numbers 4 (death), 5 (negative), and 7 (change) were avoided. The train also includes two dining cars, a saloon, a bar, an observation car, two staff personnel cars, a generator car, and 14 sleeping cars, making a total length of 440 m (480 yards). As far as the Thai border the train is hauled by a 2,200-hp (1,641 kW) diesel locomotive of the Thai railway service (SRT), built in France. The track gauge is 3 ft 6 in (1067 mm).

On the River Kwai

Leaving the metropolis of Bangkok takes about an hour. The first highlight the passengers experience is the world-famous Bridge on the River Kwai, the location of the 1956 novel by Pierre Boulle and the film that was made from it.

It is about 80 km (50 miles) west of Bangkok, a few kilometres after the little town of Kanchanaburi. After the train has left the bridge, it moves through the most spectacular part of the journey, the valley of the River Kwai. Here the railway was built along rocky cliffs, and in some places it rests on wooden posts surviving from its original construction; here there is a speed limit of 10 km/h (6 mph). The train travels for four hours through the wonderful River Kwai valley.

Tokens

The maximum speed allowed on Thai lines is 80 km/h (50 mph), but single tracks and numerous places where slow speed is required mean that even that speed is not always reached. In the stations the driver always slows the train down a bit to throw a ring or token representing the travel authority for the section just passed onto a post. Further ahead he picks up a second token, which is his authority to enter the forthcoming section of the line. This is a simple but effective security system preventing two trains from using the single track in opposite directions at the same time.

Through the Malacca peninsula

The Malacca peninsula extends from the border of Malaysia to Singapore Coconut and rubber tree plantations line the tracks. Now two diesel locomotives from the Malaysian state railways (KTM) haul the train. Just before Butterworth, the bridgehead to the holiday island of Penang, the E&O rumbles over a large railway bridge. On the morning of the third day of travel the train enters the Malaysian capital Kuala Lumpur. The first tracks were laid on the Malacca peninsula in 1869, and 50 years later there was a line extending the length of the peninsula to enable its raw materials to be exploited.

Eventually the E&O rolls into the city state of Singapore, which has been independent since 1965. The KTM main railway station, built in 1924, greets the travellers half-an-hour later. Then a tour of discovery of the city with its breathtaking skyline can begin.

Top: The comfortable carriages of the E&O are fitted out in colonial style.
Middle: In the valley of the River Kwai and while crossing the famous bridge.
Opposite page: Many famous buildings mark the route of the E&O.

Japanese National Railways (JNR) was founded in 1949 in Japan, whose railway lines were suffered massive damage in World War II. The first high-speed line Tokyo-Kyoto-Osaka (Tokaido Shinkansen) was begun in 1964. Even then the trains travelled at 200 km/h (124 mph). JNR was privatized in 1987 because of its high debts.

The Shinkansen has two main lines starting in Tokyo, which are owned and operated by different railway companies: lines heading to west Japan and north Japan. The Tokaido Shinkansen travels in the west of the main island. There is also the San-yo Shinkansen, which came into operation in 1975. The extension to Kagoshima in the south of the island Kyushu is still under construction. The trains on the west Japan lines are divided into three categories. Nozomi are fast, modern trains that only stop at the most important stations. Hikari stop somewhat more often than Nozomi. Kodama are trains that stop at every station and mostly carry schoolchildren and commuters. The double-deck Shinkansen have also been used in the last category since 1964.

The first north Japanese Shinkansen started in 1982: thus the Tohoku Shinkansen went from Tokyo to Morioka and the Joetsu Shinkansen to Niigata. Later additional routes to the north were added, and new construction is still in progress.

While the Shinkansen of the original type only travel in the slower categories of train, the super-fast trains now use modern electric locomotives from the 1990s. The trains of the latest generation reach speeds of up to about 350 km/h (217 mph). The total output of their motors ranges from about 5,000 kW (6,700 hp) to over 7,000 kW (9,380 hp). In order to meet the high emissions standards in Japan, the Shinkansen must travel as quietly as possible. This has resulted in the constant effort to develop ideal streamlined shapes and insulation. As a result of the higher and higher speeds and the decreasing distance between trains, both the signal system and the brakes of the train have been steadily re-worked and improved.

A new generation Shinkansen. The tested maximum speed of these trains is about 350 km/h (217 mph).

GLOSSARY

Axle loading: The axle loading is the weight with which the axles of the locomotive bear upon the rails. A given section of track is designed to carry a maximum axle loading, so locomotives with a high axle loading may not travel on every line.

Axle-hung or nose-suspended motor: The motor is supported partly by the the axle and partly the frame.The relatively high unsprung weight means that axle-hung motors are best for locomotives with a low maximum speed.

Blast pipe: A steam locomotive's short chimney may not provide enough draught through the firebox for good combustion. The blast pipe feeds excess steam from the cylinders through the chimney, creating a lower pressure in the smoke box that in turndraws more air into the firebox.

Bogie: In order to improve the performance of long wheelbase vehicles round curves, two or more sets of wheels are grouped in a bogie. In practice, each bogie acts as a separate vehicle with a shorter wheelbase. On modern passenger trains the superstructure is built on two bogies.

Bogie wheels: These are unpowered carrying wheels that improve the smoothness of the ride and distribute the weight of a locomotive, lowering its axle load.

Boiler: The boiler of a steam locomotive is filled about two-thirds full with water. It is filled with pipes that carry the smoke and heat from the firebox to the chimney. The water, also called boiler feed water, turns into steam and collects in the upper part of the boiler. The steam travels through the dome, and the superheater if any, to the cylinders where it does its work.

Compound locomotive: The steam in a compound locomotive releases its energy in two stages. First itenters a high pressure cylinder. Since there is still plenty of energy in the steam after this, it is then fed into a low pressure cylinder to perform further work. Compound locomotives are economical and powerful, but maintenance costs are high because they are complex.

Condenser tender: The condenser tender was developed for use in regions where there is little water, so that some of the steam can be recycled. The outgoing steam from the cylinders is fed into the tender where it is condensed back into water using cooling screens and fans.

Contact wire: Electric locomotives usually take the power they need from a contact wire suspended above the rails. The contact wire usually consists of a load-bearing cable and the actual contact wire itself, which is also known as the atenary. Sometimes the power comes from a conductor rail mounted bewteen or to the side of the other rails, especially in local transport systems, .

Continuous automatic train control: Traditional signals by the track are not adequate for fast and high-speed trains. Among other problems, there may not be time for trains to stop between the warning and the main signal. Therefore the driver must receive information on the route as early as possible. This is done using cables between the tracks that work like antennas. A receiver in the vehicle transmits information to the driver. Normally speeds in excess of 160 km/h (99 mph)may only be achieved on routes with continuous automatic train control.

Coupled wheels: Wheels connected to the driven wheels by coupling rods.

Cylinder: The steam under pressure expands in the cylinder, pushing the cylinder away. The power is transmitted from the piston to the driving wheels by the piston rod and connecting rods.

Diesel-electric locomotive: The diesel engine of a fast locomotive cannot drive the wheels directly, so its power must find some other form of transmission. This is usually done using electricity. A generator is attached to the diesel engine and this provides the driving motors with power. A characteristic of diesel-electric locomotives is their simple, low maintenance design, but against this the twin motors increase their weight.

Diesel-hydraulic locomotive: Thisis an alternative to the diesel-electric locomotive that is especially common in Germany. In this case a hydrodynamic drive conducts the power from the diesel engine to the wheels. Diesel-hydraulic locomotives are technically more complicated than diesel-electric ones, but they are also lighter.

Dome: This is a small bulge on the upper side of the boiler. The steam collects in the dome, from where it is conveyed to the cylinders by pipes. Many steam locomotives have a second steam dome for applying sand.

Double-headed: If one locomotive is not powerful enough to pull a train, another locomotive can be added to make a double-header. Both locomotives have crews. If the second locomotive is controlled by the driver o the first one, the arrangement is described as multiple traction.

Driving wheels: Directly powered wheels.

Electric brake: The motors of an electric locomotives can also work as generators. The power generated in this way is either eliminated by resistance (rheostatic braking) or fed back into the network (regenerative braking). Electric braking is efficient and causes little wear.

Express trains: Passenger trains with speeds form 140 or 160 and 200 km/h (87 or 99 and 124 mph).

Garratt locomotives: Articulated steam locomotives with two separate bogies. One carries the water and coal bunker. Another water tank is carried on the forward unit. The connecting frame between the bogies carries the driver's cabin and boiler.

Gauge: The gauge is the distance between the inner edges of the rails of a straight piece of track. In curves the gauge may be slightly larger, which is called widening of the gauge. This helps to increase the smoothness of the ride on vehicles with long, fixed wheelbases.

High-speed train: Passenger trains that travel at speeds over 200 km/h (124 mph).

Light signal: The simplest method of transmitting information to the driver consists of lights arranged in a particular pattern. Light signals require little maintenance.

Mallet locomotive: Articulated locomotive with two separately driven groups of bogies. The front bogie can be turned in its frame.

Motor coach: A locomotive and coach combined in one. It operates singly or coupled to trailer units or control units.

Motor coach train: A train consistingof several units that are fixed together, some driven and some unpowered. In addition to the combination of motor coach and control unit, as implemented for example in the German Railways 628 series, there are also vehicles with drive units similar to locomotives and middle cars with no drive. This concept was implemented in the first ICE 1 high-speed train. In modern motor coach trains the drive is distributed over the entire train.

Multiple unit control: in order to control several locomotives from one driver's cabin, multiple unit controls are installed. Locomotives so equipped are suitable for multiple traction.

Operating number: Every railway service has its own system of locomotive designation. In Germany the number consists of a three-digit description of the series and the three digit sequential number for each unit within the series. A check digit is added at the end so that typos can be detected when entering the numbers in computer systems. Train coaches also have operating numbers.

Permanent way: The track, consisting of bottom ballast, sleepers and rails. Today new tracks are built using a fixed roadway, meaning that the rails are mounted on a concrete foundation.

Push-pull train: Traditional trains consist of a locomotive and a varying number of coaches or wagons. At terminus stations, the locomotive must be rotated and moved to the other end of the train, or a new locomotive must be attached. Push-pull trains have a control cab at each end. To change direction the driver simply moves the other end of the train.

Rack railway: If the gradient of a route is more than 1 in 14, normal trains can no longer use the route safely. To overcome this problem, a toothed rack is mounted between the rails with which gearwheels mounted in the locomotive engage, so that the train conveys itself up the incline. The train must be able to come to a halt safely whether travelling uphill or down. The top speed oof a rack railways is comparatively low.

Reversible motor coach train: This can be controlled from either end. A multi-strand cable transmits the commands directly. Alternatively, timed multiplex reversible train control is used, which uses a collector rail on the train for data transmission. The computers in the locomotive and control cars are in constant communication and monitor each other.

Regulator: The driver uses the regulator to control the supply of steam to the cylinders, and therefore the speed of the train.

Rod drive: In the first diesel and electric locomotives, the power to the driving wheels was transmitted by rods, similar to the connecting rods used in steam locomotives. Coupling rods transmit the power to other coupled wheels.

Rotary current motor: Also called asynchronous motors, these are used in modern electric and diesel-electric locomotives. The current taken from the contact wire is converted into rotary current in the locomotive. The control of speed is infinitely variable by changing voltage and frequency. Rotary current motors are wear little and are economical.

Saturated steam locomotive: The first steam locomotives worked exclusively with steam with a temperature just below the boiling point of water. Since some steam condensed on its way to the cylinders and inside them, the performance of such locomotives was limited. To overcome this problem locomotives were fitted with superheaters.

Semaphore signals: Orders from the signalmen to the driver of a train used to be transmitted by mechanical semaphore signals with one or two hinged wings operated by cables connecting them to the signal box. The mechanism had be serviced regularly. They have therefore largely been replaced by light signals, but many semaphore signals still exist, operated by twin cables leading to the lever frame in the signal box.

Signalman: The signalman in a signal box monitors the operation of a section of track or in a station, being responsible for the correct positioning of points and signals, and also for the running of the trains.

Smoke box: The exhaust gases from the firebox of a steam locomotive collects in the S. before it escapes through the chimney.

Smoke deflectors: The purpose of smoke deflectors is not to improve the aerodynamics of the locomotive but to give the driver an unobscured view of the line and signals ahead. They do this by creating an airflow to route the escaping steam and smoke away from the locomotive.

Steam pressure: The principle of the steam engine depends on the fact that water expands when turned to steam. The boiler is permanently under pressure, the degree of pressure depending on the type of boiler. If the pressure increases beyond the value allowed, the boiler is likely to burst. This is prevented by safety valve that releases the steam before the permitted pressure is exceeded.

Superheated steam locomotive: These use steam superheated to a temperature of up to 380° C (716° F). This means that the steam does not condense in the cylinders so quickly as saturated steam and can thus work more efficiently.

Superheater: The device in which saturated steam is raised to a temperature of up to 380° C (716° F)

Tank locomotive: These carry their supplies of coal in a coal bunker and water in one or more water tanks. The containers are permanently mounted on the locomotive. This is convenient for short-range work but not enough fuel and water can be carried for long journeys.

Tender locomotive: This pulls a tender containing larger supplies of water and coal or oil than a tank engine can accommodate. It can be attached to locomotives of different series.

Thyristor control: This solid-state technology controls the power delivered to the modern electric locomotives. Compared with the tap changer, there are no contacts and the system is therefore largely maintenance-free. The switching of the driving power is stepless.

Tilting technology: This enables a train to travel faster round curves without distressing the passengers. The body of the car tilts up to 8° to one side or the other using electric or hydraulic power. The purpose of tilting technology is exclusively for comfort while traveling. The lateral forces increase with the speed, so the track must carry a heavier side load when carrying coaches with tilting technology.

Wheel arrangement: Locomotives are described by their driving wheels and bogie wheels, which support the load but are not powered. The axle arrangement describes their sequence. In the continental system, driving wheels are described by letters of the alphabet: A means a single axle, B means two axles coupled together, and so on. Bogie wheels are described with Arabic numerals, 1 for a single axle, 2 for two axles, etc. Each group of axles in a bogie frame is separated by an apostrophe. A letter "o" indicates axles individually driven, common in electric locomotives for instance. The Whyte system is normally used for steam locomotives in English-speaking countries. Here the number of wheels is counted, so 0-6-2 would indicate no bogie at the front of the locomotive, three pairs of driving wheels, and one carrying axle.

6: AH-Archiv; 6/7: Hubrich;
8/9: Hubrich;
10/11: Eckert;
12/13: Hubrich;
14/15: Hubrich;
16/17: Eckert;
18 — 29: AH-Archiv;
30: Heilmann, Vollmer;
31: AH-Archiv;
32: AH-Archiv;
33:AH-Archiv,Sammlung Hehl;
34: AH-Archiv, Ssammlung Hehl;
35: AH-Archiv, Sammlung Hehl;
36 — 41: AH-Archiv;
42: AH-Archiv, Sammlung Hehl;
43: AH-Archiv;
44/45: AH-Archiv;
46: AH-Archiv;
47: AH-Archiv;
48: AH-Archiv;
49: Sammlung Hehl;
50: AH-Archiv;
51: AH-Archiv;
52: AH-Archiv;
53: Sammlung Hehl;
54: AH-Archiv;
55: AH-Archiv;
56: AH-Archiv;
57: Sammlung Hehl, AH-Archiv;
58: AH-Archiv;
59: AH-Archiv;
60: AH-Archiv;
61: AH-Archiv;
62/63: Nelkenbrecher/Archiv EJ;
64: Nelkenbrecher/Archiv EJ;
65: Schmidt/RioGrande-Video;
66: AH-Archiv;
67: Hubrich;
68: Hubrich;
69: AH-Archiv;
70: AH-Archiv;
71: Hubrich;
72/73: Eckert, Gußmann, Eckert;
74: EuropMedia Verlag;
75: Hubrich;
77: Schmidt/RioGrande-Video;
78: Schmidt/RioGrande-Video;
79: Schmidt/RioGrande-Video;
80: Nelkenbrecher/Archiv EJ, Hubrich;
81: Hubrich;
82: Schmidt/RioGrande-Video;
83: Schmidt/RioGrande-Video;
84/85: Nelkenbrecher/Archiv EJ;
86/87: Nelkenbrecher/Archiv EJ,
Nelkenbrecher/Archiv EJ, Hubrich;
88/89: Nelkenbrecher/Archiv EJ;
90: Hubrich;
91: Schmidt/RioGrande-Video, Hubrich;
92: Hubrich;
93: Nelkenbrecher/Archiv EJ;
94: Schmidt/RioGrande-Video;
95: Hubrich;
96: Nelkenbrecher/Archiv EJ;
97: Schmidt/RioGrande-Video,
Schmidt/RioGande Video,
Nelkenbrecher/Archiv EJ;

98: /99: Nelkenbrecher/Archiv EJ;
100/101: Schmidt/RioGrande-Video;
102/103: Schmidt/RioGrande-Video;
104/105: Schmidt/RioGrande-Video,
Nelkenbrecher/Archiv EJ,
Nelkenbrecher/Archiv EJ;
106: Schmidt/RioGrande-Video;
107: Nelkenbrecher/Archiv EJ;
108: Hubrich;
109: Nelkenbrecher/Archiv EJ;
111: Hubrich;
112: Nelkenbrecher/Archiv EJ;
113: Schmidt/RioGrande-Video;
114: Schmidt/RioGrande-Video;
115: Nelkenbrecher/Archiv EJ, Hubrich;
116: Schmidt/RioGrande-Video; Eckert;
117: Nelkenbrecher/Archiv EJ;
118: Hubrich,
119: Schmidt/RioGrande-Video; Eckert;
120: Nelkenbrecher/Archiv EJ;
121: Hubrich;
122: Kampmann, Eckert, Off, Eckert;
123: Hubrich;
124/125: Eckert (2), Hubrich;
126/127: Heilmann,
Schmidt/RioGrande-Video (3);
128: Lux;
129: Schmidt/RioGrande-Video;
130: Schmidt/RioGrande-Video;
131: Schmidt/RioGrande-Video;
132: Hubrich;
133: Hubrich;
134/135: Hubrich,
Nelkenbrecher/Archiv EJ;
136: Grosch, Sammlung Hehl;
137: Gutjahr,
Schmidt/RioGrande-Video;
138: Pischek;
139: Schmidt/RioGrande-Video;
140: Lux, Schmidt/RioGrande-
Video,Eckert,
141: Schmidt/RioGrande-Video;
142/143: Eckert, Chessum;
144: Eckert;
145: Chessum;
146: Hubrich;
147: Hubrich;
148: Schmidt/RioGrande-Video;
149: Hubrich;
150: Eckert;
151: Hubrich;
152: Hubrich;
153: Hubrich;
154/155: Eckert, Hubrich, Berndt,
Hubrich;
156/157: Kampmann,
Nelkenbrecher/Archiv EJ;
158: Schmidt/RioGrande-Video,
Nelkenbrecher/Archiv EJ;
159: Kempf;
160: Wollny, Rotthowe, Wollny;
161: Wollny, Nelkenbrecher/Archiv EJ;
162: Eckert;
163: Eckert;
164: Heinrich;
165: Schmidt/RioGrande-Video;

166 — 172: Eckert;
173: Hubrich;
174: Schumacher; Dr. Beckmann;
175: Eckert, Dr. Beckmann;
176/177: Eckert;
178: Eckert;
179: Dr. Beckmann;
180: Eckert;
181: Hubrich;
182: Hubrich, Nelkenbrecher/Archiv EJ;
183: Hubrich;
184: Eckert;
185: Kampmann, Eckert, Hubrich;
186/187: Hubrich (2), Eckert;
188/189: Hubrich;
190/191: Eckert (2), Hubrich;
192: Hubrich;
193: Hubrich;
194: Eckert;
195: Hubrich;
196: Eckert;
197: Gutjahr;
198: Heisig;
199: Heisig, Hubrich;
200/201: Hubrich, Eckert;
202: Hubrich;
203: Henschel; Heisig;
204: Dr. Beckmann;
205: Dr. Beckmann, Hubrich;
206/207: Dr. Beckmann;
208: Sammlung Hehl (2),
Dr. Beckmann;
209: Dr. Beckmann;
210/211: Eckert;
212: Gutjahr, Eckert;
213 — 223: Eckert;
224/225: Gutjahr, Eckert;
226 — 251: Eckert;
252/253: Eckert (2), Gutjahr;
254/255: Eckert, Hubrich;
256/257: Hubrich;
258/259: Eckert;
260/261: Gutjahr, Eckert;
262: Hubrich,
263: Eckert;
264/265: Eckert;
266/267: Eckert (2), Wilhelm;
268/269: Eckert (2), Hubrich;
270/271: Hubrich, Heisig;
272 — 279: Eckert;
280: Pischek;
281: Pischek;
282: Pischek, Wohlfahrt;
283: Pischek;
284: Eckert;
285: Hörstel;
286: Hubrich;
287: Hehl;
288: Eckert;
289: Schmidt/RioGrande-Video, Eckert;
290: Eckert, Hubrich,
291: Eckert;
292: Eckert;
293: Schmidt/RioGrande-Video;
294/295: Eckert, Dr. Beckmann;
296: Eckert, Dr. Beckmann,

297: Eckert;
298/299: Eckert, Dr. Beckmann;
300 — 311: Eckert;
312 — 325: Hubrich;
326: Eckert;
327: Eckert;
328 — 331: Hubrich;
332: Schmidt/RioGrande-Video;
333: Hubrich, Sammlung Hehl;
334: Sammlung Hehl;
335: Sammlung Hehl, Grosch;
336/337: Hubrich;
338: Hubrich;
339: Schmidt/RioGrande-Video, Hehl;
340/341: Hubrich,
Schmidt/RioGrande-Video;
342 — 347: Hubrich;
348: Sammlung Hehl;
349: Sammlung Hehl;
350/351: Vollmer (2),
Schmidt/RioGrande-Video;
352/353: Schmidt/RioGrande-Video,
Vollmer (2);
354 — 359: Schmidt/RioGrande-Video;
360/361: Eckert;
362: Eckert;
363: Vollmer, Eckert (2);
364 — 375: Vollmer;
376 — 383: Küstner;
384/385: Hubrich;
386: Hubrich;
387: Schumacher;
388: Hubrich;
389: Hubrich;
390/391: Hubrich;
392 — 395: Schmidt/RioGrande-Video;
396: Hubrich;
397: Schmidt/RioGrande-Video;
398/399: Hubrich;
400: Schmidt/RioGrande-Video;
401: Schmidt/RioGrande-Video;
402: Schmidt/RioGrande-Video;
403: Hubrich,
Schmidt/RioGrande-Video;
404 — 425: Hubrich;
426: Hehl;
427: Eckert;
428: Eckert;
429: Hehl;
430: Hehl (2), Eckert;
431: Hehl; Eckert;
432: Schuhböck;
433: Schuhböck;
434: Borell;
435: Borell,
Japanisches Tourismusbüro;